LOOK EAST
TO
ACT EAST

Transforming India-ASEAN Relations in Modi Era

LOOK EAST
TO
ACT EAST

Transforming India-ASEAN Relations in Modi Era

Editor

Sudhir Singh

in association with

SOCIETY FOR SOCIAL EMPOWERMENT, NEW DELHI,

INDIAN COUNCIL OF WORLD AFFAIRS, NEW DELHI

&

MAULANA ABUL KALAM AZAD INSTITUTE OF ASIAN STUDIES,
MINISTRY OF CULTURE, GOVT. OF INDIA, KOLKATA

PENTAGON PRESS LLP

Look East to Act East: Transforming India-ASEAN Relations in Modi Era
Editor: Sudhir Singh

ISBN 978-81-942837-1-3

First Published in 2020

Published by
PENTAGON PRESS LLP
206, Peacock Lane, Shahpur Jat,
New Delhi-110049
Phones: 011-64706243, 26491568
Telefax: 011-26490600
email: rajan@pentagonpress.in
website: www.pentagonpress.in

Printed at Aegean Offset Printers, Greater Noida, U.P.

Contents

Preface

Act East Policy is a new incarnation of Look East Policy that was launched in the year 1991 in the backdrop of the culmination of the Cold War. India has had excellent relations with Southeast Asian countries since millennia due to synergy of civilizational convergences. Prime Minister Narashimha Rao had launched the Look East Policy to mark India's presence in the important region. During the Cold War our bilateral relations with this region were largely absent due to a gamut of factors. India also adopted LPG process in the backdrop of the end of the Cold War that was responsible in forcing the policy makers to ensure good relations with like-minded countries. After the end of the Cold War, China emerged as an important Asian as well as global power. Look East Policy provided adequate level playing field to India to mark her presence in the region. Act East Policy was launched by Prime Minister Narendra Modi in 2014. By 2014, the Look East Policy had performed well but after 23 years of its implementation, many new challenges had inevitably cropped up that needed to be contained at the earliest. Act East Policy is one of the hallmarks of Modi's foreign policy to cope up with these emerging challenges. With the passage of time, the focus of the policy has extended from Myanmar up to Australia.[1] Modi has adopted a proactive foreign policy. Prior to that Indian foreign policy was reactive in nature. Modi changed the contours of Indian foreign policy by adopting ample proactiveness. Moreover, countries from Myanmar to Australia had really desired India to ensure a kind of counter balance to China.

Since its inception, India and China has had a turbulent relationship. Conflict, competition and cooperation has dominated the landscape of this relationship despite the high voltage trade. Pakistan remains a pawn of China to contain India within South Asia. Despite the prevailing reality, China is afraid that India might join the American umbrella that could be detrimental for the larger Chinese interests. In August 2019, Modi government scrapped special status of Kashmir but the Chinese were guarded despite visits of various high-profile Pakistani leaders and suggested both countries to settle the problem on the basis of existing bilateral framework of resolving disputes.

After Pakistani foreign minister's Beijing visit in August 2019 in the backdrop of scrapping of article 370, joint statement stressed "China recognises that the Kashmir dispute must be properly resolved based on the UN Charter, relevant UN Security Council resolutions and bilateral agreement".[2]

Post Pulwama terror attack (February 2019), China blocked French move to designate Masood Azhar as a global terrorist. But in May 2019, China lifted its technical objections (veto) and Azhar was declared a global terrorist by the United Nations. This was a balancing act undertaken by China. China has been in the state of prisoner's dilemma in terms of dealing with India. China is apprehensive of India's embrace of the American orbit. In contrast, Pakistan has no practical importance for China. It has a mere psychological appeal. Pakistan is a weak state with a failing economy and negligible global importance.

According to an eminent strategic thinker Pervez Hoodboy, Pakistan's status at the global stage has diminished to a great extent.

"Third, patrons have their own interests. To call a friendship higher than the Himalayas, deeper than the oceans, and stronger than steel may be good poetry. But patrons act after a cold calculation of losses and gains. China's silence on Kashmir and its climb-down in May at the United Nations on Masood Azhar's blacklisting shows just how carefully it weighs things. Saudi Arabia, on which Pakistan pins its hopes, went along with India."[3]

In Wuhan (2018) which took place in the backdrop of Doklam crisis, both Prime Minister Modi and President Xi pledged to manage the divergences. When both met in Bishkek for SCO summit in June 2019 they agreed for another Wuhan type summit and that was held at Mahabalipuram (near Chennai) in October 2019. It is noteworthy that President Donald Trump has launched a trade war against China since July 2018 and it has also accelerated the Chinese woes on multiple fronts. PM Modi met President Trump in Paris in the backdrop of Kashmir crisis and again during his September 2019 United States trip and beside bilateral meeting they jointly addressed rally at Houston (Texas) known as 'Howdy Modi'.

PM Modi has also perceived that cooperation with China is essential at least in the areas of convergence. Conflict and competition have also remained the order of the day in Sino-Indian relations. China had launched maritime silk route in 2015. It is intended to expand its naval activities. Right from Sitwae (Myanmar) to Gwadar (Pakistan), China has developed the existing ports and besides trade promotion, containment of Indian naval activities has remained the moot point. Yet only two weeks before Modi's election (2019), a different and first-of-its-kind quadrilateral exercise had quietly taken place away from the glare of the campaign, as two Indian naval ships in a rare exercise sailed jointly with ships from the US, Japan and the Philippines through the South China Sea. This would normally be a red rag to China, but what was striking was that shortly before the joint sail, the same two warships had sailed all the way to Qingdao to represent India at a fleet review to mark the 70th anniversary of the Chinese navy – another carefully considered decision that saw India's warships sail beside China's, when ships from the US – and not to mention China's close "all-weather" ally Pakistan – were missing.[4]

"China is also (one) of the countries across the world concerned about terror," Modi said. He added, "The India-China relationship is one of mutual respect. When the world is speaking of this century being Asia's century, they are speaking about the rise of both China and India becoming the powers they used to be historically. So, we are working together, with the knowledge that we are both focusing on growth. Even if there are some differences, both the countries understand there is a lot we agree upon as well."[5] This was a balancing act and it is slated to sustain with slight timely modification in Modi-2 as well.

India's Act East Policy, finding an alternative to the Chinese Belt and Road Initiative in conjunction with the US, Japan and IOR countries, Security and Growth for All in the Region (SAGAR) initiatives are a part of its concerted focus on the IOR that has gained primacy in the Indian calculus. India is concerned to contain Chinese maritime silk road innovation which is intended to reduce traditional Indian dominance in the Indian Ocean Region. India has developed strategically located Andaman Islands in recent years to protect and promote its interests. Commissioned by Admiral Sunil Lamba, chief of the naval staff, this new airfield is the fourth military airfield in the Andaman and Nicobar archipelago (the Andamans). The 572-island archipelago dominates the Malacca Strait that links the Indian Ocean with the South China Sea.

The Andamans also straddle the vital Indian Ocean sea lanes, through which 1,00,000 merchant vessels carry $3 trillion worth of cargo each year, including much of China's oil supplies and trade.

This region which stretches from Myanmar to Australia and parts of Africa has been named as 'Indo-Pacific' by the United States. Clearly, the concept is not new to the geopolitical discourse. The German geopolitician Karl Haushofar first used it in the 1920s in his academic work called "Indopazifischen Raum".[6]

Former Secretary of State, Hillary Clinton had stressed on this region and centrality of India within the region in 2011. Trump administration is also sustaining this policy to consolidate American hegemony in the region.

In April 2018 Trump administration stressed that India had the "capability and potential" to play a weightier role in the Indo-Pacific region. Briefing reporters on the Trump administration's Indo-Pacific Strategy, the Deputy Assistant Secretary of State for East Asian and Pacific Affairs, Alex Wong said it is in the U.S.' interest as well as of the entire region that India plays an increasingly weighty role in the region.

According to Mr. Wong "India as a nation has invested in a free and open order. It is a democracy. It is a nation that can anchor free and open order in the Indo-Pacific region. And it's our policy to ensure that India does play that role and that it becomes over time a more influential player in the region,"[7] China was never comfortable with this nomenclature which has been emphasised by the United States since last one decade. In June 2019, Chinese trawler sank a Philippines boat and over 20 of its fishermen in serious crisis who have been finally rescued by the Vietnamese boats.[8]

ASEAN in its 34th summit held at Bangkok gave adequate stress for the compliance of UN Law of the Sea and freedom of navigation. The US and other important powers like Japan and India have also stressed that freedom of navigation operations to vindicate that Chinese dictates are not acceptable to them. India under Modi has devised its own Indo-Pacific policy and put ASEAN as the fulcrum of this policy. Modi's 2018 Shagari-La-Dialogue was the official articulation of India's strategy. Modi has returned into power with improved majority for the second term (2014-19) in May 2019 and pledged to sustain its proactive policy for the region. In its dissuasion with the United States and Japan with India formed a trilateral platform called JAI (Japan, America and India) and stressed that centrality of ASEAN is must for evolving Indo-Pacific strategy.

India's Act East Policy, finding an alternative to the Chinese Belt and Road Initiative in conjunction with the US, Japan and IOR countries, Security and Growth for All in the Region (SAGAR) initiatives are a part of its concerted focus on the IOR that has gained primacy in the Indian calculus.

Under president Donald Trump administration, United States has launched multi-faceted offensive against China. Since July 2018 trade war is on going between the United States and China and which has reduced Chinese reserves. On the military front also, United States has been active in Indo-Pacific region. In Shangri-La- Dialogue, US deputy defence secretary Patrick Shanahan stated "China can and should have a cooperative relationship with the rest of the region.... But behaviour that erodes other nations' sovereignty and sows' distrust of China's intentions must end."

"Until it does, we stand against a myopic, narrow, and parochial vision of the future, and we stand for the free and open order that has benefitted us all, including China."

Washington has been pushing back against Beijing's militarisation of the South China Sea, where China has built installations to enforce blanket sovereignty, pitting it against partial claims by Taiwan, Brunei, Malaysia, the Philippines and Vietnam.

Shanahan asserted that the US was investing heavily in the Indo-Pacific region to maintain its military superiority and capability to defend its Asian allies. "The Indo-Pacific (region) is our priority theatre. We are where we belong. We are investing in the region," he added. "When we talk about preparedness, we mean having the right capabilities in the right places to respond to crises, and to compete with and deter high-end adversaries," the Pentagon chief said. "While the US does not seek conflict, it knows that having the capability to win wars is the best deterrence. We want to ensure no adversary believes it can successfully achieve political objectives through military force," he further added.

He insisted that the Pentagon had requested for $104 billion globally—its most ever—for research and development in the next fiscal year and $125 billion in operational readiness.[9]

United States and Australia have been durable allies since decades and sustained it even today. The arc of democracy (United States, Japan, India and Australia) has emerged as a new realignment in Indo-Pacific. Despite high profile trade volume between China and ASEAN, basic reason of the formation of the ASEAN (1967) was containment of China and it remains a prevailing reality till today. It could be felt in the prevailing trust deficit between disputant ASEAN countries and China over South China Sea issue. Australia is another major country in the Indo-Pacific region that desired a multipolar Asia. Australia-India relations has also improved particularly in the backdrop of November 2014. It was a maiden Indian PM visits after three decades which was successful in accelerating the pace of deepening the bilateral relationship. Australia is India's maritime neighbour and our deepening bonhomie has saddened China. India has been engaged in joint maritime exercises with coincidently democratic countries. (Japan, United States, Australia and many ASEAN countries). This has created apprehensions in Chinese strategist thinkers. China's naval watchers have in particular been suspicious of naval exercises involving India, Japan, Australia and the United States, ostensibly aimed at balancing Chinese maritime power in the Asian littorals.[10]

India has enormous soft power imprint in Indo-Pacific region. Indian culture is immensely embedded in the region and can be witnessed in the day to day life of the region. India has no territorial or maritime conflict with the countries of Indo-Pacific region. Prevailing security architecture in Indo-Pacific region is turbulent and China is willing to catch many fishes within these troubled waters. Countries of the region perceive India as a natural counter balance to China. India also has a huge trade relation with the region. It has also accelerated its strategic presence in the region. India would never willingly accept Chinese dominance in the region. India wishes to ensure a multiple power system in the region along with the possibility of relations with like-minded nations Act East Policy is intended to achieve these egalitarian objectives of Indian foreign policy. PM Modi has returned in power for the second term (2019-2024) and has pledged to upgrade Indian economy $ 5 trillion economy by 2024. All round broader relations with Indo-Pacific region will further embolden these projections for India. Strategically also, it is a positive area for larger Indian security calculus. The transformation from Look East to Act East policy launched by Modi-1 has been intended to strengthen Indian strategic foot prints in the larger canvass of 'Indo-Pacific' in general but in Southeast and East Asia in particular. Since Act East Policy is signature foreign policy innovation of Modi-1 government so it is all set to accelerate the process during Modi-2. The papers included in this book is intended to highlight these cardinal and pertinent issues in a comprehensive manner.

NOTES

1 Singh, Antara Ghosal, India's Vision for Connectivity; A Discourse Analysis in India and Connectivity Frameworks, *Delhi Policy Group Report,* 2017.

2 Naveed Siddiqui, China to 'Uphold justice for Pakistan on Kashmir Issue, *Dawn*, Karachi, August 9, 2019.

3 Pervez Hoodbhoy, Client and Patrons , *Dawn,* Karachi, July 6, 2019.

4 Ibid

5 Ibid

6 Karl Ernst Haushofer, Lewis A Tambs, Ernt J Brehm. An English translation and analysis of Major General Karl Ernst Haushofer's *Geopolitics of the Pacific Ocean: Studies on the relationship between Geography and History.* (Lewiston, N.Y, Edwin Mellen Press: 2002)

7 India can play a weightier role in Indo-Pacific region: U.S., *PTI,* New Delhi, April 3, 2018.

8 Indrani Bagchi, ASEAN Links its Indo-Pacific Strategy to India's Outreach, *Times of India,* New Delhi, June 24, 2019.

9 China must stop eroding neighbour's sovereignty, US, *AFP*, June 1, 2019.

10 'Australia woes India to Counter balance China' , *The Global Times*, July 27, 2017.

About the Contributors

Ms. Aaradhana Singh is teaching in the Department of Political Science, Central University of Himachal Pradesh, Dharamshala.

Dr. Alok Gupta is teaching Political Science in Central University of Bihar, Gaya, Bihar.

Dr. Amulya Kr. Tripathi is teaching Political Science, in Behrampur University, Orrisa.

Dr. Bachchan Kumar, Consultant, South East Asian Studies, Indira Gandhi National Centre for the Arts, Ministry of Culture, Govt. of India, New Delhi.

Dr. Bibhuti Bhusan Biswas, Assistant Professor & Coordinator, Department of International Relations, School of Humanities and Social Sciences, Central University of Jharkhand, Brambe, Ranchi, India.

Dr. Chandra Mohan Upadhaya is teaching Political Science in Kisan P.G. College, Bahraich, Uttar Pradesh.

Dr. C.S. Anuradha is a UGC Post-Doctoral Fellow, Department of Politics and Public Administration, University of Madras.

Prof. D. Gopal, School of Social Sciences, IGNOU, New Delhi.

Dr. Debashis Chakraborty is teaching in , Indian Institute of Foreign Trade, Govt. of India, Kolkata.

Ms. Devina Shukla is teaching in DDU College, University of Delhi, New Delhi.

Prof. Gangantha Jha was teaching in the Centre of Indo-Pacific Studies, Jawaharlal Nehru University, New Delhi.

Dr. Geeta Kochhar, Assistant Professor (Chinese) in the Centre for Chinese and South East Asian Studies, Jawaharlal Nehru University, New Delhi.

Dr Jayshree Tandekar is teaching Political Science in Gargi College, University of Delhi, New Delhi.

Prof. K. Jayprasad is Pro Vice-Chancellor, Central University of Kerala, Kasaragod.

Dr. Mohar Chakravorty is teaching Political Science in South Calcutta Girls' College, Calcutta University, Kolkata.

Dr. Nirmal Jindal is teaching Political Science in Satyawati College, University of Delhi, New Delhi.

Ms. Nisha is an independent scholar based in New Delhi.

Ms. Pragya Pandey is Research Associate at Indian Council of World Affairs, New Delhi.

Mrs. Rakhee Viswambharan, teaching Political Science & Head, Department of Political Science, Sree Narayana College, Chempazhanthy, Thiruvananthapuram, Kerala.

Dr. Ramesh Kumar is teaching in Shyamlal College, University of Delhi, New Delhi.

Ms. Remya R, Research Scholar, Department of Political Science, University of Kerala.

Dr. Sabu Thomas is teaching Political Science in Post Graduate Department of Political Science, Government Brennen College, Thalasserry, Kerala.

Dr. Santhanam Prabhakar is Dy-Director, Lok-Sabha, New Delhi.

Dr. Sumit Kumar is Research Fellow, Maulana Abul Kalam Azad Institute of Asian Studies, Ministry of Culture, Govt. of India, Kolkata.

Prof. Suresh R is teaching Political Science & Hon. Director, V K Krishna Menon Study Centre for International Relations, Department of Political Science, University of Kerala, Kariavattom, Thiruvananthapuram, Kerala.

Dr. Sudhir Singh is teaching Political Science, Dyal Singh College, University of Delhi, New Delhi.

Prof. Tridib Chakraborti, Former Professor, Department of International Relations, Jadavpur University, Kolkata, Currently Dean, School of Social Sciences , ADAMAS University, Kolkata.

Prof. Utham Kumar Jamdagani is head of the department, Defence department, University of Madras, Chennai.

1

Geopolitics of Indo-Myanmar Relations and Its Relevance for India's Act East Policy

Aaradhana Singh

Since the inception of human civilization, geography remains an important element for the formulation of policies. Former PM, Atal Bihari Vajpayee once stated that you cannot change geography so you have to cope up with geographical challenges. Kautilya propagated the theory of realism in the spheres of international politics 2400 hundred years ago. In the middle of the 20th century E.H. Carr and Morgenthau campaigned for the cause of realism in the realm of international politics, however a sizeable component of idealism was mixed with their theories.[1] In the latter decades of the 20th century an important development was the emergence of neo-realism, associated in particular with Kenneth Waltz whose key argument was that the international behaviour of states derived from the anarchical character of international politics.[2] States had to protect themselves in a situation where there was no overriding authority. Balancing behaviour was the most obvious example of how states sought to achieve their security goals. In Waltz's view international politics was best explained in terms of the nature of the system as a whole, rather than by focusing on the characteristics of states or even human nature. He gave less explicit attention to moral issues than did Carr and Morgenthau. Nevertheless, goals such as peace and security are important to Waltz. His concern is to show how the achievement of such goals is dependent upon understanding how states function in international politics. Liberalism (or liberal institutionalism) provides an important alternative to the various versions of realism.[3] As an approach to international politics, liberalism places some emphasis on the role of states but also gives attention to other actors such as international organizations, transnational corporations, and non-governmental organizations. Whereas realism focuses on the high politics of security issues, liberalism puts more emphasis on issues concerning economic and social interactions.

The interdependence of all actors in the international domain is a particular theme. In general, liberalism is not explicitly concerned with moral issues. There is, however, an assumption that increasing interdependence will promote international peace and promote human welfare. Some of the themes in liberalism are developed further in globalization theory.[4] Globalization as a theoretical approach is particularly important in fields such as sociology and international political economy, but it also has implications for understanding international politics. The key point is that increasingly political, economic, social, and cultural processes need to be understood on a global level. In the economic domain there is an assumption (no doubt oversimplified) that the global marketplace is dominant. Individual states have less control over their destiny in such a situation (although this can vary with the particular state, of course). From this perspective the high politics of realism is dealing with only one aspect of a very complex world, and is thus grossly oversimplified.

Located among India-China and ASEAN-Myanmar has had immense geo-strategic importance since ages. In Vedas, which is considered 10,000 years old and perhaps oldest global literature, it is mentioned as 'Swarnbumi'.

Myanmar has a great geo-strategic location and is one of the important balancing actors in rapidly changing security architecture of Asia in post-Cold War era. Myanmar formally known as Burma is geo-strategically a trifurcation among ASEAN, India (South Asia) and China (East Asia). It has a huge sea coast with Bay of Bengal and considered as one of the best geo-strategically located countries within Asia. It has emerged as one of the important places within Asia due to its geo strategic location. It is also the largest country within ASEAN in terms of landmass. In post-Cold War era, an intensive power struggle is going on in Asia to restructure the security architecture. Myanmar has a great similarity with Pakistan because military have been prominent power centres in both countries and have also ruled directly for a sizeable number of years in their post-independence period.

In light of India's changing foreign policy over the last three decades, particularly after the end of the Cold War, Indo-Myanmar relations have also changed radically. The reasons thereof pertain principally to four factors: the economic development of India's North East, India's increased interest in trade with ASEAN, India's search for energy security and increased Chinese involvement in Myanmar and its geo-strategic importance in the chessboard of balance of power in Asia.

PM Modi had visited Myanmar in November 2014 during his first term (2014-19) to participate East Asia Summit and India-ASEAN bilateral summit also. He launched 'Act East Policy' during this visit. It is a new avatar of 'Look East Policy' which was invented by PM Narasimha Rao in 1993 to connect with the countries of Southeast Asia. In fact, Act East Policy is the furtherance of Look East Policy. Only major transformative difference is it that it is more proactive and has stretched its geographical span from Myanmar to Australia. This paper intends to dwell upon the importance of Myanmar in India's Act East Policy. It has become more important when PM Modi has been reelected for the second term (2019-2014) with bigger majority. His government has become a maiden one after 1971 to return in power with full and accelerated majority with the same leader. It is bound to accelerate the proactive implementation of the foreign policy further, which has been hallmark of Modi government since 2014.

Myanmar was not in the focal agenda of India's Foreign policy in first decades of independence despite the fact Myanmar was one of the pioneers of Non-Aligned Movement super headed by Prime Minister Nehru to maintain neutrality during the Cold War era. Nehru was a Wilsonian idealist and never tried to understand Kautilayan notion of realism in the realm of foreign policy. Nehru's utopia was shattered into pieces after 1962 war. China has resolved boundary disputes with Burma almost at the same time. The interesting thing is that in case of demarcation of its boundary with Myanmar, China had conceded McMahon Line, which it had refused to accept with India just after the 1962 war and till date opposes. Former Chinese Prime Minister, Wen Jiabao (2003–2013) met 15 times with his Indian counterpart Dr. Manmohan Singh and Present Chinese President Xi met over 13 times with PM Modi but boundary dispute remains unresolved. When PM Vajpayee visited Beijing in June 2003 it was agreed that high-voltage talks headed by both countries NSAs will take place to resolve the long-standing border issue. Till date even after 21 rounds of the high-voltage talks no progress has been made to resolve it. It has further broken the tall claims of the harbingers of the process of globalization that they have the capacity to resolve thorny conflicts between two big adversaries.

Myanmar is of course a different country for India in comparison with China. Myanmar was part of India till 1935 and even today a good number of Indians are in Myanmar. India and Myanmar share over a 1600 km land border and four Indian northeastern states (Manipur, Mizoram, Nagaland & Arunachal Pradesh) have porous border with Myanmar. China is intended to protect its southern flank from possible future Indian threats and needs access to the sea to export goods from land-locked southern China. India fears encirclement by Chinese client states, like Pakistan and to some extent Myanmar. Both major powers need Myanmar's natural gas to fuel their rapidly expanding economies. Since independence, however, Myanmar sought autonomy in managing relations with India and China.

Since the post-Cold War, India has upgraded the contours of its Myanmar policy and discarded promotion of democratic values and adopted realism to deal with it. This strategic competition worries members of ASEAN, who are concerned that an apparently weak and vulnerable state like Myanmar will fall into Beijing's orbit and become a Chinese stalking horse in the region. Prevailing divergences between China and ASEAN countries over South China Sea have further eroded trust deficit despite high voltage trade. Other Asia-Pacific countries, like Japan and South Korea, are concerned about the impact this competition will have on their sea lanes of communication to the Middle East, on which they depend for oil. Meanwhile, Russia is keen to consolidate its foothold in the region, and secure energy contracts with Myanmar, which it is wooing through the sale of arms and a nuclear reactor.

The United States fears that left abandoned by the western countries, Myanmar may slip in the full ambit of China and could become another pariah country. The United States is worried about containing Chinese influence a in Myanmar therefore it is engaging Myanmar.

President Obama visited Asia-Pacific just after his re-election in November 2012. Interestingly, he visited Myanmar also and has established a minimum level of bilateral relationship between two estranged countries for many decades. Months before, Secretary of State, Hillary Clinton had also visited Myanmar and it was a maiden visit by any top US officials after 1955. At the same time India–US bonhomie is also propelling and this has been a push factor for the softening of the US attitudes towards Myanmar. All these efforts of engagements have taken place despite a long rhetoric against military government and now military controlled government by India and all other important Western countries including the US. It is merely due to geo-strategic importance of Myanmar. Since the end of the

Cold War, the architecture of Asian balance of power is changing therefore Myanmar has started to exploit its excellent geo-strategic position to maximize its interests through keeping diversity in foreign relations.

Over the previous two and half decades, Myanmar has skilfully exploited its sensitive geo-strategic position, and the fears about its close relationship with China, to win favourable deals from India and some of the key ASEAN countries, notably Singapore and Thailand. Yet Myanmar's military government still feels threatened by the US and other Western countries. To contain the wrath of the Western countries and the US, Myanmar has started to diversify its foreign policy. To achieve this it has started to engage India with full will power and also with the Western countries and the US.

During the expansion of European imperialism even Myanmar was important among competing imperil powers due to its geo-strategic importance. Myanmar has always in some sense been a focal point of political and economic interest or contention. Starting in 1820, the British colonial empire absorbed Myanmar into British India through a series of three expensive and contentious Anglo-Burmese Wars.

Post-Cold War and post-9/11 global architecture of power has given a new twist to Asia. It is widely argued by the pundits of the international politics that Asia will dominate the global system in the 21st century. Two decades of the 21st century are almost coming to an end, but there is hardly any possibility of emergence of Asia. This situation has arisen due to conflict of interests among major powers of Asia. In the case of Myanmar, although all important stakeholders of Asia are involved but India and China are involved deeply due to their geo-strategic clash of interests, and needless to say that Myanmar is of strategic interest for both. Kautilya had stated that two big geographical neighbours cannot be friends. India and China are not only big geographical neighbours but nursing great ambitions as global powers.

Myanmar has abundance of natural resources which both countries need to feed their expanding economies. Myanmar's geo-strategic location is also important for both countries because it is sandwiched between both countries, landlocked areas which despite their all-round progress remain underdeveloped. For maritime point of view, it is again important for both countries. Myanmar is also important because it connects South Asia to Southeast Asia and thus remains extremely important for India, China, ASEAN, Japan, South Korea, Indonesia and of course also to the US due to its unipolar status in global politics.

Geo-Politics of Myanmar and Sino-India Relations

Myanmar is strategically located between ASEAN and India and also between two fastest growing Asian economies China and India. The relation between 'territoriality' and foreign policy has always interested students of both Geopolitics and Foreign Policy analysis. These fields of study are much more interrelated than is traditionally acknowledged.

Geopolitics was born in the late 19th century and disappeared from universities with the end of the Second World War. International Relations as a separate academic discipline was born during the interwar period. Despite the fact that both IR and geopolitics deal with common issues and share many common assumptions, IR theory never directly mentions geopolitics or its prominent branch. This was at first due to the idealist character of American IR when it emerged during the interwar period. After the Second World War realists came to the fore. Unlike the idealist's worldview, realists viewed IR as power politics and competition between self-interested states in an anarchical international system. It is ironic that the Second World War marked the victory of realism and at the same time loss of geopolitics. Just like the term race, geopolitics was erased from academic literature in accordance with its close association with Nazism. It is assumed that mainstream IR theories cannot be properly understood or analyzed without addressing the theories of geopolitics that abounded and informed them during the period of their genesis. The fields of geopolitics and political geography were central to political thought long before IR grew of its own as a separate academic discipline in the aftermath of the First World War. Although the term geopolitics was only coined in 1899, by Rudolf Kjellen, the field of geopolitics as an intellectual tradition and an expression of state interest and identity politics[5] dates back further to the universities, geographical institutes, and centres of learning in the rival empires of the late nineteenth century.[6] Some of the eminent writings by intellectuals in this field over the years are: Alfred Mahan, Halford Mackinder, Friedrich Ratzel, Rudolf Kjellen, Karl Haushofer, Nicholas Spykman, and George Kennan, as well as some others. Political geography developed as a branch of the discipline of geography and was in common use until the invention of geopolitics in 1899. Political geography argued that states' politics emanated from their geography. As territory is one of the constitutive elements of states, geography is essential to inter-state politics. That is why the age of discovery was sponsored by states. That is why Napoleon, who argued that every state pursues the politics of its own geography, founded the first chair of geography at the Sorbonne University.[7] According to the Dictionary of Human Geography, political geography is:

> "[t]he study of the effects of political actions on human geography, involving the spatial analysis of human phenomena. Traditionally political geography was concerned with the study of states—their groupings and global relations (geopolitics) and their morphological characteristics, i.e. their frontiers and boundaries. In the last 20 years increasing interest has been shown in smaller political divisions, i.e. those within states, involving an appreciation of the interaction between political processes and spatial organization, e.g. the nature and consequences of decision-making by urban government, the relationship between public policy and resource development, the geography of public finance and electoral geography."[8]

India was pursuing promotion of democracy as an agenda of its foreign policy in terms of Myanmar since last independence but changed the discourse while anticipating growing Chinese imprint and geopolitical importance of Myanmar in post-Cold War scenario. ASEAN was also apprehensive about the credentials of military dominated governments in Myanmar and therefore was hesitant to include Myanmar in ASEAN, but was finally compelled to incorporate it to maintain cohesion. China is known for its arm-twisting tactics as far as boundary issues are concerned with all of its neighbors but with Myanmar it has accepted the same McMahon's Line as legitimate boundary which Chinese have rejected with India.

It is vindicating Napoleon's assertion that every country is basically pursuing its own geography in the realms of foreign policy. In mid-April 2013, Chinese troops entered 19 km deep into Eastern Ladakh within Indian territory and after great efforts returned in the first week of May 2013. Such incursions into the LAC (Line of Actual Control) are still on and well thought out Chinese ways to test India's courage and send a candid message to India that it should not be allied with its competitor particularly the United States. China is making regular incursions and violating McMahon Line, but has accepted the same line as legitimate in case of Myanmar. Chinese have also occupied strategic Pakistani port of Gwadar in February 2013 and developing it to consolidate its geo strategic status. But through this it has almost surrounded India from all sides. It is estimated by intelligence experts that a strong presence of PLA is already in Pakistan occupied Kashmir. These incidents are indicators that many negative things are occurring in this part of the world and India must correct this situation while offering new vistas of cooperation with Myanmar and other like-minded countries of the region.

India-China Thrust for Energy Security and Myanmar

The demand for energy in Asia is growing exponentially. A 2011 State Department Public Affairs document projects that:

> "if Asia continues its current trajectory, the region will likely account for nearly one-half of the expected growth in the world oil demand between 2008 and 2030."[9]

In particular, the growing economies and populations of China and India are placing an incredible strain on the domestic energy resources of their respective countries. Decision makers recognize that diversity in energy supply will strengthen their economic and political stronghold in the region. In general, their consensus is that a country that relies on a few sources of energy risks being at the mercy of those suppliers and comprises the security of its economic, political, and military agendas. Energy security is thus closely tied to national security, and can even be considered an aspect of it.

Merging the elements of security and energy is a concept that has garnered more attention in the last few decades, accompanying the general realization that energy resources such as gas and oil are becoming scarce. The sustainable growth of India and China despite many global and regional odds has further aggravated the issue. But many of the newly discovered gas and oil deposits are in politically tenuous and unstable regions of the world. Increased demand plus restricted supply drives many governments to re-evaluate this heightened risk; they stretch beyond their borders and political comfort zones to secure access to a cheap and diverse supply of oil and gas, thus establishing energy security.[10]

The competition between China and India, specifically over energy, has regional implications for security. These countries have practiced an energy resource tit for tat, seeking a competitive advantage in securing energy supplies. They use the full array of their diplomatic and economic "arsenal" in securing energy supplies with the "overall strategy to forge closer strategic and political ties with oil-rich countries."[11]

In most instances, both countries directly compete for energy contracts in which the "winner reasoned that the risk of pursuing oil in the "distant and insecure oil supplies in Persia" (present day Iran) was outweighed by the oil's promise of "strategic benefits... of greater speed and more efficient use of manpower."[12] Moreover, Churchill saw that oil would not only improve the operational ability of the British Fleet, but also diversify the energy supplies of the British Empire.[13]

The challenge that Churchill faced in the early 1900s is not dissimilar to that faced by contemporary China and India. China and India are "two of the fastest growing economies in the world...(and) are expected to consume a substantial share of the World's energy resources in the coming decades."[14] The pursuit of energy security is an important component of China and India's national strategies and shape their political and economic decision-making process. The need is so acute that both countries have diversified their energy supply from all possible energy surplus countries of the globe.

Sino-Indian competition is not entirely centered on the pursuit of energy, and the geopolitical facet of their overall competition is a clear illustration of the dynamics between the two countries in the region. Politics and economic interests are inseparable and "there are still considerable strategic misgivings between the two countries that hamper bilateral cooperation in the energy sector."[15] Yet, as Chatterjee contends, both countries have realized that the "lack of energy cooperation...will not only impair their own energy security, but may also have negative implications on regional stability, as has happened in the case of Sino-Japan relations."[16] The intricate and often despairingly political dynamic between these two countries is best exhibited by their energy interests in Myanmar.

In contemporary Myanmar, China and India pursue the same priorities: resource extraction and regional dominance. Their approach toward Myanmar is both comprehensive and competitive in their political support of the Burmese regime.[17] Their support of the current regime is merely a choice of strategic benefit as they have "supported the Myanmar government's seven-step roadmap to democracy and strongly opposed Western sanctions against Myanmar."[18] China and India have chosen in many instances to ignore questionable actions by the Burmese regime, specifically in domestic politics, in order to gain lucrative oil and gas contracts.

China's appetite for energy has significantly grown throughout the recent years. In late 2010, "China's energy import dependency had already amount(ed) to 50% of its total consumed energy, and according to some sources, even 60% or higher."[19] The importance of establishing a consistent and reliable supply of energy is intricately tied to the infrastructure of the Chinese economy. The economy depends on this growing infrastructure, which in turn depends on a consistent and reliable supply of energy.

The rapid lust for more space for energy security in Myanmar by China and India has created environmental problems. The Burma Environmental Working Group (BEWG) published a report on environmental issues concerning Burma.[20] Of particular interest was the impact of multinational companies on the environment; because those companies often represent the interests of various host governments, the report contains useful data on Chinese investment in energy resources. The authors concluded that, "Chinese companies have invested $8.2 billion USD in the resource sector in March 2010 alone, including $5 billion in hydropower, $2.15 billion in oil/gas sector, and nearly $1 billion in mining."[21] Additionally, Burma has been benefited from a: "30-year interest-free loan (from China) in September 2010 amounting to 30 billion Yuan (4.2 billion USD)...for economic development."[22] In short, the revenue and investment figures presented by the Harvard Kennedy School Ash Center for Democratic Governance and Innovation, the National Bureau of Asian Research, and the BEWG show a trend of significant investment and energy associated revenue in Burma by China.

India's energy security is a critical component of its national strategy. The population of India amounts to an estimated "16% of the world's population."[23] But the country only has "0.4% of the world's oil reserve" to support the energy consumption of the high population.[24] India must therefore import a considerable amount of its oil which currently is estimated at 75 per cent and according "to an estimate by the International Energy Agency, by 2030, India will need to import 91 per cent of its total oil demand."[25] India relies heavily on its ability to secure energy reserves and supplies outside of its borders.

Yet even with this demand for import oil, India was still initially hesitant in its engagement with Myanmar. The relationship started to become focused in 1988 and is characterized by scholars and policy makers to have evolved from "more pragmatic to less moralistic."[26] Initially, that is, India was quick to condemn the domestic policies of the neighbouring Burmese regime. As a result, the relationship between the two countries suffered and long-standing disagreements concerning border disputes, the treatment of the Indian diasporas population in Burma, and trade were aggravated.[27] However, India's "state socialism gave way to economic liberalism" and national policy became more focused on establishing itself as a regional influence in Southeast Asia.[28]

Myanmar as a Pivot of India-ASEAN deepening ties

The year 2012 witnessed many changes in economic and strategic dynamics of India and ASEAN. India's bilateral trade with ASEAN has reached to $80 billion in 2012 even surpassing India-China trade of $67 billion in the same period. The bilateral trade volume between India and ASEAN was $71.6 billion in 2016-17; interestingly in the same year, ASEAN-China bilateral trade was $452.31 billion.[29] ASEAN-India trade is likely to touch $100 billion by 2020, Union Urban Development and Housing Minister Hardeep Singh Puri stated, calling for greater cooperation between the two sides in economic sector.[30]

Significantly Indo–Myanmar bilateral trade remains $2.05 billion in 2015-16 to $2.18 billion which is extremely low given the proximity of both countries.[31] In FY of 2017-18 it was $1.6 billion.[32]

It vindicates the deepening of relations between both partners. India and ASEAN have also inked much awaited trade agreement in December 2012 at New Delhi. Since 1992, when Look East Policy was launched India has become members of many ASEAN platforms. Meanwhile, discord between ASEAN and China is also growing due to several prevailing differences, but particularly due to the South China Sea. Many among us have perhaps forgotten that ASEAN came into being in 1967 and one of the most important goals of its formation was to contain Chinese expansionism. It is also an open secret that ASEAN and China have a huge trade relation, far ahead than India–ASEAN, but at the same time it is also true that it has not been translated into strategic front. One of the important concerns of China has been the acceptance of its peaceful rise by their neighbourhood. Deng initiated a low-profile foreign policy in late 1980s but it is at stake due to the pursuance of present hawkish policy. A sizeable section of Chinese foreign policy thinks tanks believe that it is time when China must translate its economic power into a strategic arena. Some ASEAN countries who have land and maritime border problem with China are seriously concerned with assertive China and intended to contain it by promoting other regional and global power to ensure their presence in the region. The core issue that China's foreign strategy faces is how to respond in the international community's anxiety towards China and how to make China's rise acceptable to other Asian powers. The real goal for China is to reduce external pressure to win the acceptance and support of other key actors. The Chinese government has paid more attention to surrounding areas than ever before by declaring its 'surroundings Area First' strategic since 2003.[33] But the arrogant behaviour of China towards ASEAN has reminded them to back the ambience of its formation in 1967. ASEAN is now trying its level best to diversify their foreign policy and engage many outside powers, like India, United States, Japan, South Korea, Russia and Australia, to neutralize China. ASEAN wishes that Asia must be multipolar and this will promote and protect their national interests. It is vindicated with the editorial of leading Indonesian daily Jakarta Post:

> "The evolving geo-strategic framework inexorably impels countries in Southeast Asia to accept China and India as major regional powers. In the first case, it is necessary consequence of the former...Beijing has also shown an unequaled zest in its economic diplomacy with the Association of Southeast

> Asian Nations, ASEAN. Delhi on the other hand has been a late bloomer....ASEAN wants India's presence as much as India needs to be active in the region....ASEAN makes available a strategic framework and regulated forum which India can bluntly interact with economic powers Japan and South Korea along with fellow regional power China. This is an opportunity in which Delhi must not be hesitant. It cannot afford to miss the boat again."[34]

International players are also concerned for engaging Myanmar due to its geo-strategic importance and changing security architecture of Asia. The US has been most critical of Myanmar due to its dismal human rights and democracy record. In August 2011 putting the pundits of international system under deep surprise, the Obama administration announced the appointment of Derek Mitchell as special representative and policy coordinator for Myanmar, an office integral to the administration's 'dual track' approach of engagement and sanctions. He visited Myanmar and cleared the way for the most significant development in improving relations. It was the visit of US Secretary of State, Hillary Clinton, in November 2011, which was a maiden visit since 1955, and it came in the light of what President Obama described as " Flickers of Progress" in Myanmar. The Secretary met the President, Thein Sein, in Naypyidaw, and a day later in Rangoon they met with Aung San Kyi, both of whom described the visit as "historic".[35] President Obama himself visited Myanmar in November 2012 and reinforced deepening of ties. So is the case of many high profile visits from the Western world. Japan has also shown keen interests to develop warm relations with Myanmar. Japanese Prime Minister, Shinzo Abe visited Myanmar in the first half of the 2013. British PM has also visited Myanmar. Myanmar's President has also visited Washington in May 2013 and further cemented the ties. The US is aware about growing Myanmar importance in Asia-Pacific. These significant visits by US and allied leaders should be seen in the backdrop of America reinserting itself as a key player in Asia-Pacific, becoming a counterweight to a rising and assertive China, and rallying Asian countries under the banner of the stars and stripes.[36]

This opinion by a leading ASEAN daily justifies the urge of the region. We have witnessed a smooth relationship between India and ASEAN since the adoption of Look East Policy in 1992. But the actual fruit of deepening relationship with ASEAN will only be realized when connectivity will be established between both sides. It was conceived almost 20 years ago but till date proper land route has not been established. Once it gets established, it will be a game changer for both India and ASEAN in the areas of trade and commerce, cultural relations, tourism and people to people exchange. It will also be accelerating the pace of growth and development of our northeastern states. Majority of road network has already been constructed in Myanmar, only few bridges and missing links have yet to be constructed. Once network will be ready in Myanmar, it will be extended up to Thailand and then it will be connecting India to Hanoi, Vietnam. According to Union Minister of Road Transport, Mr Nitin Gadkari, India-Myanmar-Thailand Trilateral Highway is likely to be operational by December 2019. According to him, extension of trilateral highways to Cambodia, Laos and Vietnam is being planned and are at different stages of implementation.[37]

We had been obsessed with the policy of democracy promotion in Myanmar therefore we had some problem of trust deficit. Historically, Myanmar has been pursuing diverse foreign policy. While facilitating connectivity with ASEAN, Myanmar will be intensifying its strategic independence and maximize its national interest. India and ASEAN have neither land nor maritime boundary problem. The proposed connectivity will provide India an important foothold within the security architecture of Asia-Pacific. PM Modi visited Myanmar in November 2014 and it was followed by other high-profile visits from both sides.

The ASEAN-India Commemorative Summit was held in New Delhi on 20-21 December 2012. The Vision Document that was adopted proclaimed a Strategic Partnership and underlined the importance of regional integration and connectivity. The Commemorative Summit was attended by the Sultan of Brunei, Presidents of Indonesia and Myanmar, Vice President of the Philippines and PMs of Cambodia, Lao PDR, Malaysia, Singapore, Thailand and Vietnam.[38] In January 2018, all ASEAN heads of states were collective guests for India's Republic Day celebrations. It coincided with India-Summit also. Many bilateral agreements were inked.

The report by the Asian Development Bank (ADB) records the extraordinary rise of Asia and points out that, " Asia is in the midst of a truly historic transformation. If it continues to grow on its recent trajectory, it could by 2050, account for more than half of Global Domestic Product (GDP), trade and investment, and enjoy wide spared affluence."[39] Likewise Robert Kaplan, Senior Fellow at the Center for a New American Security, observes that the world's new centre of gravity is in 'monsoon Asia. According to him, "...the sum total effect of US preoccupation with Iraq and Afghanistan has been so fast forward the arrival of the Asian century, not only in the economic terms that we all know about, but in military terms as well."[40] But the question remains that Asia is fighting within much before its dominance over the global system has been established. In this new security architecture of Asia, Chinese interests are not converging with India, ASEAN, Japan, Vietnam, South Korea and Australia. United States of course has propelled containment of China policy tacitly and trying to expand the alliance. In this calculation too, Myanmar has immense use for India because of its geo-strategic location.

Importance of Myanmar for India's Act East Policy

The growing Myanmar-India relationship could be detrimental for the insurgents in northeast India. The northeastern states of Mizoram, Manipur, Nagaland and Arunachal Pradesh share a long porous border with Myanmar. Consequently, almost all rebel groups of the Northeast maintain sanctuaries in remote areas on the Myanmar side of the border. Many parts of North and Northwest Myanmar bordering India are not in control of the establishment. The policy of Myanmar towards Indian insurgents has been a mix. Because India was earlier supporting pro-democracy elements therefore, Myanmar was also supporting northeast insurgents to contain India. But it is also a fact that Myanmar has never had an inimical attitude towards India in terms of supporting insurgents' groups despite Chin, Mizo and Kachin ethnic groups being spread on both sides of the border. The fact remains that when India is not supporting Myanmar it was extending a temporary support to the insurgents. Myanmar cannot sustain the process of supporting insurgents because the Naga insurgent groups like NSCN (K)'S aim of 'Greater Nagaland' includes large areas of Myanmar is a direct threat to Myanmar's national integrity.[41] Many insurgent groups active in Manipur and Assam have bases in Myanmar also. All these rebel groups obtain weapons from various clandestine sources on the Sino-Myanmar border. Some of these weapons originate in China's Yunnan province and while others are made in secret gun factories in areas in Northeastern Myanmar. Myanmar is the corridor to Yunnan where a low-profile Chinese organization known as 'Five Tigers' runs arms deals with tacit understanding of the Chinese authorities.[42] China is very happy to witness that insurgency will sustain in India. Only Myanmar has a common concern with India due to its own vulnerability from the synergy of ethnic groups on its side too. Myanmar has taken practical steps to curb insurgent training centres from its soil but many training centres are still active and need to be dealt with. In June 2019, Myanmar and Indian forces jointly executed operations against insurgents in their territories.[43]

Myanmar has been their natural habitat since decades but since the last one decade their natural habitat has been devastated in Bhutan, partially in Bangladesh and now Myanmar has extended its cooperation to weed out insurgents from its soil. Modi government has taken proactive interest in these affairs and convinced

Myanmar that insurgents' sanctuary in deep Myanmar is not only detrimental for India's security but for Myanmar also, given the fact that it has a larger ethnic spectrum and majority are fighting against the state. Besides this important prevailing cooperation to eliminate insurgents which will facilitate normalcy in northeast India, we need to contain drug menace too that originated from Myanmar known as Golden Triangle. In northeast India this drug trade has created a social havoc where sizeable numbers of youth are suffering with HIV-AIDS. The drug trade is also providing lucrative financial base to insurgent groups. Myanmar is eager to cooperate in this regard because of its own similar problems.

At the same time, one should not forget that Myanmar is a unique country which believes in diversity in its foreign policy options. The changing security architecture of Asia-Pacific has given this opportunity to Myanmar due to its geo-strategic location. China and India have already become the engine of growth in Asia and expected to sustain the process in foreseeable future. As mentioned above western block is also seriously engaging Myanmar for maximizing its national interests in prevailing situation. Myanmar has also become important within ASEAN.

The US and other important members of western block are reengaging Myanmar. India has also renewed its deepening relationship with Myanmar.

PM Modi visited Myanmar in September 2017. It was his second visit after coming into power in May 2014. During this visit many new agreements were inked. In May 2019, PM Modi returned to power for the second term (2019–24). PM Modi had launched 'Act East Policy' while participating in India-ASEAN summit in November 2014 in Myanmar. Act East Policy is a new incarnation of Look East Policy and came out with a new comprehensive mechanism to cope up with new challenges in India's relations with the region. Myanmar also participated in the swearing-in ceremony of PM Modi in his second term on 30 May 2019. We should not forget that Myanmar is the only land bridge between India and ASEAN.

Myanmar has an important geo strategically location in Asia. During the Cold War period it was not vindicated. In the post-Cold War period too, it was not been reflected since few years back. It is connecting South Asia to Southeast Asia. Myanmar has been dominated by the military both overtly and covertly since its inception. China has been dominant in Myanmar since last two decades and invested in energy and infrastructure sector in a huge way. Although in 2011, a mega Dam project was withdrawn from China by Myanmar but still China has a dominating role.

Till recently, India was obsessed with the idea of promotion and protection of democratic values in Myanmar but growing Chinese muscle has motivated India to reconsider its policy towards Myanmar to cope up with the emerging situation. China has given military equipment to Myanmar in a huge volume. China also provides the Myanmar Army with training in the technical use of weapons and weapon systems. Goods bought from China over the years have included amounted personnel carriers, tanks, fighter aircraft, radar systems, ammunition, surface-to-air missiles and short-range air-to-air missile systems. China has already nurtured Pakistan since early 1960s and availing the status of 'all weather friendship' and their deepening relations with Myanmar could mean that India would find itself surrounded on three sides by Beijing and its area of influence leaving no buffer states. We have noticed the arrogant Chinese behaviour since last few years particularly with the growing incidents of border incursions. In this situation we need to be proactive instead of reactive. Narasimha Rao had initiated this policy engaging Myanmar when his foreign secretary J.N. Dixit visited Myanmar and laid the foundation of convergence. Since the NDA regime (1998-2004) India has accelerated the Kautilyan realism to engage Myanmar. Former PM Manmohan Singh (2004–13) has sustained the process. In the year 2011 and 2012, Myanmar President visited India and it was reciprocated by high-profile visits from the Indian side.

It has created a good opportunity for India. Historically, Myanmar has been pursuing diversified foreign policy and never allowed any particular country to dominate it. Myanmar bilateral relation is not simply important for us but it also connects India to Southeast Asia and that is extremely important for the unexpected growth of India. We could establish connectivity by road and rail with ASEAN only through Myanmar.

Conclusion

Engaging Myanmar will pay lucrative dividends to us on the chessboard of Asian balance of power. It will be another fulcrum of India's Act East Policy. We are moving on the right direction. The arrival of Modi government for the second term in May 2019 has given a boost to Act East Policy. Myanmar-India bonhomie is all set to grow with prevailing security architecture of Asia. The geopolitics of Myanmar will be a facilitator of our role as an Asian power.

Need of the hour is that we have to deepen our relationship with Myanmar, which will not only be a win-win situation for both but in addition it will facilitate justice-based order in Asia.

NOTES

1 Carr, *The Twenty Years' Crisis, 1919–1939;* Morgenthau, *Politics Among Nations.*
2 Waltz, Kenneth, '*Theory of International Politics*', in *Neorealism and Its Critics*, Robert O, Keohane (ed.), New York: Columbia University Press.
3 See in particular Keohane and Nye, *Power and Interdependence.*
4 See Held et. al., *Global Transformations.*
5 Stefano Guzzini, "Self-fulfilling geopolitics? Or: The Social Production of Foreign Policy Expertise in Europe," 15 June 2010, p. 17.
6 Gerard Toal, *Critical Geopolitics: The Politics of Writing Global Space*, London: Routledge, 1996, p. 21.
7 Alexandre Defay, *Jeopolitik*, Ankara: Dost, 2005, p. 13.
8 Brian Goodall, *Dictionary of Human Geography*, London: Penguin Books, 1987, p. 362.
9 *Asia's Rising Energy and Resource Nationalism: Implications for the United States, China and the Asia Pacific Region.* United States, Lanham: Federal Information & News Dispatch, Inc, 2011, accessed July 15, 2011. http://search.proquest.com/docview/864830733?accountid=12702.
10 Daniel Yergen, 'Energy Security of Markets', in *Energy and Security: Toward a New Foreign Policy Approach,* Jan H. and Goldwyn, David L. (eds.), Baltimore: 2005, p. 51.
11 Mingjiang Li, 'Sino-Indian Energy Politics', in *The Geopolitics of Energy in South Asia,* Marine-Carine Lall (ed.), Singapore: Institute of Southeast Asian Studies, 2009, p. 154.
12 Op. cit., No. 2, p.12.
13 Op. cit., No. 2, pp.11-12.
14 Rayadurgam, Indu. *Linkages in Urban and Energy Policies: An Analysis of China and India.* Singapore, Singapore: Institute of Southeast Asian Studies, 2009, accessed July 15, 2011. http://search.proquest.com/docview/189254692?accountid=12702.
15 Op. cit., No. 3, p.157.
16 Neeladri Chatterjee, 'A Political Perspective on Energy Security Cooperation between India and China' [paper presented in 58th Political Studies Association Conference, Swansea University, 1–3 April 2008]: 3.
17 Li Chenyang, 'The Policies of China and India toward Myanmar', in *Myanmar/Burma: Inside Challenges Outside Interests*, Lex Rieffel (ed.), Washington, DC: The Brookings Institution Konrad Adenauer Foundation, 2010, p. 118.
18 Ibid, p.118.
19 Jose Roberto Concha Velasquez and Berhard Pichler, 'China's increasing economy and the impacts on its energy strategy', *Estudios Gerenciales* 26, no.117 (Oct-Dec 2010): 133.
20 Burma Environmental Working Group (BEWG), *Burma's Environment: People, Problems, Policies* [Thailand: BEWG, June 2011] accessed on Aug. 31, 2011 http://www.shwe.org/campaignup date/ burma-environment-working-group/].
21 Ibid., p.45.
22 Ibid., p.45.
23 Census Report 2011, Government of India, New Delhi, 2012.
24 Op. cit., No. 3, p.153.
25 Op. cit., No. 3, p.153.
26 Gurmeet Kanwal, 'A Strategic Perspective on India-Myanmar Relations', in *Myanmar/Burma: Inside Challenges Outside Interests,* Lex Rieffel (ed.), Washington D.C.: The Brookings Institution Konrad Adenauer Foundation, 2010, p. 134.

27 Ibid., pp.143-149.

28 C. Raja Mohan, 'India and the Balance of Power', *Foreign Affairs* 85, no.4 (July-August 2006): 19.

29 Surojit Gupta, Indo-ASEAN trade rises 10% to $ 72 billion in FY 2017, but its long way of potential, *Times of India*, New Delhi, January 26, 2018.

30 ASEAN-India trade likely to touch $100 bn by 2020: Hardeep Puri, *the Hindu Business Line*, July 20, 2018.

31 Shine Zaw-Aung, 'Myanmar-India Relations – Trade and Economic Perspectives', Mizzima.com, 10 December 2016.

32 Nisha Taneja et al., India: Myanmar Trade, ICRIER, New Delhi, June 2019, p.11.

33 Zhao, Kejin, 'China's Internal Debates on Strategic Choices in the Asia Pacific Region', *Korea Observer*, Vol. 43, No. 2, Summer 2012, p.309.

34 'Is India Ready to be a part of Southeast Asia Again?', Editorial, *Jakarta Post*, June 18, 2007.

35 Ba Kaung,' Clinton Concludes Landmark Burma Trip', *The Irrawaddy*, December 2, 2011, <http;//www.irrawaddy.org/article.php?art_id=22591.

36 Pranay Sharma, 'The Burma Road', *Outlook*, December 19, 2011.

37 Peter Warr, 'Boom, bust and beyond', in *Thailand Beyond the Crisis*, Routledge, Peter Warr (ed.), 2005, p. 57.

38 *Annual Report 2012*, Ministry of External Affairs, Government of India, New Delhi, 2013, p.11.

39 'Asia 2050; Realising the Asian Century', Manila, *Asian Development Bank*, May 2011, p.17.

40 Robert, Kaplan, 'Monsoon Asia's Rise', *On Point*, October 27, 2010.

41 Brian McCartan, 'India, Myanmar; Reluctant Brothers in Arms, *Asia Times Online*, February 19, 2010. See: http//www.atimes.com/atimes/south_Asia/LB19DF01.HTML

42 Ibid.

43 *The Hindu*, New Delhi, June 16, 2019.

2

India-South Korea Relations: Expanding Contours of India's Act East Policy

Alok Kumar Gupta

India has gained a place of primacy in South Korea's foreign policy over last few years. There is imperative on both sides as each is in the need of the other. For the first time in the history of India-South Korea relations South Korea has formulated a foreign policy initiative for India and documented it as "New Southern Policy". The change and convergence is owing to changing geopolitical landscape of Northeast Asia and shifting strategic and political dynamics on the Korean peninsula. There has also been hectic diplomacy, involving South Korea, North Korea and United States directly and China and Russia indirectly. South Korean President Moon Jae-In is as dynamic and forward looking as Indian Prime Minister Narendra Modi. Both leaders have ambitions to provide a strong boost to their countries' economies, and expand their global footprints, strengthen their international and regional personalities and have been shaping their foreign policies based on their own visions. Modi visited South Korea in May 2015 and in response to which Moon visited India in July 2018. The visits by both leaders speak volumes about their commitment to improve bilateral ties and redefine their roles in regional and wider global context. Meeting between the two leaders and subsequent talks between them provided opportunity to review the entire gamut of bilateral relations and contextualise the same in terms of evolving new challenges and opportunities. This makes it imperative to explore the dynamics of their relationship to better comprehend the necessities for their convergence and future opportunities amidst changing regional and global political and strategic scenarios.

India and South Korea have been endeavouring to expand their partnership, particularly in the economic domain under the present political dispensation on both sides. Their recent visits are evidence to this fact. Indian Prime Minister Narendra Modi had visited South Korea (ROK) in May 2015; in response to which South Korean President Moon Jae-In made his maiden four-day visit to India during July 8 to 11, 2018. Undoubtedly, ever since South Korea established formal ties with India in 1973, it has been a valued economic partner for India with ever growing bilateral trade and each other's economic imperatives.[1] South Korean companies are household names in India and are now partnering in many of India's flagship projects like 'Make in India', 'Skill India', 'Digital India', 'Start-up India', and the likes. South Korea has also made a financial arrangement of USD 10 billion for infrastructure development in India. To facilitate and fast-track Korean investments in its economic activities, India has set up a cell "Korea Plus" within India.[2] Therefore, there are increased activities on both sides to facilitate each other in number of ways to enhance economic and strategic engagements. The growing convergence makes it imperative to explore and analyse the gamut of bilateral relations between the two countries and its future implications on regional geopolitics and global order. This paper attempts to put South Korean President's visit and consequent growth of convergence in proper perspective to better understand the dynamics of the convergence and engagement between the two nation-states amidst changing geopolitical environment and geo-economics of Northeast Asia.

India-South Korea Relations: Foreign Policy Imperatives

Modi-I government took oath in May 2014 and unfolded its foreign policy choices one after the other. Alongside, 'neighbourhood first' foreign policy choice his dispensation announced the transformation of erstwhile 'Look East Policy' into 'Act East Policy'. Since then India has been strongly proactive towards expanding its outreach and engagement with the countries of the East and ASEAN. Therefore, the strong partnership between India and South Korea is undoubtedly a logical extension of India's Act East Policy. Prime Minister Narendra Modi visited South Korea in pursuance of his Act East Policy in May 2015. His visit had elevated India-South Korea's relations to a 'Special Strategic Partnership'. It was during his visit that Korean government agreed to provide $10 billion to support India's priority infrastructure sectors. Since then the relations between the two countries have expanded in several dimensions including defence and security.

South Korean President Moon Jae-In came to power in May 2017. It was during his election campaign that Moon pledged that he would elevate ties with

India to level off Korea's relations with the four major powers in and around the Korean peninsula—China, Japan, Russia and the United States. This was a significant departure from Korea's traditional foreign policy, and was a timely and even necessary development.[3] Even during his tour to three ASEAN countries, when Moon outlined his "3Ps" vision to build a people-centred, peace-loving, and mutually prosperous community through the "New Southern Policy", he aimed at boosting ties with India as well as ASEAN member countries.[4] This was further established during Moon's visit to India when he visited Akshardham Temple in New Delhi on his first leg and said that India and Korea may be having different cultures, but the two countries share commonalities in values such as peace, harmony and unity in diversity.[5] Therefore, it is an ambitious move by Moon to diversify his diplomatic engagement owing to changing geopolitical scenario in his proximity and in larger Asia. Undoubtedly, South Korea's new foreign policy choice of 'New Southern Policy' is a hedging strategy amid the US-China tug-of-war in the region, and partly a forward-looking move to address how Korea and India can together meet the demands of a dynamic future. Therefore, South Korea has aptly understood the pitfalls of putting all its eggs into one basket, i.e. China, especially when China is at loggerheads with USA. South Korea is always in need of USA hence it cannot earn its wrath. India thus becomes an obvious choice in South Korea's urge to diversify its foreign relations portfolio.

Both countries also share historical ties that date back over 2,000 years and have been building relations bit by bit since then. South Korean president Roh Moo-Hyun had visited India in 2004 which resulted in the establishment of the 'Long-Term Cooperative Partnership for Peace and Prosperity' that paved the way for the commencement of bilateral Free Trade Agreement (FTA) negotiations.[6] Therefore, Moon's endeavour has been for an extension of the close economic ties that the two countries have been sharing. His commitment to build and expand India-South Korea ties is further reiterated by the fact that, The Korean National Diplomatic Academy has opened the 'ASEAN-India Research Centre' within its Institute of Foreign Affairs and National Security in February 2018, and the government is currently working on an institutional framework that will oversee the development and implementation of the policy.[7]

It makes it quite obvious that India and South Korea are moving closer at a fast pace since both countries came to be governed by a new political dispensation. There seems to be a strong urge on both sides to enhance economic and strategic engagement that too at a very fast rate. Given their commitment it seems the relations will soon develop potentials to redefine the regional and global geo-economics and subsequently the geopolitics under Modi-II regime. Alongside both countries will have tremendous opportunities to develop economically and generate employment for their citizens.

Bilateral Economic Engagement: Prospects and Problems

India and South Korea are Asia's third and fourth largest economies respectively. Trade between the two countries hit the $20-billion mark in 2011 after signing of the Comprehensive Economic Partnership Agreement (CEPA). However, there is a huge trade deficit in South Korea's favour which is a cause to be worried about for India.[8] It is this situation probably one of the strong reasons that has prompted India for a further opening-up with South Korea. Moon's visit was thus an opportunity for South Korea to cultivate a new destination of investment for Korean business communities; and an opportunity for India to attract investments in India as well as open windows of investments for Indian business communities. This is indeed the mutual need for both these countries.

South Korea has long played a key role in India's economic growth story since the early 1990s when India liberalized its economy and opened its market. Since then their economic engagements have come a long way and are expected to grow continuously as there is renewed buoyed spirit on both sides. During President Moon's visit to India, India and South Korea signed 11 Agreements to further enhance business ties and more than double their mutual trade to $50 billion by 2030 alongside India's reiteration of its commitment to deepen strategic cooperation between the two countries. The agreements included Internet of Things (IoT), Artificial Intelligence (AI), Big Data, and anti-dumping[9], which are upcoming areas and have prospects of investment and employment.

Moon's visit to India has initiated discussion and engagement on many fronts. Leaders from both the countries also asked their respective business communities to expand investment and promote joint ventures. Both sides discussed various issues in the realm of defence and security, artificial intelligence, and trade besides resolving to work together for regional peace and prevent the proliferation of weapons of mass destruction (WMD).[10] South Korea is indeed a valued economic partner for India as trade and economic relations have started to gather momentum following the implementation of CEPA in 2010 as stated above. Bilateral trade in 2011 crossed $20.5 billion, registering a 70-percent growth over a two-year period. However, bilateral trade declined to $18.13 billion in 2014-15, $16.56 billion in 2015-16, $16.82 billion in 2016-17, which finally recovered and posted a positive growth of 30 per cent in the first seven months of 2017.[11]

According to Statistics Korea, a Korean Agency, Indian exports to the country accounted for $2.91 billion and imports accounted for $8.707 billion during January-July 2017, marking a growth of 26 per cent and 30.1 per cent respectively. Upgrading and revising CEPA was mandated by both leaders in 2015, and both countries initiated negotiations to upgrade CEPA to enhance bilateral trade between the two countries.[12] Therefore, economic relations between these two countries have seen several ups and downs, yet willingness to arrest the decline and move forward has never been sagging.

Investments from South Korea are increasing, despite severe setback caused due to the Posco experience. Posco is a South Korean steel giant which has not been able to execute a $12 billion investment in Odisha, and pulled out finally after 12 years of waiting for approvals. Major conglomerates such as Samsung, Hyundai Motors and LG have made significant investments with consequent inroads in India, estimated at over $4.43 billion (as of March 2017). Kia Motors, a sister company of Hyundai Group, has announced $1.1 billion investment to set up a manufacturing unit in Andhra Pradesh, and Samsung Electronics announced a $760 million investment to expand production facilities in India. There are 603 large and small Korean firms, which have offices in India. Indian investments in South Korea are nearing $3 billion.[13] Thus, investments too have seen ups and downs yet the spirit to work on the same with ever greater vigour has never deterred the business communities on both sides, because there is also strong political will among political leaders for several reasons discussed later. Moon's visit became a landmark in India-South Korea relations when head of both these countries together inaugurated the biggest mobile manufacturing unit in Noida city of Uttar Pradesh.

Samsung: The Economic Citadel of India-South Korea Relations

Samsung announced on July 9, 2018, that it would double the capacity of its mobile phone factory in Noida making it the largest phone factory in the world. The factory is spread over an area of 35 acre. Media reported that it was scheduled to provide 1,000 more jobs directly. Modi and Moon together inaugurated the plant which was to produce up to 120 million smartphones every year.[14] About 30 percent of all phones made in the new unit were to be exported. India's growing middle class is a huge opportunity for mobile companies. Today, India is the second largest mobile manufacturing hub in the world with 120 mobile factories, from just two in 2014. Out of the 120 factories 50 of them are in Noida.[15] Samsung is indeed a rare blend of South Korean technology and Indian manufacturing capabilities. This will also be an example worth emulating for many other mobile manufacturing companies to invest in India.

Joint Vision Statement

Modi and Moon together announced a shared vision for building a new era of India-Korea 'Special Strategic Partnership'. The vision spelt out a number of initiatives in the foreign policy and strategic realm. It reflected regional anxieties and tensions and a shared approach to address the same. Together they emphasised freedom of navigation, overflight, and unimpeded lawful commerce, resolving disputes on the basis of sovereignty, territorial integrity, and international law, as well as containment of the proliferation of weapons of mass destruction, which is a shared priority.[16]

The two countries had signed a Framework of Cooperation in the areas of road transportation and highways and another MoU in maritime transport and logistics during Modi's visit to South Korea. The two sides are now eyeing development and infrastructure projects in third countries such as Afghanistan.[17] This has revealed a symbolic token towards shared interest in the joint capacity-building programme in Afghanistan. The leaders of both the interacting countries also pledged to strengthen various elements of military-to-military cooperation as well as through areas like training, exchanges, and research and development. However, all is not smooth as Korean companies have been citing problems in doing business in India, despite a special "Korea Plus" desk set up by the Prime Minister's office in 2015 as stated above. Tourism between the two countries has always been low, and strategically both are preoccupied with tensions in their immediate neighbourhoods and ties with the big world powers.[18]

Therefore, what becomes obvious from the economic engagements and joint vision released during the Moon's visit to India is that both countries have rightly identified the areas in accordance with their stated goals of national interests and regional environment and have been engaging each other to march forward. They have also identified the new areas in which they need to cooperate and work together to reap benefits in future.

Relations between North and South Koreas: Implications for India

The changing equations and strategic environment on the Korean peninsula on account of convergence between two Koreas and the commencement of constructive engagement between North Korea and USA has thrown a new challenge before the Indian diplomatic community. Accordingly, India needs to comprehend and analyse the changing equations on the peninsula and start redesigning its diplomatic interventions in a manner that it is able to play its due role in peace-making and nurturing its own relations to further national interest. Undoubtedly, the development on Korean peninsula is a strategic one and would have major implications for India.

Accordingly, the then General V K Singh, Minister of State for External Affairs, Government of India met North Korean officials in Pyongyang in May 2018 and held discussions on a host of issues with Kim Yong Dae, Vice President of the Presidium of the Supreme People's Assembly, Ri Yong Ho, foreign minister, Pak Chun Nam, Minister of Culture, and Choe Hui Chol, Vice Foreign Minister of the Democratic People's Republic of Korea. The discussion included political, regional, economic, educational and cultural cooperation between the two countries. It has been speculated that Mr. Singh's visit was preceded by a historic diplomatic breakthrough when Moon Jae-In and his North Korean counterpart Kim Jong Un signed a peace treaty to remove nuclear weapons from their backyards.[19] However, later India's the then External Affairs Minister, Late Ms. Sushma Swaraj, made it clear in a Press Conference that while India did not intend to play the role of a mediator between the US and North Korea, it would continue to nurture its democratic ties with the former.[20] Thus, India seems to have geared-up its diplomatic machinery to play its role.

Futhermore, Moon before his visit to India had sent former Cultural Minister, Chung Dong-chea, as Special Envoy to India to explain his diplomatic vision and deliver his wish for enhanced bilateral relations. This was followed by the official announcement of the policy in November 2017.

India on its part asserted its place as a 'stakeholder' in the Korean peace process and as a beneficiary too; while South Korea had for the first time shown an interest in talking about an Indo-Pacific policy. This indeed has been a welcome move for both sides.

There is another serious dimension of the North Korean nuclear proliferation which is a major cause of concern for India. There are reports of established linkages between North-East Asia and South Asia in the field of nuclear proliferation. The proliferation linkages between the two said regions is a serious security concerns for India. The North Korea-China-Pakistan alliances have led to the building of North Korea nuclear programme. It was in this context that Prime Minister Modi revealed to President Moon in a veiled reference that India too is a stakeholder in the Korean peace process.[21] India thus expressed its willingness to play its role in the ongoing peace process on Korean peninsula. President Moon while discussing the peace process on Korean peninsula with Mr. Modi expressed his confidence about the positive outcome of the talks in spite of bumps and bruises along the way. This revealed his willingness that India too could play a constructive role in it and thus it provides an opportunity to India to further broaden its global footprint and Asian personality under Modi-II regime.

Growing Convergence between South Korea and India: The Imperatives

There are critical shifts in foreign policies of India and South Korea which have opened new vistas of immense possibilities for the future. Both countries agreed to upgrade their economic partnership CEPA, trade remedies, railway safety research, cyber strategy, and cultural exchanges, and signed a joint vision statement on strategic ties in the region. There is thus renewed spurt in the bilateral relations. There are several reasons for the same which are being discussed below.

First, despite formal announcement of a strategic partnership a decade ago, India and South Korea have struggled to impart any considerable real content into it. Now both Mr. Modi and Mr. Moon have an opportunity to change that scenario. On his part, Moon has announced a "New Southern Policy" that looks beyond Northeast Asia to focus on Southeast Asia, Australia and India.[22] Modi's Act East Policy has a much wider theatre by now, i.e. Indo-Pacific for which he had to extend his outreach to as many countries as possible. Accordingly, South Korea is one more in this keg.

Second, both the countries urgently need to strengthen their economic partnership. As trade war unfolds between the world's major economies, India and South Korea have an urgent need to liberalise their own bilateral trade relations. Amidst the unfolding technological disruption of the global economy, South Korea and India have a stake in binding the innovation ecosystems of the two countries.[23] Improving business and investment ties were one of the chief bilateral agendas of two leaders' visit to each other's country in view of the fact that the bilateral trade witnessed slump during 2014-16 as enumerated above. Accordingly, both leaders agreed to double their bilateral trade from current level of $20 billion to $50 billion by 2030 as stated above. Moreover, India has been worried about its trade deficit with South Korea that stood at $12 billion in 2017, whereas Korean businessmen were complaining about problems in the 'ease of doing business' in India.[24] Since both countries have been facing hiccups in their bilateral trade engagements they needed to address it at the highest level.

Third, both these countries need to focus on expanding bilateral security and defence cooperation and working together with other countries to promote a stable Asian balance of power system. Therefore, they must focus on building flexible middle power coalitions in Asia to limit the impact of the current volatility in the relations between US and China.[25] This is more relevant given the fact of Asian balance of power where India is continuously trying to contest China's attempt at keeping Asia as unipolar. The US under its 'Pivot to Asia' foreign policy choice is improving ties and supporting countries which have potentials to check Chinese dominance in Asia and its vicinity.

Fourth, Moon as president of South Korea was truly instrumental towards breaking the ice between the US and North Korea, i.e. Trump and Kim meeting to ease the ever tense relations and save the Korean peninsula as well as many other Asian countries from a possible future ruin owing to nuclear conflict. Moon may be still apprehensive about the disruption of the dialogue between North and the US leading to further escalation of the conflict. The fact remains that it is quite difficult to synchronise the implementation of the American technical demands for a quick and comprehensive denuclearisation and the North Korean agenda on political and military trust building. Therefore, he is out on a diplomatic mission to ensure that North's promise of denuclearisation is sustained and taken to its logical conclusion. India could be truly instrumental in that as being the second largest population on the earth a favourable public mood in India in favour of denuclearisation of North Korea would really help Moon in his endeavour. The changing geopolitics of Korean peninsula has opened a new window of great opportunity to India where it can play its role and enhance its international personality as it has been instrumental earlier also. India maintained balanced relations with both North and South even during the Cold War. India has always maintained its diplomatic mission in North Korea and thus has a leverage to influence North Korea. India being one of the leading global powers, has considerable influence in world politics, it has a voice in the Korean peninsula as well and has always played a constructive role under situations of conflict and animosities. When North Korea suffered from famine India provided food articles to them. Therefore, it has leverage and considerable engagement in issues of Korean peninsula which would be of great help to Moon's mission of peace and subsequent unification of South and North. India thus can continue to do so even today and hammer out peace to the peninsula. Since Moon is seeking reconciliation with the North, India could be instrumental towards the realisation of that dream of Moon.

Fifth, when India adopted the policy of liberalization to integrate its economy with the global economy and reap the benefits of globalization in the 1990s, South Korea became an important participant in India's economic rejuvenation. However, post-Soviet Russia and China stepped up their collaboration with the economic powerhouse that South Korea had become thereby leading to the isolation of North Korea. Subsequently, North Korea started developing nuclear capability as an insurance against the loss of old communist allies. This made the South Asian subcontinent also a part of the strategy owing to convergence for atomic quest between North Korea and Pakistan. This worsened the relations between North Korea and India with growing collaboration between North Korea and Pakistan for nuclear and missile cooperation. Therefore, when South Korea is trying to cement its ties with North Korea even India may do so. Therefore, convergence between South Korea and India will lead to cementing of ties between North Korea and India as well.

Sixth rationale in the convergence of the two is that Moon is trying to diversify South Korea's relations, particularly with significant countries in the region, beyond just China.[26] This indeed is timely and necessary development in the Korean foreign policy to lessen its over-dependence on China which has grown over last couple of decades. This is obvious from the fact that when a comparison is made regarding South Korea's relations with India and China it is found that South Korea's trade with China was $240 billion while with India it was mere $20 billion. Similarly, Korean investment in India was $6.8 billion, including Samsung and LG, while in China it was $57 billion. Therefore, South Korea is all out to seize the opportunities that Indian market provides. Only, the future will reveal the extent of potentials that is there. However, in the present circumstances both countries are trying to strengthen their bilateral ties to maximize upon their own national interests.

Seventh, the geopolitics of Indo-Pacific has been changing in the recent past as it is evident from the nomenclature itself. The expectation of both Modi and Moon would have been to drive bilateral relationship from an economic and trade to a security and strategic perspective. Though the bilateral engagements and agreements signed by the two sides reveals that economic and commercial ties dominated the relationship; yet there are strong overtones of security and strategic concerns given the changing geopolitical dynamics in South China Sea and Indo-Pacific. Both South Korea and India need each other to extend their outreach to address their growing strategic concerns in the region.

Eighth, there have been accusations of China flying military aircraft into the Korean air defence identification zone without providing prior notification. This may have been a glimpse of China's combative reactions to the South Korean decision to deploy a US Terminal High Altitude Area Defence (THAAD) system, in South Korea. Thus Chinese actions shook South Korea's confidence in China. Though China and South Korea relations have shown signs of warming up; yet South Korea's quest for a broader foreign policy approach is quite obvious in Moon's endeavours to expand outreach. South Korea thus is in need of new strategic partners amidst changing geopolitical scenario in its Asian vicinity. India is one such partner which could be cultivated to suit Korea's strategic national interest.[27]

Ninth, given the scale of economic development that South Korea has achieved by now, it is also in dire need of new markets. This has come as a corollary of the previous reason as South Korea's business was hit hard owing to China's reactions to US THAAD deployment. Accordingly, it has forced South Korea to look for diversifying its economic presence and India offers plentiful opportunities to this effect.[28] India offers a huge export market for South Korea and this can indeed give a strong boost to India-South Korea economic relations with mutual benefits.

Tenth, both countries could also cooperate in areas of defence technology. South Korea's expertise in developing high-end defence electronics should be of particular interest to India. One of the agreements signed during Moon's visit to India pertains to defence industry collaboration. In the year 2017 they signed an agreement for the development of artillery guns under the 'Make in India' initiative.[29] They have also agreed to enhance their military exchanges and experience-sharing, and research and development including innovative technologies for mutual benefit. One Korean defence manufacturer Hanhwa Techwin has partnered with Larsen and Tourbo to produce K-9 Vajra artillery guns for the Indian Army at a factory near Pune.[30] This is in accordance with Modi's endeavour of promoting his 'Make in India' programme. Though it won't be without hurdles yet there are ample opportunities in the field of defence production to collaborate.

Conclusion

India and South Korea have suffered mutual political neglect for a long time. Meanwhile, South Korea has emerged as a large economic powerhouse and a member of the developed nations. However, the worldview of South Korea has largely remained riveted on North East Asia. India has begun to adopt the notion of an Indo-Pacific; South Korea has not been at the top of its regional priorities in Asia for sometimes. Now both are in need of each other on account of their economic and strategic concerns. Therefore, it is high time that both should expedite their multi-faceted engagements at all levels.

India now seems to be the central pillar of President Moon's foreign policy choice of 'New Southern Policy" and he wants to elevate Korea's relations with India at the same level as it has with China, Japan, US and Russia as discussed above. Therefore, it has opened a new horizon for the Indian economy which needed to be tapped and put considerable substance into it. Moon's endeavour will certainly gear-up the relationship between the two countries. The bilateral vision statement has also revealed commitment to build a peaceful, stable, secure, free, open, inclusive and rules-based region, incorporating President Moon's slogan— "3Ps: People, Prosperity and Peace." His visit will thus expand cooperation with India and would develop strategic understanding, cultural appreciation, and people-to-people engagement. Once it succeeds it shall have tremendous potentials to generate employment for both the interacting countries. Both countries have tremendous opportunities to enhance cooperation in areas such as technology, cyber-security, tourism, defence, and culture which must not be lost sight of.

India's global footprint has been growing. India under the present political dispensation has been investing in relationship both in the region that has been helping it to minimize the polarization of confrontation and also with the larger global community. India has set a goal for itself to become a $5 trillion economy for which it is in dire need of foreign investments and cooperation in the field of infrastructure projects, heavy industries, and skilled professionals. Undoubtedly, Moon's vision of people, peace and prosperity is no different from those of Modi's. Under the given circumstances of each other's need and aspiration it is an excellent move that the two countries are recalibrating their ties to further their national interests.

A clear road-map is the need of the hour under Modi-II dispensation. Undoubtedly, Samsung will bring investments and create jobs in India. However, more Korean companies should be persuaded to invest, by projecting a counter-narrative to the failed bid by the steel company Posco to set up its plant in Odisha. All is not lost because of the Posco fiasco either for India or for South Korea. This should be treated as an isolated case and not a norm.

It has been rightly pointed out in media that at a time when US foreign policy is capricious and unpredictable, and China is making purposeful moves towards global domination, it is important that the South Korea-India partnership grows and consolidates, to contribute to stability in the region. Hurdles are there and will be there in the future as well but spirit to move forward is important. Leaders on both sides have political will to prevail under all circumstances and that shall pay rich dividends. India continues to be a new frontier for the Republic of Korea's strategic and business interests. South Korea is yet another major addition to India's Act East Policy.

NOTES

1 It was on the eve of Moon's visit to India that South Korea's presidential Blue House had announced that India is becoming a crucial partner for Seoul not only in terms of the economy, but regarding its plans for peace and prosperity on the Korean peninsula as well. "Moon Jae-in to arrive in New Delhi today; South Korean President's four-day visit will focus on economic cooperation", July 08, 2018, www.firstpost.com
2 Aishwarya Kumar, "On his Maiden Visit to India, South Korean President Moon-Jae to Inaugurate Samsung Factory", July 09, 2018, www.news18.com
3 Soyen Park and Ramandeep Singh, "South Korea's 'New Southern Policy' Reaches the Shores of India", July 03, 2018, *The Diplomat*, www.thediplomat.com
4 Ibid., no.3.
5 PTI, "South Korean President Moon Jae-In on 4-Day Visit to India", July 08, 2018, www.ndtv.com
6 Ibid., no.3.
7 Ibid., no.3.
8 Editorial, "Moon Shine: on India-South Korea ties", *The Hindu*, July 13, 2018, www.thehindu.com
9 Rajeswari Pillai Rajagopalan, "What Did Moon's India Visit Achieve?", July 13, 2018, *The Diplomat*, www.thediplomat.com
10 Express Web Desk, July 10, 2018, www.indianexpress.com
11 C. Raja Mohan, "Raja Mandala: India and the Korean Dream", July 10, 2018, The Indian Express, www.indianexpress.com
12 Ibid., no.11.
13 Ibid., no.11.
14 Anuj Bhatia, "PM Modi, Prez Moon Jae-In inaugurate world's largest mobile phone factory, will produce 1 crore sets a month", *Indian Express*, July 9, 2018, www.indianexpress.com
15 Ibid., no.14.
16 Ibid., no.9.
17 Ibid., no.9.
18 Ibid., no.8.
19 Ibid., no.2.
20 Ibid., no.2.
21 Suhasini Haider, "India a stakeholder in Korean peace", *The Hindu*, July 11, 2018, www.thehindu.com
22 Ibid., no.11.
23 Ibid., no.11.
24 Ibid., no.21.
25 Ibid., no.11.

26 Ibid., no.9.
27 Ibid., no.9.
28 Ibid., no.9.
29 Ibid., no.9.
30 Ibid., no.21.

3

Revisiting Modi's Act East Policy: A Study on Trade and Cultural Relations of Odisha with Indonesia-Java, Sumatra

Amulya K Tripathy

Introduction

The Look East Policy was launched in 1992 by P.V. Narasimha Rao in the post-Cold War period. It aimed at strengthening cultural and economic relations, developing political contacts, and forging security cooperation with countries of Southeast Asia, that had till now escaped India's attention. I.K. Gujral had stated that, "What look east really means is that an outward looking India, is gathering all forces of dynamism, domestic and regional and is directly focusing on establishing synergies with a fast consolidating and progressive neighbourhood to its East in Mother Continent of Asia".[2] Besides the central government some state governments in India started building linkages with various countries of Southeast Asia. These were mostly coastal states which in the past had rich cultural and trade relations with several Southeast Asian countries. For example, the traders of Kalinga travelled to Indonesian Islands, like Java and Sumatra, through Sea. Although the journey by sea was very risky, Kalinga Traders not only conducted trade and commerce but they also carried India's religious and cultural values.

Much before India articulated its "Look East" and "Act East" policies that aimed at embracing countries of Southeast and East Asia, a prominent political figure from India had set up close ties with Indonesia. It was the legendary leader from Odisha, Biju Patnaik (1916-97) who had continued with the civilizational and cultural links that his state had shared with the Southeast Asian archipelago in the past, to have an enduring relation with the Sukarno family. Patnaik, is also credited with naming the daughter of Sukarno—Indonesia's first president—as Megawati, who was born on a rainy day (hence the daughter of clouds). Megawati also went on to become Indonesia's president in 2001 and ruled for three years.

Patnaik, who was Odisha's third chief minister and father of the current incumbent Naveen, reached out to Indonesia during its years of colonization under the Dutch. In July 1947, he flew to Jakarta to bring leaders of Indonesia's independence movement to India at the order of Jawaharlal Nehru. His role in rescuing Indonesia's first prime minister Sutan Sjahrir from the house arrest imposed by the Dutch is still remembered as a daring act. Indonesia did not forget Patnaik's contribution and conferred him with its highest honour—Bintang Jasa Utama—in Jakarta in 1995, two years before he died.[2]

The present state of Orissa once formed part of the ancient kingdom of Kalinga. As early as 4th and 5th centuries BC ports flourished in this area. There was regular interaction via sea-route between the ports of Orissa and Ceylon, Java, Sumatra, Borneo and Bali. By the beginning of the Christian era the merchants from Orissa established cultural and trade ties with countries like Indonesia, Malaysia and Cambodia. Bali, Java and Sumatra were the ports most frequented by the merchants from Orissa. Maritime history of Kalinga sailors lies scattered in these islands of Indonesia. The ancient sailors and sea-faring merchants did not care to leave their footprints upon the sands of time as kings have left in the form of inscriptions. But even today glimpses of their adventurous voyages to distant lands are presented through celebration of popular festivals.

In countries like Indonesia and Thailand various Hinduism and Buddhism are very much visible. The Kalinga Traders sold various local products in those countries. This maritime trade, though difficult and dangerous was adventurous and a source of wealth for Kalinga. Even today the memory of this trade and cultural ties with Southeast Asia are celebrated in Odisha on the day of Kartik Purnima. In many parts of Odisha, especially in the coastal areas women in villages, town and even in cities like Cuttack, Bhubaneswar and Brahmapur sail handmade boats made of banana tree in ponds/rivers/in the way of Bengal to remember the past glory. Orissa has a long history of maritime trade with other countries. The strategic location of Orissa with its long coastline was mainly responsible for its maritime activities. The coast of Orissa was the stepping-stone from which traders and artisans set out to colonize different corners of the globe. The influence of Orissan culture can be seen in such diverse locations as the South-east Asian countries and the Eastern shores of Africa. Orissa is actually the central portion of historic Kalinga of medieval fame, whose commercial and colonial enterprise had spread as far as China in the east and Rome in the west. The Kalinga of that time had a number of ports like Dantapura, Tamralipti, Manda, Konark, Kati-Kardama, etc., from which ships sailed regularly to Malaysia and beyond. Fa-Hien, the Chinese pilgrim of the 5th century AD, has left many detailed accounts of the various seaports of Kalinga. Kalinga was a nation of traders and mariners as is evident from the stories of trade with far off lands woven into the religious beliefs, traditions and folk legends of the state. Many south and South-East Asian countries reflect the influence of Kalinga in their art, culture, literature and even names of places. Such was the dominance of Kalinga ships in the modern Bay of Bengal, that it was then known as Kalinga Sea. The Car festival and procession of the Tooth Exhibition of Ceylon are similar to the car festival of Lord Jagannath at Puri. Even today, the annual festivals of "Bali Yatra" and "Boita Bandana" where hundreds flock to the riverside to float tiny boats on the water, are reminiscent of those early times when the brave and hardy traders used to set out in their fralf ship to trade in foreign lands. This commercial trade with people of other countries made Kalinga an economically prosperous nation. On the temple walls at Bhubaneswar, Puri and Konark, we can see sculptures depicting boats, which reflect the maritime activities of that time. The people of Kalinga were also skilful boat builders, for their ships had to be both swift and strong to carry them and their goods to different countries across unpredictable seas.

Former Chief Minister Biju Patnaik (Odisha, 1990–95) made serious and sincere efforts to relive this history of Kalinga by organising seminars, meetings, publications and sea voyages to Indonesia. Cultural activities like dance and drama depicting the old stories of Kalinga Traders were organized. A ship being properly decorated sailed from the port of Paradeep to Indonesia. Several eminent historians, artists, traders and others travelled in the ship. Since then Paradeep Port Authorities have been organising meetings and Cultural activities on the day of Kartrik Purnima in memory of Kalinga's sea trade and cultural lines with Southeast Asia. The Buddhist pilgrimages of Odisha, Ratnagiri, Lalitgiri, Udayagiri, Khandagiri, Dhauligiri, Chandragiri are great attractions for Buddhists of Far East and Southeast Asia. This has enlisted Odisha's tourism industries and re-connected Odisha to various East Asian countries. The government of Odisha has taken several steps to improve the infrastructure for Buddhist pilgrimages in order to increase their attraction. For example, every year an International Seminar is held in **Ratnagiri** of Jajpur District of Odisha where Buddhist scholars from many countries including those of East Asia are invited. Ratnagiri (Jewel Mountain) is an excavated area comprising two quadrangular monasteries, along with the remains of 8 temples and about 300 minor stupas. The development of Buddhist art and architecture at Ratnagiri, whose ancient name was Ratnagiri Mahaviharaya Arya Viksu Sangha, took place between 5th century AD and 13th century AD. Most of the sculptures found here date back to 8th and 9th centuries. It was a part of the Puspagiri University, together with Lalitgiri and Udayagiri. **Lalitgiri** set in the valley of two rivers, Birupa and Chitrotpala, was a monastery discovered by a local British official in 1905. A seven-year excavation of the site by the Archaeological Survey of India beginning in 1985 yielded a number of stone inscriptions, seals, sealing, and potsherds, which established the site as having flourished between 2nd-3rd and 14-15th century AD. It is a popular tourist destination and pilgrimage site for its enormous brick monasteries. If Lalitgiri is the oldest Buddhist site in the area, **Udayagiri and Khandagiri** are the most picturesque. Located at the base of verdant rolling hills forming a semi-circle, this site exemplifies the blissful and tranquil natural surroundings selected for the construction of Buddhist monasteries in ancient India. It is a Buddhist complex in Odisha comprising major stupas and monasteries and is also famous for its Jain monuments.

Dhauligiri is also famous for its Buddhist monuments. It happens to be the place where the bloodiest of battles were fought and won by Emperor Ashoka. This monument marked his transformation from an ambitious king of a prospering kingdom to a follower of Buddha and his teachings. The evidence of this transformation can be seen at Dhauli, 8 km from Bhubaneswar, in the form of a rock edict marked by the image of an elephant sculpted from the overhanging rock. There are two such rock edicts still surviving in Odisha.

Chandragiri was inaugurated in 2010 by His Holiness Dalai Lama and is South Asia's biggest monastery at Chandragiri near Berhampur. Spread over 10 acres, the monastery houses a 21-feet high idol of Buddha, 17-feet high second Buddha Padma Sambhav and the idol of Avaloketeswara The foundation stone for the monastery was laid in 2003 and the construction was completed in 2009 at a cost of rupees eight crore.

Recently, air travel had started between Bhubaneswar and Bangkok but because of technical difficulties it was suspended. Resumption of this air service will help to establish cultural and economic links between Odisha and Southeast Asia. Though government of Odisha has taken some steps like sending trade delegations to the countries of Southeast Asia to improve Trade relations, not much progress has been achieved on this front. What is needed is a visionary approach, practical measures and sincere and sustained efforts. Regular cultural exchanges will help to establish understanding and Cooperation between peoples as well as governments. The revival of Kalinga history should be linked to India's policy of improving its cultural, economic and strategic presence in East Asia through pursuance of its Look East to Act East Policy.

The 21st Century is Known as the Asian Century

The Look East Policy registered impressive gains for 20 years after its inception. India became a sectoral partner of ASEAN in 1992 and a dialogue partner and member of the ASEAN Regional Forum in 1996. India and ASEAN entered into a summit partnership in 2002 on the 10th anniversary of the Look East Policy, and launched negotiations for a free trade agreement (FTA) in goods in 2003. These discussions culminated in a bilateral deal in 2009, which took effect the next year. Bilateral trade and investment showed impressive gains in the first decade of the century. While bilateral trade increased from $2 billion in 1992 to $12 billion in 2002, registering annual growth of 12 percent, it increased to $72 billion in 2012, with a cumulative annual growth rate of around 22 percent over the preceding decade. In the past few years, however, the relationship has not been able to maintain the same momentum. Even Hillary Clinton, the then US Secretary of State, during her visit to India in 2011 said that India should not merely "look" towards the East, but more importantly, "act" and "engage" with the East.

Modi: Revisit of Act East Policy

Continuing the "Look East" policy and in keeping with the "enhanced" Version of the policy, the new government has given a push in engaging the neighbourhood. During her visit to Singapore in August 2014, Late External Affairs Minister Sushma Swaraj had sought Singapore companies to invest in connectivity and infrastructure projects in the region along with other major corridors in the country. The NDA government outlined the Act East Policy in November 2014, within six months of assuming power in May 2014. The policy seeks to revive and reinvigorate India's relations with ASEAN as well as expand the country's engagement beyond the region to encompass the Koreas in the North to Australia and New Zealand in the South, and from neighbouring Bangladesh to Fiji and Pacific Island countries in the Far East. During Bangladesh President Abdul Hamid's visit to India in December 2014, the first after a gap of 40 years, Modi said that India's Act East Policy would begin from Bangladesh. A key component of the AEP has been India's maritime engagement in the Asia Pacific. Through regular ship visits, naval exercises, and maritime capacity building programmes with partner navies, the Indian Navy has striven to lift New Delhi's geopolitical profile in Southeast and East Asia. Regular warship deployments in the Bay of Bengal and the South China Sea have stressed the nautical dimension of Prime Minister Modi's "neighbourhood-first" policy, even as high-end bilateral and multilateral naval exercises in the East Asian littorals have exemplified India's maritime outreach in the Asia Pacific region.[3]

The new government under Narendra Modi brings in a renewed focus on the neighbourhood since coming to power. Over the past two decades, India's Look East Policy (LEP) has served as New Delhi's principal foreign policy instrument in the Asia Pacific region. Originally conceived as a strategy for closer economic relations with Southeast Asia, the policy has deepened India's political and institutional linkages in the Asia Pacific, burnishing its credentials as a dominant engine of regional growth. In November 2014, when Indian Prime Minister Narendra Modi rechristened the LEP as the Act East Policy (AEP), many saw it as a defining moment in India's Asia policy'. As a political strategy, the AEP attempts to infuse vigour into India's regional Diplomacy, emphasizing New Delhi's desire for closer economic and security relations with its Asian neighbours.

Modi government continues on prioritizing political ties within the South Asian neighbourhood, and the AEP signals a more action-oriented policy towards the Association of Southeast Asian Nations (ASEAN). In seeking closer political interaction with its eastern partners, New Delhi has expanded the scope of its economic, security, and connectivity endeavours across a wide arc in the Pacific littorals, including Japan, South Korea, Australia, and the Pacific Island states. Odisha government is taking all steps to attract Southeast Asian countries to invest in state and attract people, particularly Buddhists to visit the Buddhist monuments by which economic development will be there.

NOTES

1 "Statement By His Excellency Mr. I.K. Gujral, Minister of External Affairs of India", ASEAN Post Ministerial Conference, Jakarta, 20–21 July, 1996: http://www.asean.org/?static_post=joint-press-release-the-first-asean-india-joint-cooperation-committee-meeting-new-delhi-14-16-november-1996.

2. By Shubham, Updated: Tuesday, May 29, 2018, 15:20 [IST]

3. Scott Cheney Peters, "India's Maritime Acts in the East", Asia Maritime Transparency Initiative, June 18, 2015: at https://amti.csis.org/indias-maritime-acts-in-the-east/

4

Act East Policy and Emergence of India-ASEAN Cultural Relations

Bachchan Kumar

Introduction

India shared cultural heritage with the South East Asian Nations. It can be traced back before the Christian era. This reveal in religion, art, architecture, language, literature and other cultural spheres of life. In this paper, I have discussed the Act East Policy and its ASEAN cultural connections. Guru Rabindra Nath Tagore while in the island of Bali (Indonesia) with the king of Karengasem in July 1927 commented on the prevailing culture "this region is culturally a part of ancient India". However, South East Asian Nations had hardly been brought to the notice of policy and planning makers. The Look East Policy was officially formulated and enacted during the year 1991 which led India to become a Sectoral Partner of ASEAN in 1992, a Dialogue Partner in 1996 and a Summit-level Partner in 2002. The up gradation of this partnership to Strategic Partnership during the celebration of 20th anniversary Commemorative Summit at New Delhi in 2012 was a natural corollary to the growth of India-ASEAN relationship during last two decades. The India-ASEAN Strategic Partnership acquired a new momentum with the announcement of "Act-East Policy" in the 12th Summit in 2014. It conveyed a clear intent on the part of India to up-scaling its engagement with the ASEAN Member States. The Act-East Policy emphasizes Connectivity, Commerce and Culture as the focus areas of action for a greater ASEAN-India integration.

Look East Policy

India's Look East Policy was officially launched in the year 1991 during the tenure of Prime Minister Narasimha Rao, although the term 'Look East Policy' was mentioned for the first time in the Annual Report of the Ministry of External Affairs in 1996. Shri I.K. Gujral had stated that 'What look east really means is that an outward looking India, is gathering all forces of dynamism, domestic and regional and is directly focusing on establishing synergies with a fast consolidating and progressive neighbourhood to its East in Mother Continent of Asia'. The relations with ASEAN were pursued with a lot of vigour and dynamism which saw India became sectoral dialogue partner with ASEAN in 1992 and full dialogue partner in 1995. In 1998, Prime Minister, Atal Bihari Vajpayee intended to accelerate India's Look East Policy. The concept of "extended neighbourhood" was popularized by Indian leaders such as I.K. Gujral and Jaswant Sinha. After almost a decade, the policy assumed a more pronounced strategic flavour and expanded to the countries other than ASEAN member like Australia, Japan and South Korea. India's then Foreign Minister Jaswant Sinha heralded the second phase of the Look East Policy in 2003. While in the first phase, the emphasis was on political, diplomatic and people to people relationships, improved connectivity and enhanced trade, the second phase revolved around strengthening of economic relations, defence and security cooperation besides strengthening relationships in other areas. During the second phase, though the dominant impulse remained the economic engagement, increasingly it also acquired strategic orientation. This policy has, though, without any doubt, brought India closer to the ASEAN nations, but was not fully able to tap the opportunities that such relations could have born.

Act East Policy

India's Look East policy required to be undertaken as more active. Keeping this, the Look East policy was transformed as Act East Policy by the active policy makers and planners. It was envisaged to be accelerated across-the two growth poles of a vibrant Asia. This has been reflected in a spate of two-way visits in the first few months of the Modi government. President Pranab Mukherjee went on a landmark visit to Vietnam in September, followed by the visit of Vietnam's prime minister to New Delhi in October. External Affairs Minister Sushma Swaraj chose Myanmar as one of her first few foreign destinations abroad in August, and met a spectrum of ministers from ASEAN countries as well as East Asian countries. She has already visited Vietnam and Singapore and looks set to travel to most of other ASEAN countries in the months ahead. During her visit to Singapore,

India's foreign minister articulated the need for an Act East policy forcefully: "Look East is no longer adequate; now we need Act East policy."

The present government has strengthened and enhanced India's foreign policy perspective on multiple fronts. The participation of Prime Minister Narendra Modi to the India-ASEAN Summit in Myanmar in November 2014 led the foreign policy decision to a prioritization of relations within India's own neighborhood.

The Objectives of "Act East Policy" are to:

1. Promote economic cooperation, cultural ties and develop strategic relationship with countries in the Asia-Pacific region through continuous engagement at regional, bilateral and multilateral levels.
2. To increase the interaction of the North-Eastern Indian states with other neighboring countries.
3. To find out the alternatives of the traditional business partners like; more focus on the Pacific countries in addition to the South East Asian countries.
4. To curb the increasing impact of China in the ASEAN region. Two-way trade between India and ASEAN are to be revamped.
5. Experts say that under the "Act East Policy" the government is relying on the 3-C's (Culture, Connectivity and Commerce) to develop better relations with ASEAN nations.

In order to ensure the success of the policy, NDA government is putting steady efforts to develop and strengthen connectivity of Northeast Indian states with the ASEAN region through people-to-people contacts, trade, culture and physical infrastructure (airport, road, power, telecommunication etc.).

With the visit of Prime Minister Modi to Myanmar, India-ASEAN relations headed for a substantive upgrade in both economic and strategic arenas. Looking ahead, the two sides will be exchanging notes on the next steps in their partnership in the form of the 2015-2020 action plan, which is expected to be firmed up and unveiled at the India-ASEAN next summit. The strategic content of the relationship is set to deepen in days to come as the two sides step up their collaboration across a range of strategic issues, including trans-national terrorism, maritime piracy and nuclear proliferation.

India's Culture Creativity with ASEAN

In the Act East Policy, India-ASEAN relations was paid due attention. Culture and Creativity provided mental and spiritual fodder to nurture this growing engagement. Known in ancient times as Suvarnabhumi, the land of gold, Southeast Asia bears deep impress of the Indian culture. The *Ramayana* and the *Mahabharata* are not just Indian epics, but civilizational memories India shares with many Southeast Asian countries like Indonesia, Thailand, Myanmar, Laos, Vietnam and Cambodia. Buddhism forms the spiritual nucleus of India-ASEAN relations as Buddhists from all over the region flock for pilgrimage to revered shrines like Bodh Gaya, the place where Lord Buddha attained enlightenment under the Bodhi tree.

Blending the ancient and the modern, the Nalanda University, an ancient seat of learning, is no longer a dream, but a living reality and has started functioning. People-to-people contact was also given due priority. The leaders of India and ASEAN have identified forging a knowledge and culture bridge as the enduring way to fructify the full potential of the relationship. Cultural linkages of the ASEAN countries, on issues like language, religion, traditions, dress, and our traditional crafts," will taken up as priority sector says Anil Wadhwa, secretary (east) in India's external affairs ministry.

With the mind and the heart in the right place, the multi-hued India-ASEAN relations are set to soar high and quicken the realization of an Asian century. It is in this spirit Prime Minister Modi is expected to renew at the summit in Myanmar India's unflinching support to the creation of an ASEAN Community by 2015. Intertwining collective dreams of 1.8 billion people, India and ASEAN are set to expand an arc of prosperity across the region and script a new narrative of an Asian renaissance.

"For India, ASEAN leadership and centrality is essential for peace and prosperity for the rapidly changing Indo-Pacific region," External Affairs Minister Sushma Swaraj said in her inaugural address at the Association of Southeast Asian Nations (ASEAN)—India Pravasi Bharatiya Divas, a gathering of the Indian diaspora from the region, in Singapore.

"ASEAN has reached the golden milestone of 50 years," she said. The bloc was formed when "southeast Asia was a global faultline, a theatre of a brutal war, and a region of uncertain nations," but has now "unified 10 countries to become an economic hub and an anchor of broader regional integration and cooperation".

India places ASEAN at the heart of its 'Act East Policy' and centre of the dream of an Asian century. India was making efforts on all fronts to enhance physical and digital connectivity with ASEAN, said Swaraj earlier. "ASEAN and India are natural partners that share geographical, historical and civilizational ties."

The strength of India's engagement with the ASEAN region lies in the clarity of the vision both sides share, the minister said: "We believe that when all nations adhere to international rules and norms, when we conduct relations on the basis of sovereign equality and mutual respect, our nations feel secure and our economies prosper." Given China's aggressive posturing in the South China Sea and growing influence in the Indian Ocean region, Ms Swaraj's remarks were cautionary. India and ASEAN have a future full of possibilities and also of enormous responsibilities "as much as this creates synergies for us, from democracy to the dynamism of our economies, from proximity to the talent of our people", she said.

Prime Minister Narendra Modi's government understands that any security partnership can only be strengthened by close economic ties, another area on which the external affairs minister laid emphasis. Deeper economic integration with ASEAN was a crucial aspect of India's Act East Policy. "ASEAN is India's fourth largest trading partner, accounting for 10.8 per cent of India's total trade," she said. "India is ASEAN's seventh largest trading partner. Trade is back on track and registered an 8 per cent increase in 2016-17, as compared to the previous year."

There have been continuous efforts to promote dialogue among ASEAN and Indian business and trade associations, to further enhance bilateral trade and investment.

North East India and Act East Policy

It was observed that without significantly developing all the states in the Northeast, realising the vision of the Act East policy from all dimensions remain to be a difficult proposition. Prime Minister Modi in a whirlwind tour covering Assam, Nagaland, Manipur and Tripura, coined a new acronym for the region: NEZ, or Natural Economic Zone, and called for the region to be developed through economic corridors to Southeast Asia. The Prime Minister on this visit also announced a slew of much needed projects, including scholarships for students, a national sports university, agricultural colleges, upgraded power and digital connectivity and new railway lines.

A number of recent developments in the North East region of India are notable. The level of education has certainly risen in the region, as has the demand for professionals from this part of the country. Some of these growth patterns are a result of the establishment of the Ministry of Development of North Eastern Region in 2001. The Ministry is entrusted with the responsibility of ensuring security. There is a need to "rebrand" the North Eastern part of India. Many "movements" are on to restore greater integration and prominence to the region. Nagaland and Myanmar have hosted many cultural events that are an evidence of this movement. Shillong is being promoted as the "Education Capital" of the North East. Similarly, Sikkim is being hailed as India's "brand ambassador" in terms of zero plastic consumption, organic produce, and ecofriendly industries. A number of laboratories have also been set up to study the innovative methods of entrepreneurial activity in this area. Google has also set up some enterprises in the region. The government has also taken multiple initiatives recently. The Prime Minister has taken a serious initiative of developing organic farming, making the entire region as a major economic hub for organic farming. The government also proposed to have an airstrip at Rupshree in Dhubri district bordering Kokrajhar, that it would be upgraded to an airport for both Air Force and civilian use. The PM also strengthened the need for education as a base while unveiling the plaque for the foundation of the Indian Institute of Information Technology (IIT), Guwahati.

India-ASEAN Connectivity

By promoting tourism sector, India-ASEAN connectivity could be established. India-ASEAN Tourism Ministers Meeting signed a MoU on Strengthening Tourism Cooperation thereby making India the first Dialogue Partner to sign a MoU on Strengthening Tourism Cooperation with ASEAN. An ASEAN Promotional Chapter for Tourism (APCT) has been established in Mumbai in 2011. A number of activities are conducted every year to promote mutual tourism. People-to-people connectivity Several projects on people-to-people connectivity are held annually to increase interaction between India and ASEAN Community. Projects which have been carried out on this front are as follows: (i) ASEAN-India Network of Think Tanks: ASEAN-India Network of Think Tanks established since 2009-10 held its 4th Meeting in Kuala Lumpur, Malaysia in August, 2015. The 5th meeting is slated to be held in Indonesia in 2017. (ii) Exchange of Parliamentarians: Indian parliamentary delegations have been regularly attending the ASEAN Inter-Parliamentary Assembly (AIPA) since 2010. (iii) ASEAN-India Media Exchange Programme: Forty media personnel visit AMS and India annually under the ASEAN-India Media Exchange Programme. (iv) Students Exchange Programme: A Student Exchange Programme has also been institutionalized under which 250 ASEAN Students visit India annually from ASEAN Member States. The participation has been increased to 500 students in the Commemorative year 2017. (v) ASEAN-India Eminent Persons Lecture Series: AIEPLS is an annual event where Eminent Persons from ASEAN Countries and deliver lectures on topics of relevance and similarly Eminent Persons from India visit the ASEAN Member States to deliver the lectures. (vi) Special Course for ASEAN Diplomats: Annually 30 ASEAN Diplomats including 3 Officials from the ASEAN Secretariat are provided special training at the Foreign Service Institute (FSI) in New Delhi. Delhi Dialogue: Delhi Dialogue is a premier annual track 1.5 event since 2009 to discuss politico-security and economic issues between ASEAN and India. Nine editions of Delhi dialogue have been held so far at New Delhi. Delhi Dialogue has an Inaugural Ministerial Session, a Business Session and an Academic Session. It has evolved into a premier event for taking stock of global geo-political movements and their impact on ASEAN-India relations and making recommendations for future direction of this landmark relationship. ASEAN-India Plan of Action (2004-2010) was developed to implement the ASEAN-India Partnership for Peace, Progress and Shared Prosperity. The 3rd Plan of Action for 2016-2020 has been finalized after successful implementation of previous one and a list of prioritized activities chalked out for 2016-18. It envisages functional cooperation in a range of sectors in the political, economic and socio-cultural spheres with the objective of capacity building and development, particularly to narrow the development gaps between ASEAN member states under their Initiative for ASEAN Integration (IAI) programme. The financing of POA projects is done through ASEAN-India Fund, Science & Technology Development Fund and Green Fund.

Under Act East Policy, the following are the India–ASEAN country wise cultural relations boosted:

Thailand

Thailand has emerged as an important trading partner of India in Asean and is also one of the important investors in India from Asean. Bilateral trade between India and Thailand has more than doubled over the last decade. Relations between India and Thailand are extensively spread across many areas. We are important regional partners linking South and Southeast Asia. We cooperate closely in the ASEAN, East Asia Summit and BIMSTEC (the Bay of Bengal Initiative for Multi-Sectoral Technical and Economic Cooperation), as also in the frameworks of Mekong Ganga Cooperation, Asia Cooperation Dialogue and Indian Ocean Rim Association. Thailand's prime minister's state visit to India in 2016 has made a long-lasting impact on bilateral relations.

The whole of India mourned with their Thai brothers and sisters the demise of the great and popular King Bhumibol Adulyadej. The people of India also join the friendly people of Thailand in praying for the long, prosperous and peaceful reign of the new king, His Majesty King Maha Vajiralongkorn Bodindradebayavarangkun.

Vietnam

The traditionally close and cordial relations have their historical roots in the common struggle for liberation from foreign rule and the national struggle for independence. Leaders like Mahatma Gandhi and President Ho Chi Minh led our peoples in the heroic struggle against colonialism. During the visit of Prime Minister Nguyen Tan Dung to India in 2007, we signed the Strategic Partnership agreement. This strategic partnership has grown into a Comprehensive Strategic Partnership with my visit to Vietnam in 2016.

India's relations with Vietnam are marked by growing economic and commercial engagement. Bilateral trade between India and Vietnam has increased about 10 fold in 10 years. Defence Co-operation has emerged as a significant pillar of strategic partnership between India and Vietnam. Science and Technology is another important area of cooperation between India and Vietnam.

Myanmar (Burma)

India and Myanmar share a land-border of over 1600 km as well as a maritime boundary. Religious and cultural traditions flowing from our deep sense of kinship and our common Buddhist heritage bind us as closely as does our shared historical past. Nothing illuminates it more gloriously than the gleaming tower of Shwedagon Pagoda. The cooperation to restore Ananda Temple in Bagan with assistance of the Archaeological Survey of India also is emblematic of this shared heritage.

During the colonial period, political bonds were forged between our leaders, who displayed a great sense of hope and unity during our common struggle for independence. Gandhiji visited Yangon several times. Bal Gangadhar Tilak was deported to Yangon for many years. The clarion call of Netaji Subhash Chandra Bose for India's independence stirred the souls of many in Myanmar.

Our trade has more than doubled over the last decade. Our investment ties are also robust. Development cooperation has a significant role in India's relations with Myanmar. This assistance portfolio is presently worth over $1.73 billion. India's transparent development cooperation is in line with Myanmar's national priorities and also builds synergy with the Master Plan of ASEAN Connectivity.

Singapore

Singapore is a window to the heritage of India's ties to the region, the progress of the present and the potential of the future. Singapore was a bridge between India and ASEAN.

Today, it is our gateway to the East, our leading economic partner and a major global strategic partner, which resonates in our membership in several regional and global forums. Singapore and India share a strategic partnership.

Our political relations are infused with goodwill, warmth and trust. Our defence ties are among the strongest for both.

Our economic partnership covers every area of priority for our two nations. Singapore is India's leading destination and source of investments.

Thousands of Indian companies are registered in Singapore.

Sixteen Indian cities have over 240 direct flights every week to Singapore. Indians make up the third-largest group of tourists in Singapore.

Singapore's inspirational multiculturalism and respect for talent have nurtured a vibrant and dynamic Indian community that is contributing to deeper cooperation between our nations.

Philippines

I had a very satisfying visit to the Philippines a little over two months ago. In addition to attending the ASEAN-India, EAS and related Summits, I had the pleasure of meeting President Duterte and we had extensive discussions on how to carry forward our warm and problem-free relationship. We are both strong in services and our growth rates are amongst the highest among major countries. Our business and trade potential holds great promise.

I laud President Duterte's commitment to bringing about inclusive development and to fighting corruption. These are areas where both countries can work together. We are happy to share our experience with the Philippines in universal ID cards, financial inclusion, making banking accessible to all, facilitating direct transfer of benefits, and in promoting cashless transactions. Making affordable medicines available to all is another priority area for the government of the Philippines that we are ready to contribute to. From Mumbai to Marawi, terrorism knows no boundaries. We are enhancing our cooperation with the Philippines in facing this common challenge.

Malaysia

The contemporary relations between India and Malaysia are quite extensive and spread across many areas. Malaysia and India shares Strategic Partnership and we cooperate in a number of multilateral and regional fora. Malaysian Prime Minister's State visit to India in 2017 has made a long-lasting impact on the bilateral relations.

Malaysia has emerged as the third largest trading partner of India in ASEAN and is one of the important investors in India from ASEAN. Bilateral trade between India and Malaysia has increased more than two-fold in 10 years. India and Malaysia have a bilateral Comprehensive Economic Cooperation Agreement since 2011. This Agreement is unique in the sense that both sides have offered ASEAN Plus commitments in trade in goods and have exchanged WTO Plus offers in trade in services. The Revised Double Taxation Avoidance Agreement between the two countries, signed in May 2012, and the MoU on Customs Cooperation, signed in 2013 further facilitate our trade and investment cooperation.

BRUNEI

Bilateral trade between India and Brunei has more than doubled over the last decade. India and Brunei share common membership of UN, NAM, Commonwealth, ARF, etc., and as developing countries with strong traditional and cultural ties, Brunei and India enjoy a fair degree of commonality in their perceptions on major international issues. The visit of the Sultan of Brunei to India in May 2008 was a landmark in India-Brunei relations. Vice-President of India visited Brunei in February 2016.

People's Democratic Republic of Laos

Relations between India and Lao PDR are extensively spread across many areas. India has been actively involved in power transmission and agricultural sectors in Lao PDR. Today, India and Lao PDR cooperate in a number of multilateral and regional fora.

While the trade between India and Lao PDR is still below potential, India has extended Duty Free Tariff Preference Schemes to Lao PDR, encourage exports of goods from Lao PDR to India. We also have immense opportunities in services trade that goes in building the economy of Lao PDR. Implementation of the ASEAN-India Services and Investment Agreement would help facilitate our services trade.

Indonesia

Separated by a mere 90 nautical miles in the Indian Ocean, India and Indonesia share a continuity of civilizational relationship that spans over two millennia.

Whether it is the annual Balijatra celebrated in Odisha or the legends of Ramayana and Mahabharata, which are visible across the entire landscape of Indonesia, these unique cultural threads umbilically bind the peoples of Asia's two largest democracies in a special neighborly embrace.

'Unity in Diversity' or Bhinneka Tunggal Ika is also a key facet of the shared societal value structures that both countries celebrate, as also the common values of democracy and rule of law. Today, as Strategic Partners, our cooperation spans across the entire gamut of political, economic, defence & security, cultural and people to people fields. Indonesia continues to be our largest trading partner in ASEAN. Bilateral trade between India and Indonesia increased 2.5 times in the last ten years. President Joko Widodo's State visit to

Cambodia

Culturally, India and Cambodia are deeply rooted. The massive monument Angkor Wat is a testimony of the glory of past. India was proud to undertake restoration and preservation of Angkor Wat temple during the difficult period from 1986-1993. India continues this valuable association in the ongoing restoration of Ta-Prohm temple.

After the collapse of Khmer Rouge regime, India was the first country to recognize the new government in 1981. India was also associated with the Paris Peace Accord and its finalization in 1991. These traditional bonds of friendship have strengthened through regular exchange of high level visits. We have expanded our cooperation in diverse fields such as institutional capacity building, human resource development, developmental and social projects, cultural exchanges, defence cooperation, tourism and people-to-people contact.

In the ASEAN context, and on various global platforms, Cambodia is an important interlocutor and a supportive partner for India. India is committed to remain a partner in Cambodia's economic development and looks forward to further deepen its traditional ties.

And, India and ASEAN are doing much more. Our partnership in ASEAN-led institutions like East Asia Summit, ADMM+ (the ASEAN Defence Ministerial Meeting Plus) and ARF (the ASEAN Regional Forum) are advancing peace and stability in our region. India is also an eager participant in the Regional

Comprehensive Economic Partnership Agreement, seeking a comprehensive, balanced and fair agreement for all 16 participants.

The strength and resilience of partnerships come not just from arithmetic of numbers, but also from the underpinnings of the relationship. India and ASEAN nations have relations free from contests and claims. We have a common vision for the future, built on commitment to inclusion and integration, belief in sovereign equality of all nations irrespective of size, and support for free and open pathways of commerce and engagement.

The ASEAN-India partnership will continue to grow. With the gift of demography, dynamism and demand—and with rapidly maturing economies—India and ASEAN will build a strong economic partnership. Connectivity will increase and trade will expand. In an era of cooperative and competitive federalism in India, our states are also building productive cooperation with Southeast Asian nations. India's Northeast is on a resurgent path. Links with Southeast Asia will accelerate its progress. In turn, a connected Northeast will be a bridge to ASEAN-India ties of our dreams.

As Prime Minister, I have attended four annual ASEAN-India Summits and East Asia Summit. These have reinforced my conviction in ASEAN unity, centrality and leadership in shaping the region in this vision.

This is a year of milestones. India turned 70 last year. ASEAN reached the golden milestone of 50 years. We can each look to our future with optimism and to our partnership with confidence.

At 70, India exudes the spirit, enterprise and energy of its young population. As the fastest growing major economy in the world, India has become the new frontier of global opportunities and an anchor of stability of the global economy. With every passing day, it is easier and smoother to do business in India. I hope that ASEAN nations, as our neighbours and friends, will be an integral part of New India's transformation.

We admire ASEAN's own progress. Born when Southeast Asia was a theatre of a brutal war and a region of uncertain nations, ASEAN has united 10 countries behind a common purpose and a shared future. We have the potential to pursue higher ambitions and address the challenges of our times: from infrastructure and urbanisation to resilient agriculture and a healthy planet. We can also use the power of digital technology, innovation and connectivity to transform lives at unprecedented speed and scale.

A future of hope needs a solid bedrock of peace. This is an age of change, disruptions and shifts that comes only rarely in history. ASEAN and India have immense opportunities—indeed, enormous responsibility—to chart a steady course through the uncertainty and turbulence of our times to a stable and peaceful future for our region and the world.

Indians have always looked East to see the nurturing sunrise and the light of opportunities. Now, as before, the East, or the Indo-Pacific Region, will be indispensable to India's future and our common destiny. The ASEAN-India partnership will play a defining role in both. And, in Delhi, ASEAN and India renewed their pledge for the journey ahead. Modi government had launched 'Act East Policy' once it came into power in 2014. It was a new avatar of 'Look East Policy'. It has taken a proactive stance for the compliance of larger national interests. Modi has returned into power for the second term with the bigger majority and all set to infuse new lease of energy into its much-coveted Act East Policy. It is not only win-win situation for both but could ensure international law based order in 'Indo-Pacific' region.

REFERENCES

ASEAN-India Centre at RIS (2016), "ASEAN India Relations" [Online: http://www.mea.gov.in/aseanindia/20-years.htm] retrieved on 16th August, 2019.

Coedes, George (1967), *The Indianized States of Southeast Asia*, Honolulu: East-West Centre Press.

De, Prabir and Sreya Pan (2019), *Act East: ASEAN-India Shared Cultural Heritage*, New Delhi: RIS.

Institute of Cultural Diplomacy (NA), [online: http//www.cultural diplomacy.org/index.php?en_culturaldiplomacy] retrieved on 16th August 2019.

Kumar, Bachchan ed. (2011), *Art and Archaeology of South-East Asia*, New Delhi: IGNCA and Aryan Books International.

—— (2014), *The Art of Indonesia*, New Delhi: B.R. Publishing Corporation.

Murari, Dr. Krishna (1985), *Cultural Heritage of Burma*, New Delhi: Inter-India Publications.

Northeast India (NA), [online: https://en.wikipedia.org/wika/Northeast_india] retrieved on 14th August, 2019.

Rabindranath Tagore to Mira Devi, 31st August 1927 (in) Tagore *Java Jatrir*, pp. 483-489.

Rooney, Dawn F. (2006), *Angkor: Cambodia's Wondrous Khmer Temple*, Hong Kong: Odyssey.

Sarkar, Himansu Bhusan (2001), "The Migration of Ramayana Story to Indonesia" (in) *Glimpses of Early and Indonesian Culture: Collected Papers of H.B. Sarkar*, ed. Bachchan Kumar, New Delhi: IGNCA & Aryan Books International.

Sen, T. (2009), *Buddhism, Diplomacy and Trade: The Realignment of India-China Relations*, Hawaii: University of Hawaii Press.

Sharma, Anjana ed. (2013), *Civilizational Dialogue: Asian Inter-connections and Cross-cultural Exchanges, ASEAN-India*, New Delhi: ICCR, Nalanda University and Manohar Publications.

Vien, Nguyen Khac (2007), *Vietnam: A Long History, Hanoi*: The GIOI Publishers.

Zaide, Joyce Iris (NA), *Tagore Asian Voyage 1927*, India: Nalanda Srivijaya Centre & Singapore: Institute of Southeast Asian Studies.

5

Role of Andaman and Nicobar Islands to Promote Act East Policy of India

Bibhuti Bhusan Biswas

Introduction

India has very close socio-cultural and trade links with East Asian countries even before emerged as a sovereign country. The colonial period could not snap these old links. The prominence of Southeast Asia was recognised by K.M. Panikkar, who is considered as one of the India's first strategic analysts, way back in the 1940s. It was also realised by Pt. Jawaharlal Nehru that of these links and articulated the idea and conceptualized the Asian regionalism. Mr. Nehru understood the significance and hence invited Indonesian President as the Chief Guest of first Republic day in India and organised Asian Relations Conference in New Delhi at the eve of India's Independence. Such gesture shows India's strategic importance of Southeast Asian region.[1] India was very much supportive of towards Southeast Asia region to protest against of anti-colonial movement, which shows India's mature foreign policy not to surrender or compromise with sovereignty.

While the world was experiencing certain changes in early 1990s and moving towards globalisation, India was initiated a new policy of reform, i.e. 'Look East Policy' by the then Prime Minister Mr. Narasimha Rao. This initiative has changed the world perspective on India strategic shift. In this period India had launched its economic liberalisation reforms to boost its economy and trade. After lunching 'Look East Policy' India and ASEAN came closure and shown interest to work closely for economic and trade reforms. However, this policy has been meticulously followed by the successive governments of Atal Bihari Vajpayee and Dr. Manmohan Singh. Though the next successive government was formed by the National Denotative Alliance (NDA) has given boost to the greater strategic role for India in the Asia-Pacific, as it was a landslide victory for Mr. Narendra Modi in the May 2014 general election in India. Mr. Modi clearly given the signal to the world during swearing in ceremony that India's policy would be neighbourhood first and collective development, and hence, he intensified relationship with ASEAN. Besides, China compelled India to enhance India's role in East and Southeast Asia, due to China's intensifying presence in Indian Ocean and maritime dispute in East Asia. Mr. Modi has upgraded India's 'Look East Policy' to 'Act East Policy' during the India-ASEAN Summit in Myanmar in November 2014.[2] Though New Delhi viewing ASEAN is one of its core strategic interface and have acquired a wider canvass, encompassing the Asia-Pacific as a whole, nevertheless some scholars and analysts seeking this policy as balance China's influence in the region. However, New Delhi repeatedly reiterated that neither India competing with China not trying create obstacle for China in any manner.

The most important thing that India is doing is to nudge these Asian countries to move towards a pan-Asian economic grouping. There has been a pan-African movement, a Pan-Latin American movement. But there has been no pan-Asian movement. But today, the time for such a grouping has come. India is taking lead in pushing this idea. Two-thirds of the foreign exchange reserves are held by Asian countries, mainly China and India. With this, Asian countries have mostly been able to ward off monetary crisis without taking the help of the International Monetary Fund.[3] The region is home to bustling centres of trade, investment and financial resources, a manufacturing hub, and a sophisticated sphere of science and technology development, alike. Initiated in 1991, India's "Look-East" Policy framed towards the nations of South East Asia (ASEAN), though subsequently expanded, marked a strategic shift in New Delhi's perspective on and perception of, the 'MO-JO' Region. In the words of former Indian Prime Minister Dr. Manmohan Singh, it is "not only an external economic policy; it's a strategic shift in India's vision of the world and India's place in the global political economy."[4]

Incumbent Indo-ASEAN cooperation traverses a wide gamut of domains, from trade and investment synergies, to collaboration in various front, such as science and technology, health and pharmaceuticals, tourism and human resource development, transportation links, infrastructural projects,[5] etc. India's signed of the cornerstone "Long Term Cooperative Partnership for Peace and Prosperity," in 2004, morphing into the landmark conclusion of the "Indo-ASEAN Free Trade

Agreement" in August 2009.[6] India's trade with ASEAN has grown in bilaterally as well as through regional platforms in many ways. India's trade with ASEAN gone upto $76.52 billion in 2014-15. India's export to ASEAN is worth $31.8 billion and imports $44.7 billion.[7] India's trade with ASEAN is going to boost up in near future and hence, bilateral trade is likely to increase in near further of US$100 billion.

To give a new direction to the Act East Policy, Andaman and Nicobar Islands impart India with immense strategic importance for India as it is located in the eastern Indian Ocean and its close proximity with ASEAN countries. The Islands contribute about 30 percent of the Especial Economic Zone (EEZ) to India's total EEZ area. India is having 7,517 kilometre of coastline of over and out of which Andaman and Nicobar Islands covers 1,962 kilometres. Andaman and Nicobar Islands (ANIs) consist of 572 Islands and these Islands are separated from main land India and isolated. Nevertheless, India has an opportunity to play an important role in the security of sea lines of communication in the region, which is a busy shipping communication lines. Though ANIs are approximately 1,200 km far away from main land India, though it is nearer to several ASEAN countries. Its southern-most part (Indira Point) is located only about 160 km away from the northern tip of Sumatra.[8] India is engaging Southeast Asian countries through joint military operations, due to islands proximity to the Southeast Asian countries, which is enable India to foster friendly relations. It is also giving a tough challenge to Chines dream to encircling India. And hence, Andaman and Nicobar archipelago act as the first line of defence and four unsinkable aircraft carriers at Diglipur, Port Blair, Car Nicobar & Campbell Bay. As ANIs are strategically very important for India due to its location and hence it can play a vital role towards promoting India interest in the East. On the other hand Ten-degree and six degree channels also provide pre dominating position of India in this region.[9] It's also provide a better opportunity for India to counter the influence of China in the region and further strengthening cooperation will provide opportunity for India to countering poaching, piracy, illegal fishing, drug trafficking, maritime pollution. The Modi Government has a determined plan to transform the archipelago into the country's first maritime hub, as the Islands contribute about 30 percent of the Especial Economic Zone and hence, pushing for infrastructure needed to boost the tourism, fisheries, utilisation of forests resources.

Importance of Straits of Malacca

Former Prime Minister of India Pt. Jawaharlal Nehru said "to be secure on the land, we must be supreme at sea". Importance of Indian Ocean is very much understood by several scholars and one can understand from the statement of Admiral A.T. Mahan in 1890 that "Whoever controls the Indian Ocean will dominate Asia. In the 21st century, the destiny of the world would be decided on its waters". Former Prime Minister Shri Atal Bihari Vajpayee also clearly stated India's strategic priorities in November 2003 "the strategic frontiers of today's India, grown in international stature, have expanded well beyond confines of South Asia. Our security environment, ranging from Persian Gulf to Straits of Malacca across the Indian Ocean, includes Central Asia and Afghanistan, China, and South-East Asia. Our strategic thinking has also to extend to these horizons." Hence, Andaman Sea has become a strategic important place to play a major role in maritime security for India. Human civilisations has used Sea extensively for trade and commerce. Due to geographical location of India and long coast line provide a huge opportunity in trade and security for its main land. On the other hand presence of ANIs also provide a secure strategy to monitoring the world most strategic and overcrowded trafficked Malacca Strait, through which approximately 95,000 merchant, oil and gas cargos, pass through.[10] Hence, makes the strait an energy lifeline for Southeast and East Asian countries.

Strait of Malacca is one of the busiest and longest navigation routs which connects the Indian Ocean via Andaman Sea and the Strait is 900 km length. Besides, this Strait is shortest, safest and economical for ships to reach between East Asia and Europe. Though the Strait is very narrow and limited navigational restrictions, nevertheless the Strait is still an attractive and preferred navigational route for international shippers compared to other alternative routes like Sunda or Lombok-Makassar Straits in the Indonesian archipelago.[11] Malacca Straits annually provides safe transit to over 60,000 tankers, cargo vessels, passenger vessels, tug and pilot and it is likely to increase in near future. However, Chines goods and oil transportation took place in large volume through Malacca Straits and hence, due to India's territory of Andaman and Nicobar, India is having advantage in the region and any disruptions in the Straits will effects its trade and transit. China is not in a position to effort such disruption in the Malacca Straits and therefore, China is establishing its bases in different neighbouring countries of India to avoid such scenario.

However, India is a growing economy and its national interest is to promote Act East Policy to counter China in the region as well as initiate development in Northeast region of India. India's long pending development initiative in Northeast region has been initiated by taking up the projects such as the Asian highway project in South Asia to link Singapore with New Delhi via Kuala Lumpur, Ho Chi Minh City, Phnom Penh, Bangkok, Vientiane, Chiang Mai, Yangon, Mandalay, Kalemyo, Tamu, Dhaka and Kolkata. India also has taken initiative to upgrade and resurfacing 160 km long Tamu-Kalewa-Kalemyo road. Besides, Kaladan Multi-modal Transit Transport will connect Indian ports and Sittwe port in Myanmar through Mizoram.[12] Which will prove a greater opportunity for the region to development in every aspects as well as it will provides a huge market for peoples of India and ASEAN.

Andaman and Nicobar Islands and Act East Policy

Andaman and Nicobar Islands (ANIs) are having very close cultural linkage and proximity with ASEAN as well as a large number of diaspora is living in ASEAN and a section of people from Thailand and Myanmar is living in Andaman and Nicobar Islands. Due to old age linkage with ANIs and ASEAN, it is providing an easy platform to connect this region with each other. Hence, to promote Act East Policy of India as well as containing China, ANIs could play a major role.

People-to-People Contact

Andaman and Nicobar is also known as mini India, as people from different parts of India migrated and settled in ANIs. Besides, a sizable diaspora from ASEAN are living also settled in ANIs. In the Islands different culture, language, tradition, religions are practice by the people and all sects participate in most of the festivals, which is a unique feature of ANIs. Apart from that Andaman and Nicobar is a castles society, which is featuring the unique character of India, Unity in Diversity. Hence, Government of India must take initiative to start direct flight service between ANIs and ASEAN. Flight services will promote tourism in the Islands and also strengthen people to people connection. Besides, establishing High Commission of ASEAN countries in the Islands will promote people to people connection as well as it will boom trade and economic growth.

Tourism

Andaman and Nicobar is having 572 Islands but only 36 Islands are inhabited by the people, which is a very small area. As these islands are very isolated and away from mainland India and less possibility to get any industries, hence, people of ANIs gets very little opportunity for increasing living stander. Hence, tourism industry can provides large employment opportunity for the local youths of ANIs. Besides, tourism will create a platform where India's national interest of Act East

Policy will boost-up, it will also enhance positive role in the field of Inter-state and international relationships.

Boosting such sector, also provides employment opportunity to the semi-skilled and the unskilled labourers. The never-ending growth of Islands tourism main the following factors favouring the growth of tourism in ANIs are: natural beauty and free from pollution, crime, political evils, free from the rigidities of caste, creed and religion. As Andaman and Nicobar Islands has huge potential of tourism industry and ASEAN can be one of the major contributors in the growth of this industry. Hence, Government of India may take extra efforts to develop infrastructure for tourism development.

Maritime Security and Cooperation

In the present scenario, maritime security is one of the most important aspects of any country. After Mumbai attack which is known as 26/11, India has modernise its maritime security as well as installed several surveillance mechanism to secure its coastal line from entry of any terrorists or unwanted elements from outside. To secure India's maritime boundary, it was necessary to settle down all its disputes with neighbouring countries and hence, to strengthen cooperation India has settled its maritime boundaries with Malaysia, Indonesia, Thailand, Myanmar and Sri Lanka through nine boundary agreements with its neighbours.

Andaman and Nicobar Islands are one of the major important places from where India is trying to secure its maritime boundary and hence tri-command has been setup in the Islands. Besides, India has initiated cooperation with ASEAN through *Milan,* to boost interoperability and share views on common maritime issues as well as foster bonds of friendship, Indian Navy at Port Blair has initiated this biennial conglomeration of Asia-Pacific maritime navies. *Milan* is one of the successful initiatives by India to showcase its Navel power in Indian Ocean and its preparedness. Besides, India is able to gain trust in the region to contain China in Indian Ocean as well as ASEAN countries also gaining confidence to challenge and contain China in South China Sea. Hence, Andaman and Nicobar playing a major role to realise its national interest of Act East Policy. It's not only providing a common platform to jointly learn maritime security aspect also bringing likeminded countries together to strengthen their maritime security.

Securing maritime boundary is one of the biggest challenge in the present circumstances, because terrorists and non-state actors are using sea to enter into the country. Hence, ANIs would be one of the important places from where such infiltration can be monitored. Besides, piracy in the Strait of Malacca can be monitored closely. As per International Maritime Bureau piracy has been reduced in the region due to joint patrols by Indonesia, Malaysia, and Singapore. India has also built a UAV-patrol base to monitor the Andaman Sea adjacent to the Strait of Malacca in Andaman and Nicobar Islands.

The Narco-Trafficking Network known as 'Golden Triangle' comprising Myanmar, Thailand and Laos[13] is one of the major irritating aspects for India and Southeast Asian countries. Also arms trafficking are taking place through sea in the region. Hence, joint naval exercise and monitoring may ensure safety and security of the region.

Duty free Port in Andaman and Nicobar Islands

One of the oldest industries in transportation of goods is shipping industry which is still playing an important role in modern society. Oceans are becoming more important in transporting sector, as every day 20 million containers are traveling across the oceans. Hence, managing the traffic in the sea is becoming very challenging as well as identifying unwanted ships are becoming a hectic for each country. To maintain smooth shipment of goods and transportation it is very much necessary to increase port facilities. As Straits of Malacca is one of busiest Sea Lane of Communication and Andaman and Nicobar Islands are very close to it, hence, these islands has got huge potential to provide a safe and duty free port service to ASEAN countries as well as other friendly countries. However, China is putting several challenges before India by setting up a string of ports starting with Hambantota in Sri Lanka, Gwadar in Pakistan, Chittagong in Bangladesh,[14] and Sittwe in Myanmar as well as Chines bonhomie with India's neighbouring countries. Besides, China is keeping very close eye on India's navel movement as well as capability of missile tests from Coco Island, which is located 18 km away from the northern most islands in the Andaman. Hence, developing duty free ports in Andaman and Nicobar Islands will provide a safe and cost effective ports and also it will help to manage traffic in the sea. Besides, it will provide eyes to India's maritime security, which will reduce Chines influence in Indian Ocean. Apart from that India will be able to gain trust of ASEAN countries, which will fulfil India's national interest.

Deep Sea Fishing

Though India's one third of Especial Economic Zone is around ANIs but due to various reasons the India's coast guards are finding so much of difficulties to manage properly its surveillance. Whereas in the Andaman Sea several foreign vessels are illegally fishing despite the Fishing Federation and the Indian Ocean Tuna Commission (IOTC) and Coastguards are closely working and cooperating with each other to stop such fishing. Nevertheless, India is losing approximately US$ 200 million per year illegal fishing in India's Especial Economic Zone. Whereas fisheries sector contributes about two per cent of India's GDP.[15] To control such illegal fishing by poachers, India is taking different measures to stop it. However, large number of poachers are from Myanmar, Thailand, Bangladesh, and far off Taiwan still venturing Andaman Sea for illegal fishing and marine resources, which is imposing a serious national security threats.

On the one hand India is trying to stop illegal poachers from Myanmar, Thailand, Bangladesh, and far off Taiwan and on the other hand India is trying to promote its Act East Policy very effetely. But in this context India can very easily manage such illegal poachers by signing joint deep sea fishing with these countries. This may stop illegal fishing and strengthen maritime surveillance of India in particular and for ASEAN in general. Joint deep sea fishing will provide a platform for the fisherman of Andaman and Nicobar as well as fisherman from coastal area of mainland India to strengthen their economic status. Not only that, it will help fisherman of Myanmar, Thailand, Bangladesh, and Taiwan also to grow. This will help India to keep very close eye on Chines activities in Indian Ocean as well as other terrorist organisations those who are illegally trying to enter in India through sea. Besides, Indian Navy in Andaman can extend all possible help to fisherman for their safety and navigation while fishing in deep sea.

Way Ahead

To promote "Act East Policy" and regional cooperation with ASEAN Malacca Strait is playing a major role. India has developed the tri-command in Andaman and Nicobar Islands to strengthen its surveillance and monitoring the Malacca Strait, as it provides a gateway to the South China Sea and the Pacific Ocean. However, Andaman and Nicobar Islands is one of the components of promoting India's 'Act East Policy' and decrease mistrust among the people of India and ASEAN countries. India's engagement with ASEAN is not confined to economic partnership, as ASEAN is an important strategic entity for India and it looks forward to a multi-dimensional engagement with the emerging community. Though Andaman and Nicobar Islands isolated from mainland India but close to some of the ASEAN countries, hence, it will play a major role in promoting India's interest in East Asia. Besides, cooperation among India and ASEAN will help this region to establish peace and harmony. Apart from that it will also provide a huge opportunity for the people of this region to reduce mistrust. However, to expand India's geographical coverage up to countries like Australia, Japan, Pacific Island nations, South Korea and Mongolia, the present Government has rephrased India's Look East Policy as Act East Policy.[16] However, Indian needs to focus in various aspect to make Act East policy to be successful.[17] India and ASEAN may start People to People Contact and increase of tourism to reduce mistrust among the peoples and governments, direct flight service between Andaman and Nicobar and ASEAN, Military cooperation need to be increase, duty free Port in Andaman and Nicobar Islands, cooperation in Maritime Security, increase joint surveillance to reduce Chines influence in Indian Ocean, provide safety and security of Sea Lines of Communication, joint deep sea fishing, increase joint surveillance in Indian Ocean to counter terrorists activity. Government of India may focus to strengthen such components to fulfil the national interest.

NOTES

1 GVC Naidu, "India and Southeast Asia", *World Focus*, vol.17, nos.10–12, October–December, 1996, pp.82–84

2 Narendra Modi, "Media Statements by Prime Minister of India and Prime Minister of Vietnam in New Delhi," media statement, 28 October 2014, http://www.mea.gov.in/incoming-visitdetail. htm?24143/Media+Statements+by+Prime+Minister+of+India+ and+ Prime+ Minister+ of+Vietnam+in+New+Delhi+October+28+2014; Narendra Modi, "Opening Statement by Prime Minister at the 12th India-ASEAN Summit," (speech, India-ASEAN Summit, Nay Pyi Taw, Myanmar, 12 November 2014), http://www.mea.gov.in/incoming-visitdetail.htm?24143/Media+Statements+by+Prime+Minister +of+India +and +Prime+Minister+of+Vietnam +in+New+Delhi+October+28+2014.

3 Muchkund Dubey, *India's Foreign Policy in Contemporary International Scenario* (New Delhi: South Asian Publishers, 2009).

4 https://books.google.co.in/books?id=aAeqCQAAQBAJ&pg=PA48&lpg=PA48&dq =not +only +an+external+economic+ policy;+it%E2%80%99s+a+strategic+shift+in+India%E2%80%99s+ vision+ of+the+ world+and+ India%E2%80% 99s+place+in+the+global+political+economy& source= bl&ots=ISNLbGeF6A&sig=TXPicMEQDhNWFRBfw7rWW6aNX2I&hl= en&sa= X&ved= 0ahUKEwiYiJnn-Y3NAhUJNI8KHbWkBIMQ6AEIGzAA#v=onepage&q= not%20only%20an% 20external%20economic%20policy%3B%20it%E2%80%99s%20a %20strategic% 20shift%20in%20India%E2%80%99s%20vision%20of%20the%20world% 20and% 20India%E2%80%99s%20place%20in%20the%20global%20political%20economy &f=false (accessed on January 10,2016)

5 Thongkholal Haokip, "India's Look East Policy: Its Evolution and Approach," *South Asian Survey*, vol. 18, issue 2 (2014), pp.239-257.

6 Pal, P. and M. Dasgupta, "The ASEAN-India Free Trade Agreement: An Assessment," *Economic and Political Weekly* (Mumbai), vol. XLIV, no. 38, 2009.

7 "A New Community: For India, a unified Southeast Asian market represents special opportunities and challenges", *Indian Express* (New Delhi), November 24, 2015 available at

http://indianexpress.com/article/opinion/editorials/a-new-community/ (accessed on May 15, 2016)

8 For more details, see R.V.R. Murty, *Andaman & Nicobar Islands: A Geopolitical Perspective* (New Delhi: Northern Book Centre, 2007), pp. 1-202

9 Sam Bateman, Catherine Zara Raymond and Joshua Ho, "Safety and Security in Malacca & Singapore Straits", Policy Paper, *Maritime Security Programme*, Institute of Defence & Strategic Studies, Singapore, 2006.

10 Sudhir Devare, *India & Southeast Asia: Towards Security Convergence* (Singapore: Institute of Southeast Asian Studies, 2006).

11 Sam Bateman, Catherine Zara Raymond and Joshua Ho, "Safety and Security in Malacca & Singapore Straits", Policy Paper, *Maritime Security Programme*, Institute of Defence & Strategic Studies, Singapore, 2006.

12 Available at https://www.security-risks.com/ (accessed on 10th April 2019)

13 Supatn, Nucharee, "Regional Development of the Golden and Emerald Triangle Area: Thai Perspective," in Masami Ishida, ed., *Five Triangle Areas in the Greater Mekong Sub-region,* BRC Research Report no.11, Bangkok Research Centre, IDE-Jestro, Bangkok, Thailand.

14 "China offers to build and fund", *The Daily Star*, September 28, 2012 at www.thedailystar.net/newdesign/news-details.php (accessed on 10th March 2018)

15 Rohini Mohan, "The Great Indian Tuna Robbery", *Tehelka*, March 03, 2012, pp. 12-13.

16 Ashok Sajjanhar, "2 Years On, Has Modi's 'Act East' Policy Made a Difference for India?", *The Diplomat* (Tokyo), June 03, 2016.

17 Tridivesh Singh Maini, "Why India needs to Act East", *East Asia Forum: Economics, Politics and Public Policy in East Asia and the Pacific*, 11th April, 2015 (available at file:///C:/Users/cuj/Downloads/why-india-needs-to-act-east.pdf (cited on 11/07/2018).

6

The Chinese Dominance and the Security Concerns for India and the Region (with special reference to South China Sea)

Chandra Mohan Uppadhaya

The growing dominance of the rising China, has every potential for global instability in the 21st century. My hypothesis treads cautiously on the premise that China is emerging as a revisionist power. It has got security implications and complications for the regional states in particular and the world in general. Any hypothesis to be sound should be tested on the basis of facts and not on fancies. I am putting my hypothesis to this rigorous parameter, leaving the judgement to my honest readers and critics. By challenging the might of America in South-East Asia, China has given the first major hint of its intentions to dominate the region. China's growing economic and military power, has encouraged its initiation of military conflicts. However, the liberalist view leads us to expect that China's growth will deepen Asia's economic interdependence, thereby increasing international stability and regional integration. According to this perspective, we should be worrying not about China's rise but about fear of the rise. Given that China is expected to continue growing and eventually equal the United States in terms of the size of its economy, will we also see China become internationally more aggressive. Some scholars have compared the Chinese growth and aggression and have found that China has become more hostile to its opponents in territorial disputes. Their finding support my position that as China gained greater economic capability, it has become more hostile to its opponents. "To test the above hypotheses, we examine China's practice of initiating militarized conflicts with Asian states and major powers after the death of Mao Zedong, when it began to re-emerge... Using the Militarized Interstate Disputes dataset, which provides information on four types of military action (military threat, military display, use of force, and war, we measure the dependent variable: China's first military action against a particular state in a given year... The dataset contains 55 initiations of militarized conflict by China against Asian and major countries: 22 from 1976 to 1989 and 33 from 1990 to 2001." (Sung C. Jung and Kihyun Lee: The offensive realists are not wrong, Pacific Focus, Inha Journal of International studies, 2017)

China's greater power has made the country more assertive, rather than cooperative, toward Asian states and major powers. This leads me to hypothesise that China will maintain its current uncompromising and adamant position in the South and East China Seas and elsewhere. Renouncing its earlier charade of peaceful rise, China is now asking others to 'get used to its muscle flexing'. China has searched strategic opportunities everywhere in the world. Now it is time for China to reap the rich dividends and South China Sea provides the ample opportunities for the realization of its great game ambitions. Belying any reference to history, China claims almost the entire South China Sea, through which about $5 trillion worth of trade passes each year. The littoral and regional countries along with United States have unequivocally criticized Beijing's build-up of military facilities in the sea and expressed concerns they could be used to restrict free movement. China has shown a great deal of disdain towards its neighbouring countries. The claims and counter claims of territories in South China Sea continue to fester. China's island-building, construction of facilities, and militarization of features in the area proceed unabated.

The rise of China is not disturbing the least because we once fought a war and lost but the implications of resultant dominance is spreading far and wide. It is appropriate to understand the mindset of China, before our painstaking.

Noted Scholar Lucian Pye points out a strange uniqueness of China, which still remains a "civilization pretending to be a nation-state". Lucian Pye, "Social Science Theories in Search of Chinese Realities," (China Quarterly 132 (1992): 1162). The legendary, former US secretary of state, Henry Kissinger aptly describes this situation 'the extent and variety of territory bolsters the sense that China is a world unto itself, and its rulers presiding over ***tian xia***, or All under Heaven". For China, this is essential for a harmonious world order, where harmony emanates, to quote **Confucius** 'from knowing your rightful place in the hierarchy' (Henry Kissinger, On China). The Multi-polarity of 21st century is incompatible with this tian xia approach. It seems quite plausible that behind all the plans to integrate the world, there is a hidden agenda somewhere down the line to rediscover and regain that utopian centrality, lost long ago in the vicissitudes of time.

China has initiated a multifarious project, with a pious declaration of connecting the world economy, popularly known as 'One Belt, One Road' or OBOR. The OBOR, is basically a smoke-screen to hide the real ambitions of ruling the world. It is the part of their cultural front to believe that 'China is a world into itself. China wants to integrate Eurasia through a trillion Dollars of infrastructure. It has rightly been termed by critics As China's New **Marshall Plan**. In a world of competing economic and trade alliances OBOR needs to be compared with its contemporaries—the most famous European union has got 27-members, OPEC has 13, the organization of Islamic states (OIC) has 57. OBOR surpasses all with its 60 members. (Indian express 16 may 2017). The initiative has since been widely discussed between policy makers and academics both inside and outside China. Many questions have been asked like 'why did China come up with such a strategy at this point of time, when it is already slowing down or what are the real intentions behind it? Is it not the Pax-China in disguise? To put simply it is the long-cherished dream of Middle-Kingdom or '***zhongguo***' by another name.

India decided not to participate. India was invited to the Beijing conclave. India has got a number of reasons for staying away. None of them was more important than the question of India's sovereignty over Pak-occupied Kashmir (POK), through which an important part of China's OBOR runs. The foreign office in Delhi affirmed that "No country can accept a project that ignores its core concerns on sovereignty and territorial integrity writes. The Foreign policy expert C. Raja Mohan writes, 'international isolation is not India's biggest problem ... India is too large an economy and political entity to be isolated by another power, occupying a vertical Geographical location, India can contribute to the success of China's belt and Road initiative or create needless complications." India's real challenge is to match its claim on territorial sovereignty with effective action on the ground." (C Raja Mohan: 'the politics of territory'; Contributed to Carnegie Foundation May 16, 2017)

It is not India alone but the world community at large is quite concerned with the magnitude of initiatives around the globe. One of the most venerated scholars of international politics, Joseph S. Nye Makes a stinging observation "Marco Polo would be proud. And if China chooses to use its surplus financial reserves to create important infrastructure that helps poor countries...China's motives are not purely philanthropic. (Joseph Nye: 'Xi Jinping's Marco Polo Strategy' project-syndicate.org, June 12, 2017)

As the financial times put it, BRI "unfortunately is no more a practical plan for investment than a broad political vision". May 12, 2017. The financial part of the plan is exposed more than ever. Many countries who earlier enthusiastically participated like Pakistan and Sri Lanka, are now reeling under the debt burden. Speaking at Shangri-La in Singapore Prime Minister Modi also underlined the deliberate debt-trap in the name of connectivity: "We understand the benefits of connectivity. There are many connectivity initiatives in the region. If these are to succeed, we must not only build infrastructure; we must also build bridges of trust. And for that, these initiatives must be based on respect for sovereignty and territorial integrity, consultation, good governance, transparency, viability and sustainability. They must empower nations, not place them under an impossible debt burden." Finally, all of this is possible if we do not return to the age of great-power rivalries. I have said this before: an Asia of rivalry will hold us all back; an Asia of cooperation will shape this century. So, each nation must ask itself: are its choices building a more united world, or forcing new divisions? It is a responsibility that both existing and rising powers have. Competition is normal, but contests must not turn into conflicts; differences must not be allowed to become disputes. (PM Modi, at Shangri-La Dialogue, JUNE I, 2018', online source)

Asian and particularly South-Asian countries have tried to balance the over bearing presence of China but in the absence of a strong US backing, these countries would fall back on China, as rightly maintained by Samuel P. Huntington 'a band-wagoning propensity is likely to exist among Asian powers, which would preclude any US effort at secondary balancing'. (Huntington: The Clash of Civilizations and Remaking of World order, p.233).

America is aware of this propensity and therefore it is already ready with strategy. American defence secretary James Mattis elaborated it at 17th Asian Security Summit, Shangri-La "America's Indo-Pacific strategy is a subset of our broader security strategy, codifying our principles as America continues to 'look west'. In it we see deepening alliances and partnerships as a priority; ASEAN's centrality remains vital; and cooperation with China is welcome wherever possible." (James Mattis: speech at Shangri-La June 2, 2018)

India and US both stressed that no one nation can or should dominate the Indo-Pacific. The maritime commons, is a global good, and sea lanes of communication are the arteries of economic vitality for all. It is in the best interest of the region to preserve that vitality. US promised to help the regional players to build up naval and law-enforcement capabilities and capacities to improve monitoring and protection of maritime borders and interests. So long as littoral nations pool their resources to be a force multiplier for peace, no miracle is going to happen. Therefore, the regional states need to ensure that their military can more easily integrate with others. The strategy is to include Australia and New-Zealand also in the ambit of Indo-Pacific security cooperation. The US values the role India can play in regional and global security and views the US-India relationship as a natural partnership between the world's two largest democracies based on a convergence of strategic interests, shared values and respect for a rules-based international order.

Considering the enormity of the challenge from China, Americans are invoking the cooperation from other Pacific allies, such as the United Kingdom, France and Canada to build a strong and lasting alternative. China on its part has promised several times to play by rules but never shied away from overt to covert arm-twisting of the regional countries. China's militarisation of artificial features in the South China Sea includes the deployment of anti-ship missiles, surface-to-air missiles, electronic jammers and, more recently, the landing of bomber aircraft at Woody Island. Despite China's claims to the contrary, the placement of these weapons systems is tied directly to military use for the purposes of intimidation and coercion. China's militarisation of the Spratlys is also in direct contradiction to President Xi's public assurances. Given the precarious nature of America leadership, India should take a lead. We must seriously invest in several groupings which are lying dormant like Indian Ocean Rim countries (IORC), & BIMSTEC, BBIN and Mekong-Ganga Cooperation (GMC), which was conceived more than a decade (year 2000) ago. Our record of translating conceptions into creations is dismal. It is here that our real test lies. It is in this regard a significant development worth mentioning. India and Japan have launched a vision document for Asia-Africa Growth Corridor (AAGC). The AAGC initiative is part of Indo-Pacific freedom corridor being put in place by India and Japan with an eye on counterbalancing the Chinese OBOR. It aims for Indo-Japanese collaboration to develop quality infrastructure in Africa, complemented by digital connectivity. Let us examine the ground zero.

China Domineering Behaviour with Philippines and other Regional Countries

China claims particularly on Scarborough Shoal in the Spratly Islands have been rejected by the International Tribunal of the Permanent Court of Arbitration (PCA) at Hague. The PCA at Hague handed down its historic and sweeping award on maritime entitlements in South China Sea, overwhelmingly favouring the Philippines over China. The ruling was a major victory for the Philippines, particularly the tribunal's decision on China's "nine-dash line," through which Beijing attempts to lay claim to vast areas of the South China Sea. As expected, Beijing refused to accept the PCA ruling, hardened its legal and diplomatic positions, and. Within hours of the ruling, at least 68 national and local government websites in the Philippines were knocked offline in a massive Distributed Denial of service attack. The crippling DDOS attacks against Filipino government networks continued over several days and targeted key government agencies, to include the Department of Foreign Affairs, the Department of National Defence, and the Central Bank. Within few months after the award, under the huge pressure from China, Philippines issued a conciliatory statement even as energy official announced that Manila would soon offer investors new oil and gas blocks at Reed Bank, off the Philippine coast but within the nine-dash line. (Foreign Affairs: July 2017)

Beijing, for its part, has always made clear that it regards the tribunal's decision as "null and void" and of 'no binding force.' Statements from Association of Southeast Asian Nations (ASEAN) states in the wake of the decision were muted. None urged China to adhere to the ruling; the strongest merely called for respecting international law. The real significance of the tribunal's decision was to clarify resource rights. Its main findings were twofold. "First, it ruled that China cannot claim historic rights to resources in the waters within the nine-dash line if those waters are within the EEZs of other coastal states. Such rights were extinguished when China ratified the UN Convention on the Law of the Sea in 1996. Second, the tribunal ruled that none of the features in the Spratlys is entitled to a 200-nautical-mile EEZ. Like Scarborough Shoal, all of the Spratly features are at most rocks entitled to 12-nautical-mile territorial seas". (Foreign Affairs: July 2017)

Although technically binding only on parties to the arbitration, the tribunal's decision has bolstered the position of ASEAN littoral states in the South China Sea. It has clarified that the EEZ entitlements of the Philippines, as well as Brunei, Indonesia, Malaysia, and Vietnam, are unencumbered by China's nine-dash line or any claimed EEZ from features in the Spratlys. Areas of overlap in the Spratlys are now limited to a 12-nautical-mile ring around rock features. Beyond these areas, China has no claim recognized under international law to fish or to extract oil or gas in the EEZs of other states outside the EEZ generated from China's mainland.

In assessing the impact of the award, what China and ASEAN states do is at least as important as what they say. In official statements issued on the day of and after the judgment, Beijing appeared to expressly assert, for the first time, that China's maritime claims in the South China Sea include "historic rights." It did not specify what it means by this. China is a country whose history is best known to it. It has claims over almost all the neighbouring countries. From centuries Tibet had been an autonomous region, paying tributes to Chinese and adjoining Indian kingdoms. Suddenly China discovered its forgotten history only to capture the Tibet. It has still remnant claims over India after illegally capturing 24000 sq km of our motherland. It claims are wide ranging covering not only land-masses but sea areas also. The South-China controversy is nothing but the same kind of historical claim over a number-countries. However, if Beijing is claiming historic rights to resources within the entirety of the nine-dash line (rather than historic fishing rights within territorial seas), its assertion flies in the face of the judgment. In May 2018, Beijing also imposed an annual fishing ban, which overlapped with the EEZs of the Philippines and Vietnam but excluded the Spratlys. The Philippines has been a key ally of the United States and a territorial rival of Beijing in the South China Sea. The impact of Beijing's action could be assessed by the fact that within few days of this orchestrated drama the President of Philippines Duterte announced during a visit to China, his "separation" from Washington and realignment with Beijing. This is another form of bandwagoning.

India and South China Sea

Indian trade and economic linkages in the Pacific are becoming stronger and deeper. Not only are ASEAN and the far-eastern Pacific key target areas of the "Act East" policy, Asia's Eastern commons are increasingly a vital facilitator of India's economic development. With growing dependence on the Malacca Strait for the flow of goods and services, economics is increasingly a factor in India's Pacific policy. China must know that territorial conflicts in the SCS threaten the future trajectory of India's economic development, creating an unacceptable hindrance for regional trade and commerce. India believes that the disputes in the Southeast Asian littorals are a litmus test for international maritime law. In the aftermath of The Hague, tribunal's verdict on the South China Sea, New Delhi feels obligated to take a principled stand on the issue of freedom of navigation and commercial access as enshrined in the UNCLOS. "Beijing must know that regardless of the guarantees it seeks from India about staying neutral on the SCS, New Delhi cannot be seen to be condoning the aggression of armed Chinese naval ships, aircraft and submarines in the region." (Abhijit Singh: IDSA, New Delhi, August 2016)

Beijing must know that New Delhi recognizes the threat that Chinese aggression poses for the wider Asian commons – in particular, the exacerbation of existing power asymmetries. In order, to contribute to a fair and equitable regional maritime order, New Delhi must take a stand that restores strategic balance in maritime-Asia.

New Delhi's inability or rather the old habit of suppression of information and sometimes denial makes Indian positions unsustainable. Renowned scholar and journalist Arun Shourie has correctly summed up our position wishful construction...paste a motive, fling a doubt at the messenger, discredit him...minimize what the adversary has done...manufacture explanations and at each turn summarily pronounce "But what else could we have been done" (Arun Shourie: 'Self-Deception', Harper Collins, New Delhi, 2013, pp.7,8.)

For instance, the co-relation the Indian maritime analysts discern between aggressive Chinese patrolling in the SCS and its growing deployments in the Indian Ocean Region; or the suspicion in Indian strategic circles that China might use its SCS bases as a springboard for active projection of power in the Indian Ocean and never the less keeping studied silence. So is the case of India's aggressive encirclement by China, its permanent presence in POK, its calculated incursions in Uttarakhand. Everywhere our response is not only inadequate but at best reactive. New Delhi should really worry about China's reclamation and militarization of features in its possession – particularly the deployment of missiles, fighters and surveillance equipment in its Spratly group of islands, allowing the PLAN (PLA Navy) effective control over the entire range of maritime operations in the SCS. New developments in China's military strategy are also notable. "Recently, Beijing has strengthened its anti-access/area denial (A2/AD) strategy in order to protect its core interests, including Taiwan, from interference by external forces, such as the United States. More specically, the A2/AD entails changes in military plans and strategies for air, maritime, submarine, space, and cyber warfare. For example, the People's Liberation Army Air Force (PLAAF) has decided to develop long-range mission capabilities and high-tech equipment, such as anti-satellite weapons". (Sung C. Jung and Kihyun Lee: The offensive realists are not wrong, Pacific Focus, Inha Journal of International studies, 2017)

The People's Liberation Army Navy (PLAN) aims to expand its scope of influence from the first island chain, connecting Okinawa, Taiwan, and the Philippines, to the second island chain, connecting Guam and Saipan. In this regard, PLAN has declared a territorial sea baseline and air defence identification zone (ADIZ), has conducted regular patrols of the Diaoyu/Senkaku Islands, and has constructed artificial islands in the South China Sea, among other activities. Such military expansions present challenges to the US-led regional order that has existed in Asia since the end of World War II. Indian experts should also recognize the important role Beijing's militia forces play in achieving its regional objectives. India knows well that the main threat to maritime security in Asia isn't so much from the PLA Navy, but China's irregular forces. Chinese surveillance ships, coast guard vessels and fishing fleets are the real force behind Beijing's dominance of the littoral spaces. "With the expansion of Chinese maritime activities in the IOR, New Delhi fears a rise in non-grey hull presence in the Eastern Indian Ocean. Already, China's distant water fishing fleet is now the world's largest, and is a heavily subsidized maritime commercial entity. While an increase in the presence of such ships doesn't always pose a security threat, India remains wary of Chinese non-military maritime activity in the Eastern Indian Ocean". (Abhijit: IDSA New Delhi August, 2016)

Beijing's blueprint for maritime operations in the Indian Ocean involves the construction of multiple logistical facilities. China's 10-year agreement with Djibouti in 2015 for the setting up of a naval replenishment facility in the northern O bock region is widely seen as proof of the PLA Navy's strategic ambitions in the IOR. And this anticipation has proven right.

Djibouti is a resource-poor nation in the Horn of Africa. Its location also matters greatly to global commerce and energy, due to its vicinity to the Mandeb strait and the Suez-Aden canal, which sees 10 percent of oil and 20 percent of commercial exports annually. (Joseph Braude and Tyler Jiang: Huffington post, online retrieved)

"The greatest worry is America's diminishing military footprints. It has begun to affect the calculation of allies and rivals alike". (Joseph Braude and Tyler Jiang: Huffington post, online retrieved)

US has tried to address this fear also. In his brilliant speech at Shangri-La Dialogue on June 2, 2018, James Mattis was quite forthcoming "So make no mistake, America is in the Indo-Pacific to stay. This is our priority theatre. Our interests and the region's, are inextricably intertwined."

In fact, US and China are actually playing the role of the history. The United States embodies what Huntington considered 'Western civilization'. And tensions between American and Chinese values, traditions, and philosophies will aggravate the fundamental structural stresses that occur whenever a rising power, such as China, threatens to displace an established power, such as the United States. A conflicting situation is ensued, in the words of famous Historian Graham Allison, this is **Thucydides'** ***trap***. According to Thucydides, "It was the rise of Athens, and the fear that this instilled in Sparta, that made war inevitable." Rising powers understandably feel a growing sense of entitlement and demand greater influence and respect. Established powers, faced with challengers, tend to become fearful, insecure, and defensive. (Graham Allison, 2017 Foreign Affairs)

With its new-found self-confidence, China is building military bases next door to US AFRICOM in Djibouti. India must learn right lessons from several such episodes. China is just not any-other strong nation being satisfied by playing a second fiddle. It has its global ambitions and it is unabashed about it. No victim card will fetch security and dignity to India. Long ago Thucydides reminded the succeeding generations through his 'Melian Dialogue' that "standard of justice depends on the equality of power to compel and in fact the strong do what they have the power to do and the weak accept what they have to accept. (The Globalization of World Politics: Oxford University Press 2008, USA, p.97)

Our preparedness is not up to the mark and the kind of policy paralysis is visible even today. This is disappointing for a country which harbours the ambitions of attaining great power status. Indian leaders have not articulated the full extent of their anxieties over Chinese maritime operations in Asia. Regardless of the concessions on offer to New Delhi, Beijing must know that India will not agree to a compromise deal with China on the South China Sea.

It is in the light of this situation and Chinese overall aggressive postures in South China Sea that Indian Prime Minister Narendra Modi's visit to Vietnam in September 2016 and his Japan visit in the second week of November marked an important step forward in their ties. The fact that the PM chose to drop by Vietnam on his way to the G20 Summit in Hangzhou, China would not be lost on observers and must have ruffled quite a few feathers in Beijing. It also comes in the wake of July 12 awards handed down by the Permanent Court of Arbitration. Despite the open suggestion to India by China during the recent visit to Japan, Prime Minister Modi went to stress that "India supports freedom of navigation and over flight, unimpeded commerce, based on the principles of international law, as reflected notably in the UNCLOS." (Indian Express, July 13, 2017.)

In an age when geopolitics in the region is in a state of flux, it is essential for India to stand by our friends. Just as China has been wading into India's neighbourhood, there is no reason why India should shy away from doing the same in China's extended neighbourhood. With its soft power and lately hard power in full flow in Vietnam and Japan, New Delhi must be careful not to squander the new opportunities.

The Policy Alternative Before India and the Region

For China, order is the highest value, and harmony results from a hierarchy. In some ways, Chinese exceptionalism is more sweeping than its American counterpart. "The [Chinese] empire saw itself as the centre of the civilized universe," the historian Harry Gelber, wrote in his book, 'Nations Out of Empires'. (Harry Gilber: "Nations out of Empires", Palgrave Macmillan, UK, 2001, p.79) This notion is buttressed when we come across such kind of assertions, from no less a person than President himself. Xi claimed in his book, 'The Governance of China', that "China's continuous civilization is not equal to anything on earth, but a unique achievement in world history." (Xi: Governance of China, Foreign Language Press, 2014, p.11). China's treatment of its own citizens provides the script for its relations with weaker neighbours abroad. During a meeting of the Association of Southeast Asian Nations, then Chinese Foreign Minister Yang Jiechi responded to complaints about Chinese assertiveness in the South China Sea by telling his regional counterparts and U.S. Secretary of State Hillary Clinton that "China is a big country and other countries are small countries, and that's just a fact." (Indian Express, June 05, 2010.) China enters the global arena for ***shi*** or relative advantage. It is against the backdrop of hegemonical behaviour of China that Japan took the initiative. One of the interesting features of Japan's latest plan to revive the Indo-Pacific quadrilateral dialogue (Quad), is the move to associate the European powers with it. For Prime Minister of Japan, Shinzo Abe, who first discussed the idea of a quad a little over a decade ago, the four-nation forum is, in essence, a coalition of "maritime democracies". Abe argued that the maritime democracies have a stake in securing a rules-based global order, liberal trading system and freedom of navigation. 'As a realist Abe is conscious of the fact that the growing power imbalance in Asia amidst the rapid rise of China can't be addressed by America's Asian alliance system alone. Abe has consciously courted special relationships with India, Australia and other regional powers. He also sees the need to keep the **quad** an open-ended organisation that can also benefit from the partnership with European powers.' (C Raja Mohan October 31, 2017, Indian Express). More than 70% of European trade passes through Indo-Pacific.

Both France and Britain have military presence and security arrangements in the Indian Ocean. France has many military facilities in the Indo-Pacific, including those in Reunion, Djibouti and the United Arab Emirates. Britain continues to control Diego Garcia. It also leads the Five Power Defence Arrangement (involving Singapore, Malaysia, Australia and New Zealand) set up in 1971. France has a variety of coordination mechanisms in the Pacific with the United States, Japan, Australia and New Zealand. As India is concerned about the strategic implications of China's port building in Gwadar (Pakistan), and Hambantota (Sri-Lanka), Canberra too is concerned about Chinese push for militarization of Vanuatu islands. Similarly, Japan has also burnt its fingers at Senkaku/Diaoyu islands. Therefore, this convergence of maritime democracies is not coincidental, but rather it is of late recognition of a common-threat. India already has a strong bilateral security engagement with countries like France and Britain. Issues relating to maritime security have been at the top of the agenda. As Delhi prepares to cope with China's rapid naval advances in the Indian Ocean and deploys its ships far from the Indian shores, it needs to bring together its bilateral cooperation with individual European countries into a comprehensive strategic framework. Japan's plans to bring France and Britain on board the **QUAD** can only reinforce India's maritime partnerships with Europe.

Freedom of navigation, is one of the most essential aspect of maritime cooperation. No wonder, Prime Minister Narendra Modi found time during the busy election season to travel all the way south to Male, the capital of the Maldives. Modi's presence at the swearing-in of the new president of the Maldives, Ibrahim Mohamed Solih, underlined the renewed warmth in the relations between the two countries. Under Solih's predecessor, Abdulla Yameen, India's relations with the Maldives rapidly deteriorated even as China's influence began to rise. The intersection of Sino-Indian rivalry with domestic politics has also come to the fore in neighbouring Sri Lanka. India supported Prime Minister Ranil Wickremesinghe, while China openly sided with the former president Mahinda Rajapaksa. During Rajapaksa's decade-long rule of Sri Lanka (2004-15), Colombo seemed to steadily drift into China's orbit. Symbolising China's new influence in Lanka were the strategic contracts it won to build the Colombo port city and the construction of a new port at Hambantota in the southern part of the island. India, in turn, appeared to lose its historic primacy in the island state. Now we have regained our balance in Sri Lanka also.

Like India in the Indian Ocean, Australia and New Zealand had underestimated the scale and speed of China's power projection into their South Pacific neighbourhood. So, did the US, which failed to react in time to China's push to gain control of the small rocks and islands of the South China Sea at the beginning of this decade. We can not allow the historic opportunity, which has come to us in the name of Indo-Pacific, to be squandered, this time. To be sure, the novelty of the Indo-Pacific lies in recognising the growing strategic and economic interdependence of the Pacific and Indian Ocean littorals that we saw as separate theatres until recently. Noted strategic thinker C Raja Mohan is quite categorical here "Indo-Pacific is also a sum of its many sub-regions that include the East China Sea, South China Sea and South Pacific to the east of the Malacca Straits as well as the Bay of Bengal, Arabian Sea and the waters of Africa to the west. What India does in these sub-regions is far more important than the abstract debates on the Indo-Pacific. One such sub-region, the Andaman Sea—is likely to preoccupy India in the coming years." (C. Raja Mohan, Carnegie, November 13, 2018.)

The Andaman Sea is flanked by the Andaman and Nicobar chain of islands in the West, Myanmar to the north, the Thai-Malay peninsula to the east, and the Sumatra island to the south. It funnels into the Straits of Malacca that connects the Indian and Pacific Oceans. The large amount of shipping that enters the Andaman Sea from the east heads to Singapore, from where it turns the Pacific Ocean. After the Second World War, the partition of India and the Cold War between America and Russia, the Andamans became marginal to the new geopolitics. The rise of China and its projection of naval power way beyond its home waters is beginning to put the Andaman Sea back in play. Beijing has signed an agreement with Naypyidaw on building a deep-water port at Kyaukpyu on Myanmar's Arakan coast in the Bay of Bengal. The port will form an important part of the China-Myanmar Economic Corridor, which would connect Kyaukpyu to the Yunnan province in southwestern China via rail and highways. China is already assessing the cost of building Kra-canal to link the Andaman-Sea to the gulf of Thailand. China is also enhancing its military profile by selling nuclear Submarines to Bangladesh and Thailand, and conducting military exercises with Thailand and Malaysia.

For India Andaman sea has assumed a new significance. As a sequel to our Look-East Policy, we have conducted largest ever naval exercise with Singapore, aptly called 'Simbex', in Andaman Sea. These exercises began 25-years ago. Prime-Minister Modi's visited and renamed three islands, on the occasion of 75th anniversary of Subhas Chandra Bose flying the tricolour in Port Blair has helped highlight the role of Andaman and Nicobar Islands in India's freedom struggle. New Delhi has decided to end the isolation of the island chain and promoting economic development, tighter integration with the mainland, strengthening military infrastructure, regional connectivity and international collaboration. It is in this regard that we can also connect our efforts out of Malabar exercises. The 22nd rendition of the Malabar naval exercise, held for the first time in waters off the coast of Guam and involving aircraft and ships from Indian Navy, the U.S. Navy, and the Japan Maritime Self Défense Force (JMSDF), officially came to an end on June 16, 2018. The Malabar naval exercise began as a joint Indo-U.S. naval exercise in 1992. Japan became a permanent participant in 2015. This year, India once again refused Australia's bid to take part in the 2018 iteration of the exercise. This is very disappointing, given our penchant, particularly for cooperation among maritime democracies. It is again inhibiting to the evolution of **quad**. India does not need to be a scared partner of China's Band-wagon. We are not supporting confrontationist India. We have to search every possible opportunity to work and collaborate with China. India has shown enough maturity and courage by joining Shanghai Cooperation Organization (SCO) which is also a brain child of China. What we want is a dignified presence at decision making table. We want the respect for our unity, integrity and of course the security of our land, air and territorial waters along with the freedom of navigation across various sea-routes. The over-bearing presence and the domineering behaviour of China has really created a disequilibrium. We have to address this disbalance in the right earnest, lest we should fall prey to another deceptive design of devouring Dragon.

7

Shifting Strategic Dynamics in the Indo-Pacific Region: Implications for Australia and India

D. Gopal

Introduction

President Donald John Trump in his foreign policy propositions has indicated that his administration will be less inclined in honouring the existing alliance system in its current format, and will tend more towards economic development of the United States to "make America great again".[1] This overture raises a serious question mark as to how the new administration will respond to Barack Obama initiated and Hillary Clinton championed "pivot" or in softer terms "re-balancing" of Asia. The re-balancing was coined against the backdrop of the US's shift in its interest in the Middle East and quick fill of the power vacuum in Asia-Pacific by China.

Yet a major issue for the Trump administration will be how to respond to a rising China and its assertion both economically and militarily in the South China Sea (SCS) and the Indo-Pacific region *per se*. The Indo-Pacific region, no doubt, is passing through a flux to adjust to the evolving regional and global order, for that several permutations and combinations appear to be in the process. Major countries like India, Australia, Japan, Philippines, Indonesia, Malaysia, Vietnam and others are either openly reckoning the Chinese power and potential, or are entering in bilateral, trilateral or multilateral security and strategic agreements to maintain the status quo, balance of power, hedging or strengthening their alliance or partnership with the US.

Overall, China's ascendance, the US withdrawal or in a sense conceding to Beijing to continue its assertive power postures in the region, and the alliance countries like Japan, South Korea, Philippines and Australia's, perception of feeling jittery on being left high and dry to fend themselves or buy the US alliance with monetary contributions gives rise to a complex, uncertain and perilous situation. Placed in this critical predicament, states in the region are pushed into an imbroglio as how to respond to the evolving power shift and what options countries like India and Australia have, whether they can defy the Cold War psyche and adapt to withstand the shifting power paradigm.

China–US Strategic Manoeuvres China

China in its strategic overtures has unambiguously charted out its strategic imperatives that President Xi Jinping succinctly outlined in 2014 at the Conference on Interaction and Confidence Building Measures in Asia, "It is for the people of Asia to run the affairs of Asia, solve the problems of Asia, and uphold the security of Asia".[2] This statement undoubtedly reflected that China aims to restrict the role of external powers in the Asian security and strategic affairs. In this statement, also implicit is that Beijing considers itself as the most prominent power in Asia and intends to play an uncontested leadership role to shape an order that constitutes a unipolar Asia under the strategic and security aegis of China. This means taking the Asian affairs away from the Western patterned alliance system to one that promotes "security through dialogue".[3]

United States believes that China is number one adversary for incoming decades and particularly in Asia. Against this backdrop, China's pursuit of its publicly stated strategic delineations such as Anti-Access Area Denial (A2/AD), second island chain of defence, creation of an Air Defence Identification Zone (ADIZ) over the East China Sea and its claims over the South China Sea through the nine-dash line, have posed strategic and security challenges for the regional countries as well as for the US. These challenges were evident with the release of its ninth Defence White Paper entitled China's Military Strategy in May 2015, which outlined a new military strategy that charted a more "active defence posture". In this regard, the Paper highlighted challenges at two levels, one at regional level referred to as "some of its offshore neighbours take provocative actions and reinforce their military presence on China's reefs and islands that they have illegally occupied" and the other of "external countries...busy meddling in South China Sea Affairs".

Considering the evolving strategic challenges, China envisages winning the "local wars under informatised conditions" and the external wars by expanding "offshore waters defence" with "open seas protection". Therefore, Beijing emphasises on strengthening its determination to "strategic management of the sea"[4] and developing a robust anti-access/area denial punch that includes short, medium and intercontinental range ballistic missiles, anti-ship ballistic missiles (ASBM), destroyers bristling with cruise missiles, and nuclear-armed submarines.[5]

However, Beijing's claim of "neighbours take provocative actions... reinforce their military presence...illegally occupied" China's reefs and islands proved volte-face with the July 2016 decision by the Permanent Court of Arbitration award in The Republic of Philippines v. The People's Republic of China.[6] The Tribunal concluded that there was no legal basis for China to claim historic rights to resources in the areas that fall within the nine-dash line. It was judged that none of the features claimed by China can generate an Exclusive Economic Zone (EEZ) and that certain sea areas claimed by China were within the EEZ of the Philippines. Since these areas not being overlapped by any possible Chinese entitlement, it was decided that China had violated the Philippines' EEZ and its sovereign rights by interfering with Philippine fishing and petroleum exploration, through the construction of artificial islands, and by failing to prevent Chinese fishermen from fishing in the zone.

Instead of accepting the decision, Beijing repeatedly expressed its denouncement saying, "It will neither accept nor participate in the arbitration unilaterally initiated by the Philippines".[7] Furthermore, China negated the judgement by stating: "PRC solemnly declares that the award is null and void and has no binding force. China neither accepts nor recognises it".[8] Notwithstanding such behaviour, China still considers its rise as a peaceful development and supports amicable relations with the Asian countries. In the words of President Xi Jinping: "We believe that it is necessary to advocate common, comprehensive, cooperative and sustainable security in Asia. We need to innovate our security concept, establish a new regional security cooperation architecture, and jointly build a road for security of Asia that is shared by and win-win to all".[9]

As against China's proclamation of an order steered for common Asian security and strategic interests and challenges, Beijing is being accused by the regional states as a hegemonic power that aims to suppress the regional security ambiance and forcefully control the resources and territories in the region. Such as Beijing's claim over the SCS has connotation not just on the sea water but also on the estimated deposits in the range of 11 billion barrels of oil, 190 trillion cubic foot of natural gas, and around 12 per cent of global fisheries catch. While being energy rich, it is also strategic with $5.3 trillion sea-borne trade passing through it every year.[10] Thus, dredging and filling to create artificial islands in the SCS and sailing of its nuclear submarines in the Indian Ocean proves duality between the stated and actioned objectives of peaceful rise.[11] China's response to its territorial disputes with its neighbours has not demonstrated what has been elaborated in its statements at different forums.

These actions, against the Chinese claims of regional prosperity and win-win equation, raise apprehension at the regional level as the states support status quo in the Asia-Pacific region as a prerequisite for the peaceful development and prosperity. The arbitration judgement not only supported the regional states to aspire for their legitimate claims but also exposed China as a coercive power. In a sense, "China will almost immediately abrogate its moral and ethical right to state or stake a position in future international arbitrations of all kinds".[12]

United States

The United States acted as a guarantor of peace in the Asia-Pacific region from post-Second World War till its involvement in Afghanistan and Iraq wars. This involvement proved opportune for China to fill the power vacuum swiftly. Witnessing Beijing's increasing assertive military power projection in the region, the US in response to these overtures in turn gave impetus to its strategy of 'rebalancing', as Secretary of State, Hillary Clinton underlined in her article in the journal *Foreign Policy*, the US' "strategic turn" to the Indo-Pacific region. These strategies among others included: strengthening the existing bilateral security alliances; deepening working relationship with emerging powers including China; engaging with regional multilateral institutions; and forging a broad-based military presence.[13] In order to enforce a rebalance, a major focus of the US has been to modernise existing alliances with treaty allies such as Japan, Korea, Australia, the Philippines and Thailand, and expand and deepen partnerships with Singapore, Vietnam, India, Indonesia and others.[14]

In his address to the Australian Parliament in 2011, President Barack Obama reinforced that the United States is a "Pacific power 'here to stay'" and that he had instructed his national security team to make "America's presence in the region a top priority". Furthermore, he reiterated, "Let there be no doubt, in Asia-Pacific in the 21st century, the United States of America is all in".[15] Thus to realise the re-balancing, the US continues to build-on and reinforce its Indo-Pacific partnerships with India, Japan, Australia, South Korea and Taiwan because it cannot defend vital national interests in Asia without them.[16] According to strategists, Hillary Clinton, as Secretary of State quite emphatically expressed her determination to "spare no effort to contain China's rise" as a result she was considered "fiercely anti-China".[17]

Against this backdrop, the entry of President Trump in the political horizon of the US gave rise to new strategic dynamics. He has indicated to radically alter focus from the strategic calculations to pressing economic imperatives. To administer this, he indicated to reduce the US military footprint in the Asia-Pacific region. Trump pointed towards a staggering $19 trillion debt, that he explained: "We're sitting, probably, on a bubble. And it's a bubble that if it breaks, it's going to be very nasty. I just think we have to rebuild our country". To meet this objective, Trump underlined "unabashedly noninterventionist approach to world affairs" and questioned "the value of massive military investments in Asia". To counter China, or "to halt China's military airfields on reclaimed islands" in the South China Sea, Trump supported countering by limiting China's access to American markets.[18] Thus, rather than a military threat or deterrence, China's hegemonic overtures can be neutralised through trade tariff on goods emanating from there, Trump signaled: "Who the hell cares if there's a trade war?".[19] He has threatened to impose tariff as high as 45 per cent on imports from China.[20] To begin with, Trump is projected as a repeat of President Andrew Jackson (1829 to 1837) as a "nationalist, populist, suspicious of the outside world—and willing to use force to beat it back".[21] Even the Chinese sources consider Trump as "'volatile' and 'unpredictable', less than desirable traits when it comes to handling great-power relations".[22]

Though it is difficult to extrapolate at this stage as how the Trump administration will thrust its presence in the Indo-Pacific region, however, based on the initial indicators different scenarios can be envisaged in the following section.

Implications of Trump's Policies Postures

The tribunal award and Trump's election victory took place within a gap of few months. The George Bush and Obama administrations had reflected continuation of the US's Asia-Pacific policy while flexing muscles at times, remained reticent on some of the regional issues. Even on the Arbitration Tribunal award and China's rejection of it in action and spirit, the US instead of instigating a confrontational approach, appealed the concerned parties to keep restrain, while not supporting "any one side in territorial disputes, it insisted on ensuring respect for freedom of navigation and overflight in the South China Sea". The US further cautioned the parties to avoid conflict and opt for "peaceful resolution of disputes and... all parties to respect International Law, including the UNCLOS". At the same time, Washington also set the red lines for China to not to adopt "aggressive moves" and claim "enhanced air defence identification zone" and harass the ships and aircrafts passing through the SCS.[23]

It is quite apposite to postulate that the US and China will not be involved in any direct military conflict. So the question arises, how will these two powers *manoeuvre*, challenge, or accommodate each other?

The first option could be that the Trump administration will continue to project its overtures of 're-balancing' in the Indo-Pacific region simply to remain relevant and competitive. And continue to neutralise China's hegemonic actions by navigating within the 12 nautical miles of the disputed territories and support the existing alliance and partnership network. At the same time, not initiating any action that could thrust China in an offensive mode. Thus, thwart China's ambition to exert hegemonic control over Asia in a modern tributary system. As attested by retired US Marine Corps General James Mattis, China intends to construct a "tribute model" with the intention to exert a "veto authority in each of the countries around their periphery".[24] This perception was further reinforced by the new US defence strategy launched in January 2012, when the US Chairman of the Joint Chiefs of Staff, General Martin Dempsey, without mentioning China by name outlined: "All trends are shifting to the Pacific.... Our strategic challenges will largely emanate out of the Pacific region".[25] Thus, under this approach Trump could follow a "congagement": a mixture of enhanced containment and engagement, as opposed to the "smart power" doctrine of the Obama years.[26]

The second option could be that the US retain a symbolic presence in the region and support the major regional powers to go nuclear. This will certainly pose regional deterrence to counter China and will prove restraint on Beijing to not to push any neighbour to the point of nuclear aggression. If China continues to exert its power in the region, Asia-Pacific states most likely will band together to contain and constrain China's increasing influence and power, in order to ensure their own influence is not diminished in this zero-sum game. China has already expressed its resentment over the new Indo-Pacific strategic construct in that it believes this effort is being orchestrated, not only to deny China its rightful place in the international system, but to create multi-polarity, multilateralism and a so-called rules-based international order, all interfering with China's one-on-one relations with its neighbours.[27] Inclusion of the Indian Ocean region in this calculus only raises China's apprehensions that it is being bracketed and isolated by a wider-ranging containment strategy, one where a nuclear India is considered a threat to China's ambitions in the medium-to-long term.

The third option could be the US assumes a leading role in the Indo-Pacific region but auctions its security umbrella for bidding by the regional states. This means, the states could enter a deal based on individual security requirements and accordingly pay for the cover. Thus, the regional states building a credible deterrence by procuring their security under the US umbrella. Perhaps this is the most favourable proposition that Trump is indicating at corporate style stakeholders based paradigm.

To counter such manoeuvres, Beijing has established credible economic and infrastructure initiatives with the ASEAN states. In the process, China has become their largest and most influential trading partner. In a sense, "China lobbied for the exclusion of not only the United States but also India, Australia and New Zealand...from the East Asia Summit".[28] Against this backdrop, Beijing's strategic intent and framework becomes clearer, a desire to establish a unipolar Asia-Pacific region with China at the centre. In November 2014, President Xi Jinping in his address to a Central Foreign Affairs Work Conference while propping up a carrot and stick policy affirmed that, "a proactive, balanced, and where necessary, muscular foreign policy approach is likely to be a hallmark of his rule". At the same time while assuaging the concerns of its neighbours, Xi implored, "China's rise can only be accomplished by peaceful means and will only be pursued with an eye toward achieving 'win-win' outcomes for all concerned".[29] Plying both offensive and defensive diplomacies, Beijing still remains on the defensive mainly because of lack of reliable allies other than North Korea, Pakistan and potentially Russia, China is somewhat isolated in its own region of influence, as its aspirations of a China-centric, unipolar Asia appear to be threatened by US military presence, interference and particularly military alliances.[30]

Economically, China seeks to exert financial leverage against the US strategic forte by launching parallel institutions, such as Shanghai Cooperation Organisation and the BRICS Bank aimed at "re-writing of the international financial architecture and a gradual de-coupling from American Dollar hegemony".[31] The establishment of the Asian Infrastructure Investment Bank (AIIB) can be seen as a continuation and expansion of this policy aimed to marginalise US banking and economic dominance at least in the developing countries.[32] The results of such follow up, notwithstanding conflict with China in the SCS, can be witnessed with Philippine President Rodrigo Duterte's announcement of his country's "separation" from the

US, and Malaysian Prime Minister Najib Razak's visit to China to sign new defence and investment agreements.[33]

In either of the options available to the regional states, instead of carrying the burden of the alliance and partnerships, the Trump administration is likely to develop the regional security architect on a contributory basis. In addition to the regional setup, the US will have leverage over China to needle it at a time of its choosing by imposing tariff on Chinese imports, that other countries could also follow in unison. This will prove instrumental for the US to compute its strategic framework in a way that enhances its own strategic power equations. This will also serve the US envision of a unipolar world with a multipolar Asia, including an ambition to contain an increasingly militarily aggressive and territorially expansive China at its very doorstep. This will also be instrumental in checking China's assertion of a multipolar world with a unipolar Asia.

Anyhow, it will take another twelve months or so for the Trump administration to unfold its Indo-Pacific strategy, come whatever form it takes but its basic tenets would not be very indistinct in the future.

It is quite evident that the US would like to retain its dominant role in the Asia-Pacific region otherwise there will be severe economic consequences for the US and may even erode its alliance framework that has served as the "bulwark for regional security since the end of World War Two".[34] Even if Trump administration expresses limited interest in the Indo-Pacific region, China's rise is viewed with suspicion by many regional states, fearing it will eventually pull these states into a dependent, tribute-state relationship. In an evolving China-centric Asia, ASEAN meanwhile prefers the use of ASEAN-centric, multilateral institutions, based on "strategies that promote economic interdependence, commitment to ASEAN norms, and soft balancing".[35] Considering smaller size of the ASEAN states, they would prefer to be part of larger multilateral arrangements, rather than entering in unequal bilateral relations with a much larger and more powerful China. Furthermore, with China's refusal to accept the arbitration court ruling, and a muted response by the regional countries has emboldened China's flagrant claim over the SCS. Even in a joint communique adopted on 25 July 2016 ASEAN Foreign Ministers' Meeting, under the Chinese pressure the Arbitration Court judgement was not even mentioned despite member states direct involved in the conflict.[36] As against the spirit of the ASEAN, this has reduced the status of the regional sovereign countries to less than equal and has bolstered China to continue its reclamation activities even more vociferously during the US presidential transition. This has afforded China necessary timeframe to subdue or co-opt the regional countries that are directly involved in the SCS conflict. In a sense, Beijing has laid a foundation that it would engage with the other claimants at a bilateral level. For example, the Philippine president's change in stance from a US ally to anti-US and pro-China overture. Similarly, the president of Malaysia reverted his stance and not only supported China but also entered in defence agreements.

China expressed its displeasure about Obama's announcement of an increased US presence in Australia and other states in Asia. Even Obama's visits to countries like Australia and India and other regional countries were translated by Beijing as aimed at subduing China's ambition to dominate the region by: initiating rotational stationing of the US forces in Australia, the Philippines, Japan and South Korea; signing civil nuclear agreement and Logistics Exchange Memorandum of Agreement (LEMOA) with India; installing Terminal High Altitude Area Defense (THAAD) system in South Korea; and promoting the Trans-Pacific Partnership regulatory and investment trade deal (that excludes China); as attempts to resolve the South China Sea disputes in multilateral forums, against China's insistence on bilateral discussions.[37]

These developments pose a serious security dilemma for regional states. To counter a rising China, the states are left with a few alternatives, such as increase their respective national defence budgets; unite into alliance arrangements; bandwagon against a rising China; or approach the US, the traditional regional peacekeeper, to seek assurance about its continued engagement in the region.

Strategic Implications for Australia and India

Any such transition in power, change in alliance system and assertion by a single power in the absence of a credible institutional framework will result in destabilisation in the Indo-Pacific region. Even for democratic countries like Australia and India there will be different but far-reaching repercussions. Both India and Australia are non-claimants in the SCS but both support freedom of navigation, Law of the Sea (UNCLOS), peace and harmony in the region. They also support a status quo, that is the region is not dominated by any one country and the "overall balance of power remains favourable to the liberal democracies".[38] With Donald Trump in the political horizon of the US several strategic policy variations are quite imperative, as he intends to "reduce America's role in the world...take unilateral action, move away from traditional allies and move closer to adversaries".[39] Trump has described Obama's foreign policy as a "complete and total disaster".[40] These changes will have different connotations for both Australia and India.

Australia

Since the end of the Second World War, Australia has been an ANZUS alliance partner of the US. Resultantly, it has sacrificed with blood and treasure in the wars fought by the US but at the same time has availed security without investing heavily in its defence sector. With Donald Trump's ascendancy to the White House, initial policy overtures indicate that the alliance partners will be cajoled to contribute more to maintain and withstand the alliance. As Trump indicated, "he would diminish or possibly abandon American commitments to security alliances. That includes NATO and defence treaties with Japan and South Korea".[41] Though Australia is being not named but it is implicit that similar terms will be applicable to Australia as to the other alliance members.

Geo-strategically placed in the proximity of Asia, dependent on the alliance formatting by the Trump administration, Australia will be limited to three choices. First, the ANZUS alliance continues as such, and Australia continues to provide the logistic support such as base in Darwin and facilities in Perth and on some of the islands. Second, Australia will be asked to enhance its financial contribution to retain the current level of alliance. In this case Australia, may contribute a couple of more billion dollars. Third, Australia may consider stepping out of the alliance and actively engage in the regional strategic dynamics. A rationale for this option can be that in the post-Cold War period the 1951 ANZUS Treaty has brought more pain than gain to Australia.

The above equations will require lot of thinking and retrospection among Australian policymakers and intellectuals as how to respond to this core issue as well as the addendum like Trump's suggestion that more countries should acquire nuclear weapons, and his inflection to mend fence with Russia.

Leading experts on Australia's security have opined that Australia should calibrate a space between alliance and autonomy for itself in the Asian Century. Thomas Wright while supporting this view, states: "Australia's defence relationships, including its military alliance with the United States, would be at risk" and "Australia's strategic environment will be transformed overnight".[42] In this regard Hugh White has also stressed that there is a "major blow" to Canberra's assertion that the US would "remain the primary strategic power in Asia indefinitely". Against this backdrop, White suggests that Australia should not "turn to China and seek the kind of alliance...that we have had with America or Britain". While Australia can "no longer prudently expect America to remain the dominant power in Asia", rather Australia should fathom "what kind of role might [the US] be willing and able to play, and how could [Australia] encourage it to do so?". Yet another aspect White suggests is that Australia "should start seriously adapting both...diplomacy and...defence policy for the possibility that, despite our best efforts, America's role in Asia and our alliance with America are not going to last much longer".[43]

Further sensing the evolving implications, Paul Keating supports the continuation of alliance but "what we have to do is make our way in Asia ourselves with an independent foreign policy.... Our future is basically in the region around us in South East Asia". However, John Howard while being more optimistic underlines the continuity of the alliance: "So those people who are talking about the need for some kind of radical recasting of our attitude towards the United States forget the reality that this is a relationship so deeply embedded in history and sentiment that it survives changes of personnel both in Canberra and Washington".[44] To balance between such optimisms and apprehensions, it is vital that the Australian government need to re-think its engagement with the Indo-Pacific countries. As a former Indonesian ambassador underlined:

> Politically, Australia is still stuck in 20th century mode. It is a monarchy with a head of state in London, and all its security arrangements are Cold War relics, whereby they take orders from Washington. Australia is out of sync with the emerging geopolitical environment of Asia today. Until Australia fixes this anomaly and moves into the 21st century, it is hard for Indonesia and the rest of Asia to take Australia more seriously.[45]

Similarly, Michael Wesley details the impending challenges for Australia that it "needs to become highly attentive to the strategic dynamics in a number of key areas where conflict is most likely to occur". Emphasising on the regional landscape, as per Wesley, Canberra "needs to take three bays and three peninsulas very seriously; the bay of the Arabian Sea, the Bay of Bengal and the South China Sea; and the peninsulas of the West Pacific, from Japan down to Taiwan, the Indo-Pacific from Thailand down to Malaysia; and the south Asian peninsula – the sub-continent." Furthermore, the countries in the region that have the coastlines heavily rely on their access to shipping lanes, and as a consequence the region is witnessing getting a build-up of the military might.[46]

Since 14 September 2014, when Operation Okra launched its Air Task Group (ATG) of eight F/A-18F Super Hornets, an E-7A Wedgetail AEW&C aircraft, and a KC-30A air-to-air refuelling tanker, along with a Special Operations Task Force to the Middle East to counter Daesh forces,[47] Australia has witnessed an escalation in cases related to Islamic extremism and home-grown terrorists on its soil. Yet another offshoot of Australia's involvement in US led wars is that radicalisation continues to breed in Australia, despite the government's all-out measures to combat home-grown terrorism. Prime Minister Malcolm Turnbull has continuously reassured that by collaborating with the US-led coalition force against ISIL will only deter Islamist ideology.[48] In this case, no doubt Trump has vowed to fight with extremists with force. But this will not cover the Australian citizens and the radicalisation process that is underway in Australia. In 2015–16, Australia's Defence budget increased from $29.2 billion in 2014-15 to $32.3 billion. The spending included $686 million on operations in Afghanistan, Iraq, Syria and other Middle Eastern missions. This puts defence spending for 2016 at 1.88 per cent of GDP.[49]

Notwithstanding this, a Lowy Institute report released in September 2014 indicated that the number of Islamic extremism and radicalisation cases are on increase in Australia.[50] Thus a popular opinion emerging in Australia is to surrender the ANZUS Treaty and adopt a 'Non-Military Intervention' in the Middle East conflict, this will reap benefits for Australia in terms of national security. In comparison, New Zealand's non-obligatory commitments to the ANZUS Treaty, contributed only eight New Zealand Defence Force personnel to serve as part of the United Nations Truce Supervision Organisation (UNTSO) in the Middle East proved more successful. A positive outcome of this is that there have been no reports of Islamic extremism in New Zealand since 9/11. Moreover, Trump's preference to use indiscriminate force to decimate the terrorism may result in a serious risk that Australia may be dragged into another war in the Middle East. Past experience suggests that any such war is likely to be hugely costly and difficult to "win".[51]

On the issue of developing nuclear weapons as suggested by Trump, there have been several debates in Australia, but considering its geo-strategic location Canberra remains reticent on this issue. Even Australia's affirmation to President George Bush's assertion for pre-emptive strikes in the wake of 9/11 attracted not only attention but also criticism from its Asian neighbours. Thus, it appears Australia will not create a situation of trust deficit with its neighbours hence does not plan for development of nuclear weapons.

Australia has had issues previously with the Soviet Union and currently with Russia. Mainly on issues such as use of force in Ukraine to carve out Crimea and Australia's suspicion of Russia's involvement in the downing of Malaysian Airlines Flight 17, which claimed the lives of 38 Australians.[52] Australia accused Russian-backed rebels who used Russian-supplied equipment as murderers. Moreover, Australia's "bitter manifestations from the infamous 'shirt-fronting'[53] threat by then-Prime Minister Tony Abbott to actual economic sanctions arranged by the United States and EU and joined by Australia".[54] Moscow's conduct of naval exercises with China just around the arbitration decision and presence of Russian naval vessels close to Australian waters before the G20 summit in 2014, all reflect trust deficit between the two countries.

To sum up, Australia's fight against terrorism, development of nuclear weapons, to remain in alliance and relations with Russia are all difficult issues, that appear to be out of the narrative of the strategic landscape that Trump envisages to draw. Therefore, Canberra should think out of its ANZUS alliance and consider the evolving regional strategic imperatives.[55]

India

Since independence India has followed the non-alignment policy, and since disintegration of the Soviet Union while inching closer to the US has maintained a strategic autonomy. To retain this strategic calculus, India does not subscribe to the notion that a more active America is always good for India. New Delhi envisions a multipolar world with a multipolar Asia, the objective being to match power with a militarily (and not so peacefully) rising China, while supporting a global order conducive to its aspirations of maintaining strategic autonomy in international affairs.[56] To maximise its national interest, India in its strategic competition with China, aims to exert pressure on Beijing for strategic balancing by using its improved strategic relationship with the US as a hedge against China,[57] without entering into any close strategic or security alliance but also by developing its credible strategic deterrence through launch of ballistic missiles Agni V and VI and commissioning the *Brahmos* supersonic missiles in areas claimed by China.[58] So Trump's dilution of its alliance system in the Asia-Pacific may prove advantageous to India's strategic game plan. With thinning of the US presence, the regional states are likely to hinge on India. The strategic competition between China and Asia-Pacific countries might actually benefit India and increase its value as a durable partner in 'middle power coalitions'.[59] When that happens, sovereign nations affected by China's aggressive geo-political ambition might veer towards a rising naval power like India.

Trump's rapprochement with Vladimir Putin is yet another positive factor for India. New Delhi while continuing its historic friendship treaty with Russia and orienting its strategic *manoeuvres* towards the US was hard pressed between the two big powers. The rapprochement will place India comfortably to have equally better relations with both the US and Russia. This will make India strategically at ease as the Russia that was pushed closer to China through sanctions by the NATO states, will be out of castigation and will play a more balanced role *vis-à-vis* China.

> Trump has favoured nuclear weapons option for the Asia-Pacific countries, in this regard, India already has a lead, more so the existing civil nuclear agreement with the US will further bolster India's clout as a nuclear power. This will then enhance India's credentials to seek membership of the Nuclear Suppliers Group, that China has obstructed on the basis of India being a non-NPT signatory. So, this policy posture will prove an enabler to increase pressure on China.

Yet another factor that will go in favour of India will be the cross-border terrorism issue, that India accuses emanates from its western neighbour. Trump has publicly stated to counter the Islamist terrorism through extreme measures. Even he has directly criticised Pakistan for its role in terrorism. In a talk to CNN, Trump discussed the gravity of the "cocktail of radical Islamist terrorism and nuclear weaponry that is brewing in Pakistan", yet at another occasion on a radio talk show, Trump emphatically stressed, "Pakistan is the world's most dangerous country and the US needs to work very closely with India to check it. I have great respect for India".[60]

Considering the momentum built in the security and trade relations, signing of the LEMOA, agreements to share intelligence and logistics information and on the top of this India being the biggest importer of the weapons in the world will certainly remain dear to the Trump administration. All these developments indicate a strengthening relationship between the two countries. Based on the above discussed convergence of interests, Trump can build on the platform laid by former presidents Bush and Obama. Obama in his address to the Indian Parliament specified that "the relationship between India and America will be one of the defining partnerships of the 21st century, rooted in common values and interests".[61] India considers an understanding with the US on core issues such as freedom of navigation, multilateral framework, and applicability of international law as essential to counter Chinese hegemonic postures. To give credence to its convergence with US policy postures in the region, New Delhi signed the benchmark US-India Joint Strategic Vision for the Asia-Pacific and Indian Ocean Region in 2015.[62]

On multiple occasions, Trump has expressed his intention to engage India, if not for strategic considerations, at least in business and trade. He couched in unequivocal words that if he is elected president, "Indian...community will have a true friend in the White House". Further he added, "We would be best friends....We are for free trade. We are going to have a phenomenal future together".[63]

Notwithstanding the above convergence of interests between India and the US, despite China's championing of the concept of a multi-polar world order, India remains concerned that, "alignment between Washington and its rival [China] would place it in a very difficult strategic situation".[64] Moreover, if Trump administration perceives:

> "lesser threat from China,...eager to accommodate Chinese preferences in Asia, and is less interested in upholding US primacy, it may have less of a stake in actively supporting India's rise".[65]

Under Prime Minister Narendra Modi, India seeks a more visible and leading role in Asia by achieving a broader understanding with China about its due place in the regional order, a closer security relationship with the US, Australia, Japan, Indonesia, Vietnam and other ASEAN nations, and a more prominent role in regional institutions and security architectures.[66] India understands its geo-strategic importance that Kaplan appropriately underlined, "the direction India tilts could determine the course of geopolitics in Eurasia in the 21st century. India, in other words, looms as the ultimate pivot state".[67]

Conclusion

The Trump administration will introduce tectonic changes in its security and strategic relations. No doubt, in the near future the relations with China will be a seesaw game. Initial overtures indicate that the US will accord more space to China in its vicinity but on negotiated conditions. Thus, as witnessed in the Arbitration court ruling, China in defiance has asserted its power dynamics for a unilateral Asia under its influence. This has been witnessed, while the Trump administration is in transition, China has neutralised regional countries like Philippines and Malaysia and strengthened bilateral relations with them and other states. The regional organisations like ASEAN have also not proved to take a united stand. The traditional US alliance partners will face heat to accommodate the burden sharing, however it is unclear as to under what formulae these countries will adjust and accommodate the US. India is poised to benefit from the counter-terrorism, nuclear weapons, rapprochement with Russia and being a non-alliance partner. However, Australia will be hard pressed to make a decision whether to remain in alliance and if this be so under what terms. Considering the homegrown terrorism and radicalisation, it will remain out of the scope of the Trump policy on Islamic terrorism. Again, the Russia factor and nuclear weapons issue will keep

Australia drifted from the US. In conclusion, in Trump's efforts to "make America great again" China will assertively negotiate for its role, India will turn out as a natural partner and Australia will have to consider the options that serve its interest best in the long term.

NOTES

1. Donald Trump, "Make America Great Again!", *Donald Trump 2016 Online*, 11 November 2016, http://www.donaldtrump2016online.com/ (Accessed on 8 February 2017).
2. "H.E. Xi Jinping President of the People's Republic of China", http:// www.fmprc.gov.cn/mfa_eng/zxxx_662805/t1159951.shtml (Accessed on 8 February 2017).
3. For a detailed elaboration, see Ben Schreer, "Facing the Dragon: Debating the US military response to China", in Andrew Tan (ed.), *Handbook on US-China Relations* (Cheltenham: Edward Elgar, 2016), pp.359–78.
4. *China's Military Strategy* (Beijing: Ministry of National Defence, The People's Republic of China, 26 May 2015), http://eng.mod.gov.press/2015-05/26/ content_4586805_6.htm (Accessed on 8 February 2017).
5. "Military and Security Developments Involving the People's Republic of China 2015", *USNI News*, 8 May 2015, https://news.usni.org/2015/05/08/document-pentagon-2015-report-to-congress-on-chinas-military-power (Accessed on 8 February 2017).
6. http://www.pcacases.com/web/sendAttach/1506 (Accessed on 8 February 2017).
7. *Permanent Court of Arbitration* (The Hague), Press Release, 29 October 2015, p. 1, http:// www.pcacases.com/web/sendAttach/1503 (Accessed on 8 February 2017).
8. Shannon Tiezzi, "China: Tribunal Ruling 'Null and Void', Will Not Affect South China Sea Claims", *The Diplomat*, 12 July 2016, http://thediplomat.com/2016/ 07/china-tribunal-ruling-null-and-void-will-not-affect-south-china-sea-claims/ (Accessed on 8 February 2017).
9. http://www.fmprc.gov.cn/mfa_eng/zxxx_662805/t1159951.shtml (Accessed on 8 February 2017).
10. Sue Lannin, "South China Sea tensions deter oil exploration", *ABC News* (Sydney), 11 August 2015, http://www.abc.net.au/news/2015-08-11/south-china-sea-tensions-deter-oil-exploration/6688988 (Accessed on 8 February 2017).
11. "China's Navy Extends its Combat Reach to the Indian Ocean", *US-China Economic and Security Review Commission - Staff Report*, 14 March 2014, http:// www.uscc.gov/Research/china%E2%80%99s-navy-extends-its-combat-reach-indian-ocean#sthash.JanuoBQ7.dpuf (Accessed on 3 December 2016).
12. Sanu Kainikara, "South China Sea Arbitration: Court Rules, But Who Will Enforce The Writ? – Analysis", *Eurasia Review: A Journal of Analysis and Review*, 1 August 2016, http:// www.eurasiareview.com/01082016-south-china-sea-arbitration-court-rules-but-who-will-enforce-the-writ-analysis/ (Accessed on 8 February 2017).
13. Hillary Clinton, "America's Pacific Century: The future of politics will be decided in Asia, not Afghanistan or Iraq, and the United States will be right at the center of the action", *Foreign Policy*, 11 October 2011, http://foreignpolicy.com/2011/ 10/11/americas-pacific-century/ (Accessed on 8 February 2017).
14. For details see David J Berteau, Michael J Green and Zack Cooper, *Assessing the Asia-Pacific Rebalance* (Washington DC: Centre for Strategic and International Studies, December 2014), p. 44.

15. *Obama's speech a statement of intent,* http://www.abc.net.au/news/2011-11-17/ brack-obama27s-speech-to-parliament/3678058 (Accessed on 11 November 2016).
16. Robert D Blackwill and Ashley J Tellis, "Revising U.S. Grand Strategy Toward China", *Council on Foreign Relations, Council Special Report No. 72,* March 2015, pp. 27–33, http://www.cfr.org/china/revising-us-grand-strategy-toward-china/ p36371 (Accessed on 8 February 2017).
17. Cited in Jackson Kwok, "How the Chinese media saw Trump's victory", *The Interpreter,* 11 November 2016, https://www.lowyinstitute.org/the-interpreter/ how-chinese-media-saw-trumps-victory (Accessed on 8 February 2017).
18. Philip Rucker and Robert Costa, "Trump questions need for NATO, outlines noninterventionist foreign policy", *The Washington Post,* 21 March 2016, https:/ /www.washingtonpost.com/news/post-politics/wp/2016/03/21/donald-trump-reveals-foreign-policy-team-in-meeting-with-the-washington-post/ (Accessed on 8 February 2017).
19. Cited in Katie Zezima, "Trump: 'Who the hell cares if there's a trade war?'", *The Washington Post,* 20 May 2016, https://www.washingtonpost. com/news/post-politics/wp/2016/05/20/trump-who-the-hell-cares-if-theres-a-trade-war/ (Accessed on 8 February 2017).
20. Max Fisher, "What Is Donald Trump's Foreign Policy?", *The New York Times,* 11 November 2016, http://www.nytimes.com/2016/11/12/world/what-is-donald-trumps-foreign-policy.html?_r=0 (Accessed on 8 February 2017).
21. Walter Russell Mead cited in Max Fisher, What Is Donald Trump's Foreign Policy?, *The New York Times,* 11 November 2016, http://www.nytimes.com/2016/11/12/ world/what-is-donald-trumps-foreign-policy.html?_r=0 (Accessed on 8 February 2017).
22. Jackson Kwok, "How the Chinese media saw Trump's victory", *The Interpreter,* 11 November 2016, https://www.lowyinstitute.org/the-interpreter/how-chinese-media-saw-trumps-victory (Accessed on 8 February 2017).
23. Douglas T. Stuart, *The Pivot to Asia: Can it Serve as the Foundation for American Grand Strategy in the 21st Century?* (Carlisle Barracks, PA: US Army War College, Strategic Studies Institute, August 2016).
24. J Gandy, "Mattis: US Suffering 'Strategic Atrophy'", *US Naval Institute* (USNI), 14 May 2015, http://news.usni.org/2015/05/14/ mattis-u-s-suffering-strategic-atrophy?utm_source=USNI +News&utm _campaign= 8d7 f 618f02-USNI_NEWS_DAILY &utm _medium=email&utm_term=0_0dd4a1450b-8d7f618f02-230372749 &mc_cid= 8d7f618f02&mc _eid= 7d9cd8bf7d (Accessed on 8 February 2017).
25. Ed Pilkington, "Barack Obama sets out plans for leaner military in historic strategy shift", *The Guardian,* 5 January 2012, *http://www.theguardian.com/world/ 2012/jan/05/barack-obama-plans-leaner-military* (Accessed 30 November 2016).
26. Alexander Neill, "Does Trump victory spell end of US as Pacific power?", *BBC News,* 13 November 2016, http://www.bbc.com/news/world-asia-37946719 (Accessed on 8 February 2017).
27. Martin Stuart-Fox, "Southeast Asia and China: The Role of History and Culture in Shaping Future Relations", *Contemporary Southeast Asia,* vol. 26, no. 1, April 2004, pp. 117–18.
28. Yves-Heng Lim, *China's Naval Power: An Offensive Realist Approach* (Surrey: Ashgate Publishing, 2014), p. 50.
29. Christopher K Johnson, *Xi Jinping unveils his foreign policy vision: peace through strength* (Washington DC: Centre for Strategic and International Studies), issue 15, December 2014, p. 1.
30. "Military alliances no longer relevant: diplomat", *Xinhua,* 4 December 2013, http://

eng.chinamil.com.cn/news-channels/pla-daily-commentary/2013-12/04/content_5676635.htm (Accessed on 8 February 2017).

31. Johannes Dragsbaek Schmidt, "The Asia-Pacific Strategic Triangle: Unentangling the India, China, US Relations on Conflict and Security in South Asia", *Journal of Asian Security and International Affairs*, vol. 1, no. 2, 2014, p. 204.
32. C Huang, "China-led Asian bank challenges US dominance of global economy: America's 70-year dominance of the global economy faces challenge from Chinese-led Asian bank", *South China Morning Post,* 11 April 2015, http:// www.scmp.com/news/china/economy/article/1763525/china-led-asian-bank-challenges-us-dominance-global-economy (Accessed on 8 February 2017).
33. For details, see James Hookway, "China-Malaysia Summit Marks New Test for U.S. Sway in Asia", *The Wall Street Journal*, 2 November 2016, http:// www.wsj.com/articles/china-malaysia-summit-may-mark-another-blow-to-u-s-influence-1477984216 (Accessed on 8 February 2017).
34. Alexander Neill, "Does Trump victory spell end of US as Pacific power?", *BBC News,* 13 November 2016, http://www.bbc.com/news/world-asia-37946719 (Accessed on 8 February 2017).
35. Carlyle A Thayer, *The Rise of China and Maritime Security in Southeast Asia*, 8 February 2012, http://www.ide.go.jp/Japanese/Publish/Download/Seisaku/ 120208.html (Accessed 8 December 2016).
36. Press Conference on the Outcome of the 49th ASEAN Ministers' Meeting (Vientiane), 26 July 2016, https://www.asean2016.gov.la/index.php?r=site/ newsDetail&page=25 (Accessed on 8 February 2017).
37. For details, see Udai Bhanu Singh, "Maritime Strategies of China and Southeast Asia", *Strategic Analysis*, vol. 39, no. 1, 2015, p. 88.
38. Mohan Malik, "Balancing Act: The China-India-U.S. Triangle", *World Affairs*, Spring 2016, http://www.worldaffairsjournal.org/article/balancing-act-china-india-us-triangle?utm_source =World +Affairs+ Newsletter&utmcampaign=d40ed3a0b6 (Accessed on 8 February 2017).
39. Max Fisher, "What Is Donald Trump's Foreign Policy?", *The New York Times*, 11 November 2016, http://www.nytimes.com/2016/11/12/world/what-is-donald-trumps-foreign-policy.html?_r=0 (Accessed on 8 February 2017).
40. Henry Belot and Francis Keany, "Trump election has 'serious ramifications' for Australian security interests", 9 November 2016, http://www.abc.net.au/news/ 2016-11-10/trump-election-has-serious-ramifications-for-australian-security/ 8011520 (Accessed on 8 February 2017).
41. Fisher, n. 39. *Shifting Strategic Dynamics in the Indo-Pacific Region.*
42. Thomas Wright cited in Ben Winsor, "Trump has won: Here's what that means for Australia", *SBS News*, 10 November 2016, http://www.sbs.com.au/news/ article/2016/11/07/trump-has-won-heres-what-means-australia (Accessed on 8 February 2017).
43. Hugh White, "Australia must prepare for an Asia without America", *The Interpreter* (Lowy Institute), 10 November 2016.
44. Cited in Leigh Sales and Myles Wearring, "Paul Keating says Australia should 'cut the tag' with American foreign policy", *ABC News*, 11 November 2016, http:/ /www.abc.net.au/news/2016-11-10/keating-on-american-foreign-policy-after-trump-victory/8015028 (Accessed on 8 February 2017).

45. Cited in Mathew Davies, "In defence of distance: why Australia should stay out of ASEAN", *Australian Strategic Policy Institute*, 8 October 2015, http:// www.aspistrategist.org.au/in-defence-of-distance-why-australia-should-stay-out-of-asean/ (Accessed on 8 February 2017).
46. Michael Wesley, https://crawford.anu.edu.au/news-events/news/83/australia-and-asias-new-geopolitics (Accessed on 8 February 2017).
47. Okra Home, Department of Defence, Australian Government, http:// www.defence.gov.au/Operations/Okra/ (Accessed on 8 February 2017).
48. "RAAF headed back to Iraq", *Australian Aviation*, 15 September 2014, http:// www.abc.net.au/news/2016-09-23/Malcolm-turnbull-islamic-state-fight-high-level-talks-washington/7870624 (Accessed on 8 February 2017).
49. Note 8.6, Chapter 8, *Funding Defence*, 2016 White Paper, http:// www.minister.defence.gov.au/2014/05/13/minister-for-defence-budget-2014-15-defence-budget-overview/http://www.theaustralian.com.au/budget-2016/ budget-2016-defence-policy-reads-like-a-32bn-spend-on-new-jobs/news-tory/ 9e8f1b9b6fcc394663b775dccd80ba86 (Accessed on 8 February 2017).
50. http://www.abc.net.au/news/2016-09-14/warnings-large-numbers-of-jihadists-will-return-to/7842952 (Accessed on 8 February 2017).
51. "Five ways a Trump presidency would impact Australia – for the worse", *The Conversation*, 22 March 2016, http://theconversation.com/five-ways-a-trump-presidency-would-impact-australia-for-the-worse-56366 (Accessed on 8 February 2017).
52. "Russian military provided MH17 missile launcher, says report", *The Sydney Morning Herald*, 10 November 2014.
53. In Australia, shirt-fronting means to grab somebody roughly by the shirt to give a shove.
54. Anton Tsvetov, "Australia, Russia, and a Rules-Based Order in Asia", *The Diplomat*, 8 June 2016, http://thediplomat.com/2016/06/australia-russia-and-a-rules-based-order-in-asia/ (Accessed on 8 February 2017).
55. *Geopolitics of the 2016 Australian Defense White Paper*, pp. 3 and 52.
56. Dalbir Ahlawat and Fred C Smith, "Indo-Pacific Region: Evolving Strategic Contours", in D Gopal and Dalbir Ahlawat, eds., *Indo-Pacific: Emerging Powers, Evolving Regions and Challenges to Global Governance* (New Delhi: Aakar Books, 2016), pp. 41–42.
57. Tanvi Madan, "The US-India Relationship and China", The *Brookings Institution*, India-U.S. Policy Memo, 20 January 2015, http://www.brookings.edu/research/ opinions/2015/01/20-us-india-relationship-and-china-madan (Accessed on 27 December 2016).
58. Arthur Dominic Villasanta, "India Deploys Deadliest Version of BrahMos Supersonic Cruise Missile to Arunachal Pradesh to Counter China Military Build-up", *China Topix*, 22 November 2016, http://www.chinatopix.com/articles/ 97507/20160807/india-deploys-deadliest-version-brahmos-supersonic-cruise-missile-arunachal-pradesh.htm#ixzz4QiZ3Uf00 (Accessed on 8 February 2017).
59. Rory Medcalf and C Raja Mohan, "The U.S.-China Rivalry Has Asia on Edge: Can 'Middle Powers' Create Stability?", *The Brookings Institution*, 15 August 2014, https://www.brookings.edu/opinions/the-u-s-china-rivalry-has-asia-on-edge-can-middle-powers-create-stability/ (Accessed on 8 February 2017).
60. Cited in Sreemoy Talukdar, "Donald Trump regime will be good for India, here are five reasons why", *F.World*, 11 November 2016, http://www.firstpost.com/ world/donald-trump-regime-will-be-good-for-india-here-are-five-reasons-why-3100928.html (Accessed on 8 February 2017).

61. Barak Obama, *US-India Strategic Dialogue: A Defining Partnership in the 21st Century* (Bureau of South and Central Asian Affairs), 17 June 2011, http://www.state.gov/ documents/ organization/168999.pdf (Accessed on 8 February 2017).
62. The White House, "*US-India Joint Strategic Vision for the Asia-Pacific and Indian Ocean Region*", 25 January 2015, https://www.whitehouse.gov/the-press-office/ 2015/01/25/us-india-joint-strategic-vision-asia-pacific-and-indian-ocean-region (Accessed on 8 February 2017).
63. Cited in Talukdar, n. 60.
64. Thomas Ambrosio, "The Third Side? The multipolar strategic triangle and the Sino-Indian rapprochement", *Comparative Strategy*, vol. 24, no. 5, 2005, p. 404.
65. Ankit Panda, "What Donald Trump means for India", *The Interpreter* (Lowy Institute), 10 November 2016.
66. P Cronin and D M Baruah, "The Modi Doctrine for the Indo-Pacific Maritime Region", *The Diplomat*, 2 December 2014, http://thediplomat.com/2014/12/the-modi-doctrine-for-the-indo-pacific-maritime-region/ (Accessed on 8 February 2017).
67. Robert Kaplan, *South Asia's Geography of Conflict* (Washington DC: Centre for New American Security, August 2010), p. 3.

8

India's "Act East" Policy: Potential: Implications and Limitations

Devina Shukla

Introduction

One of the noticeable aspects of the Act East strategy has been the lack of any specific articulation about it from the Indian establishment. This could well be due to the strategy being an evolving one. Apart from its own evolution through the Indian strategic prism, Act East, clearly, is trying to take note of the rapid and complex developments in the region, particularly changes in the economic and security dynamics. A more robust foreign policy driven by the conviction that geostrategic influence is a function of the length and depth of economic success achieved by India makes the Act East strategy a different instrument from its predecessor, the LEP. As India looks to deepen economic ties with countries to its East, it is also enlarging the domain of the "East" to move beyond Southeast Asia and create a strategic vision for the greater Asia-Pacific. This was hardly the objective of the LEP, which had confined itself almost entirely to the architecture of ASEAN and focused on relationships with individual Southeast Asian countries. While not neglecting Southeast Asia in any respect, the Act East approach is expected to intensify India's strategic engagement with Japan, China, South Korea, Australia, New Zealand and the Pacific Islands as part of a broader strategy for engaging the Asia-Pacific region. In this respect, Act East could be an attempt to correct India's historical neglect and lack of a strategic vision for the Asia-Pacific.

Historically, India has long exerted a considerable cultural influence over East and Southeast Asia as the birthplace of Buddhism. The British used India as the main strategic base for its colonial presence in the rest of Asia (Muni 2011) making India highly integrated with the region's economy. In the period after gaining independence however, after a promising start, India soon became largely isolated and inward focused. Upon gaining independence in 1947, India's new leaders sought to re-set Indian foreign policy to achieve a number of aims: to distinguish the nation's foreign policy from that of its colonial masters; to assert a leadership role in the international system—despite its developmental challenges—based on India's size and civilizational legacy; and to preserve the country's new found autonomy despite growing pressure to do otherwise. In the inter-war period, Indian nationalist leaders such as Mahatma Gandhi promoted the idea of a common Asian identity in opposition to the West based on ideals of non-violence, Hindu and Buddhist spirituality, anti-materialism, and communal solidarity over individualism. It was thought that this identity could then be drawn upon to unite the region in the common quest for colonial liberation under Indian leadership.

As Asia divided on Cold War lines, India's ability to exert leadership in the region based on a common Asian identity fell away and so did its economic connection with the region. This was exacerbated by New Delhi's domestic commitment to developing a semi-socialist economy, that is, an economy which had capitalist elements but was also moderated by the communal ownership of resources, a heavy reliance on state-owned enterprises in important sectors such as banking and manufacturing, extensive subsidization of important goods and services and a focus on developing self-sufficiency in production.

These features meant that India's economy was inward focused and thus became marginalized from the boom in trade and investment between Asia's maritime countries such as Japan, South Korea, Singapore and Malaysia. In terms of external trade and investment, between 1964 and 1985, the Soviet Union and India had a strong economic relationship: India was the largest non-communist recipient of Soviet aid, and its largest trading partner in the developing world. As a consequence of these policies, for almost four decades after independence, India suffered from what many derogatively termed the 'Hindu rate of growth'—where per capita GDP growth per year averaged about 1.3 per cent.

Autonomy in a post-Cold War context meant a number of things: ensuring no one state came to dominate economic and political relations in the Asian region, as well as globally; establishing strong ties—short of alliances—with states with common interests and similar strategic viewpoints in different global power centers; defending open access to key markets and securing opportunities for trade growth; securing India's geo-strategic dominance over the Indian Ocean and defending a sphere of influence in its South Asian neighborhood; and establishing the means to secure recognition of India's status as a Great Power. India's "Look East" policy, unofficially launched in 1992, which aimed to establish closer and deeper relations with countries in Asia would be key to achieving these aims.

Potential of India's Act East Policy

India's economic integration in the region has improved, but its potential has yet to be realised. The greatest scope for an expanded role for India is clearly in terms of its capacity to play a soft-balancing role to manage the rise of China. India could assist other strategic players by exerting additional costs and constraints on China to discourage behaviour that disrupts and undermines the normative and strategic basis of Asia's regional order. India's own strategic culture may be the greatest impediment to it playing this role.

India's aversion to commitment has consequences for how much can be expected of it in terms of physically challenging Chinese assertions of sovereignty in the South China or East China Seas. New Delhi's priority is maintaining a naval advantage in the Indian Ocean, and securing recognition of a sphere of influence there, and genuinely appears committed to defending free an open access to these waters for trade. Beyond this geographical theatre, however, it is unclear how committed it will be as a partner of ASEAN, Japan, South Korea or the United States should conflict arise. The participation of the Indian Navy in bilateral exercises with Japan and the annual Malabar exercises with both Japan and the United States in the Sea of Japan and the western Pacific Ocean certainly suggests contemplation of a wider role, but this has not yet been tested other than rhetorically in the regions institutions. With its history of non-alignment and commitment to strategic autonomy, there will be doubts about how credible India will be as a security partner in a time of conflict. For now, however, as part of its own strategy of ambiguity and soft-balancing India is not keen to commit explicitly to taking on any role in testing China's assertive claims. It clearly sees the United States as shouldering the major burden in terms of maintaining peace and stability in the South and East China Seas.

India is widely considered to be a major power and one of the key stakeholders in the emerging security dynamics of the South and East Asia. As a result of the Look East Policy, over the past twenty years it has become entrenched as a nation of economic, diplomatic and strategic consequence in the region. India's role in

East Asia is taking shape: whilst not yet a substantial economic force, its military capabilities and common interests with states in Asia in defending the existing norms of regional order, have raised expectations about the role it can and should play if tensions continue to rise. China's expansive claims in the South China Sea, and willingness to coerce changes to the status quo, have drawn Asian states together—and closer to India—more overtly for the purpose of soft-balancing against its rise. The primary purpose of this is to preserve the existing norms of Asia's regional order, particularly freedom of access to the maritime commons, and the resolution of disputes peacefully using accepted legal principles. Whilst major conflict is far from certain to arise over these disputes, India's greater willingness to diplomatically defend established principles of the regional order under the leadership of Prime Minister Modi, has raised expectations that India will be willing to go beyond rhetoric. India's strategic culture and preference for strategic autonomy make it an unreliable partner for this kind of endeavor.

Implications of India's Act East Policy

As the Act East policy takes shape, India–Southeast Asia relations stand poised to shift to a new trajectory. The Modi government's plans to constructively engage the Asia-Pacific and play a greater role in regional affairs are expected to significantly influence regional dynamics. Some of the potential spheres of influence are discussed here.

Regional Economic Architecture

Several upcoming sets of architecture are going to dominate the economic landscape of Southeast Asia and the Asia-Pacific in the years to come. The Trans-Pacific Partnership (TPP)—an ambitious FTA aiming to achieve seamless movement of goods and services through deep domestic regulatory convergence and new trade governance systems—has been signed by twelve APEC members, including four from Southeast Asia, and is awaiting ratification. The TPP will have a significant impact on Southeast Asia by drawing parts of it into tighter and binding U.S.–style FTA trade compacts, as opposed to ASEAN–style trade agreements that allow for greater special and differential treatment to members. The TPP has been accompanied by the RCEP, which, while having much moderate trade liberalization ambitions, is modelled on the ASEAN–style FTAs. The RCEP negotiations are at an advanced stage. Alongside the TPP and RCEP, trade discourse in the Asia-Pacific has been increasingly dominated by the vision of a Free Trade Area for the Asia-Pacific (FTAAP).

Territorial Disputes

India's increasing posturing over the tensions in the South China Sea can be taken as an example of the "multi-alignment" likely to characterize its Act East policy. While not subscribing to the formation of an anti-China alliance on the South China Sea, India is clearly keen on multi-alignment in the region through deeper engagement with various actors. Many signs are visible in this regard. These include extending diplomatic support to the Philippines in its decision to approach the Permanent Court of Arbitration in its dispute with China over claims to islands in the South China Sea—reiterating the importance of settling maritime territorial disputes through established multilateral processes—and cooperating with Vietnam in exploring offshore oil production possibilities. Prime Minister Modi's exhortation on securing the seas at his recent address in Singapore reflects India's intentions of playing a major role in the regional maritime space, both in the Indian Ocean and in the South China Sea.

A more active India in the South China Sea will likely add greater complexity to the already fragile strategic dynamics of the region. India is unlikely to play a non-committal role as it had previously, given the economic importance of the South China Sea in expanding the country's trade and business with Southeast and East Asia, particularly Japan and South Korea, but also China. South China Sea in expanding the country's trade and business with Southeast and East Asia, particularly Japan and South Korea, but also China. Strategically, a more proactive role in the South China Sea might also be a response to the similarly proactive role of China in the Indian Ocean manifesting through the proposed Maritime Silk Road Initiative (MSRI; as part of the OBOR initiative), connecting the Chinese coast to Europe through the South China Sea, Indian Ocean and the Persian Gulf. The articulation of concerns over disputes in the South China Sea marks a significant departure from past Indian policy and displays the regionally proactive dimension of the Act East strategy.

ASEAN and India

It is uncertain whether ASEAN will be entirely comfortable with India making its presence felt more forcefully in Southeast Asia and the Asia-Pacific. Many opinions within ASEAN though have been keen on a more proactive India in the region, primarily with the objective of counterbalancing the powerful strategic influence of China. China's strategic clout has led to the emergence of major divisions of opinion within ASEAN, with members failing to agree as to whether to mention China and the South China Sea disputes in official ASEAN statements. While

India's larger say in regional affairs might see it contributing more to major regional matters—like natural disaster management and healthcare—it might also see Southeast Asia becoming a more tense region, with some countries beginning to engage India more actively to pressure China. This might test the cohesiveness of ASEAN further.

As long as India was content to play a role limited to peripheral issues of the region, Southeast Asia did not have to worry much about its strategic impact. The Act East policy may introduce major shifts in this respect. Greater strategic proactivity by India would require ASEAN to study carefully the impact of such proactivity. The key imperative in this regard would be to arrive at a regional consensus on engaging a more proactive India—a consensus that might be rather difficult to arrive at.

Limitations of India's Act East Policy

India's stabilizing role in the region may not necessarily be met. Whilst the Modi government appears to be enthusiastic about forming closer ties with Japan and the United States, it is unlikely that India will reliably conform to the idea of a group of democracies working in partnership to ensure the peaceful rise of China. This is for a number of reasons.

Firstly, ideologically, Indian foreign policy remains wedded to the central aim of maximizing strategic autonomy. Whilst the concept of non-alignment has been put aside, India has remained averse to formally joining any alliance system, including the US alliance system in Asia. Rather it has sought to maximize its strategic autonomy by pursuing a strategy of multi-alignment i.e. simultaneously deepening strategic partnerships with competing global power centers without allowing any one to become supreme. To this end, India has maintained its 'special and privileged strategic partnership' with Russia, has improved relations with the United States, the EU, Japan and ASEAN states, whilst simultaneously taking contrary views to developed countries on trade and climate change alone or in concert with other BRICs nations. New Delhi has proved to be wary of Coalition of the willing' type security operations such as the US-led Proliferation Security Initiative and prefers to operate within official regional organizations such as ASEAN or the United Nations.

Second, India's key priority under Prime Minister Modi's leadership is to develop the nations' economy. For India to attract foreign investment in infrastructure and export manufacturing it must maintain a secure and stable neighborhood. India has good reasons to position itself as wary, but ambiguously independent of any moves in the region that may appear to Beijing as having the purpose of containing its rise. Like other states in Asia, India faces the dilemma that its largest trading partner is engaging in behavior that undermines its security interests. Indian strategists are also wary of the leverage China has over India in terms of re-igniting the two countries border disputes, qualitatively expanding defense cooperation with Pakistan, and and/or further using economic incentives to influence the foreign policies of India's neighbors Bangladesh, Myanmar and Sri Lanka to gain strategic advantage (string of pearls) or energy resources. The price India pays for maintaining a multi-alignment policy, is of course that should China take this path, there is a great deal of uncertainty about the level of commitment that can be expected from its new friends in the region.

Concluding Remarks

The Act East strategy is becoming increasingly distinct from the LEP in its larger geographic scope and greater strategic depth. The wider geographic scope of the strategy and its extension beyond Southeast Asia has probably been motivated by the realization on the part of India that a strategic vision for Southeast Asia is not exclusive of a similar vision for East Asia and the Asia-Pacific. Similarly, strategic views of the latter cannot be constructed without corresponding visions of Southeast Asia. The non-exclusivity is a result of the character of the regional dynamics that is intricately connected between countries and sub-regions. For India, it makes eminent sense to have a holistic strategic vision of the Asia-Pacific rather than confining itself to limited parcel views.

Taken together with the expansive geography, the greater strategic content of the Act East approach, particularly the security component, leaves little doubt about India's seriousness in working hard on its ambition to become a major regional actor. There are significant implications of India's ambition as far as regional dynamics are concerned. The most significant implications are expected to be on the political and economic balance of power in the region. The nature of these implications will become visible over time as strategic complications unravel.

The Act East strategy is expected to deepen India's engagement with Southeast Asia on a variety of issues. In this respect, the partnership with ASEAN is likely to graduate to that of a comprehensive strategic relationship, similar to those that India has already begun striking with various countries in the region. While bilateral issues might condition the character of many of these relationships, ASEAN as a whole needs to be prepared to adjust to India as a strategic partner.

REFERENCES

Anderson, Walter. 2008. Korea: an Important Part of India's "Look East" Policy. Working Paper Series 1. US Korea Institute.

Brewster, David. 2010. "India's Developing Relationship with South Korea: A useful Friend in East Asia." Asian Survey 50(2): 402-425.

Ganguly, Rajat. 2015. India's Military: Evolution, Modernisation and Transformation. India Quarterly 71(3): 187-205.

Haokip, Thongkholal. 2011. India's Look East Policy: Its Evolution and Approach. South Asian Survey 18(2): 239-257

Jaffrelot, Christophe. 2003. India's Look East Policy: An Asianist Strategy in Perspective. India Review 2(2): 35-68

Lee, John. 2015. In Defense of the East Asian Regional Order: Explaining Japan's Newfound Interest in Southeast Asia. Geopolitics, History and International Relations 8(1): 30-53.

Scott, David. 2013. "India's role in the South China Sea: Geopolitics and Geoeconomics in Play." India Review 12(2): 51-69.

9

India at the RCEP: Threat or Opportunities?

Debashis Chakraborty

Background

After India embarked on the liberalization exercise in 1991, one of the major objective of the country had been creating a steady export market. With the break-up of USSR around the same time, India lost a major trade partner. While the USA and European countries also showed interest in partnering with India, the distance and the associated trade cost as well as the political economic drivers (e.g., difference in perspective over signing in NPT, CTBT) resulted a modest and gradual deepening of relationship. In the course of time, India developed significant differences with the 'West' at the WTO negotiating forums as well (e.g., agricultural subsidy reforms, extent of service trade opening up), and the resulting discord with both EU and USA caused both the sides to move forward in a cautious manner. In that context, from early nineties, possible role of East and Southeast Asia as both business and development partners of India deepened in the calculations of both the Ministry of Commerce and Ministry of External Affairs. The relationship was subsequently formalized through the 'Look East' initiative.

Nevertheless India was never able to penetrate the 'East' very effectively owing to a number of reasons. First and foremost, the outward-oriented model, i.e., growth supported through enhanced foreign direct investment (FDI) and export, was already taking shape in the East and Southeast Asian region from eighties. Regional integration drive in East and Southeast Asia started from the consolidation of the Southeast Asian countries first, a process in which the other players joined subsequently. The 'Flying Geese' model phenomenon helped the Association of Southeast Asian Nations (ASEAN) countries initially and China later to consolidate their industries with Japanese and South Korean investments. On the other hand, India focussed on the importance of opening up to FDI only from late nineties. In a sense, therefore India suffered by being the late mover in the Asian regional trade agreement (RTA) universe at a later point. Second, in 1995 the World Trade Organization (WTO) came into existence and countries had to adopt a policy of manufacturing sector tariff reforms. As the East and Southeast Asian countries had already reduced their tariff barriers, the extent of incremental reform for them had been relatively moderate. On the other hand, India had to undertake a sizable tariff cut, in addition to removing the practice of using import quota on sensitive sectors like textile and clothing. This consequently led to considerable stress on domestic industrial sector, reflected in rising trade deficits across product segments. Third, as Figure 1 reveals the number of RTAs in the world quite paradoxically increased sharply in the aftermath of WTO formation. The seemingly counter-intuitive fact can be explained by the fact that all WTO member countries suspected the trade regulations to tighten in the upcoming period and therefore as a pre-emptive measure formed their own preferential trade agreements. While the RTAs formed in these manner 'freed' trade among member countries in varying degrees, mostly depending on initial regional dynamics, they ended up diverting trade away from countries not members of these arrangements. Fourth, given the fact that the FDI inflow in India and the extent of technology transfer never reached the desired extent, the technological sophistication of India's exports increased only modestly. Last but not the least, the entry of China in the WTO fold in 2001 with sharp rise in alleged dumping incidents, severely damaged the export potential of India in Asia and other partner regions.

India's Act East: Achievements and Challenges

After the failure of the WTO Cancun Ministerial meeting (2003), a number of Asian countries felt a rising disincentive arising from the WTO trade liberalization mechanism and embraced the RTA route instead. The ten ASEAN countries as a lucrative market caught the attention of six major Asian partners, leading to the sequential birth of the Sino-ASEAN FTA (2005), South Korea-ASEAN FTA (2007), Japan-ASEAN FTA (2008), Australia-New Zealand-ASEAN FTA (2010) and ASEAN-India FTA (2010) in that order. In particular, Japan and South Korea already enjoyed sizable presence in the ASEAN market, given their FDI flows and

Figure 1: RTAs notified to the GATT / WTO (1948 to 2017) by year of entry into force

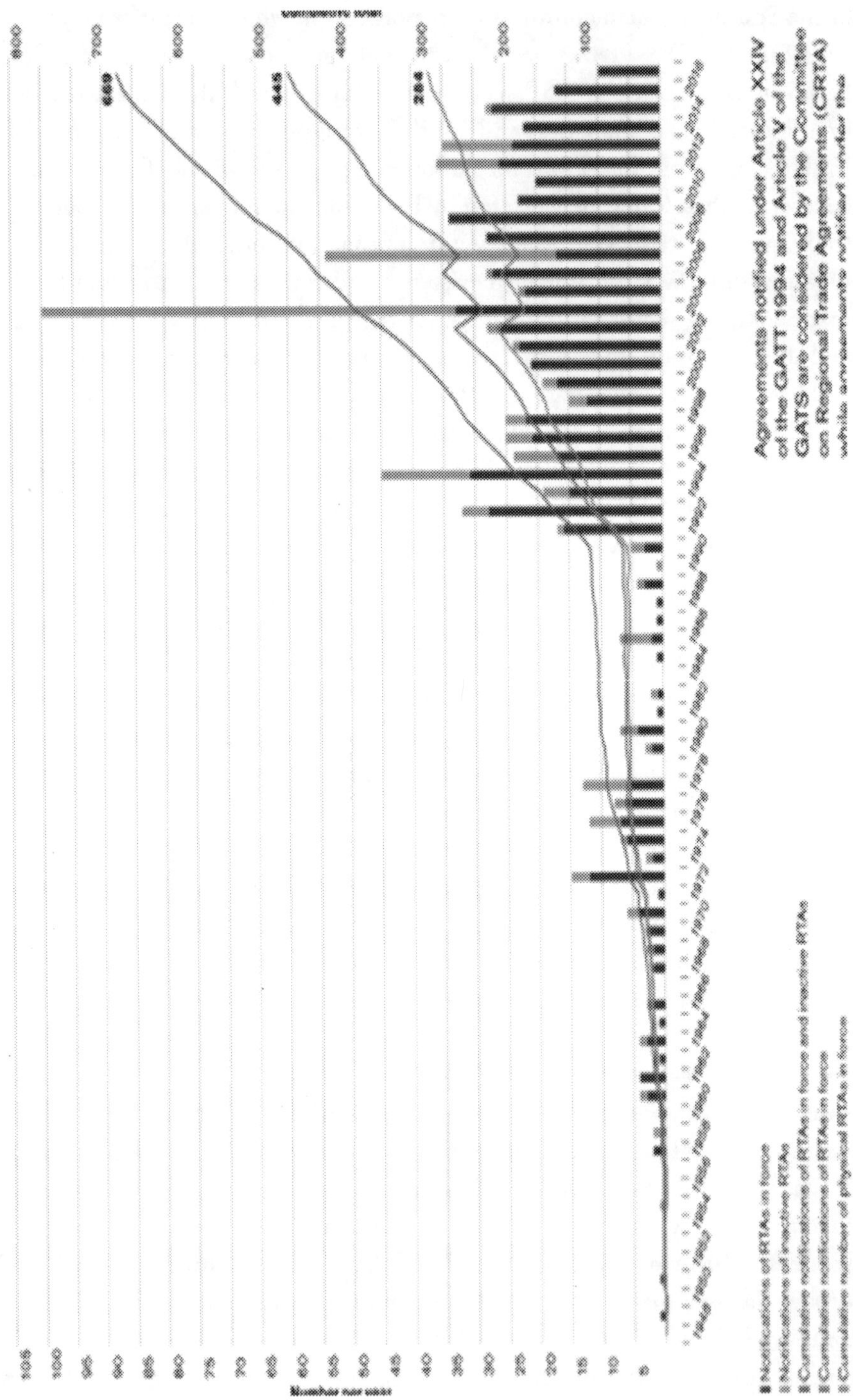

Source: WTO Annual Report (2017)

the trade relationship formalization deepened the pace of commercial exchange further. The RTA journey of the six ASEAN country's partners is shown with the help of Table 1. The table shows the launching of their negotiations with ASEAN, conclusion of a negotiation and their final entry into effect. The difference between the second and fourth columns underline the difference between the perspectives between two countries witnessed during the RTA negotiations. The last two columns show their other ongoing as well as existing RTA memberships (involving rest of the world), underlining the depth of their involvement in the regionalism process. It can be observed that India took the longest time to conclude the FTA with ASEAN as compared to other partners, given the difference in perspectives and sectoral interests (Chakraborty, 2014). It is to be noted that the number of India's active RTAs are lesser than China, Japan and South Korea.

Table 1: FTA with ASEAN–RCEP's Journey

ASEAN Partner Country	*Negotiation with ASEAN*			*RTA Agreements*	
	Negotiations launched	*Signed but not yet In Effect*	*Signed and In Effect*	*In Force/Ongoing Negotiations*	*Signed and in Effect*
Australia	2005-02-21	2009-02-27	2010-01-01	24	12
China	2002-11-04	2004-11-29	2005-07-01	28	17
India	2004-03-07	2009-08-13	2010-01-01	29	13
Japan	2005-04-14	2008-04-14	2008-12-01	25	15
New Zealand	2005-02-21	2009-02-27	2010-01-01	20	11
South Korea	2004-11-30	2006-08-24	2007-06-01	27	16

Source: Compiled from ADB ARIC database (undated)

It is obvious from Table 1 that India has entered into FTA with ASEAN quite late vis-à-vis the other five countries and can be considered to suffer from the 'Last Mover' disadvantage at the present context. The fact becomes clear from India's performance in ASEAN market post-FTA, which has remained below expectation (Chakraborty and Chakraborty, 2017a). The sharper rise in imports as compared to exports from ASEAN has worsened India's trade balance considerably. The two key policies undertaken by India since 2014 need to be viewed in this light.

First, the 'Make in India' initiative was launched to facilitate industrialization by attracting renowned foreign corporates and encouraging them to relocate and produce in India on one hand and enhancing participation of domestic players in global value chains (GVCs) and international production networks (IPNs) on the other. The newly-introduced scheme covers several employment-generating manufacturing sectors under both medium (e.g., food-processing, leather, textile and garments) and high-tech categories (e.g., auto-components, aviation, defense manufacturing, electronic and electrical machinery, pharmaceuticals). Second, India over the last decade has considerably enhanced focus on export promotion through RTA route (Chakraborty, 2018). The switch from 'Look East' to 'Act East' policy is a classic example of this evolved orientation.

Table 2 underlines the dominance of 'East' partners in Indian trade basket in terms of proportional presence. It is seen that the importance of both EU and USA has declined in percent terms in India's trade basket. On the other hand, the importance of ASEAN and Northeast Asia has improved over the same period. Even for Oceania, the rising trend has become clearly visible.

Table 2: India's Evolving Trade Orientation (percent)

Region	*Export*				*Import*			
	1997-98	*2005-06*	*2008-09*	*2017-18*	*1997-98*	*2005-06*	*2008-09*	*2017-18*
EU	26.86	22.57	21.28	17.66	26.23	17.45	14.15	10.28
SACU	1.15	0.97	1.17	1.33	1.20	1.69	1.83	1.85
Other South African Countries	0.26	0.25	0.52	0.52	0.31	0.08	0.56	1.38
West Africa	1.24	2.02	1.81	2.21	3.18	0.78	3.65	3.62
East Africa	1.40	1.20	2.43	2.15	0.24	0.15	0.12	0.30
North Africa	1.20	1.28	1.85	1.61	2.01	0.56	1.91	0.87
North America	20.91	22.49	12.51	17.85	10.16	7.02	7.58	7.58
Latin America	1.69	2.06	2.98	2.84	1.19	1.72	2.68	4.45
Oceania	1.48	1.15	0.95	1.47	3.79	3.54	3.90	3.20
ASEAN	7.09	8.76	10.33	11.27	8.19	7.30	8.69	10.12
GCC	7.80	9.32	17.34	12.98	10.49	5.23	19.40	13.76
Other West Asia	2.15	3.68	3.32	2.96	3.24	1.48	8.13	6.87
NE Asia	15.67	14.92	13.73	13.00	12.18	15.51	19.36	25.41
South Asia	4.69	5.28	4.62	7.61	0.59	0.95	0.60	0.69

Source: Constructed by author from Export Import data bank

Table 3 denotes the dominance of 'East' RTAs in Indian policy space. For the operational RTAs, the year in bracket shows when the arrangement started providing preferential treatment to each other. For the partners involved in ongoing analysis, the year within bracket depicts the negotiation launch period. It becomes clear from the table that while in the initial period India was more intent in entering merely into free trade agreements (FTAs), now the focus has shifted to comprehensive economic cooperation agreements (CECAs) and comprehensive economic partnership agreements (CEPAs). The change in attitude is in line with the growing export interest of the country in services sectors.

Table 3: India's 'East' Focus is the RTAs?

No.	*Operational*	*Ongoing Analysis, Discussion and Negotiation*
1	Bangkok Agreement (now APTA) (1976)	BIMSTEC FTA for Services and Investment (2014)
2	India-Singapore CECA (2005)	India-Indonesia CECA (2011)
3	India-ASEAN FTA (2010)	India-Thailand CECA (2014)
4	India-Malaysia CECA (2011)	India-New Zealand CECA / FTA (2010)
5	India-South Korea CEPA (2010)	India-Australia Framework Agreement (2011)
6	India-Japan CEPA (2011)	Regional Comprehensive Economic Partnership (RCEP) (2013)

Source: Constructed by author from ADB (undated) resources

India's trade growth in ASEAN however remained modest despite the FTA (Chakraborty and Chakraborty, 2017a). In 2013 India started deepening its relation with the Asian partners through the Regional Comprehensive Economic Partnership (RCEP), which involved ASEAN and all its six FTA partners. It is expected that RCEP would be enable India to increase its trade flows with the east. The negotiation for the bloc has been delayed and still continuing. The current analysis, conducted with Trade Map data, attempts to analyse to what extent the expectation has been fulfilled.

First, India's trade performance with ASEAN has been compared with other five FTA partners of the bloc, by drawing the data in Table 4. The analysis is conducted for three sub-periods, namely, 2001-05, 2006-09 and 2010-16. The first two periods indicate modest trade link of the partners with ASEAN. The last period however indicates a time when all the countries are already FTA partners of ASEAN, i.e., a period of closer integration. A few observations can be noted here. First, only India and New Zealand have witnessed a decline in their trade balance with ASEAN over the period, underlining lack of competitiveness. However, the extent of trade deficit decline has been sharper for India vis-à-vis New Zealand. Australia and Japan also experience trade deficit with ASEAN, but the extent is narrowing. Second, South Korea on the other hand witness a growing trade surplus with ASEAN over the period. Third, China register a massive turnaround as its trade deficit with ASEAN during 2001-05 narrowed during 2006-09 and finally turned into surplus during 2010-16. Fourth, the importance of ASEAN in the export basket increased for all the partners, barring the exception of Australia and New Zealand. However, the increase during 2010-16 has been quite sharp for China, Japan and South Korea. Finally, ASEAN's share declined in the import basket only for Australia. In particular, ASEAN's penetration in Chinese and Indian imports is relatively modest vis-à-vis their performance in Japan and

South Korea. The results indicate that among all the RCEP partners, India's trade performance vis-à-vis ASEAN has been quite poor so far.

The ability of a country to reach the partner markets as compared to average performance of the world, particularly for key economic sectors, can be understood through the Export Intensity Index (EII). EII can be calculated by the following formulation:

$$EII = \frac{x_{ij} / X_{iw}}{x_{wj} / X_{ww}}$$

Here, x_{ij} refers to the sectoral export of a given country pair (say, India's export to Thailand), while X_{iw} indicates India's global exports in that category. On the other hand, x_{wj} and X_{ww} represent world's export to the importing country (i.e., Thailand) and to the world respectively. The value of EII above 1 for any given country-pair (i.e., India and Thailand) indicates that the export penetration from India in the sector to the partner is 'intense', while a value less than '1' indicates otherwise. It is expected that RTA partnership would result in rise of the index value (possibly turning it to be greater than 1).

The EII indices for Garments, Knitted or Crocheted (HS 61) has been computed from the Trade Map data and compared for India and China involving their trade with key ASEAN countries. The EII results from Table 5 indicate that India's EII is not greater than one with any ASEAN country, in sharp contrast with China. A similar scenario is observed for other ASEAN countries as well (Chakraborty and Chaisse, 2018). This result indicates the growing competitiveness of China in ASEAN and its urge to push for speedy resolution of RCEP. This further The EII observations underline India's negotiating perspective in RCEP in light of its practical gains in Indo-ASEAN FTA. The non-intense relation in several sectors with the FTA partners is reflected in India's rising trade deficits shown in Table 4. Such sectoral non-intense relations with the ASEAN and RCEP partners, despite the tariff preferences on its exports, may prompt India to adopt a cautious approach during RCEP negotiations. On the other hand China enjoys an intense export relation with India, which it would like to formalize through further tariff reforms in India under RCEP. India however would be cautious against possible Chinese dumping in the post-bloc period, which is already a major area of concern (Chaisse and Chakraborty, 2016). Japan and South Korea on the other hand look forward to further trade reforms and economies of scale for investment projects through RCEP in a wider geographical region. Given India's CEPAs with Japan and South Korea and their interest in speedy conclusion of the RCEP bloc (owing to huge investments in China and ASEAN), the Indian negotiators are indeed on a tricky turf.

Table 4: Comparison of Trade Balance Scenario of RCEP Members with ASEAN

RCEP Members	*Average Trade Balance (USD Million)*			*Percentage Share of ASEAN in Export Basket (%)*			*Percentage Share of ASEAN in Import Basket (%)*		
	2001-05	*2006-09*	*2010-16*	*2001-05*	*2006-09*	*2010-16*	*2001-05*	*2006-09*	*2010-16*
Australia	−5772.19	−17366.60	−17124.63	11.753	10.586	9.693	16.226	19.900	18.073
China	−13709.33	−8777.47	31391.35	7.176	8.019	10.811	11.033	10.854	11.061
India	−858.69	−6118.11	−9639.31	9.323	10.152	10.638	8.331	8.989	9.388
Japan	3018.28	−1161.14	−1085.55	13.041	12.753	15.227	14.929	13.989	14.663
South Korea	1398.24	5810.91	24995.20	10.198	10.865	13.969	10.397	9.675	10.299
New Zealand	−448.84	−1468.74	−2030.41	7.930	10.094	9.827	9.468	14.037	15.148

Source: Computed by author from ITC (undated)

Table 5: Comparing Export Intensity of India with China (Garments – HS 61)

ASEAN / RCEP Partners	*India*			*China*		
	2001-05	*2006-09*	*2010-16*	*2001-05*	*2006-09*	*2010-16*
Indonesia	33.49	0.83	0.13	12.28	6.73	6.42
Malaysia	5.65	1.56	0.92	8.66	14.37	9.59
Philippines	0.70	0.63	0.88	14.72	15.92	22.51
Singapore	0.40	0.61	0.51	1.80	2.59	1.36
Thailand	0.56	0.42	0.70	1.34	2.52	2.61
Viet Nam	0.07	0.10	0.03	5.31	13.09	22.75
India	—	—	—	2.20	2.86	4.82
China	0.03	0.11	0.37	—	—	—

Source: Computed by author from ITC (undated)

Table 6 summarizes the intra-RCEP trade pattern from an Indian perspective trade, by focussing on the origin of value added in base metal and fabricated metal products for 2011. It is seen that the percentage share of domestic value addition is declining for India, signifying increased sourcing from ASEAN and RCEP members and from other parts of the world. This might result both from rise in import of intermediate products in India given the tariff preferences and possible lack of competitiveness in semi-processed and intermediate product categories. However, participation by Indian players in upstream activities for ASEAN's exports still remains modest, which is a matter of concern for Indian policymakers (Nag, 2016). Chakraborty and Chakraborty (2017b) noted that increased participation from ASEAN in India's production pattern had been much weaker as compared to China, which is an indicator of China's growing competitiveness in manufacturing sector. This is in line with China's export pattern to other RCEP countries, where the country is expanding its share in the partner's export value content for several manufacturing categories. Chakraborty and Chaisse (2018) has noted that the contribution from South Korea and Japan has also increased in India's exports, given the tariff and trade facilitation reforms implemented through the respective CEPAs. Nevertheless, their contribution in India's value chain still looks quite modest in comparison with the corresponding figures for China. In other words, the RCEP in short run is more likely to increase trade deficits for India and the country's cautious moves at the RCEP negotiating forums need to be viewed in this light.

Table 6: Production Integration in Basic metals and fabricated metal products – Contribution of Value Added in Exports (% in 2011)

	China	*India*	*Indonesia*	*Japan*	*Malaysia*	*Singapore*	*South Korea*	*Thailand*
China	67.48	2.79	1.64	1.89	6.01	4.28	5.77	5.30
India	0.78	59.78	0.53	0.23	1.51	1.63	0.94	0.85
Indonesia	0.92	0.89	76.25	1.45	3.97	3.79	1.99	2.79
Japan	2.87	1.21	1.83	78.49	8.52	4.16	6.33	11.87
Malaysia	0.42	0.45	1.47	0.49	44.26	1.80	0.64	1.31
Singapore	0.26	0.34	0.53	0.13	1.75	48.55	0.27	0.75
South Korea	1.20	0.73	0.80	1.02	2.29	1.24	49.72	2.54
Thailand	0.23	0.29	0.40	0.23	1.32	0.61	0.26	37.23

Source: Constructed by author from OECD (undated)

Conclusion

While India is quite serious in engaging with the Asian partners for trade facilitation, the modest manufacturing sector performance and the constantly evolving China factor is a major area of concern. China's Belt-Road Initiative (BRI), which intends to connect with Europe though the Siberian rail network on one hand and deepen presence in Asia through newer initiatives like Kra Canal project in Thailand, recent inroads in South Asia in the name of infrastructure building etc. is being viewed cautiously. The recent USA pull-out from Trans-Pacific Partnership (TPP) has changed the perspectives of China and Japan in RCEP, and both countries are intent to obtain more market access in their global markets in general and in India in particular. One saving grace for India would be the manufacturing sector tariff reforms under the RCEP arrangements, but the rising de-globalization wave in the world otherwise does not offer a bright future for India's Make-in-India campaign. It is noted that the 'East' countries in general and China in particular are enjoying competitiveness over India in manufacturing segment, and hence India's participation in Asian IPNs would only widen the trade deficit in short run. To counter the possible negative implications of the RCEP bloc, India need to focus on two crucial steps. First, the country must push for deeper reforms in the area of trade in services among RCEP members. Presently the partner countries are showing inclinations to open up only areas like Intra-Corporate Transfer, which will not effectively serve India's purpose. India should not settle for anything less than hassle-free movement of natural persons across all professional service categories. Second, massive infrastructure investment needs to be made in the Northeast region so that the states bordering ASEAN can be developed as a gateway to the 'East' and reap the full benefits of the RCEP RTA.

REFERENCES

Asian Development Bank (undated), 'Asia Regional Integration Centre', available at: https://aric.adb.org/fta (accessed February 6, 2019).

Chaisse, J. and D. Chakraborty (2016), 'Normative Obsolescence of the WTO Anti-Dumping Agreement: Topography of the Global Use and Misuse of Initiations and Measures', *Asian Journal of International Law*, 6(2): 233-263.

Chakraborty, D. (2018), ''Picking the right alternative: Should India participate in TPP instead of RCEP?', in J. Chaisse, H. G. & C. Lo (eds.), *The Transpacific Partnership: A Paradigm Shift in International Trade Regulation*, pp.501-519, Singapore: Springer.

Chakraborty, D. (2014), 'The Upcoming Indo-ASEAN CECA: Of Great Expectations and Areas of Concern', *China Report*, 50(3): 259-276.

Chakraborty, D. and J. Chaisse (2018), '*Great Expectations and Modest Outcome: Reflections on the ASEAN-India FTA*', Conference on Contemporary Issues in Economic Policy, Maulana Azad National Urdu University, Hyderabad, March 22-23.

Chakrabortry, D. and A. Chakraborty (2017a), 'India's Act East Policy: Walking the Talk', *Politico*, 6: 22-40.

Chakrabortry, D. and A. Chakraborty (2017b), 'Economic and Political Cooperation between India and East Asia: The Emerging Perspective', *Journal of Economics and Political Economy*, 4(2): 144-158.

International Trade Centre (undated), 'Trade Map Database', available at: http://www.trademap.org/ (accessed February 6, 2019).

Nag, B. (2016), 'Emerging Production Network between India and ASEAN: An Analysis of Value Added Trade in Select Industries', in D. Chakraborty and J. Mukherjee (eds), *Trade, Investment and Economic Development in Asia: Empirical and Policy Issues*, pp. 41-67, Abingdon: Routledge.

Organization for Economic Cooperation and Development (undated), 'Trade in Value Added (TIVA) database', available at: http://stats.oecd.org/Index.aspx?DataSetCode=TIVA_OECD_WTO (accessed February 6, 2019).

World Trade Organization (2017), 'WTO Annual report 2017', Geneva: WTO.

10

India-Indonesia Relations

Ganganath Jha

The fraternal ties evolved in India-Indonesia relations in course of our freedom struggle, could not be properly nurtured in the post-independence era. It is noteworthy to point out that methodology for liberation struggle in both the countries were different. Indonesia under the leadership of Sukarno had adopted revolutionary means to gain freedom. He had organized volunteers to fight against the Dutch colonial rulers. He had the courage to announce the liberation of the country in 1945 when the Dutch were still in full command and subsequent developments showed that the Dutch were forced to agree for transfer of power. On the contrary, India under the leadership of Jawaharlal Nehru preferred dialogue and other peaceful means to gain freedom and totally agreed to Mountbatten Plan as a condition for the transfer of power. Hence, India was partitioned causing immense problem of refugees, riots and bloodshed for decades to come. Although both India and Indonesia have diversity of religion, ethnicity, culture and language, Indonesia gained sovereignty and occupied all the areas of Netherlands East Indies, but India lost huge chunks of the territory on the Western and Eastern frontiers because of the implementation of Mountbatten Plan. How Indian leaders agreed to divide the nation is difficult to understand even now, but majority of intellectuals hold the view that partition was not a solution and it could have been avoided if we had accepted Indonesian line of action and adopted revolutionary means.

India had adopted non-violent means to fight freedom struggle and Congress Party was unwilling to deviate from it. It was therefore that Netaji Subhas Chandra Bose, the architect of revolutionary means, was ignored. Netaji had left the country to organize Indian National Army (INA) and Southeast Asia had welcomed him. Netaji had personal rapport with President Sukarno and other leaders supporting "Asia for Asians". INA had popular support in Southeast Asia where it got volunteers, soldiers and funding to run the organization. INA also attracted large number of soldiers engaged in the British Army to fight for the freedom of their motherland. There was a consensus in Southeast Asia that if India wins freedom, the rest of Southeast Asia are bound to be liberated. Netaji was a charismatic leader with great organizational skills, but Congress Party did not approve his method. Netaji remained active in Southeast Asia and had conquered Assam and Meghalaya during the Second World War. In 1945, he boarded a plane to go to Japan and he disappeared, possibly killed with the help of conspirators aligned with British Intelligence agencies. Therefore, INA became leaderless and the Congress Party got a free hand to negotiate issues for transfer of power. It is humiliating to find that our negotiators were more Britisher than the British themselves as they accepted Mountbatten plan in toto.

The partition of India was accepted without the conduct of referendum. It adversely exposed the negotiating skills of Indian leadership and their concern for larger national interests. Some leaders of independent India were educated in Britain and whenever they went to Southeast Asia, they talked of Indian civilization, culture and democracy displaying lot of superiority complex and arrogance. Although the Constitution promoted the idea of "Unity in Diversity", but deeper analysis of the statements of our leaders indicated "diversity in unity". Little attention was given to strengthen the economy and defence system. The nation remained divided, unable to respond to the challenges posed by hostile neighbours. This prompted China to attack India in 1962 and occupy large chunk of territories on the common frontier. India's defeat was indeed humiliating, yet our leaders talked of non-alignment, socialism and Panchasheel, ignoring the realistic assessment of the situation.

If we glance over the Indian landscape, most of our territories were interconnected. We shared same civilization, culture and urge for freedom but the result was the partition of the country. While, Indonesia is territorially disjointed as it is a country of more than 17000 islands. Each island had separate history, culture, climate and language. Yet Indonesia remained united in the post-colonial period. All those separatists who had declared the foundation of Republic of Maluku in Ambon had to retrace their steps to join in the Republic of Indonesia in due course. West Irian, which had also opposed integration with Indonesian Republic and had been referred for adjudication to the United Nations as a disputed territory, had ultimately been resolved in the favour of Indonesia. Indonesia had been recognized as an archipelagic nation, whose voice was anti-colonial, favouring the sovereignty of the developing nations, was respected by new emerging forces (NEFOS) at the global level.

President Sukarno had a revolutionary outlook in the field of economic and security affairs. He fought battles to throw out the colonial rulers and wanted to secure the economic interests of the Afro-Asian world through revolutionary means. He argued to support "independent and active foreign policy" to escape from being called as pro-American or pro-Russian. He supported the emergence of "New emerging forces" which symbolized a desire to be free from colonialism and neo-colonialism for the Afro-Asian countries and that can be neutralized only through the revolutionary means. On the other hand, India supported evolutionary means and it always wanted to avoid controversy and confrontation. Hence when Sukarno revealed his "crush Malaysia Plan", our bilateral relations were damaged. If we analyze political developments of Sukarno era in early 1960s, we find that our perception differed, which did not prove pragmatic either for India or for Indonesia.

Here an attempt is made to analyze how India faced setbacks in pursuit of peaceful means and depending on the wisdom of Lord Mountbatten. First due to acceptance of Mountbatten Plan, the nation was partitioned into two parts, unleashing migration of millions of people from one part to another due to riots and arson. Subsequently Pakistan was born which wanted to expand its frontiers towards Kashmir. They invaded Kashmir in the post-1947 era and occupied a great chunk of the territory. Indian leadership in pursuit of peaceful means, did not try military means to reoccupy those territories and instead referred the matter to the United Nations for arbitration. This matter became controversial in due course and crisis resolution became elusive. The territories of Kashmir in Pakistan gradually became a matter of intense security concern to India and now every path to conflict resolution in that region is obstructed because Pakistan has leased parts of its territories to China for BRI Plans. If India, after so many decades will ever try military means to regain those territories, the war will involve both Pakistan and China, which is not desirable. Secondly, China did not agree with the demarcation of boundaries as per McMahon line with India. They had declared their objection during the colonial period also, but when communists came into power, they asserted to redraw the map as per their historical claims and hinted at military means to occupy them. Yet our leaders did not make suitable preparations for the battle. They depended on dialogue and other peaceful means to deter the

Chinese and when the Chinese forces finally invaded on Indian territories in 1962, our troops were not suitably equipped to fight and hence we suffered the losses. If we analyze political and strategic developments in India during 1947 to 1962, we find the lack of realism and pragmatism. Unlike Sukarno, "son of soil", Nehru was educated and trained in England. Nehru disliked the approach of Netaji Subhas Chandra Bose to fight to protect our legitimate claims. Nehru supported peaceful democratic means even on matters where military means were required. In retrospect, we find that the approaches of Sukarno or Netaji were more pragmatic. Had Netaji succeeded in his efforts to throw out the colonial rule through revolutionary means, the prospects of partition or Chinese invasion would not have arisen.

Despite differences in outlook, India-Indonesia relations developed on a sound footing. When Indonesia declared independence from the Dutch in 1945, Indian National Congress had opposed the use of Indian troops in British army against Indonesian armed resistance. India offered diplomatic support to Indonesia. It facilitated to build Indonesian embassy opposite PMs residence in Teen Murti and raised Indonesian question at the UN Security Council for termination of the Dutch aggression. India helped in rescue operation of some of the top nationalists in Indonesia. It is noteworthy to mention that Biju Patnaik had been entrusted by government of India to look after the rescue act. He himself piloted a Dakota to rescue Indonesian leaders entrapped on isolated islands despite Dutch blockade. Mohammad Hatta and Sutan Syahrir were some of those leaders held hostage and rescued through Biju Patnaik mission. This act had been appreciated both by Sukarno and Nehru.

India also organized a conference on Indonesia in which 18 Asian and Arab countries participated. This conference denounced the Dutch Colonial rule and expressed support for independence of Indonesia. Indian actions had generated goodwill in Indonesia, which led the two nations to organize Bandung conference for unity and solidarity of the Afro-Asian world. It was thereafter that cramps were witnessed in bilateral relations. The relations deteriorated so rapidly that Indonesia started supporting Pakistan, which was India's greatest enemy. On the eve of Indo-Pakistan war in 1965, Sukarno projected India as an aggressor, and offered open moral, diplomatic and material support (in the air and naval fields) to Pakistan.

The year 1965 is a landmark in the history of Indonesia. It was this year when Sukarno rule was replaced by the armed forces under the leadership of Suharto. The new President of Indonesia embraced closer friendship with the US and hence became a party in Cold War politics. India on the other hand, was supporting the Soviet bloc. Hence our relationship continued to suffer setbacks till the end of the Cold War in 1991. India became a sectoral partner of ASEAN in 1992 and thereafter trade, investment and tourism along with science and technology were favoured sectors of co-operation between India and ASEAN countries.

Indonesia strategically is of crucial importance to India as it controls the southern shores of the straits of Malacca and therefore commands the passage between the Indian Ocean and the Pacific. Indonesia due to its strategic location controls sea routes from India to East Asia and on the other hand to Australia and America. When Japan had occupied Indonesia during the second World War, it had cut off all communications between Europe and India with the Pacific. The German submarines stationed on Indonesian ports, had posed obstructions to Allied powers for movement of the ships in the Indian Ocean. Malacca Straits have great significance for sea-borne trade not only for India, but for the entire ASEAN countries. They visualize a common threat for the security of the sea-lanes of communication in the region ever since China announced sovereignty rights over the entire stretch of the South China Sea. China is economic power and industrially developed. It is the largest trading partner of all the nations in South and Southeast Asia. The nations in the neighbourhood are seeking co-operation and good neighbourly relations. The ASEAN evolved a policy of preventive diplomacy to deter China from military adventurism, and established ARF to promote track II, track III channels for understanding of perception and policies and confidence building. They have signed a code of conduct regarding their policies on South China Sea, yet frictions exist and apprehension about Chinese military action to occupy South China sea cannot be discounted.

The ASEAN countries are concerned about security environment in the region and they have included India in ARF to evolve a collective strategy for preventive diplomacy. Hundreds of seminars, workshops and lectures have been organized in which Chinese are invited to understand viewpoints of countries in the neighbourhood, yet Chinese stand haven't changed much to accommodate the views of Vietnam on the Spratlys or of the Philippines on Reed Bank areas. Hence ASEAN countries along with India and others are taking part in joint exercises. They are exchanging intelligence reports with ARF partners for peace and development in the region. India has provided defence equipment including sophisticated missiles to Vietnam and it is ready to co-operate with all the countries in ASEAN region. India's naval doctrine gives priority attention for surveillance in the periphery of Andamans and it contributes significantly for security in the neighbourhood.

India and Indonesia are territorially very large and very resourceful and therefore they have a special responsibility to ensure security and stability in the Indo-Pacific region. Indonesia had signed Treaty of Friendship with India long back in 1951 which had underlined that, "there shall be perpetual and unalterable friendship" between the two countries. It had also stated that representatives of the two shall meet from time to time to exchange views on matters of common interest. There were frequent exchange of air and naval goodwill missions between the two countries, which had facilitated Indonesian military personnel to come to India for training. In February 1955 an air agreement had been signed between the two which provided co-operation between Indonesian and Indian Air Force. In December 1958 a naval agreement was concluded for five years for developing and improving of the Indian and Indonesian navies, joint training exercises and exchange of goodwill visits. All these had generated goodwill for one another but in the post-1965 era, Indonesia embraced American friendship in strategic and economic matters, and all those who were opposed to American strategic thinking including India, were discarded. The Cold War of the two superpowers were intensified and decades passed when there was a realization that India should not be ignored if developing Third World is to be protected from superpower domination and subjugation. A series of high-level meetings took place after India was included as a dialogue partner of ASEAN both in New Delhi and Jakarta. Subsequently, Strategic Partnerships Document was signed with Indonesia in 2005, outlining core areas of co-operation in ship building, trade, investment and defence co-operation. Several Indian companies like Adani, Tata and Reliance Power subsequently bought equity in many Indonesian coalfields. India is interested in increasing investments in food, automotive, manufacturing and infrastructure sectors. India has already made investment in mining, textile and automotive sectors in billions despite constraints raised by vested interests.

India and Indonesia have signed several Memorandum of Understanding to boost trade, investment and cultural ties. Special mention must be made of Indonesian Presidential visits to India by Abdurrahman Wahid, Megawati Sukarnoputri and Susilo Bambang Yudhoyono to strengthen bilateral ties which were reciprocated. Several agreements have been signed to boost co-operation in different areas and in that endeavour, the visit by President Yudhoyono in 2011 is a landmark. During this visit, 16 inter-governmental agreements were signed between the two countries such as extradition treaty, mutual legal assistance treaty and an air services agreement. The memorandum of understanding on exchange of financial intelligence related to money laundering and financing terrorism had been signed. Besides proposal to establish a biennial trade ministers forum, cooperation in oil and gas, cooperation in urea manufacturing, cooperation in the field of micro, small and medium enterprises, etc., were signed. MOU was also signed between the BATAM free trade zone and Santacruz Electronics Processing Zone (SEEPZ) for cooperation. Again, MOU for cooperation in marine and fisheries, weather and climate services, science and technology were signed. Besides cooperation between the press councils between the two countries, cooperation in the field of education and a cultural exchange programmes were agreed through MOUs.

Bilateral trade volume is increasing, and it has crossed 20 billion US dollars after 2015. India imports palm and vegetable oil, crude and processed coal, petroleum, paper products and spices from Indonesia. While, Indonesia imports textile yarn, chemicals, electric power machinery, refined petroleum products, iron and steel goods, wheat, rice and sugar. India is the largest importer of crude palm oil from Indonesia. India exports gems and jewelries, mechanical equipment and raw minerals to Indonesia. The trade is mutually beneficial, and avenues are explored to expand cooperation in information technology, bio-technology, pharmaceuticals and health care sectors. On the other hand, there is immense scope for expanding cooperation in tourism sector. Indonesia's Borobudur temple, Prambanan temple, Bali, Aceh, Ambon and Bandung are worth visiting in Indonesia. On the other hand, Bodh Gaya, Sarnath, Ayodhya, Hastinapur, Benares, Kolkata and Chennai are of historical importance and it may be of great interests for Indonesians. Besides, there are several other places in both the countries to provide new insights to sociologists and anthropologists to analyze contemporary issues facing the mankind.

Finally, it can be stated that India-Indonesia relations are bound to develop. However, the decision makers in both the countries must remain careful that people in India and Indonesia are very sensitive. Indonesian society can be mobilized based on a myth, if it is spread in an intelligent manner. There are different types of spirits in different parts of Indonesia and they have different names. The popular leaders are supposed to have the support of not only the general people, but also of some of the spirits. The Chinese diaspora have been dominating in business and trade activities in Indonesia for centuries and they have a strong network to protect their interests. They view the arrival of Indian business community in Indonesia as a challenge to their business monopoly. Hence, they have been articulating the view that the business conducted by Indians in Indonesia are benefiting the Indians only and Indonesian government should be concerned about it. They have Pribumi spokespersons instead of the Chinese to spread misunderstandings. The ultimate objective is to reduce Indian business in Indonesia, so that China will remain predominant forever in commercial activities.

> India is a rising power and geopolitically connected to Indonesia. We share common sea frontiers and common heritage. Indonesians are satisfied with the behaviour of Indian diaspora inhabiting mainly in Medan, Surabaya, Bandung and Jakarta. Some of them are engaged in business of textiles and sports goods and there are some recent arrivals including IT experts, engineers, consultants, chartered accountants, bankers and others, whose performance is highly appreciated. Indonesians are pragmatic in their decision making and realist in their approaches. When the US under Donald Trump is saying "America First" and China is striving for a superpower status, Indonesia has to promote its national interests in time with "independent and active foreign policy" that they had evolved in the post-colonial era. India was solidly behind Indonesia in the post-1945 era and geo politics demand that now we should stand together and walk together to fulfil our regional objectives at a time when both of us are under democratic rule promoting democratic values.

11

China's MSR and India's SAGAR: Opportunities of Cooperation and Challenges of Contestation of Big Powers in ASEAN

Geeta Kochhar

Introduction

The world is undergoing global transformations, especially in terms of the power asymmetry that was in place for decades. Many scholars opine that there is a shift of power from the West to Asia that is fast becoming a hub of all activities and rapid changes. There are economies that are rising at a fast pace, especially with China already leading the Asian region and challenging the US economic dominance. There is also India and other powers that are considered as fast emerging economies. However, the focus of most of these changes in Asia is linked to the propositions of the rising economies to have greater connectivity and linkages of both land and sea that can create an interconnected world with shared prosperity for the entire region.

Hence, we have new models mooted through connectivity projects like People's Republic of China's—'One Belt, One Road (OBOR)' (一带一路 *yi dai yi lu*) initiative that is commonly now known as BRI initiative financed by the USD 40 billion Silk Road Fund and USD 100 billion in commitments from other initiatives; South Korea's EurAsia initiative; India's Act East policy (向东看 *Xiang dong kan*) that was earlier commonly known as Look East policy; US "New Silk Road" (美国"新丝绸之路" *Meiguo 'Xin sichou chi lu'*); TPP; Japan's Asia Economic

Corridor (日本亚洲经济走廊 *Riben yahoo jingle zoulang*); Japan's US$100 billion Partnership for Quality Infrastructure; ASEAN's Master Plan for Connectivity, financed through the USD 500 million ASEAN Infrastructure Fund, etc. Besides, there are BIMSTEC's Transport Infrastructure and Logistics Study with 166 projects, SAARC and ASEAN corridors, SASEC corridors, GMS corridor, BCIM Kolkatta-Kunming corridor, Delhi-Hanoi Rail Link and many more such infrastructure development and connectivity projects.

It is evident that with the focus on connectivity in Asia, many states have put up proposals to link through land and sea. India is no exception to this larger transformations of Asia and is surely reflected in its reinvigoration of linkages with the South East Asian countries. On 25 January 2018, Delhi hosted the ASEAN-India Commemorative Summit with the theme "Shared Values, Common Destiny", which was attended by the leaders of the ten ASEAN States. The Delhi Declaration issued then formed the clarity of India-ASEAN future engagement and India's vision of 'Act East' policy. India's maritime cooperation with ASEAN under Modi's proposition of 'Security and Growth for All in the Region' (SAGAR) has parallels and opportunities for cooperation along with the challenges of contestations with China's 21st Century Maritime Silk Route (MSR) plan of the BRI (Belt and Road Initiative). The Southeast Asian countries are the focus in both these parallel strategies with the aim of a shared development vision of Asian region.

However, the underlining factor is also the changing dynamics of the global world order, where both India and China want to play a bigger role. Particularly, ASEAN as a regional cooperative and security architecture will reshape the regional dynamics and the power sharing among the big powers. The paper explores the new opportunities of economic engagement with the ASEAN countries while looking at the threats of economic interdependencies in the region. It posits that the Chinese new economic power challenges the neutrality of states and will reinforce choices of building alliances. India being the alternative power challenging the Chinese grand vision, the expectation of balancing the power in the region are high, yet the cooperative framework of India will pressurize the states for multipolar realignment.

Theoretical Discourse on Economic Interdependence and War

The crux of change in Asia is based on the interplay of economics and the power of geo-economic and geopolitical entanglement. China, which is now the second largest economy in the world has been quite active to utilize the power of economic clout to build trans-border and trans-regional linkages. Many scholars have looked these linkages from the prism of economic dependencies. It is argued that as most of the economies in the Asian region are developing and are in greater need for infrastructure developments, China is playing the 'cheque book' diplomacy to offer soft loans at high interest rates, which most of these countries in the long run will not be able to repay. Hence, there are notions of 'debt-trap' being floated with some even arguing that these might lead to possibility of greater contestation in the region. However, in order to comprehend the role of economic interdependence on states and the possible outcome, there is a need to look at the theories that give more clarity of the possible future scenarios. There are mainly three broad schools of thought that talk of economic interdependence and the possibility of war:

1. In 1913, David Starr Jordan, President of Stanford University, in his speech talked of 'Costs of war'. After calculating the outstanding debts from previous wars and estimating the costs of a general conflagration, he made strong prediction that high costs rule out warfare. In his conclusion, he makes a strong point that no sane statesman would pay such a price. Hence, if there is greater economic interdependence between states, then there is no likelihood of war.
2. In 1910, Norman Angell published an outstanding work titled *The Great Illusion*, breaking the myth of no possibility of war. He clearly stated that economic logic should—but wouldn't—avert war. Therefore, even if we are to believe that with greater interdependence no sane statesman will act in a manner to engage in war, but the possibility of it still exists.
3. In 2005, Thomas L. Friedman published another remarkable work titled *The World is Flat: A Brief History of the Twenty-first Century*, which talked of the "Dell Theory of Conflict Prevention". He stated that economic interdependence raises the costs of geopolitical competition, yet cannot root out the possibility of war.

Having looked at these major schools, it seems that none of these perfectly fit the current scenarios building in the Asian region, where multiple projects are floated from various actors that are expected to change the regional scenario; while many economies have fallen below the expected level. The situation for many economies is thus not just of economic interdependence, but total dependence, whereby China has plans to create military alliances with the dependent states. Hence, this paper is premised on Dale Copeland's 2014 *Trade Expectation Theory* relating to the costs of war and peace. The main premise of the theory is State's expectations of the future trade and investment environment. The theory makes two main arguments:

- When a dependent state has positive expectations about future environment, it is more likely to see all the benefits of continuing the current peace and all the opportunity costs of turning to war. Economic interdependence would then be a force for peace.
- When a dependent state has negative expectations about the future economic environment—seeing itself being cut off from access to foreign trade and investment, or believing that other states will soon cut it off—then the state will tend to believe that without access to the vital raw materials, investments, and export markets needed for its economic health, its economy will start to fall relative to other less vulnerable actors. If this economic decline is anticipated to be severe, the leaders of the dependent state will begin to view war as the rational choice, better than allowing their state to fall to a point where rising states can attack it later or coerce it into submission.

China's BRI: Regional Trade and Connectivity and Indian Ocean

China proposed OBOR to revive the old silk route linking across countries and regions utilising China's foreign reserves of 4 trillion USD, to resolve the problem of overproduction of steel and cement in China through trade. It has two components: Silk Road Economic Belt and 21st Century Maritime Silk Route. The initiative is geographically structured along 6 corridors:

- New Eurasian Land Bridge, running from Western China to Western Russia
- China–Mongolia–Russia Corridor, running from Northern China to Eastern Russia
- China–Central Asia–West Asia Corridor, running from Western China to Turkey
- China–Indochina Peninsula Corridor, running from Southern China to Singapore
- Bangladesh-China-India-Myanmar Corridor, running from Southern China to India
- China–Pakistan Corridor, running from South-Western China to Pakistan
- Maritime Silk Road, running from the Chinese Coast through Singapore to the Mediterranean

In 2016, OBOR was renamed as Belt and Road Initiative (BRI). It is a mega plan that has combined many other regional connectivity projects of China under process for last few decades. The official stated objective of those projects is to boost intra-regional trade cooperation. Hence, China has national highways, superhighway, and Railway network construction linking the inland, coastal, and South Asian cities. There is Kunming-Bangkok highway for which China provided US$30 million for Laos section, Singapore-Kunming Rail link (Bat Deng-Loc Ninh), etc., are also the other major projects. There is Greater Mekong sub-region linking waterways in Laos, Myanmar, Thailand, Cambodia and Vietnam, a stretch of 5,000 km that is regarded as a crucial economic link. Bangladesh-China-India-Myanmar (BCIM) corridor earlier known as "Kunming initiative" is also an initiative to increase connectivity, culture, trade and tourism ties and people-to-people contact in the border regions along with addressing the issues of trans-border crime, such as drug-trafficking, gun-running, illegal immigration. China has also proposed a "Two Corridors and One Rim" regional cooperation between the northern provinces of Vietnam and Laos with the southern Chinese provinces of Guangxi and Yunnan. Trade transportation, tourism and the development of special economic zones are all part of this proposal to revive transport ties along the former trade routes of the area. Hence, we see a multitude of projects floated by China across regions and countries to build a network of connectivity; while the most significant as an umbrella project is the BRI.

An important component of the BRI is the Maritime Silk Road initiative with which China proposes to build three blue economic passages connecting China and the world with one to four trillion of investment projects that include roads, railways, ports and other infrastructure projects. In the first half of 2017, Chinese companies planned to purchase or invest in nine overseas ports, all of them in Indian Ocean (Szechenyi, 2018: 21). It is interesting to note that each of the 10 busiest container ports in the world are situated along the shores of either the Pacific or Indian Ocean, and more than half of the world's maritime trade in petroleum transits the Indian Ocean alone. The ocean's commercial shipping volume has increased four-fold since 1970, with an estimated 9.84 billion tons of products being transported each year (Szechenyi, 2018: 21). Exports from Asian economies are expected to rise from 17 per cent in 2010 to 28 per cent in 2030, further indicating the economic vibrancy of the region (Szechenyi, 2018: 21).

Historical Roots of the Chinese Maritime Route

BRI has mooted the idea that it is reviving the old historical roots and creates future connectivities based on the older concepts. However, history gives a different reflection and insights to the proposed idea of connectivities and linkages. The maritime silk route that China proposes under the BRI is a concept taken from the Ming dynasty, whereby Admiral Zheng He made seven voyages to explore the connections with other states of Southeast Asia, South Asia, Western Asia, and East Africa from 1405 to 1433. (See Map 1 & 2) The most fascinating fact about

Map 1: Area Covered during Admiral Zheng He's Voyage

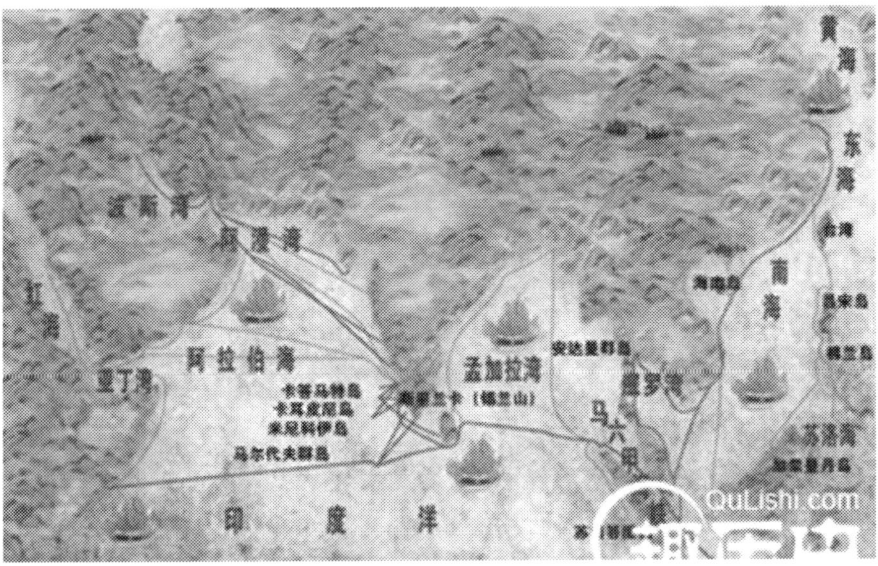

Source: http://www.qulishi.com/huati/zhxxy/

Map 2: Admiral Zheng He's Seven Voyages and the Route (1405-1433)

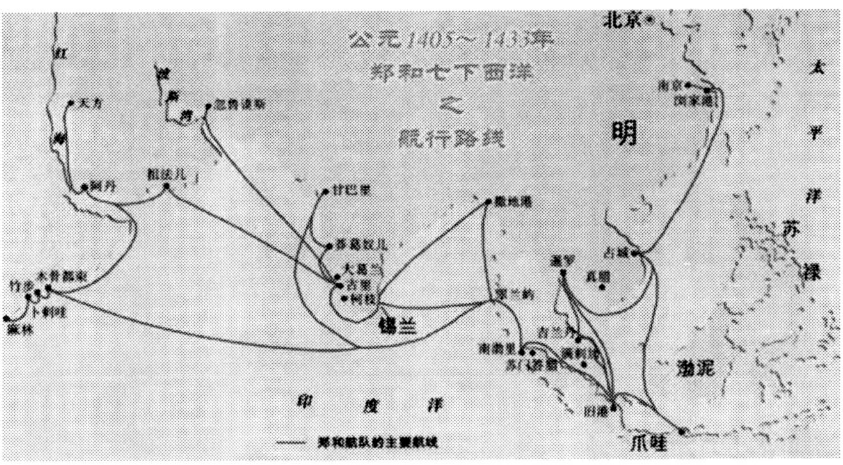

Source: http://www.t-winexpo.com/news/content/id/467.html

Zheng He's voyages is that most of these voyages were under the rule of Emperor Zhu Di (明成祖朱棣) of the Ming dynasty (1368-1644CE) during the most flourishing period of the dynasty called the 'Yongle flourishing age'. What is most striking is that during the Ming Dynasty, China controlled large territories including some of the northern part of Vietnam (See Map 3). Zheng He had the role of propagating the State power/might, which unprecedentedly influenced many ASEAN countries, though there are multiple stories to the actual purpose of his visits.

Emperor Zhu Di (1360-1424) is a very significant person in Chinese history. He is considered unmatched to other Emperors of the Ming dynasty. He is known for hiding his capacities and biding his time, strengthening his resolve, taking advantage of the chance for guarding the frontier and wipe out the rebellion in the northern area. In the northern desert, he launched the campaign, pacified the Annan State, connected to the West, and amended the Yongle Canon. He had built Beijing City and led to the creation of "Yongle flourishing age". As per the historical Chinese records, Emperor Zhu Di had the concept of "Abide by the heavens, not bully few people because you have more people, not let strong bullying the weak, and share the happiness of peace" (尔等祇顺天道，恪遵朕言，循礼安分，毋得违越，不可欺寡，不可凌弱，庶几共享太平之福) (History Topics). 'Share the happiness of peace' was based on the concept of giving huge gifts to show the supremacy of China and to appease other Kingdoms to ally with the Chinese Emperor. This is also the concept of Chinese Sun Zi 'Art of War' strategy, where the war is won without actually engaging in a war (不战而胜 *bu than er sheng*). The notion proposed by the Emperor Zhu Di indicates the kind of world order under the heaven that Ming dynasty wanted to create, which also implies that present—day China sees few powers that are dominant in South Asia with a huge population (read India) and that China has the responsibility to bring peace to the region.

India's SAGAR

The vision SAGAR was enunciated by Prime Minister Modi in March 2015 when he put forward the concept of "Security and Growth for All in the Region". This is a clear, high-level articulation of India's vision for the Indian Ocean. SAGAR has distinct but interrelated elements and underscore India's engagement in the Indian Ocean, which relate to enhancing capacities to safeguard land and maritime territories and interests; deepening economic and security cooperation in the littoral; promoting collective action to deal with natural disasters and maritime threats

Map 3: Ming Dynasty Kingdom of Zhu Di

Source: http://www.qulishi.com/huati/yongleshengshi/

like piracy, terrorism and emergent non-state actors; working towards sustainable regional development through enhanced collaboration; and engaging with countries beyond the shores with the aim of building greater trust and promoting respect for maritime rules, norms and peaceful resolution of disputes.

The vision was envisaged considering the importance of Indian Ocean in diplomacy and the changing geopolitics of the region. The Indian Ocean is linked to forty littoral states with over 40 per cent of the world's population. Two-thirds of the world's oil shipment, one-third of the world's bulk cargo, and half of the world's container traffic transit through the Indian Ocean (Padmaja, 2018). Connectivity is one of the major themes of Prime Minister Modi's 'Neighbourhood First' policy. Indian government continues to work on a range of projects to improve maritime logistics in Sri Lanka, Maldives, Mauritius and Seychelles. Other initiatives include the Kaladan transport project leading to Sittwe port in Myanmar; the Trilateral Highway to Thailand; and, the Chabahar port project in Iran (Swaraj, 2017). With SAGAR, Modi government plans to deepen economic and security engagement with maritime neighbours, as well as assist in building their maritime security capabilities. With SAGAR, India wants to reinvigorate the blue water economy and make a push of 'Act East' policy for greater connectivity.

Significance of Indian and Pacific Ocean

It is said that the 10 busiest container ports in the world are situated along the shores of either the Pacific or Indian Ocean, which makes the Oceans very important and geopolitically significant. More than half of the world's maritime trade in petroleum transits the Indian Ocean alone. Since 1970, Ocean's commercial shipping volume has increased four-fold, with almost 9.84 billion tons of products transported each year (Funaiole, 2018). In addition to this, the exports from Asian economies are expected to rise from 17 per cent in 2010 to 28 per cent by 2030, most of which will be from the sea routes (Funaiole, 2018). For China's growing population, energy demands are multiplying rapidly. Hence, China's 'vision and Actions' clearly state that communication in procuring and transportation is a major goal of the OBOR. Besides, Oil and gas procurement is the reason for transport networks. In 2016, China imported above 7.6 million barrels of crude oil from countries along the Persian Gulf (Barron, 2017). By 2017, China surpassed USA in importing crude oil and by 2035 China will need to import 80 per cent of the domestic demand for oil (Ghiasy, 2018: 7). The transit route for oil imports are through Indian Ocean or South China sea with almost 80 per cent through Malacca Strait. Hence, security interests of China are deep routed in these sea routes. In addition, 90 per cent of India's trade by volume and 90 per cent of its energy imports transit through Indian Ocean (Padmaja, 2018).

Expansion of the Chinese Empire or Debt-trap Colonialism

Much of the literature points to the expansion of Chinese footholds in various parts of the region. There is increased literature which talks of Chinese expansion to gain ports through failed debt return. Sri Lanka Hambantota port, 15,000 acres of land given to China for 99 years lease is a case in point. It is evident from many reports that the port has no commercial profitability and in fact during negotiations with India, the project was found unsuitable in terms of commercial feasibility (Koh, 2018). However, the Chinese invested billions of dollars for the port by grant of loan on interest. Result is that the Sri Lankan government was unable to repay the loan as there was no commercial profits made out of the port, which finally led the government leasing the entire port to the Chinese for 99 years (Basu, 2017). The port is now seen as China's control over crucial trade routes and international supply chains under a well-planned strategy, which sounds similar to the pattern of British colonial ways of leasing Hong Kong.

Before Hambantota was taken over by the Chinese, a lesser debated and discussed case is that of Port of Darwin in Australia, which was also leased for 99 years to a Chinese Landbridge company's head Ye Cheng for A$506 million in 2015. In 1940, Darwin was an important staging point for US sailors fighting in the Pacific and the US Peary was sunk in Darwin harbour during the Japanese bombing on 19 February 1942 (Garrick, 2018). Hence, the Chinese strategy is to take control of ports for military purposes to be recognized as a parallel to the superpower USA with military bases. What is worth noting is the fact that Landbridge company has been operating a "people's militia" at its home base of Rizhao, which means that the company is not just interested in commercial engagements, but has deeper interests (Tanaka, 2019).

Darwin is also a specific case study for the US-China contestation in the region, where China is expanding its reach at a time USA is withdrawing. Besides, increasingly it is clear that Kenya is also likely to lose Uganda's Mombasa port to China due to huge loan debt. Hence, the crucial issue is why China is investing huge amounts in commercially non-viable ports and whether it is just a simple take over on lease for the default payment of loans by lenders or more of a strategic plan to acquire ports?

If we look at Chinese actions from the historical lens, we might find easy comparison of the expansion of British Empire and the rise of the USA as the superpower. The detailed analysis of it will show that most of the agreements to take over ports have been for 99 years lease that are somewhat similar to the strategy of the East India Company, which did not look for direct intervention or expansion of the British government, but resulted in the expansion of British Empire. It is therefore right to posit that Chinese government that has greater control over all its large-scale companies is indirectly playing a role in these acquisitions for expansion of its sphere of influence and control in the region.

Moreover, if we look at the US military strategy of building alliances and acquiring military bases, many of the actions of Chinese government are parallel moves, even though China at present does not have that trust and alliance relationship with countries in the region. However, it will be just a matter of time for China to coerce states to board its ship, which is clearly articulated in Xi Jinping's vision of building 'communities of common destiny'.

Comparing the Visions of India and China

India has called for "shared destiny"; while China is emphasizing on building "communities of common destiny". The clear understanding of Chinese proposition is that China seeks to build alliances with states in the region, mainly focusing on military alliances. The notion of sharing the development and prosperity as stated in India's vision is missing. Indian PM Modi only made an oblique reference to the BRI project and expressed the need for respect to territorial and sovereignty issues of the countries at the SCO summit in 2017; while extending full support to the initiatives that are inclusive in nature. It was clearly articulated that India wants an inclusive connectivity project; while what is offered on the table by the Chinese seems to be exclusive and power oriented goal. Hence, in principle, India supports BRI, but the main concern of traditional security along with economic trade deficit with China remains high.

India is apprehensive of China's motives and interest to raise regional clout, including the entry into SAARC. India is promoting east-west connectivity through Myanmar, Thailand and on to Vietnam, which some view as a counter balance to China's north-south connectivity to South-East Asia. India is advocating 'Act East' as an alternative expansion of linkages. Many advocate that these projects mooted by India are parallels to China's MSR projects. However, China's vision comes from its historical legacy of ruling and controlling the region; while India wants an interconnected world with universal recognition of international norms, good governance, rule of law, openness based on equality and inclusiveness. If we see the grand vision of India and compare it with China, there seems more convergence than competition, yet no parallels can be drawn with the motives of SAGAR and MSR, except connectivity as the bottom line.

One of many reasons cited by some scholars for China's control of ports in the region is its desire to expand its sphere of influence. In the 2015 China Military White Paper, China explained the plan to develop a blue-water navy fleet, able to carry out operations for offshore protection (远海护卫 – *yuanhai huwei*). It also talked about the offshore protection as "frontier defense" for its own national and security interests (Berkofsky, 2019: 50). Although China's coastal fleet would have been sufficient, yet China is carrying out defence operations near the coast (近海防御 –*jinhai fangyu*). This reflects the strategic "1.5 war" doctrine, which calls for the development of Chinese naval capabilities able to fight one major war while being able to contain a second military conflict (Berkofsky, 2019: 51).

The greater issue worth examining is whether the debt trap created by China can lead to tension in the region or not? In particular, whether is entails the possibility of war or not? The region sees economic decline of small players that are highly supported and assisted by the Chinese. Pakistan is a good example to ponder, where CPEC project is highly funded by the Chinese under the BRI. In case the CPEC project also fails, as reflected in some of the reports, the possibility of Pakistan waging war in the region will be high. Same may be the future of Nepal that has had engaged in war with China over small trade related issue. Sino-Nepalese war or the Sino-Gorkha war of 1788–92, initially fought between Nepal and Tibet over a trade dispute relating to low quality coins manufactured by Nepalese for the Tibetans, resulted in Treaty of Betrawati whereby Nepal had to accept the suzerainty of the Qing Emperor.

As of now, many small and medium powers in the region are optimistic of reaping the benefits from China's growth as well as from India's rise. However, as China is also marching towards slow growth and its internal demands are growing, it will not be a long term supplier of benefits to the neighbouring countries. Hence, when the neighbouring states will fall in the debt burden of China and their expectation of future environment will be bleak, the leaders that are currently engaging in giving thrust to military buildup, are likely to make choices whereby war will seem to be a rational option as David Copeland suggests. This could be one of the possibility to avoid submission to joining the China camp as an ally or even the fear of threat. These dependent states also look at India as an option to rely on any fall out with China. This creates a space for contestation between the big powers—India and China; while areas of cooperation in connectivity and other infrastructural development are plenty.

ASEAN Dilemma and India-China Contestation

According to estimates, by 2050, ASEAN will expand to become world's fourth largest economy (ASEAN, 2017). Since its inception of MSR, China had focused on cooperation with ASEAN as a main objective. There have been three main lines of importance for China under the grand project: South China sea, Indian Ocean and the Mediterranean Sea, and the Atlantic. ASEAN member countries have close land connectivity with China and majority of them are unsure of China's naval expansion. There is contradiction in their dealing with China, whereby on the one hand, they have regional territorial disputes with China, but on the other hand want greater cooperation with China. Hence, most of the meetings of the member states lack strong decision for or against China.

The ASEAN connectivity 2025 plan would need USD 110 billion every year for infrastructure development to support future growth (Ghiasy, 2018: 19). It is here that ASEAN member states see both China and India as an opportunity, but specifically view India as a viable option to balance Chinese threat. The South China sea dispute of some ASEAN members like Philippines, Brunei, Vietnam, and Malaysia often creates heightened tension among the players, and most of these small countries fear to wage war with powerful China. India's support at a time when US is withdrawing from the region, is greatly sought for balancing the region and maintaining peace. The failure of these states to diplomatically resolve the issues has resulted in arms buildup in the region. To cite, Vietnam has increased its military expenditure by 127 per cent from USD 2.2 billion in 2006 to USD 5 billion in 2017 (Zachary, 2016).

In order to make its claims for all kinds of disputes, China is engaging with the states in building connectivity with a leverage. This can eventually help China to alter the status quo in its favour by refusing to engage in multilateral tribunal procedures or negotiations. Many of such concerns have been raised where China might use its economic and military power to its advantage. The eastern side of the Indian Ocean region connects ASEAN member states to South Asia. In order to avoid excessive dependency on China and to remain cautious of the debt traps, many member states look at India as the other influential power in the region.

However, there seems to be lack of trust over India's commitment to deliver. Besides, this balancing strategy of ASEAN member states only leads to greater competition between the big powers—India and China, with many emerging areas of contestation. Countries like Vietnam desire India to play greater role to safeguard its territorial and security interests in the region along with providing defence material to upgrade their defence capabilities. However, excessive presence of China in the Indian ocean region raises India's concerns of encirclement and leads to tensions in bilateral relations. Eventually the small powers in the region will have to make clear choices as the power of hint will break the neutrality of the states to form alliances. India, on its part, will compel to recreate a multipolar world order where many rising and emergent power will be equal player.

REFERENCES

Angell, Norman, 1933, *The Great Illusion*, London: Simkin Marshall, Hamilton Kent & Co.

ASEAN, 2017, *Investing in ASEAN*, ASEAN, Jakarta, at https://asean.org/storage/2017/01/Investing-in-ASEAN-2017-.pdf (accessed on March 20, 2019)

Barron, Jeff, 2017, "More Chinese Crude Oil Imports Coming from Non-OPEC Countries", *US Energy Information Administration*, April 14, at https://www.eia.gov/todayinenergy/detail.php?id=30792 (accessed on April 26, 2019)

Basu, Narayani, 2017, "China Buys Hambantota Port: Should India Be Concerned?" *The Diplomat*, July 29, at https://thediplomat.com/2017/07/china-buys-hambantota-port-should-india-be-concerned/ (accessed on March 30 2018)

Berkofsky, Axel and Sergio Miracola (eds.) (2019) *Geopolitics By Other Means: The Indo-Pacific Reality*, Italy: Ledizioni Publishing.

Copeland, Dale C. 2014. *Economic Interdependence and War*. New Jersey: Princeton University

Press, at http://assets.press.princeton.edu/chapters/i10403.pdf (accessed on January 21, 2019)

Friedman, Thomas L., 2005, *The World is Flat*, US: Farrar, Straus and Giroux.

Funaiole, Matthew and Jonathan Hillman, 2018, "China's Maritime Silk Road Initiative: Economic Drivers and Challenges", *Asia Maritime Transparency Initiative*, April 4, at https://amti.csis.org/maritime-silk-road-economic-drivers-challenges/ (accessed on April 25, 2019)

Garrick, John, 2018, Darwin Port's Sale is a Blueprint for China's Future Economic Expansion, *The Conversation*, December 7, at http://theconversation.com/darwin-ports-sale-is-a-blueprint-for-chinas-future-economic-expansion-108254 (accessed on March 20, 2019)

Ghiasy, Richard, Fei Su, and Lora Saalman, 2018, "The 21st Century Maritime Silk Road: Security Implications and Way Forward For the European Union", *Stockholm International Peace Research Institute*, at https://www.sipri.org/publications/2018/other-publications/21st-century-maritime-silk-road-security-implications-and-ways-forward-european-union (accessed on March 20, 2019)

History Topics, available at http://www.qulishi.com/huati/zhxxy/ (accessed on March 20, 2018)

Jordan, David Starr, 1924, "The Last Cost of War", *Advocate of Peace Through Justice*, Vol. 86, No. 2, February, pp. 110–14.

Koh King Kee, 2018, "An Ungrounded Accusation", *Beijing Review*, Issue no. 34, August 23, at http://www.bjreview.com/Opinion/201808/t20180820_800138627.html (accessed on April 20, 2018).

Padmaja, G., 2018, "Revisitng 'SAGAR': India's Template for Cooperation in the Indian Ocean Region", *National Maritime Foundation*, at http://maritimeindia.org/View%20Profile/636602941847320911.pdf (accessed on January 10, 2019)

Swaraj, Sushma, "SAGAR: India's Vision for the Indian Ocean Region," *India Foundation*, Nov-Dec 2017, inaugural address delivered by Smt. Sushma Swaraj, Minister of External Affairs, Government of India, on 31st August, 2017 at the 2nd Indian Ocean Conference at Colombo, Sri Lanka organised by India Foundation, at http://www.indiafoundation.in/sagar-indias-vision-for-the-indian-ocean-region/ (accessed on March 21, 2019)

Szechenyi, Nicholas, "China's Maritime Silk Road: Strategic and Economic Implications for the Indo-Pacific Region," *Centre for Strategic and International Studies*, March, at https://www.csis.org/analysis/chinas-maritime-silk-road (accessed on March 20, 2019)

Tanaka, Yasuto, 2019, "Concerns Raised as Australian Port Rolls Out Red Carpet for Chinese Investment", *Japan Forward*, February 2, at https://japan-forward.com/concerns-raised-as-australian-port-rolls-out-red-carpet-for-chinese-investment/ (accessed on March 20, 2019)

Zachary, A. and Nguyen A., 2016, "Vietnam's Military Modernization", *The Diplomat*, October 28, at https://thediplomat.com/2016/10/vietnams-military-modernization/ (accessed on January 20, 2018)

12

China as a Factor in Indian Foreign Policy Towards ASEAN: A Case Study of United Nations

Jayshree Tandekar

India and China started their journey of growth and progress at around the same time but somewhere India lagged behind. Since the end of Cold War, China has emerged as a powerful economic giant aspiring to become an undisputed 'pole' both at regional and global levels. In fact, China has emerged as 'threat' to India's international, regional and national interests. At the international level, India's aspirations to become a major power have been countered by the Chinese position at various international forums such as United Nations, World Trade Organization and International Labour Organization. At the regional level, India is threatened by growing close relations between its neighbours and China such as Pakistan, Bangladesh, Sri Lanka and Nepal. China has exploited troubled relations between India and its south Asian neighbours (China is an observer at SAARC). In particular, China has cultivated special relations with Pakistan by providing it with the necessary economic, military and nuclear supplies. In recent years, maritime strategy with regard to Indian Ocean has accelerated tensions between the two countries. At the national level, India's territorial interests have been challenged by Chinese position over Line of Actual Control along the Himalayan ridges, Aksai Chin, Ladakh, Arunachal Pradesh and Sikkim. To counter and balance Chinese position and influence, India decided to engage itself with a region which emerged significant in post-Cold War: Southeast Asia (ASEAN).

This article is an attempt to present a general understanding of China as a factor in Indian foreign policy towards ASEAN. It starts by describing the contesting relations between India and China. It then provides an overview of India's foreign policy for ASEAN during Cold War and post-Cold War, and the need for the Look East and Act East Policies. It also gives an outline of the participation of India and ASEAN countries in the United Nations. The central focus of this article is to analyze how the Act East Policy can strengthen India-ASEAN relations and help India in countering the Chinese challenge in the United Nations. The article ends with the lessons that can be drawn from the contribution of the Indian foreign policy towards ASEAN in the United Nations.

India and China: Contesting Relations

Both India and China began their journey of independent governance almost at the same time, India in 1947 and China in 1949. When the People's Republic of China (PRC) was established in 1949, India was the second non-communist country to accord recognition to it and the first non-communist country to establish an embassy in China. In 1950, India and China established diplomatic relations. In fact, India was one of the first Asian countries to sponsor a resolution for the admission of China in the United Nations. To strengthen ties with India, the Chinese Premier Zhou Enlai visited India in 1954, 1957 and 1960, and the Indian Prime Minister Jawaharlal Nehru visited China in 1954. The historic India-China Agreement on Trade and Intercourse between India and the Tibet Region of China signed in 1954 enshrined the five principles of the *Panchsheel*. However, the outbreak of war between India and China in October 1962 changed the course of relations between the two countries.

Though over the years, diplomatic and economic relations between India and China have resumed, there are several issues which have prevented the normalization of relations between them. The most significant amongst them have been the Indian permission for the operation ofTibetan Government in Exile in Dharamsala; territorial disputes over Arunachal Pradesh, Sikkim, Ladakh, Aksai Chin and the Line of Actual Control; Chinese financial, military and technical support to Pakistan; disagreement over maritime supremacy in South China Sea; and conflictual interests in Southeast Asian region.

India's Foreign Policy for ASEAN

The Association of Southeast Asian Nations (ASEAN) is a prominent regional organization in Southeast Asia. ASEAN, established in 1967, consists of ten member countries, namely, Brunei Darussalam, Cambodia, Indonesia, Laos, Malaysia, Myanmar, Philippines, Singapore, Thailand and Vietnam. India shares territorial borders with Myanmar and maritime borders with Indonesia and Thailand. Apart from geographical proximity, India enjoys historical and cultural relations with many of the ASEAN countries such as Cambodia, Myanmar, Thailand and Vietnam.

Despite close geographical, historical and cultural ties, India did not favour pursuing active foreign policy towards ASEAN during Cold War. This was primarily because India saw the establishment of ASEAN as an American attempt to contain communism in Southeast Asia. Further, India's Friendship Treaty with Soviet Union, its position on Vietnam War and its recognition of Hang Samrin's administration in Cambodia placed India in one ideological camp while ASEAN was seen as being supportive of the other ideological bloc. Hence, the Cold War prevented India from cultivating strong relations with ASEAN. As one scholar has put it, "the story of ASEAN-India relations throughout the Cold War can be appropriately summarized as missed opportunities due to political mistrust, economic inconsequentiality, and occasional military threats" (Desai 2017).

However, the end of Cold War increased the significance of ASEAN region for the Indian foreign policy as is evident from the 'Look East Policy' which was initiated under the leadership of former Prime Minister P.V. Narasimha Rao in 1992. The Look East Policy was the Indian response to the changes that took place at the domestic, regional and international levels in the early post-Cold War years. At the international level, the dismemberment of the Soviet Union not only resulted in economic and strategic void for India but the end of bipolar division diminished the significance of India's non-alliance. At the regional level, the emergence of China as "the face of the East" led India to rethink its strategy in the Southeast Asian region. This was important because the dominant Chinese position could relegate India to a secondary economic and political role in the region (Yeravdekar and Gupte 2014: 1). At the domestic level, the Indian economy was affected by recession and balance of payment crisis which needed immediate attention. At the same time, India realized that it was necessary to develop and stabilize its north-eastern region as it suffered from the insurgency problem. It was believed that the Look East Policy would provide India with ample economic opportunities in the regions to its east and thus help in its economic growth (Rajendram 2014: 3).

The primary objective of the Look East Policy was to renew political relations and build security and economic cooperation with the ASEAN countries. Also, through this Policy, India wanted to prevent the dominance of any one major power in the Southeast Asian region (Singh 2015: 16). Therefore, as part of the Look East Policy, India became a sectoral dialogue partner with the ASEAN in 1992. It became the full dialogue partner with ASEAN in 1995, a member of the ASEAN Regional Forum (ARF) in 1996 and a summit-level partner in 2002. India was accorded the status of strategic partner of ASEAN in 2012. India and ASEAN have together established almost thirty annual dialogue mechanisms which comprise of a summit at the level of the Prime Minister, seven sectoral dialogues at the level of ministers and three funds as well. These funds are the ASEAN-India Cooperation Fund, the ASEAN-India Science and Technology Fund and the ASEAN-India Green Fund. India has also set up separate Mission to ASEAN and East Asia Summit in Jakarta and the ASEAN-India Centre in New Delhi (Kumar 2016). Apart from this, India has entered into several sub-regional cooperation arrangements with many ASEAN countries. Table 1 provides a list of all these sub-regional arrangements.

Table 1: Indian Participation in Sub-Regional Initiatives as part of its Look East Policy

Name of the Sub-Regional Initiative	*Name of Member Countries*
Bangladesh-China-India-Myanmar Economic Corridor (BCIM-EC) Forum for Regional Cooperation	Bangladesh, China, India and Myanmar.
Bay of Bengal Initiative for Multi-Sectoral Technical and Economic Cooperation (BIMSTEC)	Bangladesh, Bhutan, India, Myanmar, Nepal, Sri Lanka and Thailand.
East Asia Summit	Member Countries of ASEAN, Australia, China, India, Japan, New Zealand and South Korea.
Mekong-Ganga Cooperation	Cambodia, India, Laos, Myanmar, Thailand and Vietnam.
Regional Comprehensive Economic Partnership (RCEP)	Member Countries of ASEAN, Australia, China, India, Japan, New Zealand and South Korea.

Source: http://www.tribuneindia.com/news/comment/asean-the-pivot-of-india-s-act-east-policy/194609.html Accessed on 18 July 2019.

The Look East Policy was upgraded and renamed as the Act East Policy in 2014. The Act East Policy aims to not only enhance economic and political relations with the Southeast Asian countries that were built during the 'Look East' days but also develop geo-strategic cooperation and uphold soft power ties with them (Singh 2015: 16). Thus in pursuit of the Act East Policy, the Indian President, the Prime Minister and the Minister for External Affairs have visited numerous countries such as Myanmar, Singapore, and Vietnam in the last few years. Also, some of the prominent projects which are either ongoing or in final stages of approval are: India-Myanmar-Thailand Trilateral Highway; Tracking Data Reception/Data Processing Station in Ho Chi Minh City, Vietnam; Telemetry Tracking and Command Station in Biak, Indonesia; and Centres of Excellence in Software Development and Training in Cambodia, Laos, Vietnam and Malaysia (MEA website).

India and ASEAN Countries in the United Nations

India and ASEAN countries are committed to the principles enshrined in the UN Charter. They believe that the international cooperation achieved through the United Nations is essential for resolving challenges that threaten the existence of the mankind. Thus, working through the United Nations forms an essential component of the foreign policy of these countries. The membership of most of these countries spans over several decades. Table 2 illustrates the time when these countries became members of the United Nations. Of these countries, India and Philippines were signatories to the UN Charter in 1945 and hence they are referred to as the founding members of the United Nations.

Table 2: Date of Admission of India and ASEAN Member Countries to United Nations

Name of the Country	*Date of Admission*
Brunei Darussalam	21 September 1984
Cambodia	14 December 1955
India	30 October 1945 (Founding Member)
Indonesia	28 September 1950
Laos	14 December 1955
Malaysia	17 September 1957
Myanmar	19 April 1948
Philippines	24 October 1945 (Founding Member)
Singapore	21 September 1965
Thailand	16 December 1946
Vietnam	20 September 1977

Source: http://www.un.org/press/en/2006/org1469.doc.htm. Accessed on 15 July 2019.

Countering Chinese Factor at United Nations through Act East Policy

The activism and involvement of these countries in the United Nations can be determined from their personnel and financial contribution to this international organization. As far as the finances are concerned, India and ASEAN countries provide about three to five percent of the total UN budget annually (UN website a). Apart from finances, many of these countries have the distinction of having served as the non-permanent member of the Security Council on several occasions.

For instance, India served as the non-permanent member seven times, Malaysia and Philippines—four times each, and Indonesia—thrice (UN website b). In addition, countries such as India, Indonesia, Philippines and Vietnam have had the opportunity of being elected as the President of the General Assembly at different points of time.

Further, India and ASEAN countries have contributed significantly to UN peacekeeping. Over the years, these countries have seconded military troops, civilian police and experts on mission to UN peacekeeping operations set up in Bosnia-Herzegovina, Congo, Haiti, Liberia, Namibia, South Sudan and Timor-Leste. India has consistently sent personnel for UN peacekeeping. Apart from India, countries such as Cambodia, Indonesia, Malaysia and Philippines have emerged as the major contributors to UN peacekeeping operations in recent years though in the period between 2000 and 2004, Thailand was the main contributor (UN website c). The current contribution of India and ASEAN countries to UN peacekeeping operations is shown in Table 3.

Table 3: Current Contribution of India and ASEAN Countries to UN Peacekeeping Operations (June 2019)

Name of the Country	*Police*	*UN Military Experts on Mission*	*Troops*	*Total*
Brunei Darussalam	0	0	29	29
Cambodia	0	11	755	766
India	310	37	5,877	6224
Indonesia	327	24	2,546	2897
Malaysia	2	13	814	829
Myanmar	0	0	0	0
Philippines	24	11	0	35
Thailand	10	6	273	289
Vietnam	0	4	63	67
Total	673	106	10357	11136

Source: https://peacekeeping.un.org/sites/default/files/1_summary_of_contributions_12.pdf. Accessed on 18 July 2019.

Moreover, these countries have actively participated in various social and economic activities of the United Nations such as promotion of human rights, protection of environment, disarmament and non-proliferation, sustainable development, and gender equality. Also, India and ASEAN countries share similar views on number of issues. For instance, they strongly believe in the need to reform the United Nations in order to make it an efficient and cohesive international organization capable of addressing the challenges of the 21st century (Kyodo 2015).

Countering China through Act East Policy in the United Nations

The objectives of India's Act East Policy and the Indian participation in the United Nations are similar. The Indian foreign policy towards ASEAN and the United Nations aims to consolidate the image of India as benign and responsible member of the international community. As a member of the United Nations, India is an ardent believer of the principles enshrined in the UN Charter. However, there have been occasions when it has faced difficulties in following these principles in the United Nations due to the Chinese position. These difficulties can be reduced through the Act East Policy. This is because the Act East Policy can assist India in earning the requisite support of ASEAN countries in the United Nations to strengthen its position on issues which lack the Chinese support, such as the reform of the Security Council and ensuring effective decision making on issues of global concern.

'China' is a factor that is common to India as well as to the countries to its east. Despite being a neighbour, China is involved in several disputes with India and ASEAN countries. But these disputes remain unresolved because of the defiant Chinese position. For instance, the Indo-Chinese territorial dispute at the Line of Actual Control (LAC), the ambiguous Chinese support to Pakistan and the growing Chinese presence in the Indian Ocean region threaten the Indian national interests. Moreover, the subtle economic and military rivalry between India and China has been a cause of constant worry for the former (Schmidt 2011: 9). Similarly, many ASEAN countries are locked in maritime disputes with China in the South China Sea. Countries such as Brunei Darussalam, Malaysia, Philippines and Vietnam have conflicting claims in the South China Sea with regard to their respective territorial sovereignty and maritime borders. In particular, Vietnam and China have disagreement over the 'Paracel Islands' and twice it has been the cause of military confrontation between the two countries. Likewise, Philippines and China have differences over the ownership of the 'Spratly Islands' (Ba 2011: 269-270). Though not a direct claimant in the dispute, the interests of Indonesia are at stake as the Chinese claim in the South China Sea includes the rich fishery and seabed natural gas area north of Indonesia's Natuna Islands (Simon 2012: 997; 1009).

Since 2008, the conflictual claims in the South China Sea have intensified as China has objected to all those hydrocarbon explorations in the disputed waters which exclude its companies and in some cases China has even detained and expelled the Vietnamese and Philippine fishing boats from the contested maritime boundaries (Fravel 2011: 299; Simon 2012: 1000). The authoritative position of China on the maritime territorial disputes (due to its economic and naval power) in the East and South China Sea has made ASEAN countries turn to India (Rajendram 2014: 3). These countries want India to play a balancing role in the region. Such a development highlights the fact that these countries have confidence in the ability and intentions of India to counter the Chinese influence in the Asia-Pacific region. Also, India has no territorial disputes with any of ASEAN countries nor is it seen as a potential threat by these countries (Kumar 2016).

Given this scenario, the Act East Policy can play an important role in cementing this confidence of ASEAN countries further and transferring it to the United Nations for a longer term. This is to say that the Act East Policy can rally ASEAN countries behind India in the latter's efforts to counter and possibly reduce the Chinese influence on number of issues in the United Nations that affect India directly or indirectly. Of particular interest for India have been the reforms in the Security Council. However, China has not been enthusiastic enough to support the reforms because of its vested interests in the status quo (Schmidt 2011: 8; Thakur 2011: 901). Moreover, there are indications that China might not back India's claim for permanent seat in the Security Council if the latter continues to support the Japanese bid for permanent membership (Fullilove 2006: 68). The following section briefly discusses the issue of reforms in the Security Council.

Reform of the Security Council

One of the principal organs of the United Nations, the Security Council is primarily responsible for maintaining international peace and security. It consists of fifteen members: five permanent members with power of veto (China, France, Russia, United Kingdom of Great Britain and Northern Ireland, and United States of America) and ten non-permanent members elected for a term of two years.

Over the years, there have been demands to reform the Security Council. This is because it neither reflects the changing membership of the United Nations nor is it transparent in its functioning. The demands for the Security Council reform covers number of issues such the need to address inequality between permanent members and other members of the United Nations, the power of veto enjoyed by permanent members alone, inclusion of more non-permanent members to make the Security Council truly representative, increasing the number of permanent seats, granting of the veto power to new permanent members, regional representation as the criteria for membership and the tenure of office in the Security Council (Rivlin 2005: 368; 375).

India has been a strong advocate for the reforms in the Security Council. It believes that an ineffective Security Council has been unable to prevent or contain wars and conflicts. It is important to address these wars and conflicts as they have produced massive human, economic and environmental loss for the mankind (PTI 2015). In order to reform the Security Council, India along with Brazil, Germany and Japan has recommended addition of six permanent and four non-permanent seats to the Security Council, thus increasing the membership of the Security Council from fifteen to twenty-five. They prefer the issue of veto to be postponed for the next fifteen years (Swart and Pace 2015). Further, India aspires for a permanent seat in the reformed Security Council. India has laid its claim for the permanent membership on the basis of several factors. For one, India is home to about 1.2 billion people which make it the second most populous country of the world. Also, India has consistently provided large number of personnel for UN peacekeeping operations and currently, it ranks fourth amongst the 122 contributing countries by sending 6,322 peacekeepers (UN website d). Moreover, India is a responsible nuclear armed country committed to the objectives of the United Nations (Thakur 2011: 902).

The Act East Policy can help India realize its dream of becoming a permanent member of the Security Council. The relations cemented through the Act East Policy can provide the basis on which ASEAN countries can emerge as cosponsors for Indian claim to permanent membership. Several countries such as Brunei Darussalam, Cambodia, Laos, Malaysia, Myanmar, Singapore and Vietnam explicitly support the Indian candidature for permanent membership and this support has been demonstrated by the leaders of these countries during the state visits or official visits. The regional cooperation attained through the Act East Policy can reinforce the support of all these countries in the United Nations and help India garner the support of all those countries which have not yet consented to its bid for a permanent seat in the Security Council. The support of so many countries would certainly increase the credibility of India and strengthen its case in the United Nations.

However, China along with the other permanent members of the Security Council is not in the favour of reforming the Security Council in the immediate future (Rivlin 2005: 375). This is obvious because the reforms are perceived as a threat to their position in the 'elite club' of the United Nations. Apart from the reforms in the Security Council, China has also been reluctant to support the involvement of Security Council in managing international crises as they demand intensive investment of time, effort and resources. This is evident from its voting record in the Security Council. In the period between 1991 and 2019 (June), China has abstained from voting in 74 Security Council resolutions which also makes China the permanent member with the most abstentions in the voting procedure of the Security Council (UN website e). Moreover, China believes that if the Security Council looks into non-traditional issues (such as climate change, terrorism, human trafficking and organized crime), it will not only infringe upon the authority of other organs but it will also raise doubts about the principles of the United Nations (Lei 2014: 5; 16-17).

Conclusion

It would not be easy for India and ASEAN countries to challenge the Chinese position in the United Nations. This is because China is a permanent member of the Security Council with the power of veto. Also, it has been a consistent contributor to the UN budget with its present contribution being more than the three permanent members of the Security Council (namely, France, Russia and United Kingdom). Further, it has regularly provided personnel for UN peacekeeping operations with its current contribution being 2,519 peacekeepers. Its contribution to UN peacekeeping operations in terms of personnel has been more than the total contribution of the other four permanent members of the Security Council (UN website c). Moreover, ASEAN countries have taken different positions in the South China Sea dispute: Cambodia, Laos and Myanmar support the Chinese position whereas Philippines and Vietnam favour an American intervention which however is not acceptable to Malaysia and Indonesia (Simon 2012: 997). These differences can make it difficult for India to align with ASEAN countries against China in the United Nations.

If implemented well, the Act East Policy can strengthen the Indian position in the United Nations on the basis of the 'China' factor. It can bring India and ASEAN countries on the same platform which would give greater voice to the Indian concerns in the United Nations. For this, India would have to 'act' vigorously. However, this is not to deny the significance of the measures that have already been implemented under the Act East Policy. It means that India would have to move beyond conducting joint military exercises and bilateral defence agreements to more concrete and active engagement with ASEAN countries.

To begin with, India can increase its exports to ASEAN. As is evident from Table 4, in the period between 2009-10 and 2015-16, the Indian exports to ASEAN have mostly declined, though in the recent years, Indian exports have registered a marginal increase. As understood from the Table, the share of Indian exports to China, United States and the European Union has increased more than the increase in the share of Indian exports to ASEAN. Given the goals of Act East Policy, it would only be better if India could increase share of its exports to ASEAN. This would considerably strengthen economic relations between India and ASEAN countries which in turn would strengthen their much needed trust and support for India in the United Nations.

Apart from cementing economic relations, it would be beneficial for India if personal relations are also promoted. Personal relations can be built in several ways. For one, apart from the official visits at the dignitary level (such as president, vice president, prime minister and foreign minister), regular ministry to ministry exchange should be encouraged. Also, frequent and greater people to people exchange in the field of culture, education and sports would be useful for India. This is because personal relations have a more lasting impact than economic relations. Organization of food festivals, film fests and music programmes showcasing the diversity of its eastern neighbours, setting up of academic and research centres dedicated to its neighbouring eastern countries, and planning of sports meet with participation from its eastern neighbours can go a long way in deepening India's relations with ASEAN countries. The personal relations can be further advanced by improving connectivity between India and ASEAN countries. This would involve identifying and building new roadways, waterways and airways. Some progress has been already made in this direction but more needs to be achieved.

Table 4: Indian Exports to the World (2009-10 to 2019-20 {April-June})
(% Share in Total Indian Exports)

	ASEAN	*Australia*	*China*	*European Union*	*Japan*	*United States*
2009-10	10.13	0.77	6.49	20.15	2.03	10.92
2010-11	10.25	0.68	5.67	18.42	2.03	10.12
2011-12	12.00	0.80	5.90	17.17	2.06	11.35
2012-13	10.98	0.78	4.50	16.78	2.03	12.03
2013-14	10.53	0.73	4.71	16.40	2.16	12.44
2014-15	10.25	0.89	3.84	15.89	1.73	13.67
2015-16	9.59	1.24	3.43	17.00	1.77	15.37
2016-17	11.22	1.07	3.69	17.14	1.39	15.30
2017-18	11.27	1.32	4.39	17.65	1.55	15.77
2018-19	11.35	1.06	5.08	17.31	1.47	15.88
2019-20 (April-June)	11.94	0.70	5.52	17.36	1.60	15.80

Source: http://www.commerce-app.gov.in/eidb/default.asp. Accessed on 14 July 2019.

Moreover, India can take the initiative in setting up a centre that is dedicated entirely to identifying the areas where its interests and those of ASEAN countries converge in the United Nations. Particularly, the research carried out by this centre can help India to identify those areas where it can seek support and cooperation of ASEAN countries in the United Nations. Accordingly, specific agreements can be concluded which would positively contribute to the Indian position in the United Nations.

REFERENCES

Ba, Alice D. (2011), "Staking Claims and Making Waves in the South China Sea: How Troubled are the Waters?", *Contemporary Southeast Asia,* 33. 3: pp.269-270.

Desai, Suyash (18 November 2017), "Revisiting ASEAN-India Relations", *The Diplomat,* 15 July 2019, http://thediplomat.com/2017/11/revisiting-asean-india-relations/.

Fravel, M. Taylor (2011), "China's Strategy in the South China Sea", *Contemporary Southeast Asia,* 33. 3: p.299.

Fullilove, Michael (2006), "Angel or Dragon? China and the United Nations", *The National Interest,* 85: p.68.

Kumar, Dinesh (10 February 2016), "ASEAN: The Pivot of India's Act East Policy", www.tribuneindia.com, 18 July 2019, http://www.tribuneindia.com/news/comment/asean-the-pivot-of-india-s-act-east-policy/194609.html.

Kyodo (24 April 2015), "Asia, Africa Leaders Call for U.N. Security Council Reform", *The Japan Times Online,* 16 July 2019, http://www.japantimes.co.jp/news/2015/04/24/national/politics-diplomacy/asia-africa-leaders call-u-n-security-council-reform/#.Vxc2ncmf7IV.

Lei, Xue (2014), "China as a Permanent Member of the United Nations Security Council', Department of Global Policy and Development, Friedrich-Ebert-Stiftung, Berlin, Germany, p.5; 16-17.

Ministry of External Affairs (website), http://www.mea.gov.in/aseanindia/20-years.htm, 15 July 2019.

Press Trust of India (PTI) (25 December 2015), "Over 60 Million People Affected by UNSC Malfunctioning: India", indianexpress.com, 15 July 2019, http://indianexpress.com/article/india/india-news-india/over-60-million-people-affected-by-unsc-malfunctioning-india/

Rajendram, Danielle (2014), "India's New Asia-Pacific Strategy: Modi Acts East", Lowy Institute for International Policy, Sydney, Australia, pp.1-3; 15.

Rivlin, Benjamin (2005), "The UN Reform Conundrum", *American Foreign Policy Interests,* 27. 5: pp.368; 375.

Schmidt, Johannes Dragsbaek (2011), "India China Rivalry and Competition in Southeast Asia", First draft paper for the International Conference "India in International Relations: European and Indian Perspectives", 27-29 April 2011, Delhi, India, pp.8; 9.

Simon, Sheldon W. (2012), "Conflict and Diplomacy in the South China Sea", *Asian Survey,* 52. 6: pp.997; 1000; 1009.

Singh, Abhishek Pratap (6 December 2015), " 'Act East' in Action", *Organiser,* p.16.

Swart, Lydia and Cile Pace (1 March 2015), "Changing the Composition of the Security Council: Is There a Viable Solution?", www.centerforunreform.org, 17 July 2019, http://www.centerforunreform.org/?q=node/629.

Thakur, Ramesh (2011), "India and the United Nations", *Strategic Analysis,* 35. 6: pp.899; 901-902.

United Nations (website a), http://www.un.org/en/ga/contributions/budget.shtml, 17 July 2019.

United Nations (website b), https://www.un.org/securitycouncil/content/countries-elected-members, 17 July 2019.

United Nations (website c), https://peacekeeping.un.org/en/troop-and-police-contributors, 19 July 2019.

United Nations (website d), https://peacekeeping.un.org/sites/default/files/msrs_june_2019_1.pdf, 19 July 2019.

United Nations (website e), http://research.un.org/en/docs/sc/quick/meetings/2019, 20 July 2019.

Yeravdekar and Gupte (2014), "Preface", Devare, Sudhir T., Shivali Lawale, Gauri Tiwari and Swarnakshi Luhach (Ed.), *India's Look East - Act East Policy: A Bridge to the Asian Neighbourhood*, Symbiosis Institute of International Studies, Symbiosis International University, Pune, p.1.

13

Look East to Act East: The Changing Dimensions of India's Foreign Policy under Narendra Modi

K. Jayaprasad

There occurred a fundamental shift with regard to India's Foreign Policy under Narendra Modi and that shift was one from idealism to pragmatism. The Look East policy got a new vigor and India began to focus more on its eastern neighbours, the South East Asian Countries who were neglected earlier. The policy though conceived originally as an economic initiative, has now gained political, cultural and strategic dimensions and has even upgraded to strategic partnership (PIB 2015). When the objective of the policy is to promote economic cooperation with countries is the Asia Pacific it also aims at enhanced connectivity to the States of the North Eastern Region with other countries in the neighbourhood. So the Act East Policy provides an interface between the North East of India and the ASEAN region.

Historically India had very strong cultural bond with this region and during the freedom struggle Subash Chandra Bose formed the Indian National Army (INA) with the support of Indians in the region and also with the support of the people in the South East Asian Countries. But after Independence Indian leadership under Jawaharlal Nehru took a policy of non-alignment but that gradually moved to the Socialist world led by Soviet Union. With regime change in China in 1949, the Communist government started to increase their presence in this region. But the people of the region expected more presence of India and the Indian leaders were reluctant to give that kind of support.

With the formation of ASEAN in 1967, the region emerged as an important region of economic grouping and is one of the successful regional economic grouping after the European Union. The Chinese expansionist policies were blocked by the ASEAN collective entity. During this period India had not paid much interest in the developments of ASEAN grouping. Though the Chinese big brother attitude created much pressure among ASEAN member nations the Chinese attack on Vietnam strengthened the ASEAN unity. But India underestimated the importance of ASEAN which has the membership of 10 South East Asian Nations and Asian Strategic importance was also not taken seriously by the Indian leadership. Meanwhile ASEAN developed into a major actor in Asia-Pacific region. During 1970's and 1980's this region recorded highest growth rate up to 10 percent. In that sense it became the economic powerhouse of the world.

From Non-Alignment to Look East

From the very beginning Indian political leadership under Nehru and later by Indira Gandhi nourished non-alignment with a bias on socialist world lead by the USSR. India's internal politics and international relations developed with this socialist dream. As a result ASEAN economic grouping was not attracted to the Indian leadership till the disintegration of the Soviet Union. After 1991 India started to opt a liberal policy both at domestic and international levels. Prime Minister Narasimha Rao initiated that liberal approach in 1991 and openly declared the Look East Policy, rejecting the Nehruvian Tradition in India's Foreign Policy. It marked a strategic shift in India's outlook in South East Asia and Asia-Pacific.

The Government under Atal Bihari Vajpayee (1998-2004) paid much attention in this regard. Look East policy became one of the fundamental features of India's Foreign Policy. ASEAN also emerged one of the major economic groupings of Asia-Pacific of the 21st Century. Vajpayee signed two agreements for comprehensive economic cooperation and combatting terrorism (Asia Times, 2003). Also India became an associate member of ASEAN. With the declaration of open skies policy the connectivity between India and ASEAN improved. India allowed South East Asian Airlines to operate daily flight to Indian Metropolitan Centre. The Look East Policy of India also flourished under Manmohan Singh rule (2009-2014).

India's Extended Neighbourhood and its Significance

India's extended neighborhood in the Asia-Pacific region is one of the significant regions in terms of culture, tradition, geopolitical, security, trade, maritime security, natural disasters etc. Look East Policy started in 1991 after the disintegration of

Soviet Union and midst of the economic crisis of India by Prime Minister P.V Narasimha Rao. India was looking for more trade, regional markets and economic ties during that period. Comparatively developed nations in the Asia Pacific region offered a good opportunity for India during that time. Vajpayee and Manmohan Singh followed the policies for trade, security and diplomatic relations. The Chinese presence in this region has made this a strategic location for India. So the military cooperation is imperative for the peaceful region. Bay of Bengal, Malacca Strait Pacific and Indian Ocean are important maritime route and strategical location for India. The cooperation in the case of natural disasters, climate change and environmental considerations are vital in this region. China and East Asia, South East Asia and Oceania are included in the Asia Pacific region. India's North East region is culturally and traditionally linked with eastern nations and India is trying to strengthen this age old tradition with road, rail, air and water connectivity and people to people contacts and trade. Kaladan Multi-modal Transit Transport Project, the India-Myanmar-Thailand Trilateral Highway Project, Rhi-Tiddim Road Project, Border Haats, etc. are some of the projects in this area.

During the India–ASEAN summit in Myanmar in November 2014, Narendra Modi declared that India intensified the Look East Policy to a more action oriented strategy rechristening as "Act East" (Harsh 2017). In August 2015, India adopted the ASEAN-India Plan of Action for the period 2016-20 and focused on political-security, economic and socio-cultural realm of this region.

Indonesia, Vietnam, Malaysia, Japan, Republic of Korea (ROK), Australia, Singapore and Association of Southeast Asian Nations (ASEAN) are the strategic partners of India. The up-gradation of the relationship into a Strategic Partnership in 2012 (MEA 2018) was a natural progression. India actively involved in South East Asian region for security, trade and geostrategic reasons. ASEAN, ASEAN Regional Forum (ARF) and East Asia Summit (EAS), Asia Cooperation Dialogue (ACD), Mekong Ganga Cooperation (MGC) and Indian Ocean Rim Association (IORA) are some of the regional organizations in South East Asia. India and ASEAN together envisioned the Security and Growth for All in the Region (SAGAR) and they promoted the interests in security, maritime, trade relations as well as connectivity. Education, natural disaster management, maritime cooperation, poverty alleviation, counter- terrorism measures are some significant areas of cooperation in East Asian Summit. Bay of Bengal Initiative for Multi-Sectoral Technical and Economic Cooperation (BIMSTEC) countries participated in the swearing in ceremony of Narendra Modi. The organization is an alternative to SAARC and supports India in counter terrorism activities and against Pakistan terrorist outfit. It is important due to connectivity projects also. Kaladan Multimodal project (India and Myanmar), Asian Trilateral Highway connecting India and Thailand through Myanmar, Bangladesh, Bhutan, India and Nepal (BBIN) are some of the initiatives from the part of this regional cooperation. India, Myanmar, Thailand, Laos, Cambodia and Vietnam are together in Mekong Ganga Cooperation (MGC) and actively involved in Education, Tourism and transport etc.

From the very beginning Narendra Modi asserted that, India should focus on improving relations with ASEAN and other East Asian Countries. Within a short period, Indian Foreign Minister Sushma Swaraj visited East Asian Counties. The East Asian Summit held on November, 2014 in Myanmar opened a new avenue to Prime Minister Modi. He reassured the East Asian Leaders about investment friendly climate of India and offered changes in policies to do business in India. In this above summit Modi launched 'Act East Policy.' The policy seeks to revive India's relations with not only ASEAN countries but also included Koreas in North to Australia and New Zealand in the South and from Bangladesh in West to Figi and Pacific island countries in the East. Act East Policy also aimed at promoting economic revival through implementation of India-ASEAN Free Trade areas in services and investment and strategic co-operation to fight terrorism, freedom of navigation, maritime security and defence co-operation. Modi also gave importance to soft powers such as Buddhism, tourism, people to people contacts and cultural and historical ties with this region.

Religious and Cultural Tradition

India's cultural and religious tradition is almost similar with this region and is significant in the soft power domain. The historical linkages especially in terms of Hinduism and Sanskrit language are embedded in the East Asian culture. Theravada Buddhism which is practiced in Laos Myanmar, Thailand and Cambodia has strong connection with India. Buddhism was spread from India during the time of Ashoka the emperor of Maurya dynasty. Mahayana is comparatively a new school influenced from China but roots from India which is observed in Vietnam and Singapore. India's cultural heritage is an advancement in terms of soft power relationship. Hindu Buddhist kingdom was prevalent in Indonesia which is a Muslim majority nation currently. The island Bali fallowed Hinduism and people of Island Java converted to Hinduism because of its Hindu tradition. Ramayana has been got significant place in Indonesia. Thai culture has relationship with India. Ramayana has influential role in the country Theravada Budhism which originated in India and the Pali language of Theravada was the language of Magadha.

Several words of Thailand have roots in Sanskrit. Malaysia has large number of Hindu temples and Indian Hindu Diaspora has a significant role in Malaysia. Shaiva and Vaishnava temples are there and Ratha Yatra festival conducted every year. Ramakrishna Mission has followers in Malaysia and Modi visited there and unveiled Swami Vivekananda statue in 2015. He also visited to Penang at the time of the Thaipusam festival in Malaysia. Angkor Wat's temple in Cambodia was dedicated to Vishnu and other temples imply the strong cultural linkages between two nations. The empire Angkor vase Hindu Dynasty long back in Cambodia. Southeast Asia has significant influence from India in its culture religion art and the language Ramayana and Buddhism are vital in the culture of Southeast Asian nations.

East Asian region is significant for US as well as India. The growth of Chinese influence is a strategic threat to US. India-US alliance in this region is another milestone in this region. The 2016 US-India bilateral logistics exchange memorandum agreement (LEMOA) gives reciprocal access to respective military bases for logistics supplies and fuel. India has access to US military bases in Djibouti and Diego Garcia in the time of emergency. India has been attending the annual meetings of the ASEAN security forum since 1996 and the ASEAN Defence Minister's Meeting is the highest defence consultative and co-operative mechanism in India (MEA 2018). Security co-operation is key considering the increasing traditional and non-traditional threats to security and issues related to terrorism.

India is no doubt one of the fastest growing economies of the world and ASEAN one of the most successful regional organization. Since ASEAN is a power economic co-operation, better ties with the ASEAN nations are in the interest of India. Unfortunately that has not become a focus or priority for a long duration. The Act East Policy gives a new direction not only to the economic relationship but also to political-cultural and strategic relations. Considering the political stability of the region and economic potential of the ASEAN states, India could gain much when it comes to trade and this will in turn help to counter the presence of China in the region.

REFERENCES

Asia Times (2003): "India's Look East Policy Pays Off," *Asia Times*, 11 October.

Harsh V Pant (2017): "India-ASEAN partnership at 25," *Observer Research Foundation*, Special Reports, 04 July

MEA (2018): *India ASEAN Relations*, Ministry of External Affairs, Government of India, August.

Muni S.D. (2011): "India's Look East Policy: The Strategic Dimension," *ISAS Working Paper*, February.

PIB (2015): *Act East Policy*, Press Information Bureau, Government of India, 23 December.

14

Northeast India through the Kaleidoscope of 'Look East' and 'Act East': Potential and Priorities

Mohor Chakraborty

The National Democratic Alliance (NDA)-II Government under the leadership of Prime Minister, Narendra Modi has significantly activated India's Asia-Pacific policy in general and Southeast Asia policy in particular by the re-christening, re-defining and re-activating of the 'Look East' Policy, and taxonomically transforming it into 'Act East' Policy (AEP). This new coinage (Act East) was referred to in course of Narendra Modi's address at the 9th East Asia Summit (EAS) meeting held in Naypidaw, Myanmar, on 13 November 2014, when he said: "Since entering office six months ago, my Government has moved with a great sense of priority and speed to turn our 'Look East Policy' into 'Act East Policy'" (Narendra Modi's address at the 9th East Asia Summit meeting, 2014). In this statement, his administration's intent desire to activate and rejuvenate the erstwhile 'Look East' Policy was inherent. Within the broad scaffold of Act East, India's Northeast has emerged as a major thrust area, bolstered by a conscious and proactive effort to harness the immense natural potential of this region, facilitate its development, and enhance the region's inclusiveness within the wider national topography. It is common knowledge that the Northeast forms India's natural gateway to its eastern and southeasten neighbourhood, and its strategic importance is further augmented as Myanmar shares its border with four of the Northeastern states, viz. Arunachal Pradesh, Manipur, Mizoram and Nagaland.

The centrality of Northeast India was amply enunciated in Narendra Modi's address at the 65th Plenary Session of the North-Eastern Council, held in May 2016, wherein he acknowledged the "development of the North East region through its pro-active Act East Policy" since the Northeast is the "gateway to South East Asia and we need to take advantage of this." Towards this end, he outlined the "opening up of both road and rail routes to our neighbouring countries", in order to "give a boost to the economic development of the region." In particular, he stressed the importance of "reducing the isolation of the region by improving all round connectivity through road, rail, telecom, power and waterways sectors (Narendra Modi's address at the Plenary Session of the North-Eastern Council, 2016). It is in this backdrop that the paper proposes to analyse the following:

- The rationale of the 'Act East' Policy for prioritising the development of Northeast India;
- Analysis of the regional development projects (proposed and ongoing), specifically in the spheres of connectivity; infrastructure; tourism; etc.; and
- The facilitation of India's enhanced cooperation with its ASEAN neighbours, particularly Myanmar and its implications of the development of the Northeast.

Northeast as a Pedestal of "Acting East": Rationale

Geographically speaking, 98% of the Northeast's border territory (4500 km) is shared with China, Myanmar, Bangladesh, Bhutan and Nepal and the region is connected to the rest of India by a narrow and congested 21 km-long land corridor, known as the "chicken's neck", which runs through Bangladesh. The region has been envisioned as a "natural partner in India's 'Act East' Policy'", by virtue of its unique geographical and strategic location. Situated between China, Bhutan, Bangladesh, and Myanmar and with an international border stretching up to 4, 500 km, it constitutes our land bridge to Southeast Asia. Historically, people from the Northeast have traded and travelled across the Southeast Asian region and Yunnan for years through the ancient Silk Road, trading in Himalayan salt, spices, handicrafts, food items, silk and other goods. This region even witnessed migration of people from Southeast Asia and Yunnan to Assam and its surrounding hills, the most prominent being the Ahoms tracing their roots to the Tai race in Yunnan and Thailand (Myint-U, 2012: 225). In addition to its location, the resource abundance of the region prompted Prime Minister, Narendra Modi to christen its potential as a "Natural Economic Zone" (NEZ), underlining his priority to nourish and tap its resources for the region's holistic development (Talukdar, 2014). Acknowledged as India's "capital of organic agriculture", the region constitutes 7.92% of total land area, with diverse hill ecosystems covering more than two-thirds of its total geographical area, with agriculture and animal husbandry being the two foremost economic activities. The region's comparative advantages in producing fruits, vegetables and other horticulture products are immense. Since most of the regional states have taken to the practice of organic farming, it is poised to mature as a global organic agriculture hub. Furthermore, the region offers other investment opportunities like food and meat processing, with ample scope for dairy and fishery processing and poultry. There are tremendous opportunities for entrepreneurs to set up storage, distribution and marketing infrastructure, such as a cold storage chain along major arterial highways (Untapped Potential of North East Region: National Round Table Conference Report, 2017: 2-3).

Secondly, it is an acknowledged fact that, adequate connectivity infrastructure in the Northeast will facilitate its potential as the hub of economic activity as well as its opening up towards Southeast Asia. The 'Act East' Policy has not only taken forward the momentum of pending connectivity projects, but also encouraged the inauguration of new ones, in a bid to improve its connectivity potential and tap the region's gateway for international trade and commerce. A slew of cross-border connectivity projects, already under implementation or discussion, which would link the Northeast to the wider Southeast Asia includes the Asian Highway and Asian Railway Link. The legacy of cultural, trade ties and connectivity has been resuscitated through efforts like the construction of the Stilwell Road; the 3200-km-long India-Myanmar-Thailand (IMT) Trilateral Highway, running from Moreh to Maesot via Tamu, Mandalay and Myawaddy (to be fully operational by 2018); proposed extension of the IMT Highway to Vietnam, Laos and Cambodia in the second phase; the Kaladan Multimodal Transit and Transport (KMMTT) facility etc. These are some of the game changing projects at various stages of progress which once operational would be able to further reorient the strategic and business dynamics of the region.

Thirdly, by virtue of its geostrategic location, the Northeast acts as a gateway for sub-regional cooperation, particularly for organizations like the Bay of Bengal Initiative for Sub-regional Technical and Economic Cooperation (BIMSTEC), Bangladesh-Bhutan-India-Nepal (BBIN) quadrangle and Bangladesh-China-India-Myanmar (BCIM)-Economic Corridor. The emphasis of sub-regional cooperation in the arena of trade and commerce, energy, connectivity, people-to-people contacts etc. not only promotes the prospects of integration and synchronization of interests of the sub-region at the intersection of South and Southeast Asia, but also propels the development of the Northeast, which happens to be an indispensable link in this chain.

'Act East' Focus on Development of the Northeast: Significant Prospects

A significant stride in the developmental direction of the Northeast, regarded as "India's gateway to Southeast Asia", has been under way within the wider ambit of 'Act East'. Under the present administration, there has been a steady rise in budgetary allocation: The Ministry of Development of North East Region (MDONER) has been allocated Rs 3,000 crore for 2018-2019 in the Union Budget - 11.8% more than Rs 2,682.45 crore that was earmarked in the last Budget. Besides, the Finance Ministry announced an allocation of Rs 1,014.09 crore for the upcoming financial year towards revival of 50 airports in the region and viability gap funding for improving aviation infrastructure under the flagship Regional Connectivity Scheme. This amount is nearly five times the allocation of Rs 200.11 crore as per the revised estimates of 2017-2018. Additionally, in 2018-2019, Rs 47000 crores has been allocated for the regional states, with the Railway Budget accounting for Rs 4700 crore. (Shillong Times, 2018) It deserves mention in this context that, in the 2017-2018 Union Budget, Rs. 43285 crores was allocated for the regional states, recording a rise from Rs. 32180 crore allocated in 2016-2017 [of which Rs. 2682 crores was earmarked for the MDoNER]. This was an increase from Rs. 2524 crore allotted in the previous fiscal for the Ministry, and from Rs. 29087.93 crore allotted for the region. The 2017-18 Budget emphasized financial assistance in 90:10 and 80:20 ratios for the core Centrally-sponsored and non-core schemes respectively (Singh, 2017) An analysis of the developments – proposed and ongoing – in the region within the 'Act East' domain indicates an honest effort underway, essential not only for boosting the region's economic development, but also enhancing its inclusiveness within the wider national topography. A sector-wise assessment of this developmental vision in the following identified areas has been carried out in the subsequent section:

1. **Roads, Highways and Other Infrastructure:** The National Highways and Infrastructure Development Corporation (NHIDCL) was launched in January 2015 to fast-track road construction in the Northeast and border areas. Billed as the first "e-Public Sector Undertaking" using Information Technology solutions, it will develop and widen 3,600 km road infrastructure and build bridges and tunnels. Under the aegis of the Ministry of Road Transport and Highways' Special Accelerated Road Development Programme for North-East (SARDP-NE), out of

the 10141 km road stretches of National Highways and State Roads for upgradation, 6418 km has been approved by the Government for implementation under Phase 'A' and the Arunachal Pradesh Package of Roads and Highways, while the remaining 3723 km has been approved for preparation of Detailed Project Reports (DPR) under Phase 'B'. Also, the inauguration of the Dhola-Sadiya Bridge in May 2017 is poised to be a game-changer for boosting connectivity, trade and development and facilitating the movement of troops and military logistics in Assam and Arunachal Pradesh. Furthermore, the inauguration of the 102 km Jowai-Ratacherra section of NH-06 in Meghalaya in 2018, which passes through the coal and cement producing belt, has also been a significant development initiative for the landlocked states of the Northeast. The recent award of Rs 122 crore contract by NHIDCL to build a 450-metre bridge over the Feni river will ensure connectivity to the port will help natural gas-rich Tripura to attract investments and trigger further growth. With National Highway work worth Rs 1.5 crore currently under construction in the Northeast, the Road Transport Ministry has undertaken the responsibility of reviewing the progress of the projects, in presence of major stake-holders including the Chief Ministers of the regional states, PWD Ministers, National Highways Authority of India, NHIDCL and also the project contractors. (Arora, 2018)

2. **Railways:** The Indian Railways has undertaken a major Rs. 10000 crore expansion spree in the region, proposing broad-gauge connectivity to the capital cities of the Northeastern states by 2020 and conversion of entire rail network to broad-gauge. This is over and above an additional 750-km rail projects undertaken in the region. The plan includes 19 major railway projects consisting of 12 new lines, 3 gauge conversions and 4 doubling projects in the region. The Ministry of Railways has completed four major projects: Harmuti-Naharlagun (connectivity to Itanagar); Dudhnoi–Mendipathar (Meghalya); Rangia–Murkongselek–gauge conversion (north bank of Brahmaputra River) and Lumding-Silchar–gauge conversion (Annual Report: 2015-2016, 2016: 4) In November 2014, Arunachal Pradesh and Meghalaya were put up on the rail map, while Agartala (Tripura) has also been connected with broad gauge line, encircling Bangladesh and covering Silchar in the Barak Valley region in Assam. The line has now been extended to Sabroom, Tripura, and is proposed to be extended to the Chittagong port, barely 80 km from the Bangladesh border by 2020. Significantly enough, plans are on the anvil to bring railway connectivity to Tawang (at 10000 ft in Arunachal Pradesh) on the Sino-India border. Three strategic lines connecting Bhalukpung to Tawang, Murkongselek (Assam) to Pasighat (Arunachal Pradesh) and Silapathar (Assam)

to Bane (Arunachal Pradesh) are on the pipeline, for which surveys will commence in 2018 (Arunachal Times, 2017). The broad gauge rail line supposed to be built in Imphal by 2018 is proposed to be extended to Moreh (Manipur) and Kalay in Myanmar's Sagaing division. In addition, a 132 km part of third alternative connectivity route to the region (New Maynaguri–Jogighopa) has also been commissioned. Finally, the initiation of foundation work for the Imphal railway station and the commencement of work for the longest rail tunnel (11.55 km) in India (July 2016), along the Jiribam–Tupul–Imphal new broad gauge railway line are achievements worth reckoning.

3. Inland waterways and port connectivity: Acknowledging road and rail connectivity to ports as the key to expedited economic growth, the Government has injected Rs 25 lakh crore to strengthen inland waterways, ports and rail-road links (Indian Express, 2016). Of the 106 new National Waterways that were notified in April 2016 under the National Waterways Act, 2016, 20 are in the Northeast, including Barak, Subansiri, Ganol etc. With 3 of 5 inland water transport projects in Assam, Manipur and Mizoram completed with 100% subsidy by 2015, the Rs 6.07 crore project on the construction of 17-metre-long floating terminal pontoons at 15 Assamese sites is in its final stage. Other projects including construction of a high-level jetty and ship repair facility at Pandu port (Guwahati) has commenced, while the construction of a roll on-roll off terminal at Dhubri and bank protection measures for the Inland Water Authority of India (IWAI) terminal area at Jogighopa have been approved in the state (Annual Report: 2015-2016, 2016: 5). Furthermore, the Northeast has an important geographical position on the inland waterways map since River Brahmaputra connects it with Kolkata through the Indo-Bangladesh Protocol (IBP) route, offering a seamless connectivity between NW-1 (Allahabad–Haldia) and ports in Bangladesh via NW-2 (Pandu, Assam). Along with river Brahmaputra, river Barak too provides inland water transit between India and Bangladesh through Pandu, Karimganj and Silghat (Assam) and Bangladesh's Narayanganj, Khulna, Mongla, Sirajganj and Ashuganj.

4. Telecommunications and Internet: In order to boost the economic development and connectivity of the region, Rs 5300 crore Comprehensive Telecom Development Plan for the Northeast was launched in September 2014. Aimed to cover 20% of the uncovered villages (almost 21%) in the region as also to provide seamless connectivity on national highways, the project will increase the reliability of District and State Headquarters connectivity by providing alternative optical fibre connectivity, proposed to be completed by March 2018 (Comprehensive Telecom Development Plan for North-Eastern Region, 2014). Besides, the setting up of the International Internet Gateway (IIG) at Agartala, by availing the service from the Bangladesh Submarine Company Ltd. has catapulted Tripura to becoming the third Indian state to have such a gateway after Mumbai and Chennai.

5. Tourism: Introducing a measure to establish a separate tourism development agency devoted to the Northeast, the MDoNER has formed the "North-Eastern Tourism Development Council" (NETDC) on a public-private partnership model in January 2017, thereby reflecting the high priority that the Union Government accords to the development of the region. This is in addition to the 'Swadesh Darshan' and 'PRASAD' schemes inaugurated in January 2015. While the former identified the development of the Northeast India Circuit, the latter provides Central Financial Assistance to State Governments, focusing on the development and beautification of the identified pilgrimage destinations. Under the 'Swadesh Darshan' scheme, in 2014-2015, Rs. 49.77 crore was sanctioned for the development of Bhalukpong-Bomdila-Tawang in Arunachal Pradesh; in 2015-2016, Rs 89 crore, Rs 98.05 crore, Rs 97.14 crore, Rs 97.36 crore, Rs 95.67 crore, Rs 99.59 crore and Rs 94.91 crore were allocated for developing the Imphal-Moirang-Khongjom-Moreh (Manipur); Sikkim; Integrated Development of New Adventure Tourism in Arunachal Pradesh; Kohima-Wokha, Nagaland; Wild Life Circuit in Assam; Tripura; and Mizoram respectively. Under the 'PRASAD' scheme, Rs 33.98 crore was earmarked for development of the Kamakhya Temple and Pilgrimage destination in and around Guwahati in 2015-2016 wherein a dedicated tourist train from Kamakhya station to the religious city of Puri (in Odisha) with stoppages at Bhubaneswar and Kolkata has been introduced ('Swadesh Darshan' and 'Prasad' Schemes of Ministry of Tourism, 2016).

6. Developing Rural Areas: In an ambitious bid to transform rural areas to economically, socially and physically sustainable spaces, the Shyama Prasad Mukherji Rurban Mission (SPMRM) with an outlay of Rs 5142.08 crore, was introduced in September 2015. The Mission aims at development of rural growth clusters which have latent potential for growth. These clusters would be developed by provisioning of economic activities, developing skills and local entrepreneurship and providing infrastructure amenities, like digital literacy, sanitation, piped water supply, solid and liquid waste management, village streets and drains, street lights, inter-village road connectivity, etc., thereby promoting the development of about 330 thirty smart village clusters over the next three years (Union Cabinet approves Shyama Prasad Mukherji Rural Mission, 2015). Kohima (Nagaland) and Namchi (Sikkim) have found a berth in the Smart City list released in September 2016.

7. Civil Aviation Policy: The introduction of the National Civil Aviation Policy

2016, which envisions the strengthening of regional air connectivity by making aviation affordable and convenient, and hence promoting tourism, employment, balanced regional growth and enhancing ease of doing business through deregulation, simplified procedures and e-governance, has been a momentous stride of the AEP. With the UDAN or Regional Connectivity Scheme (RCS) aiming to connect remote areas by putting un-served and underserved airports to optimum use as its centre-piece, the Government is moving ahead towards easing restrictions wherein airlines can either withdraw or revise domestic operations to and within the identified states in the Northeast by tendering a three-month notice (National Civil Aviation Policy, 2016). The scheme has stimulated most airline service operators to show keen interest in ferrying passengers in short-haul regional aircrafts on shorter routes. In addition to ten operational airports at Dibrugarh, Guwahati, Jorhat, Silchar and Tezpur (Assam), Dimapur (Nagaland), Barapani (Meghalaya), Imphal (Manipur), Agartala (Tripura) and Aizawal (Meghalaya), feasibility studies have been commissioned to set up four more airports at Tawang, Daparizo, Anini and Koloriang. Pasighat and Tezu are two airports in Arunachal Pradesh awaiting civil aircraft operations. Besides, plans to launch a new airline—a subsidiary of Pawan Hans Helicopters Ltd (PHHL)—based out of Guwahati, which would connect all Northeastern state capitals is likely to operate a fleet of six fixed-wing planes and five helicopters (Mukherjee, 2016). Notably, the proposed laying of foundation stone for building a greenfield airport (an aviation facility that is planned, commissioned and built from scratch without destroying an existing structure) at Hollongi (in Arunachal Pradesh in 2018) and the inauguration of Sikkim's maiden airport in Pakyong in September 2018 have also been significant initiatives. Regional flight operations have been strengthened with the commencement of point to point operations from Kolkata to Imphal, Aizawal, Dimapur and Dibrugarh and will be further boosted by introducing services along the Delhi-Guwahati-Dibrugarh, Guwahati-Mumbai and Kolkata-Hyderabad via Bhubaneshwar routes (Hindu Business Line, 2017). In particular, Kolkata will see new routes connecting it to other locations in the eastern region under UDAN, with one on the Kolkata–Pasighat (via Dibrugarh) route on the radar (Mullick, 2017).

8. Power/Energy: The Hydrocarbon Vision 2030 for Northeast India, unveiled in 2016 is a comprehensive attempt to relocate the region in India's energy map with the rapid development of cross-border transmission and exchange. The Vision proposes to leverage Northeast India's hydrocarbon potential, enhance access to clean fuels, improve availability of petroleum products, facilitate economic development and link common people to the economic activities, with the objective of developing the region as a power generating and distributing hub (Petroleum Minister releases Hydrocarbon Vision 2030 for North-East, 2016).

9. Organic Farming: Acknowledging the potential for organic farming in the region, the National Project on Organic Farming and Value Chain Development, with a budgetary allocation of Rs. 115 crore (2016-2017) and Mission Organic Value Development for the Northeast, with an outlay of Rs. 400 crore are welcome initiatives. The declaration of Sikkim as the first Organic State of India has opened up new vistas for start-up initiatives in organic farming as well. Apart from Sikkim, Mizoram and Assam have over 12,000 hectare and 2000 hectare area respectively cultivated under organic certification process (Mitra, 2017) The MDoNER has embarked upon the project in a mission mode with the intention of reducing risks associated with climate change, disease and markets, as well as facilitating traditional ways of organic cultivation and appropriate resource-management.

The above analysis highlights the initiatives under way in a spectrum of sectors ranging from infrastructure, energy to tourism, transportation and connectivity to bolster the development of the region.

Sub-regional Cooperation and India's Northeast: Implications and Prospects

The Act East Policy emphasises the development of sub-regionalism, particularly through organizations like Bay of Bengal Initiative for Multi-sectoral Technical and Economic Cooperation (BIMSTEC) as its conduits. Sub-regional cooperation would not only bolster the development of the Northeast, but also facilitate India's enhanced cooperation with its neighbours, particularly Bangladesh and Myanmar, with the spheres of energy cooperation, trade and connectivity being the most noteworthy. To begin with, being convinced that the development of connectivity in various forms and its manifestations is the key to promoting regional integration, the BIMSTEC has achieved progress in implementation of the recommendations of the BIMSTEC Transport Infrastructure and Logistics Study, by agreeing to explore the possibility of having a BIMSTEC Motor Vehicle Agreement (MVA). The significance of BIMSTEC-MVA may be viewed in the backdrop of the proposed India-Myanmar-Thailand (IMT) Trilateral Highway, linking Manipur with Mae Sot in Thailand via Bagan in Myanmar. This road will eventually link up with other highways to form a single stretch across South and Southeast Asia—from Singapore and Malaysia to Vietnam, Laos and Cambodia ultimately reaching India. Furthermore, at the last BIMSTEC Ministerial Meeting, held in August

2017, the leaders emphasized enhanced transport and communication infrastructure as the key to regional integration and the imperative of expediting the progress of BIMSTEC Framework Agreement on Transit, Trans-shipment and Movement of Vehicular Traffic or MVA as well as the BIMSTEC Coastal Shipping Agreement, was discussed in earnest. Secondly, taking cognizance of the need for energy cooperation among member-states, measures to expedite the signing of the BIMSTEC Memorandum of Understanding (MoU) on Grid Interconnection have been undertaken, in addition to early operationalization of the BIMSTEC Energy Centre. The last Ministerial declared that the MoU on Grid Interconnection is ready for signature (Joint Statement of the 15th BIMSTEC Ministerial Meeting, 2017). Thirdly, the members have expressed commitment to the early conclusion of BIMSTEC-Free Trade Agreement (FTA) negotiations by directing the Trade Negotiating Committee (TNC) and Working Groups to expedite the finalization of its constituent Agreements (BIMSTEC Leaders' Retreat 2016: Outcome Document, 2016) significant for facilitating trade in a region populated by 1.6 billion with a total GDP of US$ 3 trillion.

Furthermore, having acknowledged that "India's Act East starts with Bangladesh" (India, Bangladesh can work on mutually beneficial projects: PM Modi, 2014) Prime Minister, Modi had clearly catapulted Bangladesh not only to the heart of the 'Act East' Policy, but also the BIMSTEC policy, as a whole. Several initiatives have been undertaken for facilitating Bangladesh's role as a prominent 'Act East' protagonist: for instance, **first**, the MoU on the Use of Chittagong and Mongla Ports for Movement of Goods to and from India, signed in June 2015, providing that Bangladesh shall allow use of these ports for the movement of goods to and from India by using Chittagong/Mongla to Agartala, Chittagong/ Mongla to Dawki, and Chittagong/Mongla to Sutarkandi routes, by waterways, rail, road or multimodal transport arrangements has been a feather in the NDA-II Government's cap as well as for the development of India's Northeast to a considerable extent.

Secondly, the energy sector has emerged as the most promising promenade of Indo-Bangladesh cooperation of late and the Northeast has assumed a vital position. In a bid to support energy cooperation with Dhaka through the Northeast, the Palatana Project in Tripura is exporting 100 MW power to Bangladesh in lieu of the services provided by it in transporting project-related equipment, goods and services through its waterways (via Kolkata) and its roads to the project site. This gesture has been reciprocated by 10 gigabit/sec bandwidth gateway of internet connectivity for the regional states secured via Bangladesh (Cox Bazar landing station). India will be able to lease 10 Gigabits/second (GBPS) capacity from Bangladesh, which can later be increased to 40 GBPS, facilitating telecom connectivity issue to a great extent in the Northeast. The steady progress made between Numaligarh Refinery Ltd (NRL) and Bangladesh Petroleum Corporation (BPC) towards construction of the Indo-Bangla Friendship Pipeline from Siliguri to Parbatipur for supply of High Speed Diesel to Bangladesh is another pointer. Also, Indo-Bangladesh agreements pertaining to energy cooperation signed in the context of Prime Minister Sheikh Hasina's April 2017 visit to India are indicators of the ascending graph of cooperation in this sphere.

Thirdly, though the Indo-Bangladesh Agreement signed in October 2010 for setting up 'Border Haats' expired in 2013, four such markets (two in Meghalaya at Kalaichar and Balat and two in Tripura at Srinagar and Kamalasagar) continue to operate and six more are likely to come up soon, four along the Meghalaya border and two along the Tripura border (More Border Haats on India-Bangladesh frontier soon, 2016). On the whole, leveraging the potential of the Indo-Bangladesh economic relationship has the potential of transforming the economy of Northeast India, and also advance India's 'Act East' vision. Some critical steps to move this agenda forward would involve expanding direct connectivity between Northeast India and the rest of India via Bangladesh, while giving Bangladesh similar access to Nepal and Bhutan via India; reducing the time and cost of trading across the two borders, which will require reducing perceived and real non-tariff barriers and promoting efficient customs procedures and border facilities; encouraging Bangladeshi companies to invest in Northeast India, and Indian companies to expand their presence in Bangladesh (Kathuria, 2017). Agreements reached between India and Bangladesh to revive old land and train routes linking the Northeast to Dhaka, and from there to Kolkata and ongoing negotiations to extend rail and road connectivity with Chittagong and Paira ports, such that the proposed Tajpur and Sagar ports (in West Bengal) would be able to transport goods to the Northeast via these Bangladeshi ports are noteworthy developments

In addition to Bangladesh, the infrastructure development of the Northeast has close-knit relations with Myanmar, which is an integral part of BIMSTEC. To begin with, the Imphal-Mandalay Bus Service has the prospects of boosting people-to-people contact and improving physical connectivity; the upgradation of the Kalewa-Kalemyo Road in Myanmar across Manipur; New Delhi's active exploration of the opening of the Stilwell Road to Myanmar, in conjunction with a telecommunication network connecting Moreh through a 6 km optic fibre link to Tamu (Myanmar); the Kaladan Multi-Modal Transit and Transport Facility, designed to connect the region with Sittwe through construction of a Kaladan inland waterway; a road connecting Sittwe to Lawngtlai in Mizoram and improvement of the Sittwe deep sea port, after being operationalized (by 2019), which will open the direct sea trade from Kolkata to the Northeast and further to Southeast Asia through Sittwe port, are welcome developments envisaged in this respect. These endeavours would not only become profitable and boost direct trade flows, but also act as a check on cross-border informal trade, which accounts for almost US$ 500 million, as against the approximate US$ 15 million of formal trade volume conducted between India and Myanmar. Besides, the India-Myanmar 'Border Haats' are functioning "very well" and New Delhi is looking at opening more such facilities. An MoU on 'Border Haats' was inked in 2012, and it has been agreed to set up nine 'Border Haats' in Arunachal Pradesh, Nagaland, Manipur and Mizoram. The border has two Land Customs Stations at Tamu-Moreh in Manipur and Rhi-Zowkhathar in Mizoram, and the Land Customs Station at Moreh is being upgraded into an Integrated Check Post. In this context, the Trade Infrastructure for Export Scheme (TIES), launched in March 2017 and headed by the Commerce Secretary, Government of India, to develop export-linked infrastructure in states to promote shipments, focusing on customs checkpoints, last mile connectivity, 'Border Haats' and integrated check posts, gains import. With a budgetary allocation of Rs 600 crore for three years with an annual outlay of Rs 200 crore, the initiative will not only create infrastructure, but also ensure that it is professionally run and sustained. Thus, the revival and sustenance of the Indo-Bangladesh and Indo-Myanmar 'Border Haats', under this scheme, are important developments of AEP (The Telegraph, 2017). On the energy front, developments related to the revival of the 6900 km Tri-Nation gas pipeline project (India-Bangladesh-Myanmar) which would link most Northeastern states and West Bengal are significant. Initially the pipeline would link Sitwe to Mizoram and Tripura and Chittagong (in Bangladesh). The pipeline would extend to West Bengal, Assam and other states on the Northeast (Roy Chowdhury, 2017).

Challenges and the Way Ahead

The above analysis highlights the initiatives for the development of India's Northeast embarked upon by the 'Act East' policy over a period of three and a half years of its inauguration. It also focuses on the existing and proposed prospects for the progress of India's policy of sub-regionalism, with BIMSTEC as the principal conduit. It is an acknowledged fact that, since BIMSTEC is geo-strategically unique in embracing parts of South and Southeast Asia, with India's Northeast constituting an integral part of its topography, the successful implementation of BIMSTEC policy as a whole, and the enhanced level of cooperation with its members like Bangladesh and Myanmar, will be phenomenal in scripting further development of the region. Several measures undertaken, in keeping with the 'Vision Document 2020', reveal the Government's efforts at the conceptual and policy levels to craft the idea of "Acting East" via the Northeast. However, the pathway is yet strewn with challenges, among which, the dismal condition of connectivity in the region sticks out as the proverbial 'sore thumb'. Although many ambitious projects have taken off, several others like East West Highway, Rail link to Gangtok and Shillong, SARDP-NE Phase 'B' etc. have been pending since long. Even on the inland waterways front, the non-availability of adequate draft between Sirajganj-Daikhowa and Zakiganj-Ashuganj on the IBP route, the need for night navigation facilities; deficient infrastructure facilities like Ro-Ro, Jetties on NW-2 and IBP route, an Inland Waterways Terminal between Dibrugarh and Bogibil; loading—unloading and warehousing facilities on IWT routes in the Northeast are acting as a spanner (Developing waterways for sustainable transport in the North East: stakeholders call for ensuring adequate draft, augmenting terminal and warehousing facilities, 2017). With respect to air connectivity, it is desirable that regional airports be upgraded to international standards, in addition to the resumption of Guwahati-Bangkok and Guwahati-Dhaka flights and the introduction of flights between major Indian metropolitan cities and countries of Southeast and East Asia, for which the Kolkata-Kunming air route (China Eastern Airlines) can be a remarkable example. Air Asia had also proposed the commencement of international flights from Imphal in 2017, serving as the key point for connectivity among India, Myanmar and Thailand. Besides, the proposal for making Imphal a significant regional hub for international flights to Southeast Asia, with introduction of flights between Imphal and Monywa, Mandalay, Yangon and Kalemyo in Myanmar, should be followed up in right earnest. Furthermore, the execution of all identified projects should not be mired in bureaucratic hurdles, such that connectivity diplomacy is thoroughly expedited and encouraged. For instance, the IMT Trilateral Highway project is facing inordinate delays, and having already missed a couple of deadlines, is now proposed to be operational by 2018-2019. The main hindrances stem from the slow progress on rebuilding almost sixty-nine dilapidated bridges on the Indian side and other procedural issues like Myanmar's demand for renegotiating the trilateral MVA and its applicability on the Highway. The sustained emphasis on and follow-up of the ambitious projects would indeed go a long way in linking India with its eastern neighbours, thus serving as significant channels for augmenting connectivity between them, by optimally utilizing and thereby developing the North-eastern corridor. Thus, there is an imperative need for fructifying road, rail and air connectivity projects either undertaken or under negotiation, within the stipulated time.

Therefore, the key to the region's rejuvenation lies in deft diplomatic conduct by the Indian policy-makers, in apposition with the goodwill of the Chief Ministers of the concerned states and MDoNER; improvement of border infrastructure and trade facilities; goodwill of the South and Southeast Asian neighbours, particularly Bangladesh and Myanmar, which form significant connecting points in the region; and greater participation of intellectuals, business communities and civil society groups (Track II level) as well as the people of the region by expressing their genuine interest in this process of holistic development.

The Northeast constitutes such a strategically placed knot in the entire string of the 'Act East' policy, that by resuscitating this region, the overall complexion of India's 'Act East' doctrine can be successfully and positively transformed. The revival of 'Border Haats' may be interpreted as a new communicative diplomacy, to naturally enhance the mode of communication, economic and cultural exchanges of India's land-locked North-eastern states not only with Bangladesh, but also with the further East, albeit with Dhaka and Yangon as the successive geographical and strategic centres of gravity. It is to be noted here, that this 'Haat' initiative should not be allowed to be held hostage to the incidence of trans-national crimes and the mushrooming of cross-border terrorist outfits. Therefore, it is an absolute priority for New Delhi to bring Myanmar and Bangladesh into the core of its 'Act East' checklist even more expeditiously, in order to bolster the development of the region, situated at the doorstep of these two countries. In this respect, agreements reached between India and Bangladesh to revive old land and train routes linking the Northeast to Dhaka, and from there to Kolkata and ongoing negotiations to extend rail and road connectivity with Chittagong and Paira ports, such that the proposed Tajpur and Sagar ports (in West Bengal) would be able to transport goods to the Northeast via these Bangladeshi ports are developments worthy of mention. As India's Northeast aspires to change the narrative of its past underdevelopment, riding on various trade, energy and connectivity proposals, a recent study conducted by A.T. Kearney-FICCI has proposed the creation of a North-Eastern Corridor (to be connected to the upcoming 3000 km East-West Corridor, which in turn will connect Porbandar in Gujarat to Assam via the 'Chicken's Neck' or Siliguri Corridor) to tap the full potential of connectivity proposals under implementation between India and its Eastern neighbours, including Bangladesh, Bhutan, Nepal and Myanmar (Bose, 2017). Although highly welcome and ambitious, the actual success of such projects will depend on their prompt implementation and time-bound completion. Initiatives like the North East Connectivity Summit, being organized since November 2014, as a cross-sectoral endeavour of FICCI has been successful in highlighting the connectivity gaps and proposing a comprehensive connectivity agenda apart from encouraging private sector investment in this sector. The summits have helped bring into focus the opportunities in developing connectivity of Northeast and its associated strategic and economic advantages for the entire country. The summit has metamorphosed into a unique platform for strategic dialogue between various stakeholders, facilitating the addition of intellectual input from various expert agencies on the theme of connectivity-aided development with Northeast at the centre stage. Finally, it is worth reckoning that, though the impetus on "Acting East through the Northeast" is a welcome move to situate the region at the heart of the country's geo-economic outreach into Southeast and East Asia, unless connectivity, infrastructure facilities and the internal political dynamics of the states (including ethnic insurgencies) in the region are improved, it will be forced to languish in the throes of underdevelopment and instability.

The AEP has sustained the focus on Northeast India as initiated by LEP and over the last three years, has been vigorously following the developmental trajectory in terms of improving the state of connectivity, infrastructure, social capital, exploiting natural resource potential etc. These efforts have not only been inducing the region's development, but also fostering sub-regional cooperation and facilitating interactions with its vibrant Southeast Asian neighbourhood, with Bangladesh and Myanmar as conduits. On the whole, the achievements of the AEP pertaining to the Northeast have been encouraging, though an array of challenges looms on the trajectory. As the region is slowly, but steadily, escalating the developmental ladder, overcoming the handicaps bestowed by geography and poor connectivity, one must reckon that the panacea for underdevelopment lies in exploiting optimally the immense potential of the region's rich resources—both natural and human.

REFERENCES

Air India to enhance air connectivity in Eastern region soon (2017, February 12). *Hindu Business Line.*

Annual Report: 2015-2016. (2016). Government of India: Ministry of Development of North Eastern Region, retrieved from http://mdoner.gov.in/sites/default/files/NER%20AR%2015-16.pdf (accessed on 26 November 2018)

Arora, Rajat (2018, 21 September). Nitin Gadkari orders early completion of Northeastern highway projects. *Economic Times.*

BIMSTEC Leaders' Retreat 2016: Outcome Document. (2016, October 17). retrieved from http://www.narendramodi.in/bimstec-leaders-retreat-2016-outcome-document-532768 (accessed on 24 November 2018)

Bose, Pratim Ranjan (2017, June 25). Study Proposes Creation of North-East Corridor. *Hindu Business Line.*

Comprehensive Telecom Development Plan for North-Eastern Region. (2014, September 10). Government of India: Press Information Bureau, retrieved from http://pib.nic.in/newsite/PrintRelease.aspx?relid=109540 (accessed on 26 November 2018)

Developing waterways for sustainable transport in the North East: stakeholders call for ensuring adequate draft, augmenting terminal and warehousing facilities. (2017, May 29). Government of India: Ministry of Shipping, retrieved from http://pib/nic.in/newsite/printrelease.aspx?relid=163229 (accessed on 26 November 2018)

Government to invest Rs 25 lakh crore in inland waterways ports: Nitin Gadkari. (2016, June 10). *Indian Express.*

India, Bangladesh can work on mutually beneficial projects: PM Modi. (2014, December 19). retrieved from http://www.ndtv.com/india-news/india-bangladesh-can-work-on-mutually-beneficial-projects-pm-modi-715632 (accessed on 7 December 2018)

Joint Statement of the 15th BIMSTEC Ministerial Meeting. (2017, August 11). Government of India: Ministry of External Affairs, retrieved from http://www.mea.gov.in/bilateral-documents.htm?dtl/28862/Joint+Statement+of+the+15th+BIMSTEC+Ministerial+Meeting+August+11+2017 (accessed on 7 December 2018)

Kathuria, Sanjay. (2017, September 27). Bangladesh corridor vital to India's 'Act East' Policy. retrieved from http://www.worldbank.org/en/news/opinion/2017/09/27/bangladesh-corridor-vital-indias-act-east-policy (accessed on December 2018)

Mitra, Naresh. (2017, April 5). Northeast set to be global organic agriculture hub. *Times of India*

More Border Haats on India-Bangladesh frontier soon. (2016, October 26). retrieved from http://bdnews24.com/business/2016/10/26/more-border-haats-on-india-bangladesh-frontier-soon (accessed on December 2018)

Mukherjee, Sharmistha. (2016, October 22). Government in mission mode to expand civil aviation sector: says PM. *Indian Express.*

Mullick, Soumyadip. (2017, October 4). Kolkata airport eyes surge in regional connectivity. *The Statesman.*

Myint-U, Thant. (2012). *Where China meets India: Burma and the new crossroads of Asia.* London: Faber and Faber

Narendra Modi's address at the 9th East Asia Summit meeting. (2014, November 13). *Speeches and Statements.* Government of India: Ministry of External Affairs, retrieved from http://mea.gov.in/Speeches-Statements.htm?dtl/24238/Prime_Ministers_remarks_at_the_9th_East_Asia_Summit_ Nay_ Pyi_ Taw_Myanmar (accessed on 7 December 2018)

Narendra Modi's address at the Plenary Session of the North-Eastern Council. (2016, May 27). *Speeches and Statements,* retrieved from http://www.pmindia.gov.in/en/news_updates/pms-address-at-the-plenary-session-of-the-north-eastern-council/(accessed on 7 December 2018)

National Civil Aviation Policy, 2016: Salient Features. (2016, June 15). Government of India: Ministry of Civil Aviation, retrieved from http://pib.nic.in/newsite/PrintRelease.aspx?relid=146238 (accessed on 7 December 2018)

Northeast allocation up at Rs 47K crore. (2018, February 2). *Shillong Times. retrieved from* http://www.theshillongtimes.com/2018/02/02/ne-allocation-up-at-rs-47k-cr/ (accessed on 26 November 2018)

Petroleum Minister releases Hydrocarbon Vision 2030 for North-East. (2016, February 9). Government of India: Ministry of Petroleum and Natural Gas, retrieved from http://pib.nic.in/newsite/printrelease.aspx?relid=136255 (accessed on 7 December 2018)

Prop for export backbone. (2017, March 16). *The Telegraph.*

Roy Chowdhury, Jayanta. (2017, March 6). Tri-nation pipeline envisaged. *The Telegraph.*

Singh, Bikash. (2017, February 1). Budget increases allocation for 8 North-eastern states. *Indian Express.*

'Swadesh Darshan' and 'Prasad' Schemes of Ministry of Tourism. (2016, March 2). Government of India: Press Information Bureau, retrieved from http://pib.nic.in/newsite/PrintRelease.aspx?relid=137206 (accessed on 26 November 2018)

Talukdar, Sushanta. (2014, December 1). Northeast will be nurtured, says Modi. *The Hindu.*

Train to Tawang. (2017, February 13). *Arunachal Times.*

Union Cabinet approves Shyama Prasad Mukherji Rural Mission to drive economic, social and infrastructure development in rural areas. (2015, September 16). retrieved from http://www.pmindia.gov.in/en/news_updates/union-cabinet-approves-shyama-prasad-mukherji-rurban-mission-to-drive-economic-social-and-infrastructure-development-in-rural-areas/16_sep_2015 (accessed on 9 December 2018).

Untapped Potential of North East Region: National Round Table Conference Report. (2017, March 15). New Delhi: Indian Council of Food and Agriculture, retrieved from http://www.icfa.org.in/assets/doc/reports/6215521-souvenir-ner.pdf (accessed on 9 December 2018

15

India's Shift from Look East to Act East Policy

Nirmal Jindal

After the end of the Cold War, India shifted its attention to the East in order to materialise the benefits put forward by globalisation and liberalisation processes. The growing economy of ASEAN attracted India's attention to capitalise on its relations with East Asian nations. In the post-Cold War world as the US hegemony is declining, new centres of power are emerging. Though none of the emerging centres are in a position to emerge as a US competitor or challenge the US supremacy directly; China's rising economic and military power is perceived as a threat to the regional and global order by various Asian regional powers as well as the US. Therefore, the China factor is instrumental in India's move from Look East to Act East Policy.

In this context, the paper explains shift in India's policy from Look East adopted by P.V. Narasimha Rao's government in 1992 to the Act East Policy by the NDA government in 2014. Some of the questions highlighted in this paper are: Why East Asia is significant in India's security perception? How North East can act as an anchor of India's Look East and Act East Policy? How China is a factor in growing cooperation between India and East Asia and Southeast Asia? How India Act East policy can be contributory to maintain stable regional and global order? How India's Look East Policy is complementary to its policy of NAM?

Look East Policy

Since independence India has been interested in establishing collaborative relations with Southeast Asian nations as they shared a common history, culture and belief system. The basic objective of India was to exclude extra regional powers from Asia. However, Cold War and China factor kept the region under the influence of the US. Since the end of the Cold War, India has been making serious efforts to strengthen diplomatic, economic and strategic partnership with ASEAN.

India has always been interested in developing cooperative relations with Southeast Asian nations for the purpose of peace and prosperity in the region. Immediately after independence India opened communication with East Asian nations for friendly relations. The basic reason for India's interest in Southeast Asia was that they shared common historical and cultural bonding; India's central position in Asia; and India's interest in establishing non alignment policy in newly independent countries to keep the region free from the extra regional powers influence. India sought China's support in Asian Relations ambition. However, China did not support India's mission of Asian Relations as China never wanted India to emerge as leader of the third world. Nor it wanted India to be treated at par with China.

The South East Asian region became party to the superpower politics and got allied to the US throughout the cold war politics. Therefore, India could never establish relations with South East Asian nations.

After the end of the Cold War, there were major shifts in global politics:

1. The USSR withdrew from the Cold War and US emerged as a unipolar power.
2. China was no more required by the US to counterbalance USSR.
3. Economic globalisation led to the borderless world. The economic liberalisation was perceived as an opportunity for India to develop socio-economic relations with East Asian nations. India perceived South East Asia as economically dynamic, technologically advanced and possible source of FDI investment in India. India sought its economic integration with the region.
4. The attention shifted from military warfare to trade warfare.

India adopted Look East Policy in 1992 by the then P.M. Narasimha Rao amidst worsening economic and political conditions. The Gulf Ear led to acute recession and balance of payment crisis in 1991 (Haokip 2011: 242).

India's Look East Policy was introduced in order to integrate India in the global economy. Look East developed as a multi-pronged strategy involving many institutional mechanisms at multilateral and bilateral levels, economic links, and defence engagement. India's trade with North and Southeast Asia now represents about a quarter of its total trade; outweighing that with the United States and the European Union. China has become India's top trading partner, with bilateral trade growing from roughly $US7 billion in 2003-2004, to $US65 billion in 2013-2014. In the same period, two-way trade with ASEAN member states had grown from approximately US$ 13 billion to US$ 74 billion, making its trade with the region as a whole even more significant than with China (Rajendran: 3).

Look East Policy was a multi-pronged strategy. The policy has evolved from economic and diplomatic engagement with Southeast Asia to broaden security and defence ties across the whole Asia-Pacific. It aimed at economic development; establish links for defence engagement and also develop cultural relations and collaborate to deal with problems like terrorism. The basic objective is to counterbalance the growing influence of China in the India and Pacific ocean. India has allied with major powers in the Pacific like Japan and Australia and is engaged in joint patrolling, bilateral exercises, humanitarian assistance and disaster relief and multilateral engagements, including the biennial MILAN exercises in Port Blair since 1975 (Rajenderan: 8-10)

Indian Navy's Maritime Doctrine (2004, 2007, 2009, 2015) have highlighted India's maritime vision (Mehta 2009). In the 21st century, India has a vision of an arc from the Persian Gulf to Malacca strait which is a legitimate area of its interest. India's 50 per cent of trade is done through Malacca Strait.

It is believed that twenty-first century will be the era of trade warfares, wars for earth and sea bed resources. Oceans and waterways will be significant to secure these interests. The paradox is that on the one hand the state warfares are becoming obsolete, on the other hand the nations are deploying nuclear submarines to protect their trading routes. It causes tensions and arms race among nations. In this context, navy will act as anchor of stability and security. The hegemony or monopolisation of waterways by one nation will pose threat to rest of the countries. Therefore, it has given rise to new competition and conflict among nations and also new realignment partnership. In this regard, India's maritime focus has geographically dilated. South West Indian Ocean and Red Sea fall within primary area of India's interest, whereas Western coast of Africa and the Mediterranean Sea fall within second area of interest. In order to protect its waterways, India is conducting regular naval and coast guard exercises at bilateral and multilateral level. These exercises aim to ensure freedom of navigation and right of passage in international waterways; and also enhance mutual understanding and interoperability; conducting Search and Rescue (SAR) operations. In the last few years India's relations with East Asia and Southeast Asian countries are getting strengthened as it is in mutual interest of both India and pacific countries to collaborate to protect their economic and security interests and also to deal with China's hegemonic designs in the land and oceans around the region.

Act East Policy

India's Act East Policy was introduced in the 12th ASEAN-India summit in 2014 in which PM Modi mentioned that, "A new era of economic development, industrialisation and trade has begun in India". In 2011, the US secretary of State, Hillary Clinton had encouraged India not to Look East but engage and Act East. The policy aimed at ASEAN-India partnership—engagement for peace, prosperity and progress. India ASEAN relations involved political and security cooperation, economic cooperation and socio-cultural cooperation.

Act East Asia policy was a move from Look East Policy as Act East Policy wanted to engage India and Asia-Pacific nations in more active partnership. The Act East Policy included not only economic aspect of cooperative relations but also strategic and security cooperation between India and Asia-Pacific nations. The security aspect includes: maritime security, cyber security, anti-terrorism, drug trafficking and narcotics. East Asia stretched from Southeast Asian nations to East Asian nations, like Japan, South Korea and Beyond-Australia (Devare et. al.).

The Act East Policy aimed to reinvigorate India's relations with ASEAN and expand country's engagement with Korea in the North to Australia and New Zealand in the South and from Bangladesh to Fiji and Pacific island countries in the Far East. ASEAN forms the pillar of India's Act East Policy. Indian PM hosted a special ASEAN-India Commemorative Summit to give boost to the Indian economy. PM Modi visited various countries like Myanmar, Malaysia to attend ASEAN and East Asian summits held in 2014 and 2015 respectively.

Political and Security Cooperation

Both India and ASEAN are cooperating to counter terrorism by sharing best practices and information, law enforcement and capacity building. Cyber security capacity is also being built by use of information and communication technologies. Maritime cooperation between India and ASEAN by mechanism of Expanded

ASEAN Maritime Forum (EAMF) for better cooperation in search and rescue is also being worked on to prevent and manage accidents on sea according to ICAO and IMO guidelines. India's vision for Security and Growth for all in the region (SAGAR) has been recognised by ASEAN (Singh 2018).

China is emerging as a regional and global player which is leading to collaboration among US, India and East Asian countries to check the Chinese hegemonic designs in the Asian region. Chinese hegemony is a significant factor in Development of India's Asia Pacific Strategy. Indian PM Modi government moved from Look East to Act East policy during India-ASEAN summit in Myanmar in November 2014. It Signified that India would play more prominent and active strategic role in East and Southeast Asia.

North East an Anchor of Act East Policy

In order to deepen India's diplomatic, economic and cultural integration of the region, India has endorsed the Master Plan on ASEAN Plus Connectivity (MPAC) to enhance connectivity through land, water and sea routes. India's North East region is critical to develop such connectivity. North East had been isolated and has been a turbulent region so far which can be stabilised by economic development. India's Act East policy can be contribute to eliminate the geographical isolation of North East; it can be used as a connecting corridor to South East Asia. The economic connectivity—North East with Southeast Asian nations—will be instrumental in the economic development and stability of North East region.

The North East is the launching pad of Act Asia policy as it links ASEAN with India through Bangladesh and Myanmar. India is making serious efforts to develop its relations with Bangladesh and Myanmar due to their connectivity with North East. Earlier India and Bangladesh relations were conflictual, characterised by suspicion and mistrust. Due to Act East Policy both have recognised the convergence of their interest in the field of security, economy and energy development areas. The four North East States (Manipur, Mizoram, Nagaland and Arunachal Pradesh) in India share a 1643-km-long land border with Myanmar (Bhaumik 2014: 9). India's Act East Policy envisages that infrastructural development and human resource development in North East Region can facilitate people-to-people contact on social, cultural and economic platforms that can lead to the integration of the region with Southeast Asian nations. It means physical connectivity is to be complemented with soft connectivity. Various infrastructural development projects have been launched to facilitate trade with neighbouring countries. For instance India-Myanmar and Thailand Trilateral highway will be a significant link between India and ASEAN. India is also party to Trans Asian Railway project; Kaladan multimodal trade transit project and the Bay of Bengal initiative for multi-sectoral Technical Economic Cooperation (BIMSTEC) (Sajjanhar 2016: 6).

These projects will increase India's connectivity with ASEAN by land, air and water, which in turn will lead to peace and prosperity in the region. The extension of India-Myanmar-Thailand trilateral highway to Cambodia, Laos and Vietnam will facilitate the movement of passengers across Southeast Asian countries. It will increase people-to-people contact and confidence building among people of different countries in the region. One can also visualise the possibility of Trans Asian countries visa like Schengen to travel to all these countries. The physical and digital connectivity can be used for revival of their traditional, cultural and religious bonding. In the age of globalisation as all these countries are becoming consumerist and losing their interest in religion or god, there should be special efforts to revive the cultural values based on religious beliefs. The social cultural bonding can provide solid base for the economic and security relations between India and ASEAN nations. It is not too much to think about the integration of India and ASEAN nations. Most of the European countries used to have conflictual relations before the Second World War. After the end of the Cold War, European countries not only introduced common currency but also common visa—Schengen to travel to all these countries. Therefore the physical and digital connectivity between India and ASEAN is very critical of India's Asia Pacific strategy. Several steps have been taken in this direction. Asian Development Bank (ADB) is funding the connectivity projects in North East, for instance the Imphal-Moreh (NH39) highway. The construction of railway from Jiribam to Imphal via Tipul will facilitate the development of the development of economic zone around Moreh in India and Tamu in Myanmar border area which is the junction of land connectivity corridor. The development of such economic zones will transform the economic structure of the region. The development of economic corridors will attract investment and will stimulate the economic growth of India's Southern and North Eastern regions: and Cambodia, Laos, Myanmar and Vietnam (CLMV) countries will also be benefitted by getting integrated in the regional economic development. In order to strengthen economic relations with ASEAN nations, India needs to have harmonious political and legal relations with these countries. India under PM Modi administration announced, Line Of credit of USD 1 billion to promote project that support physical and digital connectivity between India and ASEAN. India also sanctioned fund of 500 crore to develop manufacturing hub in CLMV countries which will boost the economic and trade relations between India and ASEAN. The Act East Policy aims at access to capital, technology, energy, markets, a peaceful neighbourhood and a global trading system (Pukhrem 2018).

India perceives its North East as critical connecting point with South East Asian countries. India's trade with North and South East Asia represents about a quarter of total trade. India has developed strong relations with various ASIAN countries like Thailand and Singapore. Indonesia has become India's second largest trading partner in ASEAN countries. In 20 years India has become a sectoral partner of ASEAN. India and ASEAN entered in summit partnership in 2002 and launched negotiations for FTA in 2003.

Apart from ASEAN, India has become successful in strengthening its ties with East Asian nations like Japan, Australia and Korea to secure its economic, security and strategic interests.

China Factor and Act East Policy

The rise of China's economic and military power contributing to the possibility of it's emerging as a superpower by the end of 20th century is a serious concern of India and various other countries in East Asia and Southeast Asia. China's growing military power, in Indian ocean and Pacific ocean and South China sea is posing serious threat to the regional stability. China is developing friendly relations with South Asian countries like Pakistan, Sri Lanka and Maldives which is posing threat to Indian security and free trade. As part of "strings of pearls strategy" China is developing ports in Pakistan, Maldives, Sri Lanka, Bangladesh and Myanmar. (Goto: 27). These ports can also be used for resupplying, refuelling and strengthening Chinese position in Indian Ocean. China's strings of Pearl and New Silk Route to reach out to Africa and Asia by both land and sea are serious concerns for India and East Asian countries. China is developing trading routes via Pakistan incorporating Indian and Pacific oceans. China has deployed nuclear submarines in Indian Ocean; large number of fishing boats in the Bay of Bengal; and is building submarine base in Maldives. Consequently, India has developed the perception of "strategic encirclement." China is exporting submarines to India's neighbours and increasing its military presence in Indian Ocean as 80% of its trade shipped through Indian ocean. India's 55 per cent of trade is transiting through the Malacca straits, therefore India wants these waterways to be safe and free from any strategic domination. Due to rising military presence of China, India's geopolitical situation is changing.

In order to counter Chinese hegemonic designs in Indian ocean, India wants to have access to all sides of Indian ocean and has a strong navy, increasing its war ships, nuclear submarines and aircraft carriers in Indian ocean. India intends to safeguard its interests by deploying additional forces in the East China Sea and West China sea to maintain military balance in Asia. In order to counterbalance China's hegemonic designs in the region, India perceives East Asia significant in grand strategic policy and planning.

India is pursuing the policy of cooperation and competition with China. China is India's biggest trading partner of India. Both are enhancing cooperation in Railways. However, both have conflictual relations. India has dispute with china on territorial issue; water sharing and china's issuing stapled visas to residents of Jammu and Kashmir.

India and ASEAN

India is strengthening its relations with Southeast Asian nations by extending technical, economic and strategic assistance. India trained crews of Thai aircraft carriers and submarines forces, and fighter pilots in Vietnam. India has trained Malaysian pilots and land crews of fourth generation planes. India agreed to train and provide maintenance for the Indonesian Air Force. Singapore is currently using India and land air base for training.

India's PM Modi has adopted Act East Policy for a broader Indo-Pacific conceptualisation of Indian region. In 2015, India under Modi administration allocated $1 billion to build cultural and commercial connectivity between India and ASEAN. India has taken initiative of 'Make in India' 'skill India And 'digital India' for rapid economic development; promoting energy security and creating infrastructure.

Regional Comprehensive Economic Partnership (RCEP) agreement grouping ASEAN 10 and China, Japan, South Korea, Australia, New Zealand and India is a major initiative as it represents 40 per cent of the world population and 23 per cent of the world's gross domestic product.

India is trying to establish friendly relations with Japan, Vietnam, Australia, ASEAN and BRICS to pursue its goal of economic development and prevent imperialism expansionism in Indian ocean and Pacific Rim as well as act as a member of global governance. India is cooperating in economic development, cyber space, energy security and military and maritime security. India is becoming a prominent partner of various countries to play a great role in regional and international affairs. India, Japan, SEA and US are joining hands to promote defence cooperation to protect their mutual interests. It will benefit the US, Australia and other countries around South China Sea.

India-Japan Relations: Cornerstone of Act East Policy

Indo-Japanese relations converge on global interests—maintaining sovereignty, territorial integrity, democracy, human rights, rule of law, open global trade regime and freedom of navigation; maritime interconnection and growing international responsibilities. Japan is concerned about the issue of rising power of China, maritime security and terrorism which is posing challenge to the stability of East Asian regional as well as global order. Maritime security is significant to ensure safety of sea line of communication as well as ensuring economic and energy security. Japan intends to keep its ocean free and open. Japan seeks to ensure sea routes in Indian ocean from the possibility of threat of China and North Korea.

Japan though is not a strong economic trade partner of India. It is extending its technological assistance and economic investment to upgrade India's infrastructure and manufacturing sector. Japan and India have mutual interest in building long term economic and defence cooperation. After 2010 Senkaku (territorial dispute between Japan and China) incident, Japan has shifted towards India. India is also facing territorial dispute with China and intends to develop modern strategic roads, tunnels, railroads, helipads and airports to deal with China's challenge in Tibet. Japan is extending assistance in the field of transport, energy, forestry, agriculture and infrastructural development.

India has become one of the largest recipients of Japan ODA. India has become part of East Asian regional production network. In order to boost India's industrial production and urbanisation, India aims to develop six industrial corridors: Delhi-Mumbai; Amritsar-Calcutta; Chennai-Bangalore; Bangalore-Mumbai; and Vizag-Chennai. India intends to develop high speed passenger corridor and high speed rails (250-350 km/hour)—Delhi-Amritsar; Pune-Mumbai-Ahmedabad; Hyderabad-Chennai; Howrah-Haldia; Chennai-Trivandrum; Delhi-Patna. Japan is providing financial and technical assistance for the infrastructural development under special Terms for Economic Partnership Loans (Goto: 11-12).

Japan has been extending Official Development Assistance (ODA) programme and supported critical infrastructural development projects like Delhi Metro, Delhi-Mumbai industrial corridor and China-Bangalore industrial corridor (Kojima: 11). There is convergence of interest in economic and strategic partnership between India and Japan. The Japan International Cooperation Agency was awarded a contract (2014) to build 200 kms of strategic roads along India's disputed border with China. Japan planned to invest about $35 billion in India's infrastructural development. Japan is investing to develop smart cities; Delhi-Mumbai industrial corridor; Shinkansen bullet train between Mumbai and Ahmedabad. India and Japan's companies have entered in various joint ventures. TCS and Mitsubishi entered in joint venture. India and Japan are collaborating in IT sector. India and Japan are constructing six industrial ports in Rajasthan, Gujarat, Maharashtra and Tamil Nadu. Japan is also helping India to upgrade skills of its labour which will be contributory to India's manufacturing sector by enhancing quality production.

Both India and Japan have signed cooperation agreement in the field of defence and dual use technologies. In 2006, India and Japan entered in strategic partnership. They signed bilateral defence deal for sale of Shin Maywa US-2 amphibious SAR aircrafts for Indian navy (Rajendran 2014: 7). India and Japan have entered in civilian nuclear deal. Both have signed "Joint Declaration on Security Cooperation" between India and Japan. In 2009 India and Japan have entered in security cooperation to conduct joint naval exercises. Japan is participating in Indo-US Malabar exercises series. Earlier only India and the US had been conducting Malabar exercises since 1992. Japan was inducted as a permanent member in 2007. Both India and Japan have been conducting air-based anti-submarine warfare exercises in Indian ocean since 2012. Japan entered in naval exercises collaborative effort to realise a peaceful, open, stable, equitable rule-based order in the Indo-Pacific region and beyond.

India-Australia Relations

India and Australia also have common interests to cooperate in economic and strategic fields. Australian PM, Tony Abbott, signed a nuclear Deal with India as Australia has large reserves of Uranium. It will enhance India's energy generation. The White Paper released on 2017 acknowledged India as among the "front rank of Australia's international partnerships" as both have mutual economic, and security interest, particularly in regard to free and open regional waterways.

Australia is collaborating with countries in Asia-Pacific and extending assistance for training, exercises and capacity building. Australia has also entered in Quadrilateral alliance with the US. Both India and Australia are carrying out bilateral maritime exercises, AUSINDEX since 2015. It is a sign of increasing strategic partnership between the two countries. Both are conducting joint operations in the field of humanitarian relief and Disaster relief management

(HADR). Both India and Australia have also initiated ministerial dialogue to foster stability Indo-Pacific region. This region is significant for global trade, commerce, navigation and scientific research. India and Australia are also intending to enter in trilateral relations with Japan due to the commonality of their interests—economic, strategic and counterterrorism. The defence cooperation between India, Japan and Australia will emerge as a cornerstone of trilateral partnership.

Act East Policy contributes towards consolidating interests among the major regional players. India's 'Make in India' policy particularly in defence equipment has opened avenues of collaboration between India, the US, Japan and Australia. India has allowed 100% FDI in defence products only with new technology. It has encouraged Japan to invest in India. For this purpose Japan has relaxed its rules of export of defence equipment and technology. It also opened a new avenue for Australian defence export strategy adopted in 2018. Australia is looking for an opportunity to emerge as the top ten defence exporting countries by exporting its military equipment and services.

Vietnam in India's Regional Geopolitics

Vietnam is an important pillar of India's Look East Policy. Vietnam acts as strategic and defence partner of India. India perceives Vietnam a close strategic ally and has taken various initiatives to build healthy relations with Vietnam. In 2007, both established strategic partnership and collaborated in economic, scientific and cultural fields. Indian companies have started investing in Vietnam in the field of oil and gas exploration, agricultural, chemical and sugar processing as well as in IT field. Both have mutual interest in collaborating to counterbalance China's presence in India's China and South China sea. As China is deploying its nuclear submarines near Gwadar in Pakistan and combo in Sri Lanka ports, India's decision to deploy its nuclear submarines in Vietnam would act as counterbalance to China. India proposed to supply Brahmos, anti-ship missiles to Vietnam. India is helping Vietnam in its defence modernisation by cooperation on defence equipment and training. India is also developing its strategic partnership with Indonesia in 2009.

Act East Policy in Congruence with NAM

Apart from strengthening its relations with East Asian nations, India is also trying to develop friendly relations with developed nations to generate their financial and technical support for the development of third world countries. India is trying to keep NAM alive by uniting the third world countries. India being a founding member of NAM is playing an active role in G20. It aims to discuss the key economic problems of the world including the third world. The basic objective is to bridge the gap between North and South to establish new world order, the long cherished goal of NAM. India is establishing its relations with the US, Japan, Korea and Australia in congruence with its policy of NAM. India is emphasising the values of doctrine of non-alignment which is in the larger interest of the global humanity. India is emerging as a champion of the interests of the third world by pursuing the policy of non-alignment based on universal moral values like truth, non-violence, justice, solidarity and brotherhood. In the changed world scenario so far the inequality, injustice and exploitation continues, the relevance of NAM remains. India's policy of establishing friendly relations with different countries, membership of various regional and global institutions aims at strengthening its own economic and security position and bargain for the interest of the third world from the position of strength. India is trying to reinvigorate NAM and trying to bring its old glory back and work for the larger interest of humanity. Therefore, the emergence of multipolar or polycentric world is not contradictory to the Indian policy of NAM and India seeks to work against domination, intervention, containment, coercion, preemption and subjugation of weaker countries. Therefore, India's relations with ASEAN, East Asian countries like Japan, Vietnam and Australia and the US are not incompatible to the doctrine of non-alignment or essence of NAM. India's Act East Policy aims at security, development and fights against hegemonic ambitions of upcoming dominating powers in collaboration with Asian nations without compromising with its principle of independent foreign policy. In this context, it is significant to emphasise that India is trying to establish balanced relations with China and Russia as well. India is China's largest trading partner and engaged in defence cooperation with Russia. India seeks to establish its relations with most of the countries of the world keeping in view its broader national interest.

Conclusion

India's Act East Policy will enable India to play a leading role in establishing stable regional and global order. In globalising, world terrorism and nuclear proliferation in weak civilian governments will pose serious threats to economic development, peace and security to the world. India can collaborate with major global players to fight against terrorism. China-Pakistan factor is posing a serious threat to India's security which can be countered by India in collaboration with its East Asian nations. Therefore, Act East Policy is the cornerstone of India's foreign policy which needs to be carried forward by all means.

REFERENCES

Ashok Sajjanhar. 2016. Taking Stock of India's Act East Policy. ORF Issue Brief. May 2016, issue no.142.

Daniel Rajendran, 2014, India's New Asia Pacific Strategy: Modi's Act East, Lowy Institute for International Policy Analysis.

https://www.indiannavy.nic.in/sites/default/files/Indian-Maritime-Doctrine-2009-Updated-12Feb16.pdf

Makoto Kojima, "The evolution of Japan-India Economic Relations", in *The Rebalance within Asia: The Evolution of Japan India Relationsed*, ed. Shihoko Goto, Washington: Wilson Center

Shristi Pukhrem, *India Foundation Journal*, July-August 2018.

Shihoto Goto, *The Rebalance Within Asia: The evolution of Japan India Relations*, Washington: Wilson Center, p. 27.

Subir Bhaumik, 2014, Look East through Northeast: Challenges and Prospects for India, Observer Research Foundation Occasional Paper 51, June 2014: 9.

Sudhir T. et al. (ed) India's Look East - Act East Policy: A Bridge to the Asian Neighbourhood, Symbiosis Institute of International Studies. http://www.irconference.in/irc2017/assets/IRC_conference_proceedings.pdf

Suresh Mehta, 2009: https://www.indiannavy.nic.in/sites/default/files/Indian-Maritime-Doctrine-2009-Updated-12Feb16.pdf

Thongkholal Haokip, "India's Look East Policy: Its Evolution and Approach", *South Asian Survey* 18, no.2 (2011): 242.

Udai Bhanu Singh, 2018. Significance of India's Act East Policy and Engagement with ASEAN, IDSA, Dec. 4, 2018.

16

India-BIMSTEC Bilateral Relationship and Act East Policy

Nisha

> *"Leaders have devoted themselves to politics, little knowing, it seems that political independence disappears without economic independence that economic independence is the foundation of political independence."*
>
> **—Booker T. Washington**

Introduction

The seeds of Look East Policy to the present Act East Policy were sown even before 1991, when India's first Prime Minister Jawaharlal Nehru called the Asian Relation Conference in March 1947 at New Delhi and said:

> *"We are Asia and the peoples of Asia are nearer and closer to us than others. India is so situated that she is the pivot of western, southern and Southeast Asia. In the past her culture flowed to all these countries and they came to her in many ways. Those contacts are being renewed and the future is bound to see a closer union between India and Southeast Asia on one side and Afghanistan, Iran and the Arab world on the west. To the furtherance of that close association of free countries, we must devote ourselves. India has followed with anxious interest the struggle of Indonesia for freedom and to them we send our good wishes."*[1]

However, the Cold War divided the whole of Asia; events such as Vietnam War, Indo-China war, ideological confrontation in South East Asia, by signing Indo-Soviet treaty 1971 by India and its stand on Afghanistan and recognition of Hang Samrin regime led to further gap between India and South East Asia. Further,

India did not participate in the first summit of ASEAN countries in 1976 at Bali Indonesia.

As we know that economy and polity are interdependent on each other. The base of the Act East Policy was laid down by Prime Minister P.V. Narsimha Rao in 1991 in two forms:

1. Economic Reforms
2. Look East Policy

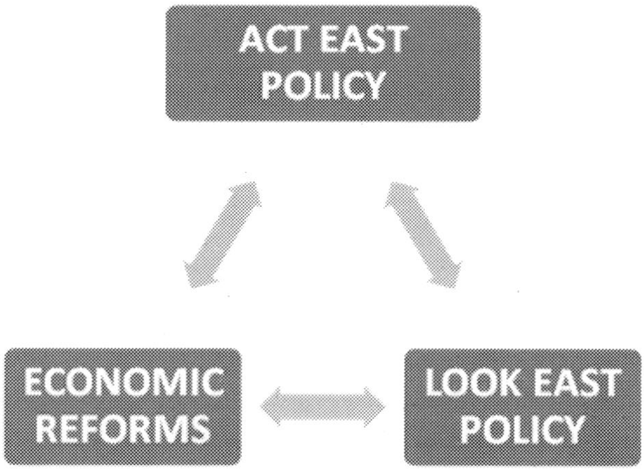

The economic reforms implemented in India when economy was in crisis. The factors responsible were high fiscal deficit and government expenditures exceeded the revenue from various sources such as taxation, earning from public sector enterprises due to high spending on social sector, infrastructure and defence.

Secondly, due to faulty policies government was unable to make repayments on its external borrowing and started taking fresh loans to repay the previous loans thus getting caught in dept trap. Foreign exchange reserves declined to a level that was not adequate to finance imports for more than two weeks.

Thirdly, long term rise in general price levels is called inflation. Price of goods increased due to slow output growth and high demand which resulted in double digit inflation in 1980-81 to 1990-91.

To solve all these issues of the economy, India approached World Bank and International Monetary Fund. India was granted loan of $7 billion as loan to manage the crisis on the condition that India would liberalize and open up the economy by removing trade restrictions on the private sector and reduce the role of the government in many areas and removed the restriction on private sector.

India agreed to the conditions laid down by these institutions and thus announced the New Economic Policy or Look East Policy consisting of wide ranging economic reforms under three heads liberalization, privatization and globalization.[2]

Look East Policy

Look East Policy was an initiative to develop closer and deeper economic integration with its eastern neighbours as a part of the new pillar in Indian Foreign Policy. This policy was focussed more on ASEAN; it improved bilateral relations with the South East Asian nations. India became a sectoral dialogue partner in March 1993 in the three areas, namely trade, investment and tourism. The aims of this policy were:

- To renew political contacts and understanding with ASEAN members.
- Achieve enhanced economic interaction including investment and trade.
- Strengthen defence and strategic links with these countries.

This policy was applied in phases and to achieve the objectives India signed a long-term cooperative partnership for peace and prosperity with ASEAN and Free trade agreement in August 2009 which turned out to be a strong base for India's Look East policy. Benefits of Look East Policy have supported India's economic transformation and growth including closer contacts between India and South East Asian countries. Infrastructure projects were also taken into consideration for connecting India with South East Asia. Prime Minister Manmohan Singh said, "The Look East Policy is not merely an external economic policy". Even Hillary Clinton, the then US secretary of state, during her visit to India In 2011 said that "India should not look towards the East but more important Act and engage towards East.[4]

To conclude India's Look East Policy was emphasising on only South East Asian countries. Role of the north eastern states was limited.[3] Therefore this policy was changed to Act East Policy.

Act East Policy

The name of this policy itself suggests being active, reviving and invigorating India relations with South East Asia and look west too towards economic security and wider dimensions externally. That focuses beyond south East Asian countries. Transformation of Look east policy to Act East Policy has also given other initiatives such as neighbourhood first.

The Act East policy began from Bangladesh. It was unveiled at the 12th ASEAN-

India Summit 2014 held at Naypyidaw. In his opening statement on the occasion said: "A new era of economic development, industrialization and trade has begun in India. Externally, India's Look East policy has become Act East policy." This was followed by plan of action for 2016-2020 aim to pursue the goals set for the next five years. To build on the achievements made in the implementation of the previous plan of action.

On this PM Modi said "The ASEAN-India plan of action for the period 2016-20 has served us well in fulfilling our objectives. We have already implemented 54 out of 130 activities identified in plan of action. This number is growing has reached to 70."

Major objectives of Act East Policy are:

- Three C's culture, commerce and connectivity.
- To promote economic growth and cooperation.
- Develop strategic relationship with countries in Asia-Pacific region.
- Engagement of countries at bilateral, multilateral and regional level.
- Focus on the development of North Eastern states which is sharing its border with Myanmar.

Significance of Act East Policy for India is to promote its national interest while taking care of economy, traditional and non-traditional threats to security. India is a huge market source for the Asia – Pacific countries. At the same time, India is the second most populous country with issues such as unemployment, poverty and recently making of India a trillion economy in the coming years. It requires economic integration with other countries for investment, development and generating employment. In this context act east policy will play a crucial role. Act East Policy has been enhanced with look west initiative too. It covers not only ASEAN member countries but other regional organisations such as BIMSTEC, MGC, BBIN, Indo-Pacific region too.

Moreover, Prime Minister Narendra Modi appealed to ASEAN member states as well as Bangladesh, Nepal and Bhutan to invest in the north east states of India, During Inauguration of the Advantage Assam: Global Investors' Summit in Guwahati. The Act East Policy envisions increased people-people contact, trade ties and other relations with ASEAN countries.

India-BIMSTEC Bilateral Relations

BIMSTEC is twenty-year old organization. This comprises five South Asian and two South East Asian countries. Hence when we analyse Look East Policy to Act

East Policy it has already build up a strong base for India with these countries being ASEAN centric. On the other hand, the five South Asian countries which could not economically engage with India due to India-Pakistan conflict will also find Act East Policy beneficial and look West which is beneficial for their economic growth. Their geographical location also plays an important role in the economic engagement.

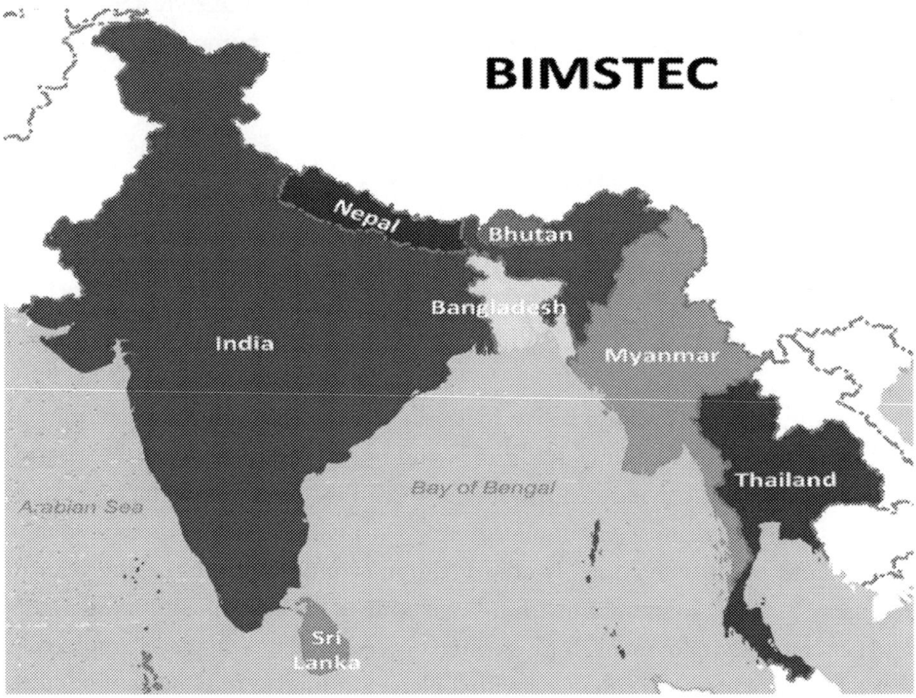

Source: www.drishtias.com

India is a peninsular plateau with water bodies on three sides which makes it a significant part of region. Both Nepal and Bhutan are landlocked countries. Nepal is located in South Asia between China in the North and India in the south, east and west. Similarly, the princely kingdom of Bhutan is mountainous and lies in the eastern Himalayas surrounded by Tibet in the North and Indian states in the west, south and east. Sri Lanka a democratic socialist republic is an island country in South Asia located in the Indian Ocean to the southwest of Bay of Bengal and to south east of the Arabian Sea. Bangladesh is a low lying, riverine country located in South Asia with a large marshy jungle coastline of 710 km on the northern littoral of Bay of Bengal.

The two South East Asian countries, one of them Myanmar (also known as Burma) is located in western portion of mainland South East Asia. It is between western border of Bangladesh and India while Laos and Thailand border the eastern side, China forms the border to the North. It is surrounded by Bay of Bengal Sea in the south and is shaped like a kite. Then Thailand is situated at the centre of peninsular South East Asia and bordered by Myanmar and Andaman Sea to the west, Laos to the northeast, Cambodia to the Southeast, the Gulf of Thailand and Malaysia to the South. It is shaped like ahead of an elephant.

To give a thought and a look at the geography of these countries is significant for the analysing India and BIMSTEC's bilateral relations. Firstly, as concluded above that Look East Policy to Act East Policy is ASEAN centric. This has already given strength to BIMSTEC member countries. Secondly, the natural resources these countries share among each other and Bay of Bengal is the major asset for them to connect and develop. To become a developed country from developing and least developed countries has many challenges and climate change is one big threat to achieve this dream. Climate change will impact the economy decision making and 22 percent of the world population. Thirdly, at present geography is related to sustainable development goals as industrialization, pollution and ignorance towards environment will impact policies in welfare of the countries. Due to these factors BIMSTEC member countries along with India signed a memorandum of understanding in the Summit in Kathmandu (Nepal) on 30-31 August 2018. To work towards maintaining peaceful, prosperous and sustainable Bay of Bengal. Under Kathmandu declaration they also signed:-

- Mutual respect for sovereign equality, territorial integrity, political independence and mutual benefit.
- Enhanced level of economic and social in the region.
- Faith in principles and purposes of UN charter and efforts to strengthen it.
- Deplore terrorist attack in all parts of the world and condemn terrorism in all its forms and manifestations.
- Terrorism should not be justified. Identify and hold accountable states and non-states entities that encourage support or finance terrorism.
- Cross-border control and monitoring of crime and drugs, disaster relief and humanitarian assistance.

In the 4th summit from 14 sectors they have reduced to four sectors. Free Trade agreement is still on the table to discuss. The Goa summit in 2016 of BRICS-BIMSTEC had put process on fast track for this organisation. Various ministerial groups were made to focus on the progress of this sub-regional organisation such as Trade and economic affairs Ministerial meeting, Ministerial meeting for managing foreign affairs. Senior official meeting precedes the ministerial meeting and is represented by the senior official of Foreign Ministers, senior trade economic officials meeting, expert group meeting and BIMSTEC working group.

Every summit meeting, visits are important for maintaining good bilateral relations between the countries Meeting work on the way forward for the future of the countries. In the first summit, the BIMSTEC meeting was held in Bangkok on 31st July 2004. Member countries emphasised on:

- The member countries agreed to annual ministerial meeting to be hosted by the member states on the bases of alphabetical rotation.
- Senior official committee to meet on regular basis as and when required.
- BIMSTEC working group comprising ambassador representatives from member states to carry on the work in between annual ministerial meeting.
- Specialized Task forces and other mechanisms are deemed necessary by the senior officials to be coordinated by member states as appropriate.

Similarly, the second BIMSTEC summit held on 13 November, 2008, which focused on:

- Agreeing on road, air and shipping links to further promote people-to-people contact to facilitate cultural exchange, business and tourism flows.
- Leaders expressed their satisfaction at the progress that has been made in the negotiation for FTA in trade in good and called for early conclusion.
- They welcomed the establishment of centres, expressed concern at the threat of terrorism possing in our region. The Summit has given a strong political impetus to the strength of our cooperation in 14 sectors.
- The member countries agreed to improve, cooperate and establish BIMSTEC into a crucial organisation.

The third summit took place on 4th March 2014 at Naypyidaw in Myanmar:

- Discussion on disaster management, environment, trade, transport and tourism.
- Proposed the establishment of a permanent secretariat in Dhaka at Bangladesh.
- Indian Prime Minister Manmohan Singh and Sri Lanka President Mahinda Rajapaksa planned to meet on the side lines of the summit to discuss United Nation Human Rights Council resolution on Sri Lanka war crimes.

Challenges they identified were terrorism and global threat it poses to peace, stability and economic progress, climate change in general, energy and food security and connectivity. Besides all this the member countries signed:

- Memorandum of association to set up permanent secretariat in Dhaka.
- Memorandum of understanding for the establishment of BIMSTEC cultural industries and observatory.
- Memorandum of Association to set up BIMSTEC centre for weather and climate in India to promote cooperation in dealing with challenges posed by climate change .These summits, visit give an overview of how collectively these countries are engaging with each other and shows that the geographical and economic bilateral relations are strengthening and building a path to walk together in the near future. Before reaching to full conclusion let us analyse the individual bilateral relation of BIMSTEC member countries with India.

India-Nepal bilateral relations are cordial and soon after the fourth BIMSTEC Summit Prime Minister of Nepal K.P. Oli said, "Summit was successful and it has provided a new hope and momentum to the regional organisation". Recently when first military exercise MILEX was conducted at Aundh in Pune (Maharashtra) in India. Theme of exercise includes counter-terrorism in semi urban terrain, cordon and search. Nepal withdrew its Army and sent three member team as observer. Nepal foreign minister stated earlier in the week, "There was no discussion held or agreement reached about the military exercise during fourth BIMSTEC summit." BIMSTEC is purely developmental forum which does not prioritise military exercise.

On the other hand, Prime Minister Narender Modi while addressing the inaugural session of summit had proposed to host the joint military exercise in India in the second week of September 2018. On this Foreign minister Pradeep Kumar Gawali said "India was free to float the agenda but we do not endorse it." Even though both the countries have deep linkages in the military area, with 30,000 Nepalese Gorkha's currently serving In Indian Army, seven Gorkha riffles and some paramilitary forces. The two armies regularly hold their annual Surya Kiran Bilateral exercise and the 13th edition was held at Pithoragarh in June. At the same time, Nepal's opinion on SAARC is to reactivate the organisation which will be possible when all issues are resolved in SAARC. It has signed Transport Transit Agreement with China and air connectivity of Nepal and China is stronger than other neighbouring countries. In India too lots of development projects are yet to be completed. Nepal wants to be a land-linked country than a land locked one and reduce its dependence for connectivity.

India-Bhutan bilateral relations share cultural and historical linkages. They are 50 year old diplomatic relations but original relations are older than diplomatic one. Bhutan is a carbon negative country and measures Gross National Happiness then Gross National Product. Their priority is to continue strong ties with India; border with China is yet to be demarcated. Doklam is a very important area where China can compromise the security of Bhutan but also of India. It is disputed area between China and Bhutan just like Jarkarlung and Pasamlung. India has signed a friendship treaty with Bhutan to intervene for the goodwill of Bhutan among many other provisions. Therefore both the countries share great bilateral relations.

India was the first country to recognize Bangladesh as a separate and independent state and establish diplomatic relations with the country. Bangladesh got its independence in December 1971. There have been high-level visits and exchanges between the two countries. There are more than 50 bilateral institutional mechanisms and share longest boundary with any of its neighbour. Both the countries have 54 common rivers. The Ganga water treaty was signed in 1996 for sharing water which has been satisfactory. Their trade agreement was first signed in 1972. India-Bangladesh trade agreement was renewed in June 2015 for period of 5 year with provisions of auto renewal cooperation in power sector and has become one of the hallmarks of India-Bangladesh relations. About 10,000 strong Indian communities are estimated to be living in Bangladesh. They are very well respected and successful.

India-Sri Lanka relations are more than 2,500 years old. Both countries have a legacy of intellectual, cultural, religious and linguistic interaction in recent years. Relationship has been marked by close contact at all levels. Political relations are marked by visits and through regional organisation. Sri Lanka has been a long priority destination to direct investment from India. India has engaged itself in education, health, transport, connectivity, small and medium enterprise development and training in many parts of the country through its grant funding. Due to the proximity of territorial waters of both countries especially in Palk Strait and Gulf of Mannar, incidents of straying of fishermen are common. Both countries have agreed on certain practical arrangement of deal such as detention of fishermen in a humane manner. They setup a joint working group of fisheries. The people of Indian origin have settled down in Sri Lanka after partition and snagged themselves in various business ventures. Even Indian origin Tamil is well placed and economically prosperous.

India-Myanmar relations share land boundary with four north eastern states and maritime border too. It is our gate-way to South East Asia with which we are seeking greater economic integration through the Act East Policy. There have been high level visits from both sides; defence cooperation between the two countries continues to strengthen. Trade agreement signed in 1970 going on with import and export of various commodities. Myanmar is partner in energy sector as future off-shore gas finds can be piped to India. These countries have strong cultural ties and given India a Buddhist heritage. Indian community in Myanmar is traced to the mid of the 19th century with advent of British rule in lower Burma in 1852. This member country is also a member of ASEAN, BIMSTEC and Mekong Ganga Cooperation has introduced a regional and sub-regional dimension to bilateral relations and imparted added significance in the context of Act East Policy.

The bilateral relations of India with Thailand are deep rooted in history, with age-old social and cultural interactions also extensive people-to-people contacts share a maritime boundary in the Andaman Sea. The language incorporates Pali and Sanskrit influences a large Indian Diaspora living and working in Thailand, which is another important aspect. Thailand has now evolved into a comprehensive partnership. India's Act East Policy is complemented by Thailand Act West Policy in bringing the two countries closer. Both countries are important regional partners linking South and South East Asia. They together cooperate in ASEAN, EAS, BIMSTEC, MGC, ACD and IORA. High level visit have taken place from both sides. Foreign office consultation was held in New Delhi. Memorandum of Understanding on defence cooperation between India and Thailand was signed on 25 Jan 2012. Since then it is strengthening day by day. Connectivity is growing through various infrastructure projects; cultural exchanges take place on framework of cultural exchange programme.

Therefore the bilateral relations of India with BIMSTEC member countries are welcoming, honest, and economically prosperous but some areas need to be looked on infrastructure development in other countries and completion of projects on time which will give boost to both the economies and polity. Of course their geographical location is an advantage as they are surrounding Bay of Bengal. On India's part first disaster management was held in India, first task force on traditional medicine, weather and climate institution was established in Noida. Its first meeting was held in July last year; Coastal shipping agreement and Motor vehicle agreement have been signed :Free trade agreement is under negotiation on custom cooperation which will give boost to trade.

Conclusion

To conclude in present international scenario bilateral relations are not only dependent on economic, political and diplomatic engagement. They are sectoral geographical, technical, immigration and employment based too. As the countries are growing in technology, economically their challenges are also growing because all countries in the world are not developed and do not have resources to combat issues. Due to this they (countries) are interdependent It is a positive sign through bilateral or multilateral inter-dependence they can be independent. There is no disadvantage in coming together with a common goal on a common platform for two or more countries.

Similarly, Indian Prime Minister invited BIMSTEC member countries on his oath taking ceremony and it showed the importance "neighbourhood first" policy and his continuous engagement with East emphasis on "Act East Policy". India plays a major role in south and South East Asia. First of all the size of India, economy, market, geographical location, science and technology, population, production and consumption is more than the other south Asian and South East Asian countries. Secondly, India is member of almost all the regional organisations. After the Cold War India association to Non Alignment Movement has made India sovereign power and encouraged other countries too. Issues of diplomacy such as debt trap by Chinese, South China Sea problems faced by south East Asian countries. Other aspect is Beijing and Washington are dominant powers in South East Asia. Both the countries are making shift from south East Asian countries towards India. These circumstances are in favour of development of India.

However, conflicts are part of the bilateral and multilateral relations that will arise. India-BIMSTEC too has individual issues such as Rohingya's problem from Myanmar, due to porous border drug trafficking, human trafficking, internal and external terrorism, Teesta water sharing dispute with Bangladesh. It depends on the member countries who must resolve any kind of disputes as soon as possible for healthy and prosperous bilateral and multilateral relations. Keeping issues on the top for long is not good for any countries. Only through peaceful dialogue method while maintaining dignity and sovereignty such issues must be solved.

Therefore, the bilateral relations of India with other countries of regional organisation such as BIMSTEC will lead to Engagement, Exchange and Empowerment of these countries and its citizens. The wide spectrum of Act East Policy is not restricted to South and South East Asian countries but also takes Asia-Pacific region under it, which is indeed significant and profitable for the BIMSTEC-India bilateral relations.

"Developing healthy bilateral relations is not only in the fundamental interests of two peoples, but also conducive for the world as a whole."

—Wen Jiabao

NOTES

1. Asian relation, report of the proceedings and documentation of the first Asian Relation Conference, New Delhi, March 1997, Jawaharlal Nehru speeches volume 1 (1946-49) and volume 2 (1949-53), Publication division, Government of India.
2. "Indian economic development", Chapter-3, *Liberalisation, privatisation and globalization,* NCERT.
3. Dr. Thongkholal Haokip, "India Look East Policy Third concept"; *An International Journal of Ideas,* Volume 24, No. 291, May 2011, pp. 7-11.
4. S.D. Muni, India Look East Policy the strategic dimension, Institute of South Asian studies, National University of Singapore no 121, February 2011.

REFERENCES

PRIMARY SOURCES

- www.thehindu.com
- www.orfonline.org
- www.bimstec.org, the e-newsletter.
- www.mea.gov.in.
- www.researchgate.net
- https://icwa.in
- The diplomat.com
- http://m.economictimes.com

SECONDARY SOURCES

Atul Sharma and Saswati Chaudhary, *Mainstreaming the North East in India Look and Act East Policy,* Palgrave Macmillan (2018).

C Raja Mohan, *Modi's Expanding India's Sphere of Influence World,* Harper Collins; (2015).

D. Suba Chandran, Tuli Sinha, Harnit Kaur Kang, An Alternative Strategy for Southeast Asia: Looking Through India's Northeast(2011)

M. Amarjeet Singh, Northeast India and India's Act East Policy, Sage Publication (2019).

Rajiv Sikri, *Challenges and Strategy Rethinking India's Foreign Policy,* Sage Publications (2009).

Prabir de, *Twenty Years of BIMSTEC Promoting Regional Cooperation and Integration in Bay OF Bengal,* KW Publishers Pvt Ltd. (2018).

S.D. Muni and Rahul Mishra, *India Eastward Engagement: From Antiquity to Act East Policy,* Sage Publications (2019).

S.D. Muni & Vivek Chadha, IDSA, Asia Strategic Review, Pentagon Press (2016).

Sanjay Chaturvedi & Vijay Sakhuja, Climate Change and the Bay of Bengal: Evolving Geographies of Fear and Hope, ISEAS Publishing (2015).

T. Nirmala Devi-*India and Bay of Bengal Community: The BIMSTEC Experiment,* Gyan Publishing House (2007).

17

India-ASEAN Relations and the Act East Policy

Pragya Pandey

The ties between India and ASEAN have been on an upswing in recent years. Recently India celebrated 25 years of its Dialogue Partnership with ASEAN. India became a Sectoral Dialogue Partner of the ASEAN in 1992, full Dialogue Partner in 1996 and Summit Level Partner in 2002 and strategic partner in 2012. India's partnership with the ASEAN can be seen as a continuation of its historical-cultural ties with the Southeast Asian countries and later the Look East policy and economic liberalization of the 1990s more recently the Act East policy. India's historical-cultural interactions with the foreign countries, since the pre-Vedic times are best observed in Southeast Asia. India's relationship with the ASEAN and the Southeast Asian countries has developed against the background of such deep rooted connections. India has been one of the founding members of ASEAN led institutions including ARF, EAS, and ADMM Plus. India's interaction with ASEAN forms the pivot of its 'Act East Policy'. The connectivity infrastructural projects underway between India's Northeast and the Southeast Asia will further enhance the ties between India and ASEAN region. The Indo-Pacific region is characterized by dynamic geopolitics with complex and at times competitive interests of regional and global powers. As economic and political centre of gravity shifts towards the Indo-Pacific region, India's relationship with ASEAN spearheaded by commerce, connectivity and culture, becomes even more crucial. In this context, pertinent issues including the historical cultural background of the India-ASEAN relationship, the Act East policy and India-ASEAN ties against the changing dynamics of the Indo-Pacific geopolitics will form the central theme of the paper.

India Historical-Cultural Connections with the Southeast Asia

Speaking at the Shagri-la-Dialogue 2018 in Singapore, Prime Minister Narendra Modi emphasizing on India's relationship with the East said "for thousands of years, Indians have turned to the East. Not just to see sunrise but also to pray for its light to spread over the entire world. The human-kind now looks to the Rising East...., because the destiny of the world will be deeply influenced by the course of developments in the Indo-Pacific region".[1]

India's cultural interactions with the foreign countries since the pre-historic days are best observed in the region which has historically carried on the names like Greater India, Farther India, East Indies, Indo-China, Swarnabhumi, Tokola or land of cardamoms, Narikeldeep or land of coconuts, before it came to be known as Southeast Asia. The region which straddled the main routes of exchange between the Indian Ocean and the South China Sea, finds mention in the ancient texts like the Ramayana, the Vayu Purana and Buddhist Jatakas.

India being centrally located in the Indian Ocean, the Ocean has played a significant role in nurturing India's contact with the rest of the world. Ships have been traversing the Ocean for several millennia carrying valuable merchandise, skills, knowledge, civilization, culture, religious ideas, inventions, artistic style, philosophers, and social customs from one end to another, responsible for the development of great civilizations of India, China, Rome, Arabia, Egypt, and Persia and helped in the foundation of the modern world. The ancient trade routes expanding across the Asia, connecting China to the Mediterranean were referred to as Silk Route or Road. These were the thriving centre of much of the maritime activities from India, China, Persia, Mediterranean, Asia Minor and, North Africa. Waters around India witnessed extensive maritime activities starting from the pre-Christian era to the middle of the 15th Century AD, in the form of trade, naval expedition and pilgrimage. As Megasthenes described, during the reign of Emperor Ashoka, the royal shipyards of the Mauryas, in the 3rd Century B.C., built a strong seagoing fleet and used it for regular commercial purposes. Later the Pandyas, Cholas, and Keralas of South India and the Kalingas of Orissa built large sailing vessels which were used for trade, naval warfare and passenger traffic.[2]

During the early centuries of the Common Era, with the intensification of seaborne trade, priests, traders, adventurers, missionaries, literati, went to Southeast

Asia, with mercantile communities dealing with trade of textiles, metals, gems, gold, pearls, salt, cloves and spices.[3] Consequently, commercial connections fostered cultural exchanges and endangered settlements of the sailors and traders during the early times. A large number of Brahmins and missionaries propagating Buddhism settled leading to spread of Indian elements of Hinduism, Sanskrit and Pali language, Dharmashastras and Theravada Buddhism, variety of subjects like philosophy, astrology, medicine and mathematics, Indian styles of art, dance, and architecture to the region. Such acceptability of Indian culture in the region is largely attributed to the absence of any political ambitions.

Figure 1: Map Showing Sea Routes between India and Greater India

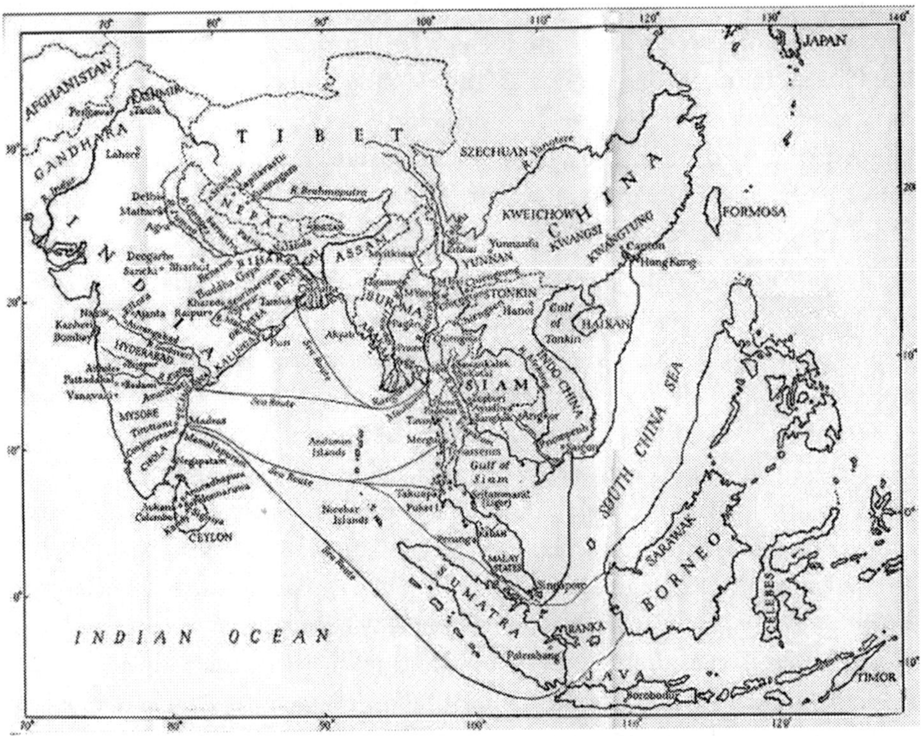

Source: K M Panikkar (1996), *A Survey of Indian History*, 4th edition, Asia Pub. House

Such exchanges also resulted in founding of Indian Kingdoms in Southeast Asia guided by the Indian political theory. These included Funan (in Cambodia, Vietnam, and parts of the Malaya Peninsula and Thailand), Champa (in present day Vietnam), Majapahit (in Java), Khemer (in Cambodia). There are both Chinese and Greek records on the existence of large Hindu kingdom and empires in Champa (Siam), Cambodia, Java, Sumatra.[4] Many artifacts in the region displayed overseas contacts especially with India, among the notables were rocks crystals, lion pendants (which were also found at Taxila), inscribed shards both in Tamil and Brahmi scripts dated to 2-4th century CE. The Andhra Dynasty (which followed Mauryas) left remarkable coins with the pictures of ships in them in Java, Sumatra, and other islands of the Pacific. Thai and Oriya scripts have similarities due to long the Kalinga rule over Thailand.[5] All this illustrates close cultural and trade relations between two regions during early Common Era.

Historians like Oliver Walters (1967) and Ian Glover (1989) and other major proponents of trade generated model of state formation in the littorals of Southeast Asia, have always been keen on emphasizing the role of trade network from India to China to Southeast Asia, since prehistoric to early historic times.[6] Historically, the term used to describe the Indian cultural influence over Southeast Asia was "Indianization". Some historians have, in fact, regarded the "Indianization" as the process of colonization but this explanation cannot be accepted, whatever the process was, it was peaceful and non-political in nature, economically also India did not had monopoly of trade with the region.

Naval powers emerged in the 10th and 11th centuries, to secure influence and access to this mammoth maritime commerce. From the 5th to 12th centuries, for nearly 500 years, the great naval powers Sri Vijaya kings based in Sumatra, controlled the entire sea between India's eastern seaboard and Far East covering Sumatra, (where its capital, Palembang, was located) Peninsular Malay, western half of Java, and numerous islands, with the Malacca Straits firmly under their control. The 10-11th centuries witnessed the emergence of the formidable Chola polity in the southern Coromandel India, which reached its zenith during the 12-13th century with the occupation of Sri Lanka. Cholas maintained a strong naval fleet during emperors Rajaraja I and Rajendra I (985-1054 A.D.). Differences arose between navies of various empires most notably Sri Vijaya and Chola towards the end of 10th century AD.[7] In 1007 A.D. Chola king dispatched a huge convoy of ships to subdue a willful Sri Vijayan King and defeated him to bring the Malayan Peninsula under their sovereignty. After their victorious maritime feat against the Sri Vijaya and successfully taking control of much of South India by the end of the 10th century, the Chola Empire increasingly began to look across the sea, sending fleets against the Andaman Islands, Maldives, and Sri Lanka along with the Persian Gulf trade.[8] With the mercantile guild of Chola and expansion of Chinese maritime trade during Song period, Chola-China link reached its climax, linking seas of Southeast Asia to the Indian Ocean and to the South China Sea.[9]

The Chola-Sri Vijaya rivalry which lasted nearly for 100 years resulted in the downfall of the Sri Vijaya's influence, weakened Chola Empire, and eventually opened the way Muslim supremacy over the Indian waters. The 8th-11th centuries argues Andre Wink, "constituted a period of expansion of Muslim (Arab and Persian) commerce on all the major trade routes in the Indian Ocean turning it into 'Arab Mediterranean', with the limited role also played by Jews and Parsis".[10] Till the 15th century, the Arabs and the Indian merchants were the vanguards of the maritime economic activity in the region. However, towards the end of the 15th century, a new pattern of rivalry emerged, among the North African, West Asian and South European countries to establish mastery over trade routes towards the East.[11] Soon Spain, Portugal and other Mediterranean countries started looking for possibilities of trade routes from Europe to India. This signaled the dawn of new era of European encroachment led by the Portuguese, followed successively by the Dutch, British and French, which approached it from west either via the Atlantic and Cape of Good Hope or the Mediterranean and Red Sea. However, "almost throughout the age of the European colonialism these routes were utilized, molded and rendered subservient to the Western capital but never torn apart completely.[12] Towards the end of the 19th century, Indian traders and financiers followed "the British imperial flag to engage in what was perhaps dependent seaborne commerce but which nevertheless enabled them to carve out sectors or pockets of local dominance in Southeast Asia, East Africa and the Middle East".[13] Indian capital was of critical importance to business like rice in Thailand, Burma, laborers in rubber plantation of Malaya. Therefore, the connections between India and Southeast Asia were never broken.

Religious-cultural influences are reflected in the fact that Indian Deities worshipped in the Southeast Asian countries: Lord Vishnu, Lord Shiva, Ganesha, Brahma and others. Some of the important temple complexes and their architectures reflects Indian influences like Sri Mariamman in Singapore, Prambanan and Borobudur in Java, Indonesia, Angkor Wat in Siem Reap, Cambodia, Pura Ulun Danu Bratan in Indonesia, Batu Caves Temples in Malaysia, Devasthan in Thailand and similar others.

Look East to Act East Policy and India's Relationship with ASEAN

The ten members grouping of Southeast Asian countries formed in 1967, has come as long way since its formation. The Association of South-East Asian Nations (ASEAN) comprises of Indonesia, Singapore, Philippines, Malaysia, Brunei, Thailand, Cambodia, Lao PDR, Myanmar and Vietnam, formed in as established on 8 August 1967 in Bangkok, Thailand, with the signing of the ASEAN Declaration (Bangkok Declaration). The institution was established, given the political and economic exigencies of time with the primary purpose of:

- To accelerate the economic growth, social progress and cultural development
- To promote regional peace and stability
- to promote active collaboration and mutual assistance
- To provide assistance to each other in the form of training and research facilities
- To collaborate more effectively for the greater utilization of their agriculture and industries,
- To maintain close and beneficial cooperation with existing international and regional organizations.[14]

India's connections with the ASEAN and its member nations have gradually evolved. During the early years of India's independence, under the Nehru government, various efforts were made to build closer partnerships with the countries of Asia and Africa including Southeast Asian countries. The Conference of the Asian relations organized in New Delhi in 1949 and the Bandung Conference in 1955 were some of the crucial initiatives undertaken on the idea of forging the Afro-Asian unity. But beyond that there was not much in terms of closer engagement with these countries. With the onset of the Cold War things became difficult with the developments like formation of blocs like SEATO (1954), the Vietnam War, India's non-alignment, and its own economic policy of import substitution and quest for self sufficiency made it difficult to develop relationship with these countries. Initially when the ASEAN was formed there were certain ambiguities about its purpose. Therefore, during the Cold War the relationship between India and ASEAN remained distant given the compulsions of the Cold War politics. India and ASEAN countries' perceptions were different on various issues like that of Vietnam War, the Soviet Union, Indian Ocean Zone of Peace (IOZP), and the nuclear proliferation issues, American presence in Diego Garcia, India's Peaceful Nuclear Explosion of 1974 and its military (especially naval) modernization in the 1980s.

The end of Cold War changed the entire scenario. The unipolar world was now witnessing the forces of globalization and liberalization. India launched its economic liberalization programme in an attempt to be integrated into liberal international economic order. Flow of western capital and technology, turnaround in India's relations with the US, was the main reason for India's entry into ARF.

India-US cooperation during the Gulf War and Indo-US naval exercise in the Indian Ocean (Malabar exercise) 1992 were in sharp contrast to India's relations with the US during the Cold War period. The launch of the 'Look East' policy was a watershed event in the history of India's integration with the world. It was launched with the aim of developing multifaceted cooperation with the Southeast Asian countries. It also marked a shift in India's perspective of the world. With the resurgence of idea of regionalism in the international environment in the post-Cold War, India gradually moved from cautions isolationism to more active engagement with regional multilateral institutions. As part of the Look East apart from establishing institutional linkages with ASEAN and strengthening bilateral relations with its member states, India has been an enthusiastic participant and supporter of multilateralism in Asia-Pacific. In the decade following the Cold War, India has emerged as one of the largest growing economies of the world. Therefore, current focus in India on a strengthened and multi-faceted relationship with the ASEAN is an outcome of the significant changes in the world's political and economic scenario since the early 1990s.

The traditional look east policy now has been reinvigorated as the Act East Policy. Prime Minister Narendra Modi formally enunciated the Act East Policy, while speaking at the 12th ASEAN-India Summit and the 9th East Asia Summit held in Nay Pyi Taw, Myanmar, in November, 2014. ASEAN is central to the Act East Policy. The Act East is the recognition of fluid geopolitical situation in the region. The entire Indo-Pacific region is undergoing an unprecedented transformation in its security outlook. China's rise and its initiatives like the 'One Belt One Road' (OBOR) can alter the regional balance of power. As an aspiring major power, it is important that India builds its relationship with its immediate neighbours and regional powers. In this context India's relationship with the countries of South, Southeast Asia and East Asia are important. In the light of the Act East Policy the emphasis is on intensifying economic, political and military engagements in the entire Indo-pacific region. However, none of this indicates, that India will enter any kind of alliance with any country.

Speaking at the ASEAN-India Commemorative summit 2018, External Affairs Minister, India Mrs. Sushma Swaraj said that "India and ASEAN are the natural partners that share geographical, historical and civilizational links. Our relationship spans 3C's—commerce, connectivity and culture".[15] Therefore, India-ASEAN relationship can be analyzed from political, strategic and economic aspects.

Politico-Security Relations

India and ASEAN observed 25 years of their Dialogue Partnership, 15 years of Summit Level interaction and 5 years of Strategic Partnership throughout 2017 by undertaking a wide range of over 60 commemorative activities, which culminated in the *India-ASEAN Special Commemorative Summit*, in January 2018 on the theme "Shared Values, Common Destiny" on 25 January 2018 in New Delhi. The Leaders of ASEAN countries also graced the 69th Republic Day function in New Delhi in 2018. ASEAN and India annual summit is in its 16th year. Apart from ASEAN, India has taken other policy initiatives in the region that involve some members of ASEAN like in BIMSTEC, MGC. On the political-security front inclusion in ARF was a major positive for India. India has been actively participating in annual ARF meetings since 1996. The ASEAN Defence Ministers' Meeting (ADMM) is the highest defence consultative and cooperative mechanism in ASEAN. The ADMM+ brings together Defence Ministers from the 10 ASEAN nations plus Australia, China, India, Japan, New Zealand, Republic of Korea, Russia, and the US on a biannual basis. India is also an active participant in the East Asia Summit (EAS) and Expanded ASEAN Maritime Forum (EAMF).[16] India and AESAN have recognized that in the face of growing traditional and non-traditional challenges, politico-security cooperation is a key emerging pillar of our relationship. Both share common concern over rising threat of terrorism, growing radicalization, piracy, climate change, and illegal migration, and trafficking (human, arms, drug) etc.

Such challenges from non-state actors are local, regional and transnational at the same time. Therefore, India's partnership with the ASEAN focuses on seeking to design a response that relies on coordination, cooperation and sharing of experiences at multiple levels. The commemorative summit also highlighted the shared belief in adherence to rule of law, freedom of navigation, respect of UNCLOS, denuclearization of the Korean peninsula etc. Speaking at the summit Prime Minister Narendra Modi, strongly pitched for "setting up of rules-based regional security architecture in the Indo-Pacific region that supports the peaceful development in the region".[17] India has reiterated at different occasions on various multilateral platforms that its objective is to build a future in an open, prosperous, stable and secure Indo-Pacific.

Maritime security remains one of the linchpins of the relationship. Much of the India's trade with its major trading partners like China, Singapore, Hong Kong, US, Japan and ASEAN nations, passes through the sea lanes of the Indo-pacific. Therefore, the security of the crucial choke points in the region, like the

Malacca Strait, Lombok Strait, and the South China Sea is critical to India and also to the international commerce. India has been vocal about the need to maintain freedom of navigation in the wider Indo-Pacific region and adherence to the United Nations Convention on the Law of the Sea (UNCLOS). In recent years, the focus is on the idea of 'blue economy', ocean led growth. In this context the vision of Security and Growth for all, SAGAR, enunciated by Prime Minister Narendra Modi in 2015 is crucial. The 10th edition of the Delhi Dialogue in New Delhi from 19-20 July 2018 was also organized on the theme of "Strengthening India-ASEAN Maritime Cooperation" to discuss ways of strengthening cooperation.

Economic Relationship

ASEAN region, along with India, together comprises combined population of 1.85 billion people, which is one fourth of the global population. ASEAN and ASEAN led institutions occupy a central place in the Indo-Pacific security architecture and in India's 'Act East' policy. India has signed an FTA with the ASEAN and is also very actively engaged in the Regional Comprehensive Economic Partnership, also known as RCEP or ARCEP, a mega trade-block which is being negotiated among the ten members of the ASEAN group and six other ASEAN-FTA countries namely South Korea, Australia, China, Japan, New Zealand and India. Latest round of negotiations was held in May 2018, in Singapore.

India-ASEAN trade relations have been growing steadily, with ASEAN being India's fourth largest trading partner. Both the sides have set a target of at least US$200 billion in two-way trade by 2022. Trade with ASEAN for 2016-17 was valued at US$71 billion, increased to US$81.34 billion for 2017-18. Investment flows are also substantial both ways, with ASEAN accounting for approximately 12.5% of investment flows into India since 2000. FDI inflows into India from ASEAN between April 2000 to May 2016 was about US$49.40 billion, while FDI outflows from India to ASEAN countries, from April 2007 to March 2015, as per data maintained by DEA, was about US$38.672 billion.[18] The ASEAN-India Free Trade Area has been entered into force of the ASEAN-India Agreements on Trade in Service and Investments on 1 July 2015.[19]

ASEAN and India have been also working on enhancing private sector engagement. ASEAN India-Business Council (AIBC) was set up in March 2003 in Kuala Lumpur as a forum to bring key private sector players from India and the ASEAN countries on a single platform for business networking and sharing of ideas.

Southeast Asian countries such as Singapore, Malaysia and Thailand have emerged as major export destinations for India. Since there are trade complementarities between India and Southeast Asian countries in areas such as agriculture, machinery and minerals, among others, trade relations have continued to expand.

Ongoing Connectivity Projects

Another major aspect of India-ASEAN relationship in the context of Act East Policy has been connectivity. As Prime Minister Narendra Modi said "enhancing connectivity in all its dimensions—physical, digital, economic, institutional and cultural—is at the heart of India's strategic partnership with ASEAN." There are transport and infrastructural barriers between India and Southeast Asian countries including poor quality of roads, missing railway links, inadequate maritime and port facilities, and lack of customs cooperation. All these have implications for any potential integration between India and Southeast Asia. Myanmar shares a land border with India's northeast, thereby providing a bridge between India and Southeast Asian markets. Attempts are being made to establish better connectivity infrastructure with this region through land, water, and air. Assam and several other Northeastern states have become critical components in the connectivity and other interactions with Myanmar and beyond with the rest of Southeast Asia through expressways and rail and air links and other exchanges. Indian Prime Minister announced a Line of Credit of US$ 1 billion to promote projects that support physical and digital connectivity between India and ASEAN and a Project Development Fund with a corpus of INR500 crore to develop manufacturing hubs in CLMV countries at the 13th ASEAN-India Summit held in Malaysia in November 2015.[20] An ASEAN-India Connectivity Summit was held on 11-12 December 2017, New Delhi

Some of the important ongoing infrastructure projects include:

- India-Myanmar-Thailand Trilateral Highway to connect Moreh, India with Mae Sot, Thailand and Myanmar (expected to be complete by 2021). A possible extension of the Trilateral Highway to Cambodia, Lao and Vietnam is also under consideration. A consensus on finalising the proposed protocol of the India-Myanmar-Thailand Motor Vehicle Agreement (IMT MVA) has been reached. This agreement will have a critical role in realizing easy movement of passenger, personal and cargo vehicles along roads linking India, Myanmar and Thailand.
- Kaladan Multimodal Project: to connect the eastern Indian seaport of

Kolkata with Sittwe seaport of Rakhine province of Myanmar. It will then link Sittwe seaport to Paletwa Chin state via the Kaladan river boat route, and then from Paletwa by road to Mizoram in Northeast India (expected to be complete by 2019). India kicked off the construction of the 109-km road project that connects Paletwa river terminal to Zorinpui on the Mizoram border in Myanmar, as part of the US$484-million Kaladan Multimodal project. India has already completed the rest of the Kaladan project work in Myanmar. This includes the construction of the Sittwe Port on Lakadan river mouth in Rakhine, construction of a river terminal 158 upstream at Paletwa and dredging of the Kaladan river.[21]

- Rhi-Tiddim road Project: road will provide connection between Zawkhathar in Mizoram and Mandalay in Myanmar.

  In addition, India is also negotiating an Agreement on maritime transport with ASEAN and also exploring ways to link our initiative with ASEAN Master Plan for Connectivity 2025.[22] India and Indonesia are setting up a Task Force to promote connectivity between Sumatra and Andaman Islands. India is also looking at developing Sabang port Indonesia (located near the strategic and vital shipping channel – the Strait of Malacca) in partnership with Indonesia.[23]

With regards to the third C i.e. culture, as mentioned earlier in the paper India shares cultural civilizational heritage links with these countries since millennia. In the cultural space the role of diaspora is important, vibrant people to people relations will provide a boost to bilateral ties between India and Southeast Asian Countries.

Conclusion

Therefore, it can be said that India and ASEAN share the quest for prosperity, stability and security. In a globalised, interdependent and interconnected world, institutional integration is crucial. ASEAN has a crucial role to play in the regional security architecture, in the light of complex geopolitical environment in the Indo-Pacific region. India's growing ties with ASEAN and the member countries bilaterally, along with the countries of Pacific and East Asia, forms the essence of its Act East policy. Relationship between India and ASEAN are a source of "balance and harmony" in the region.[24] As India looks beyond its immediate region, with its growing economic, maritime military capacities and strategic ambitions in the wider Indo-Pacific region, India appreciates centrality of ASEAN in the regional architecture.

NOTES

1 Prime Minister's Keynote Address at Shangri La Dialogue (June 01, 2018), June 01, 2018, https://www.mea.gov.in/Speeches-Statements.htm?dtl/29943/Prime+Ministers+Keynote+Address+at+Shangri+La+Dialogue+June+01+2018

2 Singh, Satyendra (1991) *Blueprint to Bluewater: The Indian Navy 1951-65*, Lancer India, p. 6, http://www.indiannavy.nic.in/about-indian-navy/blueprint-bluewater

3 Rajan 2012:187

4 Panikkar, K M (1996), *A Survey of Indian History*, p. 31, 4th edition, Asia Pub. House.

5 Rajan, K. (2012), "Emergence of Early Historic Trade in Peninsular India", in Manguin, Pierre Yves et. al. (eds.) *Early Interactions Between South and Southeast Asia: Reflections on Cross Cultural Exchange*, Institute of Southeast Asian Studies, Singapore, p.193.

6 Manguin, Pierre Yves et. al. (eds) (2012), *Early Interactions Between South and Southeast Asia: Reflections on Cross Cultural Exchange*, Institute of Southeast Asian Studies, Singapore.

7 Ibid. no. 4, pp. 32-33.

8 Prange, Sebastian R. (2013), "The Contested Sea: Regimes of Maritime Violence in the Pre-Modern Indian Ocean", *Journal of Early Modem History*, Vol. 17, pp. 9-33.

9 Sen, Tansen (2003) *Buddhism, diplomacy and trade: The realignment of Sino-Indian relations 600–1400, Honolulu: Association for Asian Studies*, University of Hawai'i Press, 2003, p.158.

10 Wink, André (1990), *Al-Hind: The making of the Indo-Islamic world: Early Medieval India and Expansion of Islam 7th -11th Centuries*, p. 65, Vol 1, Leiden, Brill

11 Ibid. no 2 pp. 8-9

12 Bose, Sugata (2oo6), *A Hundred Horizons: The Indian Ocean in the Age of Global Empire*, Permanent Black with Harvard University Press. Delhi

13 Ibid. p. 14

14 ASEAN Overview, https://asean.org/asean/about-asean/overview/

15 EAM'S Speech at India-ASEAN Commemorative Summit, http://www.iascs2018.gov.in/

16 India-ASEAN Relations, Ministry of External Affairs, http://mea.gov.in/aseanindia/20-years.htm

17 India supports regional security architecture: PM; Indicates readiness to play bigger role, Press Trust of India, http://ptinews.com/news/9236037_India-supports-regional-security-architecture—PM—Indicates-readiness-to-play-bigger-role

18 India-ASEAN Relations, Ministry of External Affairs, http://mea.gov.in/aseanindia/20-years.htm

19 Ibid. no. 16

20 Ibid.

21 Pratim Ranjan Bose, India Starts Construction of 1600cr Mizoram-Myanmar Kaladan Road, 17 April 2018, https://www.thehindubusinessline.com/news/india-starts-construction-of-1600-cr-mizoram-myanmar-kaladan-road/article23577107.ece

22 Ibid.

23 Address by Foreign Secretary on Regional Connectivity Conference: South Asia in the Indo-Pacific Context, 01 November 2018, https://www.mea.gov.in/Speeches-Statements.htm?dtl/30556/Address+by+Foreign+Secretary+at+the+Regional+Connectivity+Conference++South+Asia+in+the+IndoPacific+Context

24 Prime Minister's Address at India-ASEAN Commemorative Summit 2018, http://www.iascs2018.gov.in/

18

India-Myanmar Relations: Historical and Cultural Linkages and Possibility Factors with North-East Region of India

Remya R

Introduction

A particular region of a country may become a big factor in foreign policy decisions if it has immense strategic importance. Strategically, politically and economically, the North-East (NE) is the most sensitive region of India. Geo-strategically, the North-East is situated at the crossroads of south, southeast and east and shares much of its history and culture with Southeast Asia rather than with the rest of India. The interesting fact that, the level of geographical isolation represented that only about 1 per cent of the North-East is connected to the rest of India, with the remaining 99 per cent bordering other countries. Geographically and culturally, the seven states represent almost a separate collection of nations from mainland India.

Culture is the mirror of a society that presents before the nation those crucial features of the people within its ambit, which are sign of their identity. Focusing on culture, the values, norms and virtues occupy the foremost place in a culture. The culture of a particular country stabilizes in the heart and soul of its people. So, cultural differences of two different countries also bind strongly with common thinking and ideas of the peoples of the nations. Moreover, the governments of India and Myanmar took up ambitious initiatives to strengthen their cultural relations. (Thongam, 2017).

India and Myanmar have deep-rooted cultural, religious and historical ties. Both shares land border of over 1600 km as well as maritime boundary in the Bay of Bengal. Religious and linguistic heritage and ethnic ties shared both the countries due to its geographical proximity and even the cultural relations of the people of India particularly the North-East India with Myanmar (Govt. of India, 2014). Myanmar is one of the most important countries of ASEAN in terms of India's political, economic and strategic interest. Due to geographical proximity and cultural resemblance with the India's North-East region, the location of Myanmar is very important for India not only for its economic growth and development but also for the social and economic emancipation of North-East India. The North-East plays a major role in influencing India's foreign policy behaviour with Myanmar and stresses the fact that India's present policy of engagement with Myanmar is guided to serve its own interests, with specific relevance to the North-Eastern region. Many people in North-East share similar culture and genealogical background with the people in Myanmar.

As far as the history is concerned, Indo-Burmese contacts go back in time; Indians began to play an important part in Myanmar only after the conquest of Burma by the East India Company in 1826. The annual report of the administration of Burma in 1884-85 mentions the overwhelming presence of Indians in the country's money-lending business, retail trade, coolies in the Public Works Department or the railway stations, and even in rice cultivation. Moreover, Myanmar gained independence from Britishers almost the same period that India gained independence. The country gained independence but there were some ethnic conflicts. Even though, it has democracy, constitution, democratically elected government ruled Myanmar.

Burma was a province of British India until 1937, from which the point it became a separate British colony. The British famously exiled India's last Mughal emperor, Bahadur Shah Zafar until his death in Rangoon, simultaneously exiling Burma's last king, Thaibaw to Ratnagiri, India (Rajiv, 2011). India and Burma became independent in 1947 and 1948 respectively. Moreover, India's approach to Burma may be divided into three important phases since independence. The period 1948-62 was marked by friendship and international solidarity, while the years 1962-91 saw an unprecedented level of hostility as India embarked on its open condemnation of the Tatmadav. From 1991 onwards, as India's Myanmar policy metamorphosed into a gradual engagement with the junta, the stage was set for a new phase in the relationship (Sunniva, 2016).

However, in 1962 General Ne Win led military coup against the democratically elected government and established military rule till 2011, almost five decades Myanmar was under the military rule. Till 1962, there were no warmth bilateral relation between India and Myanmar. Following the anti-India riots of 1938, a series of laws were passed by the Burmese Government in 1938-40 targeted against the Indians, causing them huge losses. It was the friendship between Nehru and U Nu that averted any confrontation between the two countries.

The period 1948-62 marked cordial Indo-Burmese relations, and three themes stand out as important: close relations at the highest political levels, a similar ideological affinity and cooperation in international affairs, and the situation of the Indian diaspora in Burma. The relation between Indian and Burmese independent movements continued into independence and became an important factor. Personal friendship linked India's Nehru/Gandhi period to two of the most prominent families of Burma's democratic movement: the families of General Aung San and his political successor Prime Minister U Nu. Relationship between Jawaharlal Nehru and U Nu resulted annual official and private visits in the years 1948-62. To balance Myanmar's relation with neighbours including China and India was the major concern of U Nu, even though Burma nevertheless favoured India in a proper manner. India supplied arms to Rangoon's counter-insurgency efforts in 1949, and four years later U Nu and Nehru worked to counter increasing Naga demands for independence on the volatile Indo-Burmese border. Moreover, in July 1951, India and Burma signed a "Treaty of Friendship and Peace" in Rangoon's, agreeing on "everlasting peace and unalterable friendship" (Treaty of Friendship between India and Burma, 1951).

When General Ne Win in 1962 set aside U Nu in a coup condemned the move. Burma became a military one-party regime under the Burma Socialist Programme Party (BSPP), also dominating the country's external relations. While the setting aside of democracy in Burma provoked strong negative reactions in Delhi, India's attention was soon diverted by the October 1962 war with China. The Burmese military regime's neutral stand on the Sino-Indian war was in Delhi interpreted as support for China, straining Indo-Burmese relations further (Singh, 2013). Although, India-Myanmar relations were severely strained over the issue of Indian diaspora, connections at a high political level remained good, with continued close relations between influential political families. During 1960s saw the gradual progress in relations and made the visit of Ni Win to Delhi and Lal Bahadur Shastri visited Rangoon. Indira Gandhi kept this approach in her early years as prime minister, visited Rangoon in 1969, while New Delhi hosted Ni Win in

1968 and 1970. From the mid-1970s, however, relations again cooled. U Nu, exiled from Burma by Ne Win's regime, was granted political asylum by India, is a crucial point between the countries (Engh, 2016).

India's relations with Burma worsened after General Ne Win's takeover in 1962, due to the government's policy of the 'Burmese Way to Socialism' that led to a massive wave of nationalization. Although ties were close between Prime Minister Indira Gandhi and General Ne Win, in the following years, relations saw a further downturn because of India's support of the pro-democracy movement led by Aung San Suu Kyi. On the issue of Indian diaspora, the Indo-Burmese relations were more strained even though the political relations remained good to some extent. Despite the military take-over in Burma, Daw Khin Kyi remained the ambassador to India until 1967. During 1960s Ne Win visited Delhi and Lal Bahadur Shastri visited Rangoon. Indira Gandhi kept this rapprochement up in her early years as prime minister, visiting Rangoon in 1969, while New Delhi hosted ne Win in 1968 and 1970. Pragmatic concerns were also a factor.

Indo-Burmese connections reached an all-time low following the August 1988 pro-democracy demonstrations in Burma and the military administration's cruel repression of protests. India was the first and only Asian country to criticise the new Tatmadav junta of September 1988, the State Law and Restoration Council (SLORC) and its head General Saw Maung. Moreover, the Indian embassy in Rangoon helped pro-democratic activities and provided financial support for the democratic activity. Furthermore, the Indian government established refugee camps in Mizoram and Manipur states, and the government-run All India Radio (AIR) began broadcasting Burmese language reports on the SLORC repression (Garver, 260-61).

In August 1992 Burmese delegates visited India, represented the ministries of External Affairs, Home, Defence and Commerce, shared political and security concerns were identified. While India expressed concerns at the growing Sino-Myanmar cooperation (Dixit, 2000). In January 1994, Myanmar's Deputy Foreign Minister visited India and the countries signed a Memorandum of Understanding to enhance cooperation and to prevent "illegal and insurgent activities" as well as India-Myanmar Trade Treaty, aiming to expand border trade through two trading posts. In May the Indian Army Chief visited Myanmar, furthering the potential for cooperation on border stability (Malik, 1997).

Under Prime Minister Narasimha Rao, India formalized upon a new and more Pro-active direction in foreign policy, which combined a gradual approach towards the remaining super power, USA, with a turn towards East Asian region. The economically motivated policy, the Look East Policy (LEP) also aims at a strategic engagement with Southeast Asia as a result of India's search for a new friends and partners after the loss of its superpower patron in 1991. (Ganguly and Pardesi, 2009). Thus the LEP has economic, strategic and diplomatic aspects and these in totalities affect India's relations with Myanmar. Myanmar has come to attain a focal point within the LEP due to its geographical location, geostrategic relevance and natural resources.

India Cooperates with Myanmar

The major agreement signed between the two after India embarked on a policy of 'constructive engagement' was the border trade agreement of February 1995. At present, border trade is operational in Moreh (Manipur) and Zokhawthar (Mizoram). In a significant breakthrough in late 2008, the joint trade committee between India and Myanmar, led by the Indian Minister of State for Commerce and Power, Jairam Ramesh, and Myanmar's Minister for Commerce, Brigadier General Tin Naing Thein, agreed to convert the border trade at the Moreh-Tamu and Zokhawthar-Rhi border points to normal trade, paving the way for trading at Most Favoured Nation rates for all goods, except certain restricted items. It also decided to open border trade at a new border point, Avakhung (Nagaland)-Leshi (Myanmar), and to expand the current list of items for barter trade under the India-Myanmar Border Trade Agreement.

In March 2006, President A.P.J. Abdul Kalam reciprocated this by paying visits to Myanmar, the first ever visit by an Indian President to Myanmar. The visit shows the importance that India accords to a cordial relationship with Myanmar. India is currently one of Myanmar's two main military hardware suppliers, other than China. The culture of Myanmar was enriched by India. After and end of Cold-War India officially launched its 'Look East Policy' (LEP) in response to increased globalization and regionalization as well. A bilateral cultural co-operation agreement was signed in 2001 and was followed up with a cultural exchange program during 2004-2006. Between November 28 and December 07, 15 members of a cultural troupe from Myanmar visited India's North-Eastern region, particularly Nagaland, Manipur and Assam. This was organized by Union Ministry of Development of North-Eastern Region in coordination with India Embassy at Yangon, the Myanmar Embassy in New Delhi, Indian Council of Cultural Relations (ICCR), North-Eastern Council (NEC) and the North-Eastern state government.

India-Myanmar Dynamics

There are mainly four dynamics that India can regain its strategic interest in the region, viz.

Development Cooperation

This is mainly through four infrastructural or connectivity projects including Kaladan multi-modal project, 69 Bridges on Tamu-Kaleva road, Kaleva-Yargi road; these last two parts of the trilateral highway of India, Myanmar and Thailand. Rhittidam road connected Myanmar and Mizoram. All these projects have been lagging behind and will be finished by 2022.

Trade and Investment Cooperation

This is the major affair between India and Myanmar, and Myanmar basically exports agro-products or forest products to India. Currently the trade is almost 2 billion dollar less than the potential capacity that India targets, i.e. 3 billion dollar. The pulse import of Myanmar is the crucial export to India. The farmers of Myanmar found huge markets for the pulses in India. Apart from that the foreign exchange also enhanced through trade cooperation. They invested mainly on oil and natural gas but the investment can be enhanced through diversifying trade in the areas of steel, cement, power and textiles.

Security and Defence

Rohingya issue is the focal point in the security aspects of both the countries and these ethnic groups are targeted by Myanmar's military group; also it possesses a threat to Kaladan Multi Modal Transit Project. Rohingya issue is currently in the Rakine province at the capital of Sittwe, and the Kaladan project passes through Sittwe port. The disturbances in the Rakine state are a threat to this project.

Cultural Cooperation

India and Myanmar shares cultural bonds in terms of Buddhist heritage and shared the history of colonization. It also promotes strong cultural linkages and historical linkages that both countries share. The Buddhist diplomacy can be taken into account for the deeper cooperation. Building on this shared heritage, India is undertaking some key initiatives in the restoration of Ananda Temple in Bagan and the conservation of a large number of damaged pagodas.

Why India?

India is in a position to claim legitimacy in its promotion of Buddhist diplomacy for a number of reasons. Therefore, religious tourism can be promoted.

- Buddhist faith originated in India, therefore granting it singular historical legitimacy.
- India has numerous sites of importance to Buddhist faith such as Bodh Gaya, Sarnath and Nalanda.
- India has nurtured an image of being a protector of the persecuted because of the presence of Dalai Lama.

These cultural linkages enhance the people-to-people contacts, cultural activities including arts and sports, promote tourism either medical or recreational tourism, create economic or employment opportunities that altogether resulted in increased bilateral, political and trade relations between both.

North-East as a Bridge to South-East Asia via Myanmar

Until the late 1980s, the Centre saw the North-East from the strategic point of view, with security being the chief concern. But in the 1990s, several factors led to a change in strategy. The foremost among them was the end of the Cold War, which compelled leaders worldwide (including those in India) to establish relations with regions that were earlier not possible. One of these regions for India was South-East Asia, which had become remarkably successful in achieving high levels of gross domestic product. Although India had cultural linkages with the region in the past, a concrete long-term relationship did not take place due to Cold War politics.

In 1997, Myanmar became part of ASEAN, bringing South-East Asia next door to India. Hence, the 'Look East Policy' launched by India to establish trade relations with South-East Asia gained much more substance, with the added advantage being the use of the North-East as a bridge to the region. Since cultural diplomacy was a component of this policy, the presence of common sociocultural ethnic links across the borders was a strong motivating factor to promote cooperation between the two countries.

To realize peace and development in the North-Eastern region of India, stability and connectivity are the prime necessities and herein comes the importance of Myanmar. The opening of border trade can re-establish historical trade that will help the local economy. For the North-East, Myanmar is significantly important in the absence of cooperation from Bangladesh. The access to sea can also be provided by Myanmar and ports in both Bangladesh and Myanmar can be jointly utilized to promote the North-East as a commercial centre. Possibilities also lie in joint exploration of gas and oil in North-East India and Myanmar. Therefore, it is an important phase for the region and the challenge lies in employing the emerging opportunities.

Again, all the states of North-East have their breath taking, pristine natural beauty. The region is known for bio-diversity, hill stations, heritage sites, its unique culture, tradition, etc. Tourism can be a very flourishing industry for sustainable development of the region as the whole region is suitable for eco-tourism, adventure tourism and cultural tourism. If the NER is connected with South East Asia with modern communication system along with requisite infrastructural facilities, almost all tourists from the outside world visiting the South East Asia region would fly or drive a few hundred kilometers more to enjoy the scenic and cultural beauty of NER.

Since the late 1990s, the Government of India has been making concerted efforts for economic development of the North-East. Special packages of incentives aimed at industrial development were announced in 1997. This was followed by the North-East Industrial and Investment Promotion Policy in 2007. The government of India has made substantial investment for improving road and rail connectivity within the region.

Conclusion

India must also conduct people-to-people diplomacy, involving the North-Eastern provinces in such exercises. This will lead to a better understanding between the two and also re-establish the ethnic bonds among the border communities. Under its 'Look East Policy', the overall picture of North-East India has transformed from a barrier to a bridge. Indian diplomatic establishment positively hopes that by developing the North-Eastern region as a commercial hub and connecting it to South-East Asia, all-round prosperity will result. To realize this, stability and connectivity are the prime necessities and herein comes the importance of Myanmar.

The opening of border trade can re-establish historical trade that will help the local economy. For the North-East, Myanmar is doubly important in the absence of cooperation from Bangladesh. The access to sea can also be provided by Myanmar and ports in both Bangladesh and Myanmar can be jointly utilized to promote the North-East as a commercial centre. To conclude, one can say that the North-East is one of the important domestic determinants of India's policy towards Myanmar and the cooperation of the latter will be of utmost importance not only to resolve the problem areas of the region but also to connect the North-East to South-East Asia for the successful implementation of India's 'Look East Policy' and a land bridge capable of giving India a "strategic, cultural and economic space" to the East.

Boosting ties with Myanmar will also rekindle the old cultural ties generating the feeling of goodwill among the people. It is said that maintaining cordial relations with a country only on economic grounds is tardy, tiring and temporary but if it is coupled with common cultural heritage, social and religious affinities, it provides great input to have a leap not only on economic terms but also strengthening bilateral solidarity. Moreover, the present Modi led government is placing a strong accent on the use of soft power in India's foreign policy. One of the novel manifestations of these initiatives has been engagement in Buddhist diplomacy. Since the time 'soft power' was conceptualised by Joseph Nye in the 1990s. Nye posited that conventional hard power tactics predicated on military might would no longer be the sole factor in determining the degree to which a nation commanded power in the international system.

Communicating India's Soft Power: Buddha to Bollywood (book) by Daya Krishan Thussu made strong aspects of soft power rely not on the export of cultural products but on promoting certain shared religious and cultural associations. It created a platform for the further relations. It would be better to simply call these "attempts at cultural diplomacy". Today, 97 percent of the world's Buddhist population lives in the Asian continent, and a number of countries such as Bhutan, Myanmar, Thailand and Sri Lanka conceive of Buddhism as intrinsic to their national values and identity. It is within this context that one can understand the efforts of the Indian government at incorporating Buddhist heritage in order to form a basis for further diplomatic, economic, cultural and strategic associations within its foreign policy.

REFERENCES

Bhatia, R. (2011). Myanmar-India Relations: The Way Forward, *India Foreign Affairs Journal*, 6(3).

Bhatia, R. (2016). India-Myanmar Relations: Changing Contours, Strategic Analysis, 40(1), pp.67-68

Devi, S, T. (2017). Cultural Bond between India and Myanmar: Perception from the Past, IOSR Journal of Humanities and Social Sciences, 22(10)

Dixit, J, N. 'Road to Mandalay'. The Telegraph, March 22, 2000. http://www. telegraphindia.com/archives/archive.html.

Egreteau, R. (2011). A Passage to Burma? India, Development and Democratisation in Myanmar, *Contemporary Politics*, 17(4), pp.467-486

Engh, S. (2016). India's Myanmar Policy and the Sino-Indian Great Game, Asian Affairs, XLVII (1)

Government of India, Ministry of External Affairs, India-Myanmar Relations, December 2014, Accessible via http://www.mea.gov.in/portal/ForeignRelation/India-Myanmar Relations

Holliday, I. (2005). Rethinking the United States' Myanmar Policy, *Asian Survey*, 45(4), pp.607-608

Saikia, P. (2009). North-East India as a Factor in India's Diplomatic Engagement with Myanmar: Issues and Challenges, *Strategic Analysis*, 33(6), pp.877-889

Singh, A. (2013). Emerging Trends in India Myanmar Relations, Maritime Affairs: *Journal of the National Maritime Foundation of India*, 8(2), p.31

Singh, S, L. (2010). India and the Quest for Democracy in Myanmar: Rethinking India's Myanmar Policy, *The Indian Journal of Political Science*, 71(3), pp.1003-1016

Singh, S. (1998). Myanmar: The Strategic Hub of the 21st Century Asia, *Journal of the United Service Institute of India*, 128(532), p.249

Sumit G and Manjeet S. P. (2009). Explaining Sixty Years of India's Foreign Policy, *India Review*, 8(1) p. 14

Treaty of Friendship between India and the Union of Burma, 7 July 1951. Accessible via http://www.mea.gov.in/bilateral-documents.htm?dtl/6645/Treaty-of-war-and-friendsip

19

India's Act East Policy: In Retrospect and Prospects

Ramesh Kumar

Introduction

Act East Policy (AEP) constitutes the most vital defining feature of India's overall foreign policy, which is successor of the earlier Look East Policy (LEP) and is now on the trajectory of India's policy towards Indo-Pacific region. New geopolitical and geo-economic realities obtaining at the cusp of the inauguration of the post-Cold War period at the outset of the decade of the 1990s required India to embrace economic liberalization policies with effect from 1991 onwards. Emphasis on embarking upon the export-promotion led growth model necessitated identification of the potential target markets. It was in this backdrop that India launched its "Look East Policy" (LEP) in 1992 that emphasized on two-track approach: looking upon East Asian nations of Japan, South Korea and Singapore as probable potential sources of technology and investment; and exploring the emerging economies of Southeast Asia as destinations of high potential export markets.

Accordingly, India brooked no delay in fostering close ties with the member nations of Association of Southeast Asian Nations (ASEAN) by joining as Sectoral Dialogue Partner of ASEAN in 1992. The first decade of the 21st Century witnessed India consolidating its ties with the region by entering into several regional trade agreements, viz., India-Singapore Comprehensive Economic Cooperation Agreement (CECA) (2005), India-South Korea Comprehensive Economic Partnership Agreement (CEPA) (2009), India-ASEAN Free Trade Agreement (FTA) (2010), India-Japan CEPA (2011), India-Malaysia CECA (2011) etc.[1] During the ongoing second decade of the 21st Century, India's partnership with ASEAN has not only scaled new heights, albeit India has also fostered strong bilateral relations with countries in its immediate and extended neighbourhood, such as Bangladesh, Mauritius, Myanmar, Sri Lanka, Singapore, Vietnam, etc., as well as also negotiating various sub-regional programmes and projects like Bangladesh-Bhutan-India-Nepal (BBIN), the Trilateral Highway, etc., and is "actively contributing to the success of several regional initiatives such as ASEAN, EAS, BIMSTEC, IORA, RCEP, among others."[2]

From Look East to Act East

The year 2012 marked the completion of two decades of the practice of LEP and during this period multiple benefits had accrued in the form of new institutional arrangements, agreements and regular forms of engagements and cooperation between India and the ASEAN. This period was also characterized by India making attempts at fostering close ties with the stakeholders beyond ASEAN, especially with China, Japan and South Korea. The year 2012 also witnessed celebrations of the first decade of the summit-level partnership between India and ASEAN at 2012 India-ASEAN Commemorative Summit. Contemporary geopolitical and geo-economic developments obtaining at the global, regional and domestic levels required both India and the

ASEAN to invest more in cementing their multilateral relationship and India felt the need for extending its outreach beyond ASEAN and East Asia to what it called the "Extended Neighbourhood", encompassing countries of the Asia-Pacific region as well.

India's Look East Policy was rechristened as 'Act East Policy' by India's Prime Minister Narendra Modi in his opening statement at the 12th ASEAN-India Summit in 2014 held at Nay Pyi Taw in Myanmar, when he said: "A new era of economic development, industrialization, and trade has begun in India. Externally, India's 'Look East Policy' has become 'Act East Policy'."[3] While elaborating Act East Policy (AEP), India's Minister of State for External Affairs told the Lok Sabha on 23 December 2015 that India's AEP focuses on "the extended neighbourhood in the Asia-Pacific region" and it has gained political, strategic and cultural dimensions including establishment of institutional mechanisms for dialogue and cooperation. While stating that India has upgraded its relations to strategic partnership with Indonesia, Vietnam, Malaysia, Japan, Republic of Korea (ROK), Australia, Singapore and Association of Southeast Asian Nations (ASEAN). He further informed the House that India has also forged close ties with all countries in the Asia-Pacific region. He further added that objective of the AEP was to "promote economic cooperation, cultural ties and develop strategic relationship with countries in the Asia-Pacific region through continuous engagement at bilateral, regional and multilateral levels thereby providing enhanced connectivity to the States of North Eastern Region including Arunanchal Pradesh with other countries in our neighbourhood."[4]

While differentiating between LEP and AEP, Rajiv Bhatia[5] suggests that AEP encompasses wider area than just ASEAN and fits well with the change of discourse from East Asia to the Indo-Pacific. While alluding to AEP's greater stress on defence and security cooperation with the nations of the East than before, he adds that the highlight of the AEP is the stronger focus on the role of India's North East Region in cultivating relations with ASEAN along with high priority to political relations at the leadership level than in the past as a result of which AEP has acquired "a much larger profile as a sub-set of the Indian foreign policy than was the case in the preceding years."[6]

Some scholars have opined that AEP is an upgraded version of the previous LEP.[7] Viewed in a broad perspective, AEP seemingly aims at expanding India's economic and political activities beyond interactions with its immediate neighbours to the extended neighbourhood comprising countries of Southeast Asia, Northeast Asia, and part of Oceania. Apart from emphasizing on more "direct and engaging economic and security interactions"[8] with those countries, AEP's emphasis on this region can be appreciated as in response to multiple changes in domestic and international conditions. According to some scholars, India's strong foreign policy drive through AEP entails the characteristic of encompassing all ten ASEAN countries in Southeast Asia, five countries in Northeast Asia (China, Japan, South Korea, Taiwan and Mongolia) and three countries in Pacific-Oceania (Australia, New Zealand, Fiji) in addition to its immediate neighbors, Bangladesh and Sri Lanka; thereby, "proactive engagement with these countries leads India to engage directly on more global issues, from which India had historically kept its distance, even during the period of LEP governance to some extents."[9]

Economic Cooperation

Economic cooperation, in terms of trade and investment between India and ASEAN on the one hand and India and East Asia on the other hand, has registered major strides in the aftermath of AEP. In 2017, India was a sixth largest trading partner of ASEAN and the bilateral total trade between the two sides stood over $ 81 billion in 2017-2018 constituting 10 per cent of India's total trade. The services sector affords India ample advantages in its economic relations with ASEAN.

With the completion of the ratification process of the Agreement on Trade in Services under the Framework Agreement on Comprehensive Economic Cooperation between ASEAN and India, this cooperation is prone to get further impetus. This agreement is designed to "fully tap the potential, offered by the vast markets of ASEAN and India through the effective implementation of the ASEAN-India Free Trade Area, and the operationalization of the ASEAN-India Trade and Investment Centre."[10]

There are explicit indications that the ongoing negotiations between India and ASEAN as well as other countries of East and Northeast Asia with regard to Regional Comprehensive Economic Cooperation (RCEP), which are expected to be completed in 2019, is likely to be the world's largest trading bloc encompassing about 40 per cent of global GDP. In the wake of already existing India's trade deficit with many RCEP members, including with China ($ 63 billion), South Korea ($ 11.96 billion), Indonesia ($ 12.47 billion), and Australia ($ 10.16 billion); nevertheless, many domestic and international trade experts have advised for a cautious approach to RCEP.[11] The avowed objective of the RCEP is said to be to foster a "global trade environment that is open, mutually beneficial, rules-based and inclusive."[12]

India has reiterated its commitment to connectivity cooperation via land, air and maritime routes with ASEAN in consonance with the Masterplan on ASEAN Connectivity 2025 that was adopted on 6 September 2016. Completion of the India-Myanmar-Thailand Trilateral Highway Project is likely to facilitate extension of this project to Cambodia, Laos, and Vietnam; and Jakarta-based Economic Research Institution (ERIA) is likely to conduct a feasibility study on this aspect of extension.[13] While emphasizing significance of trade and investment in augmenting prosperity and security of the Indo-Pacific region, India has repeatedly reiterarted its commitment to the early conclusion of a balanced and comprehensive RCEP.[14]

Political and Security Cooperation

AEP has enabled India to further consolidate its already friendly political and security relations with ASEAN nations. Exchange of high-level visits by political leaders and participation in bilateral and multilateral summits have enabled both sides to reap good political dividends. Representing India at the 15th ASEAN-India Summit at Manila, Philippines, held in November 2017, PM Modi, while reiterating India's support, together with ASEAN, towards a rule-based order for the oceans and sea that is critical for the growth and development of the Indo-Pacific region, also underlined India's commitment to policy of zero tolerance and comprehensive approach in fighting violent extremism and terrorism, and called for the adoption of the Comprehensive Convention on International Terrorism in the United Nations.[15]

On 18 July 2018, India hosted the 2nd India-ASEAN Workshop on Blue Economy at New Delhi with a view to promoting the development of Blue Economy in the region and enhancing India-ASEAN cooperation in Blue Economy. Blue Economy is vastly perceived as a driver of inclusive and sustainable economic growth and development and interestingly, both ASEAN and India have identified Blue Economy as a new pillar of economic activity in the coastal areas and linked hinterlands through sustainable tapping of oceanic resources.[16]

India has been making efforts at deepening maritime security collaborations with willing partners in the 'East' as a part of its Act East Policy and this, according to David Scott, is often termed as a strategy for creating 'diamond necklace' against Chinese 'string of pearls' in the South China Sea.[17] India has entered into a strategic partnership with Vietnam since November 2007 and in 2011 New Delhi offered Vietnamese forces facilities for training and capacity building, reportedly in return for berthing rights at Nha Trang.[18] Indian naval ships have been paying goodwill visits to Philippines and the first meeting of the Joint Defence Cooperation Committee between the two countries was held in January 2012. In 2012 a trilateral mechanism involving South Korea and Japan was also set up.

In January 2018, during the course of the official visit of leaders of the 10-member ASEAN nations in New Delhi to participate in India's Republic Day celebrations, strong emphasis was focused on maritime cooperation under both traditional and non-traditional realms in rule-based maritime domain.[19] On 8-9 June 2018, India hosted the 3rd EAS Conference on Maritime Security and Cooperation in Bhubaneshwar (Odisha), India, in which high ranking officials from thirteen EAS countries took part and deliberations of the conference veered round issues pertaining to Maritime Cooperation, Maritime Security, Maritime Safety, Good Order at Sea, Blue Economy and Sustainable use of Ocean Resources.[20]

On 19-20 July 2018, India hosted the 10th anniversary edition of Delhi Dialogue (DDX), at New Delhi on the theme "Strengthening India-ASEAN Maritime Cooperation." Over 400 delegates, featuring political leaders, policy makers, senior officials, diplomats, business leaders, think tanks and academicians from India and ASEAN Member States (AMS also participated in the event. Delhi Dialogue is an annual Track 1.5 forum for discussing politico-security, economic and socio-cultural issues between ASEAN and India. While addressing the gathering, India's External Affairs Minister emphasized on a forward-looking agenda that seeks to recapture our common maritime heritage. Some of the areas identified wherein ASEAN and India could cooperate and work together were Blue Economy, Maritime Safety and Security to include Humanitarian Assistance and Disaster Relief (HADR), countering terrorism and piracy at sea, and countering transnational crime.[21]

Strategically vital sea-lanes-of-communication (SLOCs) are located in the region that are extremely crucial for India's maritime trade and security; hence maritime security cooperation between India and ASEAN assumes added geopolitical as well as geo-economic significance. It is in this backdrop that India is called upon to play a vital role in the Indo-Pacific region for ensuring regional, peace, security and stability in the region. The AEP initiative has enabled India to foster closer strategic and economic cooperation with the countries of this region. Concurrently, China's growing maritime influence in the India Ocean is perceived with some skepticism by ASEAN nations as well as India; therefore, Indian strategy of enhancing security and strategic partnership with ASEAN and other countries of the region is in consonance with the broader vision of China's deepening influence in Indian Ocean region.[22]

China Factor

China is a significant factor in India's Act East Policy. According to Pankaj Jha, who recently was in China and interacted with Chinese experts and intellectuals, within China, there have been apprehensions and also concerns with regard to India's Act East Policy—the successor to the much-celebrated Look East Policy. In his opinion, this skepticism is because of the nomenclature of the policy which has transited from 'Look' to 'Act'.[23] While alluding to the view of Chinese scholars that "India's increasing interactions in its periphery as well as strategic partnerships with Korea, Japan and Australia might be the blueprint for larger trans regional ambitions", Pankaj Jha opines that "Chinese scholars' view indicates that there is less knowledge about the contours of India's Act East Policy and how it will configure in the larger geo-political dynamics."[24]

On its part, India while pursuing its AEP along with emphasis on fostering close security and strategic maritime partnership with the ASEAN nations and countries of the Indo-Pacific region, New Delhi has adopted a cautious approach and has frequently made it explicitly clear that its maritime policies are not directed against China. Undeniably, India seems more vocal about China's maritime assertiveness; nevertheless, "it still remains a distant and reluctant balancer."[25] This amply demonstrates the differences between words of Indian strategic elites and pronouncements of policymakers and the Indian Navy either in Indian Ocean or South China Sea where it maintains a benign and largely constabulary operations. India is conscious of its limited naval power projection capabilities.

Limitations

India's AEP has been suffering from some limitations that have affected the realization of vast potentials entailed by this policy that were articulated at the time of its launch. The tasks as promised in the Delhi Declaration 2018 have largely remained incomplete. Among those tasks, three sets of tasks are worth mentioning. Firstly, completion and scaling up the digital connectivity projects in Cambodia, Lao PDR, Myanmar and Viet Nam still remain. Secondly, the Trilateral Highway (TH) is still incomplete and there is a need to resume the replacement of 69 bridges along the TH and negotiate the Trilateral Motor Vehicle Agreement (MVA).[26] Besides, there is also need to continue with the high impact projects like fellowships for integrated PhD programmes to ASEAN scholars; setting up a network of universities to encourage greater inter-university exchanges between ASEAN and India; celebrating the year 2019 as ASEAN-India year of tourism; along with resuming the work of the Project Development Fund (PDF), among others.[27]

India's dismal track record in its infrastructure building in its Northeast region is another indicator of its slow pace of expediting the construction of infrastructure in the neighbouring countries of Myanmar and Thailand. With regard to trilateral highway with Myanmar and Thailand, Thailand is reported to have completed its part of the highway. Apparently, the government has seeming laid more emphasis on its official statements, but there is very little to show on the ground. In the wake of India's inability to develop even its own connectivity with ASEAN, its promises of extending help to others in ASEAN with infrastructure "are bound to sound hollow. India needs to do more to convert its rhetoric into reality."[28]

Prospects

The Act East Policy affords a vast array of opportunities for India to enhance its cooperation with ASEAN nations and the countries of East Asia and the Pacific region. Concomitantly, the region is also fraught with threats and challenges. Undeniably, India along with its ASEAN neighbours is already facing new challenges in economic, security and environment. Besides, the ongoing the US-China standoff over trade, which has been exacerbating instead of cooling down; along with threat posed by China's military assertiveness in the South China Sea, together contribute to insecurity and destabilization of the region. Alarmingly, this region is also vulnerable to many non-traditional security threats like cyber security, terrorism, natural disasters, to mention a few. Another worrisome problem is the increasing indulgence of many countries in taking recourse to protectionism, both economic and otherwise.

At the initial stage of the launch of China's Belt and Road Initiative (BRI), many countries of the region were attracted by this initiative; nonetheless, with the passage of time the rising debt burden of these countries, especially Sri Lanka, Pakistan and Malaysia etc., has made these countries gradually getting disenchanted. Accordingly, Southeast and East Asia "would like India to play a more proactive role given the fact that these countries have been witnessing too much 'China' in their homeland."[29] Therefore, the region affords ample opportunities for India to take the tide at the ebb by addressing these challenges by forging new partnership. Prime Minister Modi has recently widened the ambit of Act East Policy by linking it with the term Indo-Pacific, which attained operation clarity when PM Modi unveiled India's vision in his address to the Shangri-La Dialogue on 1 June 2018 by emphasizing that for India the geography of the Indo-Pacific stretches from the shores of Africa to that of Oceania that also includes the Pacific Island countries.[30]

Act East Policy constitutes the bedrock of India's Indo-Pacific vision, with the centrality of ASEAN at the core. According to one report, India has set up an Indo-Pacific wing in its Ministry of External Affairs in April 2019; and this wing "provides a strategic coherence to the Prime Minister's Indo-Pacific vision, integrating the IORA, the ASEAN region and the Quad to the Indo-Pacific dynamic."[31] Undoubtedly, these are welcome moves; nonetheless, there is urgent need to speed up the completion of already pledged projects, especially with the ASEAN countries and a failure on India's part in this regard will not only contribute to erosion of India's credentials albeit it could pave way for expansion of Chinese sphere of influence in the region.

NOTES

1. Debashis Chakraborty & Anushree Chakraborty, "India's Act East Policy: Walking the Talk", *MPRA Paper* No. 88034, p. 1, 26 July 2018, available at https://mpra.ub.uni-muenchen.de/88034/

2. Prabir De, "Act East to Act Indo-Pacific: Agenda for the new government", *Economic Times*, June 1, 2019.
3. Opening Statement by Prime Minister at the 12th India-ASEAN Summit, Nay Pyi Taw, Myanmar, November 12, 2014. Available at http://mea.gov.in/aseanindia/SpeechStatement ASEM.htm?dtl/22566/Opening+Statement+by+Prime+Minister+ at+ the+ 12th+IndiaASEAN+Summit+Nay+Pyi+Taw+Myanmar.
4. Press Information Bureau (PIB), Government of India, "Act East Policy", pib.nic.in, 23 December 2015, available at: http://pib.nic.in/newsite/PrintRelease.aspx?relid=133837 .
5. Rajiv Bhatia, "India's Act East Policy: Gains and Prospects", gatewayhouse.org, 8 April 2019, available at: https://www.gatewayhouse.in/indias-act-east-policy/ .
6. Ibid.
7. See Kanti Bajpai, "Narendra Modi's Pakistan and China Policy: Assertive Bilateral Diplomacy and Active Coalition Diplomacy," *International Affairs*, Vol. 93, No. 1, 2017, pp.69-91. Also see Takenori Horimoto, "Explaining India's Foreign Policy: From Dream to Realization of Major Power," International Relations of the Asia-Pacific, Vol. 17, No. 3, 2017, pp. 463-496; and Jagannath P. Panda, "From 'Look East' to 'Act East': India as a Security Actor and Security Provider," *EAI Working Paper*, November, 2016, pp. 1-26.
8. For details see, Sinderpal Singh, *Modi and the World: (Re)Constructing Indian Foreign Policy*, Singapore: World Scientific Publishing Co. Inc., 2017.
9. Wooyeal Paik and Rajiv Kumar, "India's Extended 'Act East' Outreach to Northeast Asia: Its Economic and Security Interactions with China, Japan, and South Korea", *The Korean Journal of International Studies*, Vol.17, No. 1, (April 2019), pp. 1-29.
10. Ministry of External Affairs, "India-ASEAN Relations", MEA website, available at: https:// mea.gov.in/aseanindia/20-years.htm.
11. Udai Bhanu Singh, "Significance of India's Act East Policy and Engagement with ASEAN", *IDSA Backgrounder*, 4 December 2018, New Delhi: IDSA.
12. Text of Delhi Declaration of the ASEAN-India Commemorative Summit to Mark the 25th Anniversary of ASEAN-India /Dialogue Relations, MEA website at https://asean.org/ wpcontent/uploads/2018/01/Delhi-Declararion_adopted-25-an-2018.pdf.
13. Udai Bhanu Singh, "Significance of India's Act East Policy", n. 11.
14. Prime Minister Modi's speech at Singapore, see 'Visit of Prime Minister to Singapore to attend ASEAN-India Breakfast Summit, the 13th East Asia Summit and related meetings', available at MEA website, at: https://mea.gov.in/pressreleases.htm?dtl/30601/Visit+of+Prime+Minister+ to+ Singapore+to+attend+ASEANIndia+Breakfast+Summit+the+13th+East+Asia+Summit+ and+ related+meetings.
15. Ministry of External Affairs, Annual Report 2017-2018, New Delhi: MEA, p. 40.
16. Ministry of External Affairs, Annual Report 2018-2019, New Delhi: MEA, p. 88.
17. David Scott, (2013), "India's Role in the South China Sea: Geopolitics and Geo-economics in Play", *India Review*, Vol. 12, No. 2, 2013, p. 60.
18. Danielle Rajendram, (2014), 'India's new Asia-Pacific strategy: Modi acts East', Policy Paper, Sydney: Lowy Institute for International Policy, 2014, available at: https:// www.lowyinstitute.org/sites/default/files/indias-new-asia-pacific-strategy-modi-acts-east.pdf.
19. Dipanjan Roy Chaudhury, "India, ASEAN leaders agree to boost maritime cooperation", *Economic Times*, 26 January 2018.
20. MEA, Annual Report 2018-2019, n. 16, p. 88.
21. Ibid, p. 89.

22. Harsh V. Pant, (2015), 'Modi's outreach to three Indian Ocean states', The Japan Times (Tokyo), 22 March 2015.
23. Pankaj Jha, "India's Act East Policy and Chinese Perceptions", 6 December 2018, available at: https://www.vifindia.org/2018/december/06/india-s-act-east-policy-and-chinese-perceptions.
24. Ibid.
25. Cheitgi Bajpaee, "The 'China Factor' in India's Maritime Engagement with Southeast Asia", E-International Relations, 1 January 2019, available at: https://www.e-ir.info/2019/01/01/the-china-factor-in-indias-engagement-wit-sutheast-asia/
26. Prabir De, "Act East to Act Indo-Pacific", n.2.
27. Ibid.
28. Rajeswari Pillai Rajagopalan, "Minding the gaps in India's act east policy", orfonline.org, 21 September 2018, available at: https://www.orfonline.org/research/44380-minding-the-gaps-in-indias-act-east-policy/.
29. Debashis Chakraborty & Anushree Chakraborty, "India's Act East Policy", n.1.
30. Ministry of External Affair, "Prime Minister's Key Address at Shangri La Dialogue", 1 June 2018, MEA website, available at: https://www.mea.gov.in/Speeches-Statements.htm?dtl/29943/Prime+Ministers+Keynote+Address+at+Shangri+La+Dialogue+June+01+2018.
31. Harsh V. Pant & Premesha Saha, "Charting a clear course in the Indo-Pacific", *The Hindu,* 18 May 2019,

20

India-ASEAN Relations in the Era of Act East Policy: Issues and Concerns

Sabu Thomas

Introduction

Association of South East Asian Nations (ASEAN) is one of the most prominent regional alliance in South Asia. The association was founded on August 8, 1967 as an alliance of five countries, and is today home to 625 million people. The region is an area of extreme diversity and also of strategic importance to the global security architecture. ASEAN achieved greater cohesion in the mid-1970s following a change in balance of power after the end of the Vietnam War. The region's dynamic economic growth during the 1970s strengthened the organization, enabling ASEAN to adopt a unified response to many of the local and global issues. The end of the Cold War allowed ASEAN countries to exercise greater political independence in the region, and the organisation emerged as a leading voice on regional trade and security issues.

The working of ASEAN as a regional forum is characterized with informality and personal contacts which in turn prioritizes a consensus-based, non-conflictual way of addressing problems. It offers a community-model of association to address regional issues (Singh, 2013). This quiet diplomacy has actually helped the organization to smoothly travel over the troubled waters in the region. Even though the long-cherished destination of ASEAN-Southeast Asia becoming a group of countries living in peace, stability and prosperity—is still a distant dream, the group of countries contains enormous potentials to create a power balance in the region. It is in this context the Indian policy orientations toward ASEAN is to be evaluated.

The Act East Policy of Prime Minister Narendra Modi offer long term collaborative projects among the partner states in the region. These projects are aimed to bring more cohesive bonds between the state actors and to promote development in the area. It is also to share the larger benefits of development in a win-win basis. There are more avenues of cooperation with the partner states so as to make a strong unity in the region with better role for India. The Indian foreign policy quarters are in search of new partners to counter the China factor and to accelerate its journey to global economic leadership. Act East policy has contributed much to this direction. This initiative is supplemented by maintaining close relationship with regional actors and forums. ASEAN is one of the best opportunities in this direction.

ASEAN: Understanding the diversity

ASEAN is described as a potential political union with enough strength to unite the many independent political entities in the region. There were great dreams about a south Asian vision of sharing and joining. But the idea of a united South Asia under the banner of ASEAN is a too far stretched vision. ASEAN in a general sense is a mix of diversities and the projection of diversities in the organization is a great threat to any demand for unity. ASEAN consists of countries under varying stages of development and growth. There is an ASEAN member like Singapore, with an average yearly per capita income of around $82,000 and countries like Cambodia, with a yearly per capita income of $3,300. These variations are also reflected in economic growth, human development indexes etc.

Table 1: Human Development Index of Selected ASEAN countries

Country	*Singapore*	*Brunei*	*Malaysia*	*Thailand*	*ASEAN*	*Vietnam*	*Indonesia*	*Cambodia*	*Myanmar*
HDI (2017)	0.932	0.853	0.802	0.755	0.695	0.694	0.694	0.582	0.578
Rating	Very High	Very High	Very High	High	Medium	Medium	Medium	Medium	Medium

Source: World Bank Data, various sources

ASEAN is home to the world's three largest religions—Christianity, Buddhism and Islam. Different faiths and sub faiths exists in the region and there are also religious frictions across the countries. With regard to political ideologies, Myanmar, Cambodia, and Laos emphasize non-interference while older member countries focus on co-operation and co-ordination. These differences hinder efforts to find common solutions to particular issues.

The ASEAN Innings

ASEAN provides a big market and also a production hub for Asia. The economic opportunities offered by ASEAN states is highly appreciated by the regional partners. There are many ventures to establish free trade areas by neighboring countries. The region's dynamic economic growth during the 1970s strengthened the organization and the organization was capable of adapting a unified response to Vietnam's invasion of Cambodia in 1979. ASEAN's first summit meeting, held in Bali, Indonesia in 1976, resulted in an agreement on several industrial projects and the signing of a Treaty of Amity and Cooperation, and a Declaration of Concord.[1]

In the 30th anniversary meeting held in Kuala Lumpur; ASEAN leaders adapted a Vision 2020. This vision, targets the realization of a single ASEAN community, sees Southeast Asia becoming a group of countries which are: "outward looking, living in peace, stability and prosperity". The Vision 2020 also provides for peace and stability, closer economic integration, human development, sustainable development, cultural heritage, etc.

The idea of an Asian Currency Unit (ACU) is another great objective of the organization. This idea involves a proposed basket of Asian currencies, similar to the European Currency Unit. The overall goal of a common currency is to contribute to the financial stability of a regional economy, including price stability. It means lower cost of cross-border business through the elimination of currency risk. It is also expected that greater flows of intra-trade would put pressure on prices, resulting in cheaper goods and services.[2]

ASEAN lies at the heart of many important global industrial production chains in manufacturing and services trade. These allow countries to specialize in different parts of the production process, tapping the competitive advantages of each location. There is also the advantage of young and skilled labour force in the region. It is estimated that one-third of the total global migrant stock comes from this region. This gives scope for more skill mobility and competitive labour markets.

In 2006 China proposed a free trade area. Leaders of ASEAN and China decided to explore measures aimed at economic integration within the region. They endorsed the establishment of an ASEAN–China Free Trade Area. China's transformation into a major economic power in the 21st century has led to an increase of foreign investments in the region[3]. It is found that by the year 2015, ASEAN's total merchandise trade with China reached $346.5 billion and this comes around 15.2% of ASEAN's trade.

Issues and Concerns

Southeast Asia has many strengths, which include its relatively youthful workforce, its expanding middle class and its GDP growth rates. At the same time there are many issues and challenges in the region. It is not supposed to provide a security architecture for the region. Thu, (2018) observes;

> ASEAN's role in providing for regional security requires clarification. ASEAN is, and will remain, a forum for expressing concerns, and even that has been frequently challenged. ASEAN is not a vehicle to solve security related problems, nor is it a collective security mechanism (Thu, 2018:30).

The development of ASEAN as a strong regional organization is hindered by many factors-internal and external. Internally ASEAN is troubled with many territorial disputes such as the Cambodian–Thai border dispute.[4] There are also strong ideological differences among member states. Politically, there are fragile democracies like Philippines and Indonesia. Some member states are ruled by authoritarian governments. There is an absolute monarchy in Brunei. In Thailand there is a military dictatorship. Laos and Vietnam follow a single-party communist rule. Keeping ASEAN together despite these deep cultural, economic and political differences was always a hilarious task and the miracle is that it has not broken-down despite of all the differences.

The region and the individual member states are troubled by threat of terrorism. The organization of self-proclaimed Islamic State (IS) has a clear-cut agenda against some of the countries in the region. (Borelli, 2017). IS is searching for recruits from the region and consequently wants to destabilize some member states in the organisation. This threat is not limited to a single country but is a common threat to ASEAN and the region.[5] In fact ASEAN has an inbuilt principle to counter terrorism and to establish peace in the region. The mission statement of the organisation states that ASEAN shall "promote regional peace and stability". This was further expanded by the 2007 ASEAN Charter which introduces the concept of "collective responsibility in enhancing regional peace, security and prosperity".[6] On 19 October 2018, defence ministers from the 10 ASEAN nations officially adopted Our Eyes Initiative (OEI) at the 5th ASEAN Defence Minister's Meeting in Singapore. This is conceived as a platform to facilitate strategic intelligence exchange on terrorism, radicalism and violent extremism among ASEAN Member States[7]. This initiative was also supported by US, Australia, New Zealand and Japan (Ryacudu, 2018).

The Our Eyes Initiative is to be regarded as a serious initiative from the part of the organisation to offer a counter terrorism platform. But the practical operation of such an attempt raises eyebrows from many quarters. Tan (2018) argues that the prospect of a growing regional role in counterterrorism for ASEAN's armed forces raises questions over how national governments are to avoid stepping on civil liberties at home even as they work to protect their citizens from terrorism and violence. It is argued that the ASEAN mechanism for counter terrorism is general in nature and cant bring in any concrete remedies in the case of a real situation. This is because of the very organisational structure of ASEAN which is supposed to formulate policies based on consensus, respect of national overeignty and non-interference into domestic matters. Therefore, ASEAN's counter-terrorism role within the region is generally rated as a general agenda-setter and facilitator. Borelli (2017) observes:

> In practice, Southeast Asia's counterterrorism landscape is highly complex and asymmetrical in terms of member states' respective counter-terrorist capabilities, efficiency and involvement in transnational cooperation. These gaps can be exploited by terrorists, notably for the smuggling of foreign fighters and weapons. (Borelli, 2017:15)

The organization of ASEAN is criticized from some quarters for its approach to human rights. ASEAN pronounces principles such as "upholding international law with respect to human rights, social justice and multilateral trade" and these provisions make certain moral commitments over the organization[8]. As such ASEAN is supposed to protect human rights and to human rights abuses and political repression in its own backyard. It is observed that the organization failed to respond to the gross human rights violations in the region. Here they took a policy of non-interference, which is totally against the principles of UDHR and international norms. Cambodia is one of the best examples. Cambodian government has a notorious history of rights abuses. In 2017 the Cambodian government imposed a consistent crackdown on the media[9]. The opposition was cracked down and opposition leader, Kem Sokha, was imprisoned with series of interrogations. But ASEAN kept a learned silence on these violations and right encroachments.

The idea of ASEAN unity is constantly challenged from different quarters. There is the China factor which puts enormous pressure on some countries to play for Chinese interests. This is particularly evident with the territorial conflict in the South China Sea.[10] This should be read with the evident fact that China is the biggest trading partner for many Southeast Asian economies and an important source of investment and tourism in the region. Member countries were also pressurized by internal politics which demands larger subscription to national interests and lesser attention to regional and global issues.

Indian Hopes

India is a major player in the region. It has significant political and economic dominance in the regional and global politics. Politically, India is a major superpower in the region with vast political resources at its disposal. The Indian political legacy dates back to the Nehruvian era, when NAM was established as a global platform for independent countries. This forum was initiated and operated by Indian efforts. This political power was kept intact for the later period of Indian history. With the coming of Prime Minister Narendra Modi, Indian foreign policy took a new step toward establishing Indian hegemony. Modi government established closer links with the ASEAN partners.

Indian association with ASEAN dates back to the early days of the organization. In the year 1992 India became a sectoral dialogue partner of ASEAN. India was having a smooth trade relation with ASEAN. The growth rate of Indian ASEAN trade, which attained an annual growth rate of 11.2% during 1993-2003 evidences the improvement in trade relations.[11] In the year 2003, the initial framework agreement for ASEAN–India Free Trade Area (AIFTA) was signed. AIFTA is conceived as a free trade area among the members of ASEAN and India. The Framework Agreement laid a sound basis for the eventual establishment of an ASEAN-India Regional Trade and Investment Area (RTIA), which includes FTA in goods, services, and investment.[12] After many negotiations the free trade area came into effect in 2010. In the financial year 2017-18, Indo-ASEAN bilateral trade reached US$ 81.3 billion and the net growth was 14 per cent.

The Indian quest for regional peace and stability is often marred by the Chinese factor. China has established better trade relations with many ASEAN partners. As such those countries were under the long shadow of the dragon. This is also evident in regional security issues. Buszynski (2012) makes a realistic observation in the context of South China Sea. According to him ASEAN assumes a subordinate role and comes under increasing pressure to take sides.

> The Chinese have increased the pressure upon the ASEAN claimants to recognise Chinese sovereignty over the South China Sea, but the use of direct military force would provoke an international backlash and could push ASEAN to the United States. As Beijing proclaims its "indisputable sovereignty" over the South China Sea and as military representatives declare it to be a "core interest" for China it emboldens various local and central agencies to act forcefully to enforce Chinese claims. The Hainan and Guangdong provincial governments have unveiled plans to develop the fishing resources of the area and have been responsible for assertive action against Vietnam, particularly around the Paracel Islands. (Buszynski, 2012:24)

It is a fact that Chinese authorities challenged ASEAN attempts at oil exploration and maritime surveying in the South China Sea. At times they arrested Vietnamese fishermen and confiscated their vessels; and have also harassed naval vessels from external powers in this area reminding them that the waters were contested, and that China's claim should be respected. The ASEAN response to Chinese claims were too weak and dissents in the organization documents are hardly visible[13]. However, China is in a disadvantage on the use of physical force to render obedience from the opponents. This makes the Indian efforts more possible. But the Indian foreign policy quarters must work overtime to overcome this disadvantage.

The operation of the free trade area has various positive impacts to India and ASEAN. However, there are also serious concerns about the nature of trade relations and its impact in the economy. As per the agreement tariff reduction is a major tool in promoting trade. But the economies of the ASEAN countries are largely export-driven with high export-to-GDP ratios and this is feared to make India a home for ASEAN exports[14]. It is argued that India can compensate the deficit by diversifying import list. The progress of 'making India' project can transform India into a production hub. This will provide more items for the foreign market. This movement can be coupled with further focus on Information Technology and Information Technology related Services. Here India has a clear advantage over ASEAN and can benefit.

The Indian partnership with the ASEAN countries is also extended to private sector. The Indian trade organizations like Indian Chambers of Commerce and Industry (FICCI) closely associates with ASEAN partners. In the cultural context the India-ASEAN partnership is strengthening day by day. There are larger tourist exchanges and better people to people contacts. This ensures a better cultural exchange.

Conclusion

It is admitted that the achievements of ASEAN cannot be compared with many of its western counterparts. The internal and external issues limit the performance of ASEAN in establishing itself as a strong unified regional force. But it does not pose a reason for disposing the organization as such. It offers a forum for meeting and discussing relevant regional and global issues. In fact, the East Asian region is going through rough times and hard issues including strategic ones. The forthcoming scenario requires institutions that are capable of addressing complex problems that threaten development and security.

In the wake of new threats like terrorism, the role of regional organization and the need of regional cooperation is becoming significant. Many of the countries are under potential threat from terrorist organizations and ideologies. ASEAN has so far been a successful discussion forum to discuss the issue of terrorism. But when it comes to real action, it has little concrete to offer. There is a general lack of responsiveness to contemporary developments and a general lack of political appetite for collective security and responsibility in the region from the organization. These issues are to be sorted out in a business-like manner and the bonds between ASEAN members is to be strengthened in this direction.

Against all odds, the ship of ASEAN is well rowing in the troubled waters of Asian politics. The efforts at launching initiatives for communitarian models of regional integration is to be well appreciated. In spite of sporadic speculations on US-China brinkmanship, these ASEAN-centric forums represent the most agreeable regional forums for discussions on the alternative futures amongst all Asian leaders (Singh, 2013). This model promises to be far more lasting than any concert of Asia that involves the big players only. The Act East policy of Modi Government is rightly tuned towards ASEAN. It is hoped that in the near future India can reap the advantages of a regional and global power by associating with ASEAN like regional forums.

As one of the major powers in the world, India has a larger role in regional politics. Act East Policy can transform the Asian regional platforms as spring board for Indian aspirations. ASEAN can be one of the best short cuts that the south block can take to establish the Indian leadership in the region. But there are many issues and concerns in the path of developing ASEAN as a strong regional platform. However, these issues can be well sorted out with better diplomatic relations and realistic interventions. This also includes the long-term project of re asserting the cultural connections and building up the economic collaborations.

NOTES

1 ASEAN was established as a reaction against in the initial days. But very soon the power structure changed. The end of the Cold War between the West and the Soviet Union at the end of the 1980s allowed ASEAN countries to exercise greater political independence in the region, and in the 1990s ASEAN emerged as a leading voice on regional trade and security sector.

2 The path to a united currency in ASEAN is not an easy one. There are serious economic and political concerns. A common currency needs intensified intra-regional trade and the convergence of macroeconomic conditions. Member states in ASEAN currently trades more with other countries (80%) than among themselves (20%). Therefore, their economies are more concerned about currency stability against major international currencies, like the US

dollar. On macroeconomic conditions, member states have different levels of economic development, which make common currency a distant dream.

3 Majority of the Chinese investment in ASEAN was in the form of bamboo network. The bamboo network is a network of overseas Chinese businesses operating in the markets of Southeast Asia that share common family and cultural ties. These networks are highly stable and not subject to regular fluctuations and thus assure stable foreign inflows

4 The Cambodian–Thai border dispute is a century-long dispute between Cambodia and Thailand.

5 The IS-inspired generation of militants have carried out terrorist attacks in different parts of Southeast Asia including the Thamrin attack in Indonesia in 2016, the Movida club attack in Malaysia in the same year and the Marawi siege in Philippines in 2017. Several terrorist plots have since been disrupted by the security agencies, including a plan to fly an explosive-laden drone into the police headquarters in Kuala Lumpur, an attempt to mount a suicide attack against the State Palace in Jakarta as well as a plan to fire a rocket at Marina Bay Sands in Singapore (Ryacudu, 2018).

6 ASEAN has developed a substantive counter-terrorism tools since 9/11. These includes ASEAN Convention on Counter-Terrorism (ACCT) and the subsequent 2009 ASEAN Comprehensive Plan of Action on Counter Terrorism.

7 Under the OEI initiative, the Defence Minsters for Indonesia, Malaysia, Philippines, Thailand, Singapore and Brunei agreed on five main components: the creation of a common database, exchange of personnel, joint training and operations, sharing of expertise as well as the sharing of resources and experience.

8 In November 2012, the ASEAN Human Rights Declaration was unanimously adopted by all members at a meeting in Phnom Penh. The declaration is supposed to assert ASEAN nations' commitment to human rights protection. In the human rights declaration, the member states affirmed their commitment to the internationally accepted human right documents and covenants including UDHR. See, ASEAN Human Rights Declaration (2013)

9 During this period the Cambodian government banned 19 radio stations for "violating contracts". By September, Radio Free Asia had to discontinue its operations in Cambodia when the atmosphere became unbearable

10 China has significant influence over countries like Cambodia and Laos. They were provided with sophisticated aid and investment packages by the Chinese government.

11 It is admitted that much of Indian trade with ASEAN is directed towards Singapore, Malaysia, and Thailand.

12 It is argued that the signing of the ASEAN-India Trade in Goods Agreement paves the way for the creation of one of the world's largest FTAs. It has created a market of t 1.8 billion people with a combined GDP of US$2.8 trillion.

13 ASEAN's strategy over the South China Sea was to persuade China into accepting a regime of norms which would govern behavior. There were many attempts in this direction. This includes the Declaration of the South China Sea of July 1992, The Declaration on the Conduct of Parties in the South China Sea (DOC) signed with China on 2 November 2002, China's accession to the ASEAN Treaty of Amity and Cooperation (TAC) on 8 October 2003. But these tempi was not sustained as there was an evident difference in the organization which was revealed at the 20th Summit in Phnom Penh in April 2012 and showed how the regional body could be divided over the issue.

14 India has had an increasing trade deficit with ASEAN countries since the early 2000s. As a

dominant exporter of light manufacturing products, ASEAN has competitive tariff rates that make it difficult for India to gain access to the industry market in these countries. Thus, trade becomes unfair for India.

REFERENCES

ASEAN Human Rights Declaration. (2013). Jakarta: ASEAN Secretariate.

Borelli, M. (2017). ASEAN Counter-terrorism Weaknesses. *Counter Terrorist: Trends and Analysis, 9*(9), 14-20.

Buszynski, L. (2012). Chinese Naval Strategy, the United States, ASEAN and the South China Sea. *Security Challenges, 8*(2), 19-32.

Cordner, L. G. (1994). Regional Resilience: The Imperative for Maritime Security Cooperation in Southeast Asia. *Naval War College Review, 47*(2), 41-59.

Nahdohdin, M., Angelianawat, D., Prasetya, A. P., Yaoren, K. Y., Dhanaraj, J., Bashar, I., Nasir, A. A. (2019). Southeast Asia: Indonesia, Philippines, Malaysia, Myanmar, Thailand, Singapore. *Counter Terrorist Trends and Analyses, 11*(1), 6-32.

Ryacudu, R. (2018). Terrorism in Southeast Asia: The Need for Joint Counter-Terrorism Frameworks. *Counter Terrorist Trends and Analyses, 10*(11), 1-3.

Samson, A. (2012). A 'Friendly Elephant' in the Room? The Strategic Foundations of China's Multilateral Multilateral Engagement in Asia. *Security Challenges, 8*(3), 57-82.

Singh, S. (2013). Missing the Mosaic Gazing Through the Prism of Asian Futures. *Security Challenges, 9*(1), 27-33.

Tan, S. S. (2018). Sending in the Cavalry: The Growing Militarization of Counterterrorism in Southeast Asia. *PRISM, 7*(4), 138-147.

Thu, H. L. (2018). Australia and ASEAN Together for the Sake of a New Multipolar World Order. *Security Challenges, 14*(1), 26-32.

Yoon, S. (2015). Implications of Xi Jinping's "True Maritime Power": Its Context, Significance, and Impact on the Region. *Naval War College Review, 68*(3), 40-63.

21

Indian Parliament and Act East Policy: A Study of 16th Lok Sabha Inputs

Santhanam Prabhakar

India's foreign policy has always been evolved keeping in view the national interests at the core. The basic objectives of our foreign policy are to safeguard our independence, sovereignty and territorial integrity, and at the same time promote best interests of the country. No doubt foreign policy is integrated with country's fundamental security and developmental priorities.

Parliament wields enormous power in the governance of the country. The actions of government can be questioned and scrutinized by Parliament in its functioning. One can neither ignore nor overlook the contributions being made by Parliament. As such Legislature has a big role to play in the realm of foreign policy as it is the one which makes the Executive accountable.

In the 16th Lok Sabha, Members have evinced considerable interest as enumerated in this paper, on different facets of foreign policy. Members of Parliament have utilized opportunities by using parliamentary devices like Questions and Statements to get authentic information, official stand on issues of their interest, which invariably showcase the stand of the Government of the day. After assuming power, Prime Minister Narendra Modi has paid greater focus on Act East Policy. He unveiled an upgraded 'Act East Policy' during the India-ASEAN Summit in Myanmar in November 2014.

Clause (3) of Article 75 of the Indian Constitution proclaims that "the Council of Ministers shall be collectively responsible to the House of the People." Foreign policy, being a part of public policy, too is not immune from parliamentary control, at least in theory. Act East policy is in turn a part of foreign policy which comes within the scrutiny of parliamentary control.

The initiatives of Parliament in the framing of India's foreign policy are considerable. As foreign policy is based on national interests, Parliamentary initiatives too serve the national interests. Though foreign policy falls within the domain of the Executive, Parliament's contribution cannot be overlooked. As such Legislature has a big role to play in the realm of foreign policy as it is the one which makes the Executive accountable. Parliament addresses various facets of foreign policy with a view to finding an amicable and unanimous resolution. Before elaborating various parliamentary initiatives and responding to some of the questions raised above, it would be imperative to know the provisions in the Constitution relating to foreign policy.

The growing importance of foreign policy and our relationship with various countries are reflected in the discussions and debates on the Demands for Grants of the Ministry of External Affairs in two consecutive years in the 15th Lok Sabha. But in the five years of the 16th Lok Sabha, on no occasion Demands for Grants of the Ministry of External Affairs were taken up for discussion in Lok Sabha. This seems a little out of place because the Government of the day and the Prime Minister himself has been giving emphasis to our relations with the outside world, including the US, Central Asian countries and ASEAN and other East Asian countries with the announcement of Act East Policy in the line of Look East Policy enunciated by the Narasimha Rao Government in 1992.

Look East Policy and Act East Policy

In 1991, after the disintegration of Soviet Union, India relied heavily for economic and political support; India became handicapped. India embarked on free market restructuring at home and new markets and economic partners abroad.[1] As a new strategy in India's foreign policy, the Look East Policy was officially defined and articulated in September 1994 by the then Prime Minister Narasimha Rao. In his Singapore lecture, he stressed India's legacy of strong historical and cultural relations with Asia. He laid emphasis on building a strong economic and security relationship between India and its eastern neighbours (Muni: 2011).[2] Thus, India ventured into a long haul in search of spreading its reach in South East Asia.

India's Look East Policy aimed at creating inherent strength and potential in each country of South East Asia and the region so as to enable India to develop resilience to withstand internal and external threats to her security.[3] Though improvement could be seen in the states of North East, it is not by any means worth mentioning. In this scenario, there is a need to relook and reframe the erstwhile Look East Policy and make the states in the North East region with adequate internal preparation by looking North East before looking Look East or Act East policy.[4]

With the launch of India's Look East Policy, a push has been made in the region in defence and security, energy security, non-traditional security concerns like food security, water management and pandemics, India-ASEAN connectivity, improved people-to-people contact through bilateral and trilateral arrangements.[5] North-East being the gateway to South Asian nations, there is a need to give a push to ensure development and to improve connectivity in the North-East.

Connectivity in the North East is a major hurdle for the people. There is an urgent need to address connectivity issues if we want to see any discernible improvement in the North East. Improvement in the North East connectivity will help to overcome the geographical, emotional and economic distance between the North East and the rest of India and would pave way for improvement in trade and commerce with the countries bordering North East.[8]

Under the leadership of Prime Minister Narendra Modi, new government formed in 2014 had made its relations with East Asian neighbours a foreign policy priority. Indian Foreign Minister Sushma Swaraj had proposed a new outlook calling it Act East policy in the line of Look East policy which was introduced during the government of Prime Minister PV Narasimha Rao but seriously implemented during the successive administrations of Atal Bihari Vajpayee and Manmohan Singh. Over the years, all the governments followed the foreign policy initiatives of earlier governments with a few changes.

Neighbouring countries received utmost attention from the Modi Government with the maiden overseas trips by Modi and Sushma Swaraj to Bhutan and Bangladesh respectively. With the long-term aim of enhancing economic and strategic benefits, India has upgraded its 'Look East Policy' by forging closer relations with the Asia-Pacific. We need to engage on trade and commerce if we want Act East Policy to succeed. Modi government has been paying considerable attention to strengthening relations with Japan, Vietnam, Australia and ASEAN. India to exploit the benefits being accrued due to the Act East Policy, it has upgraded its relations to strategic partnership with Japan, Australia, Vietnam, Indonesia, Malaysia, Singapore and Association of Southeast Asian Nations (ASEAN), Republic of Korea (ROK) and forged close ties with all countries in the Asia-Pacific region.[6]

The renaming of the Look East Policy as the Act East Policy is justified because India's trade has shifted eastwards, that is, over 50% of the trade.[7] With only around 5% regional trade in South Asia, and the failure of SAARC, India is justified in moving eastwards. It is also opined that shifting from Looking East to Acting East is India's response to Chinese strategic inroads in India's periphery.[8]

What is required to transform the North East Region? According to an author, "The trinity of initiatives—making Bangladesh Corridor available for NER, promoting sub-regional development, cooperation and providing space for bordering States in making the neighbourhood policy—if factored into the Act East Policy, it would be able to transform the NER from landlocked entity to land-linked entity, which holds the key for the development of this peripheral region."[9] For decades, we are seeing isolation of North-East. Efforts being made are not enough. There is a need to break the economic isolation. Debate should concern connecting Act East Policy as an impetus to economic and human security in the region.[10]

Sushma Swaraj, External Affairs Minister under Modi Government in the earlier dispensation said that North East is a natural partner in India's Act East Policy. She said that the Act East Policy is a means to strengthen the stability, economy and prospects of our North Eastern region.

Major problems plaguing North East are poor infrastructure, insurgency issues, communication link not up to the mark, inadequate investment, no proper coordination and cooperation between States in the North-East, difficult terrain, long porous international border, violent conflict, etc.[11] If the governments at the state and Centre attempts to set right these issues on an emergency basis with proper policy perspective, it would go a long way in ensuring success in the implementation of Act East Policy of the Government.

A foreign policy expert has rightly said, "The Act East Policy must look to improve Indian connectivity with ASEAN, particularly between North East India and Myanmar via the Trilateral Highway and Kaladan Multi-modal Trade Transit Project, BIMSTEC, etc., to promote peace and prosperity in the North-East region."[12] Indian Parliament through its initiatives has worked towards achieving these goals during the 16th Lok Sabha.

In the 16th Lok Sabha, members have evinced considerable interest through raising varied issues concerning foreign policy, in general, and Act East Policy, in particular. How Parliament through its initiatives contributed in building and strengthening our relationship with Act East Policy are deliberated.

Parliamentary Initiatives and Act East Policy

Questions form an important device which ensures accountability of the Executive by the Legislature. Questions evince a lot of interest in the Members of Parliament as they strive to know from the government of the day as to what is happening in the realm of foreign policy, in general, and how Government is moving in successful implementation of its Act East Policy.

In the 16th Lok Sabha, only on a few occasions, Members of Parliament had raised questions on Act East Policy. But to their credit, those questions were not only very basic in nature but also very incisive in content. These questions were not related to just Ministry of External Affairs, a nodal Ministry concerning foreign policy of the country, but also to Ministry of Development of North Eastern Region. This is precisely what is emphasised in this paper that North-East and Act East are closely linked. For the success of Act East Policy, we have to develop North East in its entirety. Without finding a lasting solution to the issues of North East Region, success of our Act East Policy would be elusive. As Late Sushma Swaraj, former External Affairs Minister described 'Act East' policy as imparting 'new-found salience' to India's engagement with its 'eastern neighbourhood and beyond' taken to its logical conclusion, her desire to 'move with a great sense of priority and speed' in bolstering relations with ASEAN needs to be taken seriously.[13]

By studying in depth the questions on Act East Policy, one can easily decipher how important is North East Region. The North Eastern region is the physical and cultural bridge between India, Southeast Asia and East Asia. The prosperity of North East depends a great deal on its contact, and its relationship with the countries in the north, east and south of it, as the region is surrounded by Bangladesh, Bhutan, China, Nepal and Myanmar and shares border with them too.[14]

If India wishes to play an important part to balance China in the region, it has to bolster its Act East Policy. India has been making attempts in this direction by taking along countries like Vietnam, Japan, Australia. Mira Rapp-Hooper Director, Asia Maritime Transparency Initiative Centre for Strategic and International Studies (CSIS) has recommended that the United States should establish a mechanism to coordinate partner capacity building efforts in Southeast Asia with Australia, Japan, and India, so that training and equipment support is mutually reinforcing. This think-tank expert informed the US lawmakers that India's Act East Policy and the policies of the countries like Japan and Australia are balancing the increasing influence of China in the Southeast Asian region.[15] This is not farther from truth.

In the 16th Lok Sabha, between 7th July 2014 and 13th February, 2019 only on seven occasions questions were raised on Look Act East Policy and Act East Policy.[16] Many of these seven questions were posed by the Members of Parliament from the North Eastern Region. This shows that Act East Policy has much to do with the promotion and development of North Eastern Region.

During the 16th Lok Sabha, Members of Parliament Prem Das Rai and Muthamsetti Srinivasa Rao (Avnthi) questioned the government on projects commissioned/sanctioned under the Look/Act East Policy which connect India with ASEAN countries and wanted to know the status of connectivity projects in Myanmar from 2016 to 2019?[17] Minister of State in the Ministry of External Affairs, V.K. Singh responded that a number of connectivity projects are being undertaken by Government of India, in cooperation with the Government of Myanmar, to enhance connectivity with Myanmar and beyond to other ASEAN countries. These include the Kaladan Multi-modal Transit Transport Project, the India-Myanmar-Thailand Trilateral Highway Project, Rhi-Tiddim Road Project, etc. When it comes to implementation, he elaborated that government is ensuring meticulous planning, close monitoring and coordination with Government of Myanmar so as to facilitate timely completion of these projects.[18] This provides ample information which the Members wanted to know.

When it comes to the trilateral highway with Myanmar and Thailand, it is necessary to point out that though Thailand has completed its part of the highway, India has yet to do so on the Indian side of the border.[19] There is a need to change rhetoric into action by ensuring vast improvement on the ground when it comes to infrastructure building in the North East.

A question on Vision 2020 Document was raised by Jitendra Chaudhury of the North-East (Tripura) and he wanted to know as to how the said Document facilitated the Government of the day in achieving its set targets.[20] Minister of State (Independent Charge) of the Ministry of Development of North Eastern Region, Jitendra Singh in his reply said, "The (North Eastern Region) "NER Vision 2020" document of the North Eastern Council (NEC) has emphasised the role of "Look East Policy" for promoting economic and cultural ties, development of strategic relationship with South Asian neighbours and China and thereby ending the economic isolation of the North Eastern Region. The Look East Policy, which has been evolving since early 1990s, involves intensive and continuous engagement with countries in the Asia-Pacific region at bilateral, regional and multilateral levels."

Member of Parliament Ninong Ering from North-East and Ajay (Teni) Misra from Uttar Pradesh wanted to know whether the Government has undertaken any study on the micro and macro-economic benefits of the Act East Policy for the North Eastern Region (NER). They also wanted the details of policy proposed to be implemented across the seven sister States of the NER under the Act East Policy, State-wise, including Arunachal Pradesh?[21] The Minister of State (Independent Charge) of the Ministry of Development of North Eastern Region, Jitendra Singh replied that the objective of "Act East Policy" is to promote economic cooperation, cultural ties and develop strategic relationship with countries in the Asia-Pacific region through continuous engagement at bilateral, regional and multilateral levels thereby ending the economic isolation of the States of North Eastern Region including Arunachal Pradesh. He is of the opinion that establishing connectivity with the neighbouring countries and within North East Region (NER), and development of other infrastructure are integral part of Act East Policy. Until the connectivity with the neighbouring countries and infrastructure with in NER (road, rail, inland water transport, telecom, airports, power, etc.) are fully established the micro and macro benefit of the policy cannot be assessed.[22] This elaborate reply provides the obvious answer from the Government that without the improvement in infrastructure and connectivity, it would be difficult to achieve the objectives of Act East Policy and the economic benefits cannot be accrued to the North Eastern Region.

India's Minister of State in the Ministry of External Affairs, V.K. Singh told Lok Sabha (Parliament of India) in a written reply, "India's Look East Policy (LEP) has been a major pillar of our foreign policy since the early 1990s".[23] In the second half of 2014, LEP was upgraded to Act East Policy which focuses on the extended neighbourhood in the Asia-Pacific region. The policy which was originally conceived as an economic initiative, has gained political, strategic and cultural dimensions including establishment of institutional mechanisms for dialogue and cooperation.

With the India-Myanmar-Thailand Trilateral Highway in the pipelines and construction of Friendship Bridge connecting Moreh and Tamu on the India-Myanmar border already started, and the project Rih-Tedium Road project, an all-weather connectivity between eastern Mizoram and western Myanmar getting finalized would go a long way in helping the Act East policy work for better.[24] Myanmar is the only South East Asian nation which shares its border with India. Thus, the said Highway is not only strategically of paramount importance but also in staving off Chinese influence on Myanmar. Our efforts to strengthen its relationship with Myanmar are cemented by the visit of Modi to Myanmar in September 2017, followed by Myanmar President visit to India in December 2018. Prior to these visits, a rare eight-day visit by its Commander in Chief of Myanmar Defence Forces to India took place in July 2017.[25] To derive mutual benefit both India and Myanmar should work with a view to transform the evolving connectivity corridors into development corridors. This would lead to an enduring bond between the two countries.[26] Efforts are being made to improve relationship between two countries as is reflected in the parliamentary interventions.

On another occasion, Ninong Ering from North East wanted to know the measures taken by the Government to realise the objectives of Act East Policy in North-Eastern region[27]. Minister of State in the Ministry of External Affairs, V.K. Singh replied that India's Act East Policy (AEP) focuses on the extended neighbourhood in the Asia-Pacific region. The North East of India has been a priority in our AEP. AEP provides an interface between North East India including the state of Arunachal Pradesh and the ASEAN region. To enhance connectivity among the North Eastern states, Prime Minister has recently inaugurated the Bhupen Hazarika Setu which ensures connectivity between upper Assam and Eastern part of Arunachal Pradesh. Moreover, various plans at bilateral and regional levels include steady efforts to develop and strengthen connectivity of Northeast with the ASEAN region through trade, culture, people-to-people contacts and physical infrastructure (road, airport, telecommunication, power, etc.). Some of the major projects to develop physical infrastructure and trade include Kaladan Multi-modal Transit Transport Project, the India-Myanmar-Thailand Trilateral Highway Project, Rhi-Tiddim Road Project, Border Haats, etc. (b) & (c). Presently, there is no such proposal.[28]

Out of 55 Ministries in Government of India, every year, only three to 7 Demands of Ministries are discussed threadbare in Lok Sabha and other demands are guillotined. In the 17th Lok Sabha, Ministries of Road Transport & Highways, Railways, Rural Development, Agriculture and Youth Affairs and Sports were taken up for discussion in 2019. One of the major parliamentary initiatives is the Committee system. Departmentally Related Standing Committees are called Mini Parliament, where we can find a structured discussion and its contribution has increased manifold in the recent past as we venture to see below.

Department-Related Parliamentary Standing Committees

Committee system plays a vital role in furthering the parliamentary democracy. We find in the Committee meetings elaborate deliberations on legislative and financial business, which in the Lok Sabha Chamber is difficult due to time constraints and other compulsions. Parliamentary Committee is called Mini Parliament.

In the 16th Lok Sabha, the Departmentally Related Standing Committee on External Affairs was headed by Shashi Tharoor. The composition of the Committee is 31 Members: 21 from Lok Sabha and 10 from Rajya Sabha. Prominent Members are H.K. Dua, Feroze Varun Gandhi, Rahul Gandhi, Dr. Karan Singh.

In the 16th Lok Sabha, between 4th June 2014 and 1st March 2019, the Departmentally Related Parliamentary Standing Committee on External Affairs met 78 times. But on 18th December 2018, the topic—'India's extended Neighbourhood: Look East to Act East' was taken up for discussion.[40] During 2014-15 and 2015-16, it met on 32 occasions. In 2016-17, on 17 occasions; in 2017-18, it met 17 times, and on seven occasions; in 2018-19, on six occasions, the Committee met and took up other foreign policy related issues.

As on 13th February 2019, the Committee had submitted 25 reports. In some Reports which were presented to Lok Sabha Speaker during the 16th Lok Sabha we can find inputs on the Committee's role in examining and scrutinizing almost every aspect that is plaguing the country when it comes to our relationship with Act East and its impact on the Ministry of External Affairs and the country as a whole.

Reports prepared by the Committee took up 'Act East' and other related matters. For example, the Committee on External Affairs (2018-19) (16th Lok Sabha), in its 24th Report (Action Taken Report), on the Demands for Grants of the Ministry of External Affairs for 2018-19, presented to Lok Sabha on 13th February, made certain observations and recommendations. The Committee noted that there are ten key principles and objectives guiding our foreign policy. The Ministry expressed its surprise by the Ministry's submission that there is no overarching and formalized policy document covering all aspects of our foreign policy. But the Committee also noted that the existence of mechanisms of consultation and coordination between MEA and other arms of Government to ensure that factors shaping India's foreign policy are in tune with the country's national priorities.

To these observations of the Committee, the Government (Ministry of External Affairs) replied: "The process of formulating a road map for India's international engagement is an ongoing one. The Ministry undertakes continuous stock-taking of changes in the global landscape with a view to identify challenges and opportunities over a short, medium and long-term horizon. It is this process that has led to enunciation of the 'Neighbourhood First' policy, the "Act East" policy and the SAGAR maritime doctrine."[29] With more focus on maritime, I have no hesitation to say that maritime dimension of the Act East Policy will play an important element of India's regional policy especially when it is increasingly accepted that the security and development of the Pacific and Indian Ocean regions are interlinked.[30]

The Committee also discussed apart from India's extended Neighbourhood: Look East to Act East, Engagement of India with the African countries; India's strengthening ties with Japan: possibilities ahead; Indo-Pak relations in view of new regime in Pakistan; Restructuring and strengthening of Indian Foreign Service (IFS) Cadres, India's position in the ongoing Climate Change negotiations are some of the issues taken up for detailed discussion during the Committee meetings during 2018-19.[31]

Apart from the Departmentally Related Standing Committee on External Affairs in Lok Sabha, we have a Consultative Committee of the Ministry of External Affairs which undoubtedly plays a very vital role in creating a fine link between the Members of Parliament and the Ministry of External Affairs.

Road Ahead

Parliamentary oversight of the Executive should be strengthened with detailed deliberations in Parliament with less and less or no disruptions during the Sessions days. For this to become a reality, there is a need to have workable consensus among political parties.

We should also strive for having more number of sittings of Parliament. First Lok Sabha sat for 135 days; second Lok Sabha about 125 days; even the Eighth Lok Sabha sat for 97 days but over the past two decades or so, the number of days of Session has come down drastically. The 14th Lok Sabha sat for just 66 days and 15th Lok Sabha, only 71 days. In the 16th Lok Sabha, which sat for 331 sittings[32], the average comes to about 66 days. It may be noted here that on an average full-term Lok Sabhas sat for 468 days since 1952.[33] Efforts should be made to evolve a consensus on not only increasing the number of days of sitting to make executive more accountable to Parliament but also to ensure that more and more issues concerning foreign policy are addressed and redressed through debates and discussions in Parliament.

When it comes to total number of hours, 16th Lok Sabha sat for 1,615 hours, though this is 20 per cent more than the 15th Lok Sabha, it is 40 per cent lower than the average of all full-term Lok Sabhas.[34] According to the Lok Sabha records, 16th Lok Sabha held its sittings for more than 1612 hrs. A total of 422 hours and 19 minutes were lost due to interruptions in the House. At the same time, it tried to compensate by sitting late for 728 hours to finish its scheduled business.[35] Sixteenth Lok Sabha lost 16 per cent of its scheduled time to disruptions; the 15th Lok Sabha lost 37 per cent of its time to disruptions; and the 14th Lok Sabha lost 13 per cent of its time to disruptions.[36]

During the 16th Lok Sabha, though 219 Bills were introduced, 205 Government Bills were passed by the House and nine Government Bills were withdrawn. The percentage of Bills referred to the Committee for scrutiny and detailed discussion has come down drastically. At present, only a minuscule portion of the policy aspect is scrutinized by Lok Sabha. Only 32 per cent of the time is spent on legislative business, which is the second highest than the previous Lok Sabhas.[37] Only 25 per cent of the Bills were referred to the Committees, which is far less when compared to the 14th and 15th Lok Sabhas. In 14th Lok Sabha, 60 per cent Bills were referred to Committees; in 15th Lok Sabha, 71 per cent Bills were referred to Committees.[38] Pre-legislative scrutiny process should be given emphasis as in the UK where every draft Bill and its Explanatory Notes are made publicly available for pre-legislative scrutiny.[39]

There is a need to make parliamentary debates and interventions more effective by bringing in reforms. Efforts are being made in this direction from time to time. Speaker of the 16th Lok Sabha stated in January 2016, while addressing the 78th All-India Presiding Officers Conference in Gandhinagar, Gujarat, that people are losing faith in democratic institutions.[40] This is a cause for concern. Her statement was made in the backdrop of frequent parliament and assembly logjams.

Conclusion

There cannot be two opinions about the importance of the role being played by Parliament in addressing various concerns involving foreign policy as has been brought up in this paper. There is a need to make parliamentary debates and interventions more effective by bringing in much needed reforms. Further efforts need to be taken to strengthen parliamentary democracy.

After analyzing the functioning of the 16th Lok Sabha, one comes up with certain apprehensions and doubts. In the 17th Lok Sabha, with a clear mandate to a single party, we can expect Lok Sabha would function smoothly and would not only contribute towards fulfilling hopes and aspirations of the people but would also serve the national interests.

Parliament is bestowed with many constitutional provisions to bring up issues of national importance concerning the policies, schemes, programmes and plans of the government. Parliamentary debates, interventions should be made more effective to protect the interests of the India. As has been amply brought out in this paper, Parliament has invariably served the national interests.

Though parliamentary interventions by way of debates and discussions on foreign policy are not considerable, there is no denying of the fact that Parliament's efforts, as enumerated above, all the while are not negligible too. Hence, we can say that Parliament invariably serves the national interests in general and that of interests of foreign policy concerning Act East in particular.

NOTES

1 Gorky Chakraborty & Ashok Kumar Ray, "A roadmap of the Look East Policy", in *The Look East Policy & Northeast India,* New Delhi: Aakar Books, 2014, p. 65.

2 Ibid. p.66.

3 India & South East Asia – the Security Cooperation, Lt. Gen. Y.M. Bammi (Retd.), Chapter 8 – *Proposed 'Look East' Policy for India-2035*, New Delhi: Gyan Publishing House, 2006, p. 215.

4 C. Joshua Thomas, "Look North East before Acting East: Synergising North-East with Act East Policy", in *Act East & India's North East,* ed. C. Joshua Thomas & K. Sarda, New Delhi: Pentagon Press, 2017, p. 64.

5 Delhi Dialogue V – India-ASEAN, Vision for Partnership & Prosperity. Ed. By Rajiv K. Bhatia, Vijay Sakhuja, Asif Shuja; Delhi dialogue V: Recommendations, pp.xxv., ICWA: Shipra Publications: New Delhi: 2014.

6. *'Act East Policy' of India: Meaning and Objectives'* https://www.jagranjosh.com/general-knowledge/meaning-and-objectives-of-the-act-east-policy-of-india-1527251668-1.

7. *'India's Changing Global Priorities and the Role of Look East Policy'* by Amb. (Retd.) Pinak Ranjan Chakravarty, lecture delivered at IIT, Chennai on 30.10.2017.

8 *'From Looking East to Acting East',* by Dr. Jitendra Nath Misra, lecture delivered at Nagaland University, Lumami on 22.11.2018.

9 Chapter 14 – Making 'Act East Policy' to work for the Development of the North Eastern Region of India by Gurudas Das, Ujjwal Paul and Tanuj Mathur, p.246 from *Look East to Act East – Implication for India's North East.,* Oxon, Routledge, 2016.

10 Chapter 3 – Insider or an Outsider: Where is the Northeast in India's Act East Policy? by Rakhee Bhattacharya, p.60, in the *'Mainstreaming the Northeast in India's Look & Act East Policy'* ed. Atul Sarma & Saswati Choudhury, Palgrave, 2017.

11 Chapter 4 – 'Look North East before Acting East: Synergising North-East with Act East Policy' by C. Joshua Thomas, p.60, in *Act East & India's North East,* ed. C. Joshua Thomas & K. Sarda, Pentagon Press, New Delhi, 2017.

12 Amb. (Retd) Ashok Sajjanhar, "From Look East to Act East: India's growing engagement with ASEAN and beyond. "Lecture delivered at Tamil Nadu National Law School, Trichy on April 26, 2018. https://mea.gov.in/distinguished-lectures-detail.htm?749

13 Rohan Mukherjee, *'East by Southeast: Three Challenges for India's 'Act East' policy,* January 23, 2018. https://www.business-standard.com/article/economy-policy/east-by-southeast-three-challenges-for-india-s-act-east-policy-118012300197_1.html.

14 Chapter 4 – 'Look North East before Acting East: Synergising North-East with Act East Policy' by C. Joshua Thomas, p.59 in *Act East & India's North East,* ed. C. Joshua Thomas & K. Sarda, Pentagon Press, New Delhi, 2017.

15 "*India's Act East Policy balancing China in the region: Expert",* July 12,2018. https://m.economictimes.com/news/defence/indias-act-east-policy-balancing-china-in-the-region-expert/articleshow/48198346.cms.

16 *Indian Debates,* 16th Lok Sabha, Questions . http://loksabhaph.nic.in/Questions/qsearch15.aspx?lsno=16.

17 *Indian Debates,* 16th Lok Sabha, Unstarred Question No.1591, dated 4.3.2015, http://loksabhaph.nic.in/Questions/QResult15.aspx?qref=13436&lsno=16

18. Ibid.

19 *"Minding the Gaps in India's Act East Policy*``by Rajeshwari Pillai Rajagopalan, September 17, 2018. https://thediplomat.com/2018/09/minding-the-gaps-in-indias-act-east-policy/

20 *Indian Debates,* 16th Lok Sabha, Unstarred Question No.1498, dated 29.7.2015,http://loksabhaph.nic.in/Questions/QResult15.aspx?qref=20466&lsno=16

21 *Indian Debates,* 16th Lok Sabha, Unstarred Question No.1711, dated 9.12.2015,http://loksabhaph.nic.in/Questions/QResult15.aspx?qref=25905&lsno=16

22 *Indian Debates,* 16th Lok Sabha, Unstarred Question No.1711, dated 9.12.2015,http://loksabhaph.nic.in/Questions/QResult15.aspx?qref=25905&lsno=16.

23 *Indian Debates,* 16th Lok Sabha, Unstarred Question No.3121, dated 16.3.2016 - http://164.100.47.190/loksabhaquestions/annex/7/AU3121.pdf

24 *Editorial – Dialogue with South East.* The Pioneer, 20th February, 2016.

25 Angshuman Choudhury, *India's foreign policy for next 5 years: New Delhi must stave off Chinese influence on Myanmar through trade, development assistance",* June 20, 2019. https://www.firstpost.com/india/indias-foreign-policy-for-next-5-years-new-delhi-must-stave-off-chinese-influence-on-myanmar-through-trade-development-assistance-6846731.html.

26 V.S. Seshadri, *"Time to demonstrate an Act East' Policy",* November 13, 2014. http://ris.org.in/sites/default/files/Hindu-13-11-2014-Time%20to%20demonstrate %20an %20Act %20East%20Policy-V%20S%20Seshadri.pdf.

27 *Indian Debates,* 16th Lok Sabha, Unstarred Question No.1743 dated 26.7.2017,http://loksabhaph.nic.in/Questions/QResult15.aspx?qref=54976&lsno=16

28 *Indian Debates,* 16th Lok Sabha, Unstarred Question No.1743 dated 26.7.2017, http://loksabhaph.nic.in/Questions/QResult15.aspx?qref=54976&lsno=16.

29. http://164.100.47.193/lsscommittee/External%20Affairs/16_External_Affairs_24.pdf

30 *Interpreting India's 'Act East' Policy,* ISAS Working Paper, National University of Singapore, by Rajeev Ranjan Chaturvedy, 29.1.2018, NUS, Singapore, 2018, p.10.

31 India, 16th Lok Sabha, Committee on External Affairs, 2018-19. Subjects selected http://164.100.47.194/Loksabha/Committee/CommitteeInformation.aspx?comm_code=11&tab=1

32 *16th Lok Sabha Debates,* Synopsis, 13th February, 2019. http://loksabhadocs.nic.in/Synop/16/

XVII/Supp+Syno-13-02-2019.pdf

33 Functioning of 16th Lok Sabha (2014-2019), https://www.prsindia.org/parliamenttrack/vital-stats/functioning-16th-lok-sabha-2014-2019

34 Functioning of 16th Lok Sabha (2014-2019), https://www.prsindia.org/parliamenttrack/vital-stats/functioning-16th-lok-sabha-2014-2019

35 India, 16th Lok Sabha, *Debates,* Valedictory Address on 13.2.2019. http://164.100.47.193/Synop/16/XVII/Supp+Syno-13-02-2019.pdf.

36 Functioning of 16th Lok Sabha (2014-2019), https://www.prsindia.org/parliamenttrack/vital-stats/functioning-16th-lok-sabha-2014-2019

37 PRS Legislative Research – *Vital Stats – Functioning of 16th Lok Sabha (2014-2019)* - https://www.prsindia.org/sites/default/files/parliament_or_policy_pdfs/PRS%2016th%20LS%20Vital%20Stats.pdf

38 *Ibid.*

39 *Pre-legislative scrutiny, Commons Library Standard Note,* http://www.parliament.uk/briefing-papers/SNO2822/prelegislative-scrutiny.

40 *The Millennium Post,* 23rd January, 2016.

22

India's Act East Policy under Modi: Determinants, Dimensions and Limitations

Sumit Kumar

The coming of the BJP-led coalition government led by Prime Minister Narendra Modi in 2014 marked a profound change in India's foreign policy. While Modi focused on strengthening ties with India's neighbours under the "Neighbourhood First Policy," he also took initiatives to foster a strong relationship with all the major powers of the world. At the same time, India under the Modi government directed its attention to deepen the engagement with the East and Southeast Asian countries under the new "Act East policy." Over the last five years, the relationship between the two sides has truly transformed. It is in this context that this paper tries to take a stock of the relationship. In doing so, this paper seeks to examine as to what extent the two sides have succeeded in expanding the horizon of their cooperation. It also intends to understand the challenges that they are facing in furthering their shared interests of promoting peace, security and development among other things in the region and finally the paper prescribes some policy recommendations for India to unearth new avenues in its ties with the East and Southeast Asian countries.

India and East and Southeast Asia enjoy historical, cultural and economic ties. Though after India's independence, Prime Minster Jawaharlal Nehru organised the Asia Conference in New Delhi in 1947 with the intent to strengthen the unity of Asian countries, India did not articulate a structured policy towards the countries of East and Southeast Asia. The possibility of fostering ties between the two sides further reduced, as India chose not to join either of the blocks led by the US and the Erstwhile Soviet Union. On the other hand, several East and Southeast Asian countries decided to join the US-led western block. However, the end of the Cold War, emergence of the US as the sole superpower, India's deplorable economic conditions among other factors forced India look towards East and Southeast Asian region. Consequently, the Narasimha Rao Government in the 1990s decided to adopt the Look East policy with the aim of strengthening the economic and other ties with them. ASEAN was also on the lookout for new partners and untapped markets. The Look East Policy is being embarked upon with the presupposition that the improving trade ties between India and ASEAN will certainly elevate the North East out of the menace of insurgency, poverty and economic backwardness. The Look-East Policy is expected to usher in a new era of development for the North East through network of pipelines, connectivity, communication and trade.

Over these years, the relationship with the East and Southeast Asian countries has become one of the major bedrocks of Indian foreign policy. In fact, India became a sectoral partner of ASEAN in 1992 and a dialogue partner and member of the ASEAN Regional Forum in 1996. India and ASEAN entered into a summit partnership in 2002. Bilateral trade and investment also increased significantly from $2 billion in 1992 to $12 billion to $72 billion in 2012. In turn, India's trade with ASEAN became even more important than with China.

India also focused on exploring cooperation with East and Southeast Asian countries in the security area. The people-to-people engagement between the two sides also was also boosted. India also began several infrastructural projects including Moreh-Tamu-Kalewa Road, India-Myanmar-Thailand Trilateral Highway, Trans Asian Highway, India-Myanmar rail linkages, Kaladan Multimodal project, the Stilwell road, Myanmar-India-Bangladesh gas or oil pipeline, Tamanthi Hydroelectricity project and optical fiber network between North East India and South East Asia.

However, towards the end of the UPA government, India's policy towards ASEAN failed to maintain the pace of the engagement due to several factors including the revelation of scams, the lack of the political will to sustain the momentum in the ties and other factors.

Thus, when the Modi government came to power in May 2014 on the slogs of good governance, improving ties with its neighbours, extended neighbours and with the rest of the world, experts and scholars believed that India under Modi would take some concert steps to improve the ties with the East and Southeast

Asian countries. True to the expectations, the NDA government outlined the Act East Policy in November 2014, within six months of assuming power in May 2014. The policy seeks to revive and reinvigorate India's relations with ASEAN as well as expand the country's engagement beyond the region to encompass the Koreas in the North to Australia and New Zealand in the South, and from neighbouring Bangladesh to Fiji and Pacific Island countries in the Far East. Of course, the Association of Southeast Asian Nations (ASEAN) has been a major pillar of India's Act East policy. While the engagement between the two sides has increased significantly as the leaders of India and ASEAN frequent each other, thereby giving a boost to the relationship at the political level. This is evident from the fact that in 2015 Modi visited Singapore to celebrate the 50th anniversary of the establishment of bilateral ties between the two countries. Modi also visited Myanmar, Thailand, Vietnam, Indonesia and other countries. Also, the heads of the states of 10 ASEAN member countries were all chief guests at the Republic Day in 2018. During their two-day visit from January 25, the Association of Southeast Asian Nations (ASEAN) leaders participated in the Indo-ASEAN Commemorative Summit to celebrate 25 years of the engagement and also held a wide range of discussions with Prime Minister Narendra Modi on issues of common interests, including security, trade and commerce, terrorism, people-to-people contacts and others.

Their presence of ASEAN leaders in New Delhi was not seen merely as an exercise in commemorating the completion of 25 years of India-ASEAN relations but the occasion also underscored the seriousness with which ASEAN views India in the region. This assessment, in fact, becomes clearer from the Delhi Declaration released at the end of the ASEAN leaders' visit as it emphasised the need for greater cooperation between the two sides in a number of areas including political, security, economic, trade and commerce, socio-cultural and others.

Of course, economic cooperation is a fulcrum of India-ASEAN relations, with trade between the two sides having risen from $2.9 billion in 1993 to $76.3 billion in 2016. ASEAN being India's fourth largest trading partner, India's trade with ASEAN has increased to $70 billion in 2016-17 from $65 billion in 2015-16. India's exports to ASEAN have increased to $31.07 billion in 2016-17 from $25 billion in 2015-16. The two sides hope to increase the trade volume to $200 billion by 2022 and agreed to intensify efforts in 2018 towards the conclusion of a modern, comprehensive, high quality, and mutually beneficial Regional Comprehensive Economic Partnership (RCEP). The deeper economic engagement with ASEAN will help India sustain and increase its economic growth and thereby carry out developmental works and create new jobs. Improved ties will also play a crucial role in the development of the north-eastern states of India, since this region connects Southeast Asian countries to the rest of India. Infrastructure projects, such as the India-Myanmar-Thailand Trilateral Highway and others, have the potential to transform the connectivity between India and ASEAN. The Kaladan Multimodal Transport Project that connects Kolkata with Sittwe port in Myanmar will further improve the engagement between India and Myanmar. Thailand has established with India Comprehensive Economic Partnership Agreement (CEPA).

Defence and security are another vital ingredient of Modi's Act East Policy. It is this context that New Delhi and Hanoi have taken several steps to expand their cooperation in the recent time. During Pranab Mukherjee's visit, India provided a credit line of US$ 100 million for defence procurement. The two countries signed a vision statement for next five years in 2015 and a MoU on cooperation between the coast guards of the two countries. During his two-day visit Prime Minister Modi announced extended a new defence credit line of $500 million and elevated the strategic partnership to the comprehensive strategic partnership, signifying India's deep commitment to help Vietnam to build its defence capabilities.

The deepening defence engagement between India and Vietnam indeed is the reflection of India's deep interest in actively participating in shaping the political security order in Asia-Pacific. In so doing, the Indian strategic community believes that a strong defence relationship with Vietnam can prove a huge strategic asset for India, so far as its interests in the South China Sea are concerned. As about 50 per cent of its trade transits through the South China Sea, New Delhi needs to foster security ties with Hanoi to ensure that there is absolute freedom of navigation in this part of the world. At the same time, as Vietnam has a territorial dispute with China over the Paracel islands in the South China Sea; Beijing has in the past declared India's oil exploration activities with Vietnam as illegal, both the countries have the shared interest in containing China's efforts to convert the South China Sea into as its exclusive zone of influence. Certainly, the recent verdict of a United National court rejecting China's claim over the disputed territories with Philippines is very significant for India and Vietnam to further speed up their engagement in this regard. Prime Minister Modi's visit to Vietnam on his way to attend G-20 meeting also gave a clear signal of India's desire to use this verdict in consolidating its position in this region.

At a time when China is asserting its claim over all parts of the South China Sea and has intensified its aggressive posturing against India, both sides have a very compelling security interest to foster engagement between them. It was in this context that both sides reaffirmed their commitment to work closely together on common regional and international security issues of mutual concern and ensure an open, transparent, inclusive and rules-based regional architecture.

They also underscored the importance of maintaining and promoting peace, stability, maritime safety and security, freedom of navigation and overflight in the region, and other lawful uses of the seas and unimpeded lawful maritime commerce and to promote peaceful resolutions of disputes, in accordance with universally recognised principles of international law. Surely, one of the biggest challenges that India and ASEAN countries are facing in expanding their engagement is poor connectivity. Therefore the two sides reaffirmed commitment to enhance physical and digital connectivity in line with the MPAC 2025 and the AIM 2020 by availing the $1 billion line of credit, among others, announced by India to promote physical infrastructure and digital connectivity.

While the Modi government infused a new momentum in its first term, India needs to further take bold steps to carry out the connectivity projects on a priority-basis to foster a better transportation system with ASEAN to achieve its desired national interests. India should also explore the ways to expand security ties with them, especially when the new Indo-Pacific construct is expecting New Delhi to pay a vital role in the region.

23

Maritime Security and India's Indian Ocean Policy: Reflections on Security Dilemma in Indian Ocean Region

Suresh R

Maritime security of India is closely linked to peace and security situation in the Indian Ocean region and India's response towards it. The significance of the Indian Ocean to India's security has long been recognized. However, commensurate with the significance of the Indian Ocean to its national security no major initiative were taken during the Cold War period. India's Indian Ocean policy was centered on proposal to the elimination of external power presence from the Indian Ocean through proposals on peace zone in international forums including the UN. Thus India's Indian Ocean policy during this period was solely based on the implementation of UN General Assembly declaration on Indian Ocean as a Zone of Peace (IOZP). A marked change in India's Indian Ocean policy has been reflected in the post-Cold War period with the advent of engagement with regional countries and external powers in the Indian Ocean. Similarly, the imperatives of non-traditional threat to its national security also prompted India to collaborate with regional and extra regional countries in the Indian Ocean region to address the common threat emanating from international terrorism as it demands a multilateral approach.

Indian Ocean: Geopolitical and Strategic Importance

The Indian Ocean, which is the third largest Ocean in the world, is surrounded by Asia, Africa, Antarctica and Australia; the northern limits of the Indian Ocean are well defined by the landmass. The dividing line between the Atlantic and the Indian Ocean is the meridian of Cape Agulhas (20 deg.0 min.E). The meridian of the South-East Cape of Tasmania (147 deg.0 min.E), the western exit of the Bass Strait and the median line between North-West Australia and the Peninsula of Malay (the Cape of Talbot through Timor, Sumba, Flores and Sunda Island up to Sumatra) form the dividing line between the Pacific Ocean and the Indian Ocean. The dividing line between the Antartic Ocean and the Indian Ocean is the 60 deg. 0 min. South latitude[1]. The total area of the Indian Ocean is 74.92 million sq km^2, which is 20.7 percent of the world's sea area and 14 percent of the earth's surface[3]. The average depth of the Indian Ocean is 38.59 kilometres[4]. The main constituent parts of the Indian Ocean are the Red Sea, the Arabian Sea, the Bay of Bengal, the Andaman Sea, the Persian Gulf, the Mosambique Channel and the Great Australian Bight. The Indian Ocean differs from the Pacific and the Atlantic Ocean in two important aspects. First, it is land-locked in the north, does not extend into the cold climatic region of the Northern Hemisphere and consequently is asymmetrical with regard to its circulation. Second, the wind system over its equatorial and northern portion changes twice each year causing an almost complete reversal of its circulation. [5] Of all the oceans, the Indian Ocean offers the most suitable navigational environment round the year. Its winds are often predictable and remain at below gale force. It is mostly free from fog, mist and treacherous currents.

Geopolitics

Five narrow stretches of water, the Bab-el-Mandeb, the Strait of Hormouz, the Strait of Malacca, the Cape of Good Hope and the Sundra Strauit, guard the eastern and western entrance to the Indian Ocean.[6] The Bab-el-Mandeb is the southern tip of the Suez Canal; the strait of Hormoz stands sentinel over the oil flow by sea from Persian Gulf; the strait of Malacca and the Sundra Strait control the sea borne traffic from the western Pacific Ocean; and the Cape of Good Hope overlooks the shipping route around Africa[7]. From Pacific Ocean the Indian Ocean can be approached through Torrs Strait, the Arafura Sea, Timor Sea, Lombak, Sunda Straits, Malacca Strait, Bass Strait and even from the South of Australia. It is approachable from the Atlantic Ocean either through the Cape of Good Hope route or through the Gibraltar Straits, Mediterranean sea, the Suez Canal, the Red Sea and then through the Strait of Bab-el-Mandeb. The major sea routes, from Europe to East Asia, the Indian sub-continent, Australia and from the USA to the Indian sub-continent pass through the Indian Ocean. The minor sea routes are from Europe to West Asia, the East Africa and Mauritius.[8]

Indian Ocean Choke Points

Nine important passages provide access into the Indian Ocean, of which five are key energy Seas Lines of Communications (SLOCs). Choking any one of them would cause disruption of seaborne trade, and uncontrolled volatility in oil and commodity prices, leading to upheavals in the global economy.

The major choke points[9] are:

1 Strait of Hormuz
2 Suez Canal
3 Strait of Bab-el-Mandeb
4 Malacca Strait
5 Lombok Strait
6 Sunda Strait
7 Six Degree Channel
8 Nine Degree Channel
9 Cape of Good Hope

Map 1: Choke Points in the Indian Ocean Region

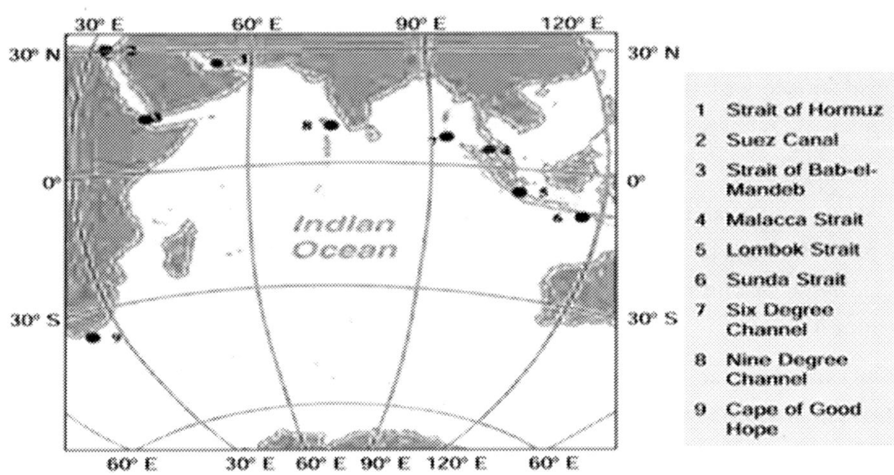

The Strait of Hormuz. Hormuz is the world's most strategic choke point. Connecting the Arabian Sea to the Gulf of Oman and the Persian Gulf, it has channels 2 nautical miles (nm) wide for both inward and outbound traffic with a Pipeline, forcing them to round the southern tip of Africa instead. This would add greatly to transit time and cost, and effectively tie-up spare tanker capacity.

The Malacca Strait. The Strait of Malacca links the Indian Ocean with the Pacific Ocean. Being on the shortest sea route connecting the Persian Gulf with East Asia and USA, it is a critical choke point in the IOR. At its narrowest point, in the Philip Channel, the Malacca Strait is only 1.5 nm wide. This creates a natural bottleneck, with potential for blockage in case of collision or grounding of ships. Closure of the strait would entail re-routing of nearly half the world's fleet, generating a requirement for additional vessel capacity and resulting in immediate increase in worldwide freight costs.

The Suez Canal and Red Sea. The Suez Canal is the gateway between Europe and Asia. It is 105.4 nm long and, being entirely at sea level, does not require any locks for its operation. Closure of the Suez Canal would cause traffic to be diverted around the Cape of Good Hope, thereby increasing the transit time and transportation costs.

The Strait of Bab-el-Mandeb and Horn of Africa. The Bab-el-Mandeb connects the Gulf of Aden and the Red Sea. Closure of the Bab-el-Mandeb would keep tankers loaded in the Persian Gulf from reaching the Suez Canal or the Sumed.

The Lombok Strait. At a minimum channel width of 11.5 nm, the Lombok Strait has sufficient width and depth and is far less congested than the Malacca Strait. Ships too large for the Strait of Malacca use this passage.

The Sunda Strait. An alternate route to the Malacca and Lombok Straits is the Sunda Strait, which is 50 nm long and 15 nm wide at its northeast entrance. Large ships avoid passage through this strait due to depth restrictions and strong currents.

The Six Degree Channel. The primary passage through the Andaman and Nicobar Islands to the Strait of Malacca is through the Six Degree Channel or Great Channel. Stretching from Indira Point on Great Nicobar to the northern tip of Aceh on the Indonesian island of Sumatra, it is an easy and wide passage without any depth limitations.

The Nine Degree Channel. The Nine Degree Channel is the most direct route through India's Lakshadweep Islands for ships sailing from the Persian Gulf bound for East Asia.

The Cape of Good Hope. The Cape of Good Hope is not a conventional choke point since adequate depth of water lies to its south and the passage of ships is not restricted by land. However, economic sense and unfavorable currents demand that ships pass close to land, which makes them susceptible to attack and grounding.

Indian Ocean—Strategic Importance

The strategic importance of the Indian Ocean lies in its geographic setting as it is a sea-line of communication between the East and West. Further since power can exercise by controlling islandic territories of the Indian Ocean they are strategically important. These include from the west to east, Mallagasy, Comoros, Seychelles, Chogos Archipelago, Socotra, Indian Coral Atoll, Laccadives, Sri Lanka, the chain of 219 islandic spots of Andaman and Nicobar stretching from South-western tip of Myanmar to the northern end of Sumatra, Mrgui Archipelago and the Cocao islands. These islands have served as the maritime station from the very beginning and were colonized in the 17th and 18th centuries to act as stepping stones to the 'Eastern treasures'. Besides the islands, the Indian Ocean cuts across the mainland at various places, thus forming a large number of gulfs, like the Persian Gulf, Gulf of Oman, Aden, Aquba, Suez and Cambay which are also strategically significant.

Geopolitical Importance of Indian Ocean Region

The Indian Ocean region includes 36 littoral and 11 hinterland[10] states making a total of 47 independent states with 30 per cent of the world population. The vast majority of the Indian Ocean littoral and hinterland countries attained their independence from the European colonial powers only after the end of the Second World War. Most of these countries in the region were either colonies, trust territories or protectorates under the British Empire which controlled the political, military and economic activities of the region till recent times. The economy of the regional countries were almost ruined by the colonialism and artificial national boundaries were drawn without any geographic, linguistic or ethnic considerations leading to intra-regional conflicts once the colonial powers left the Indian Ocean region. Moreover, in the western countries, economic and industrial revolution took place first which was followed by social and political revolution, whereas in the Indian Ocean regional countries the political revolution preceded the economic and industrial revolutions. This led to social and political tensions in these countries. Politically, the region has a strange admixture of democracy, military dictatorship, totalitarianism, absolute monarchy and constitutional monarchy; several regimes in the region are politically unstable and provide a fertile ground for external intervention. In 1960 the commercial activities in the region increased enormously and the presence of natural resources of oil aroused the interests of the great powers in the region. All the countries in the region, except Australia, South Africa and Israel are developing countries. The above-mentioned three countries and Thailand are not members of the Non-aligned Movement (NAM).[11] It is the memories of colonialism, the desire to avoid entanglement in great power rivalries and the need to devote their resources to development that have led the vast majority of the countries in the Indian Ocean region to adopt the Non-aligned policy.[12]

Map 2: Indian Ocean Region

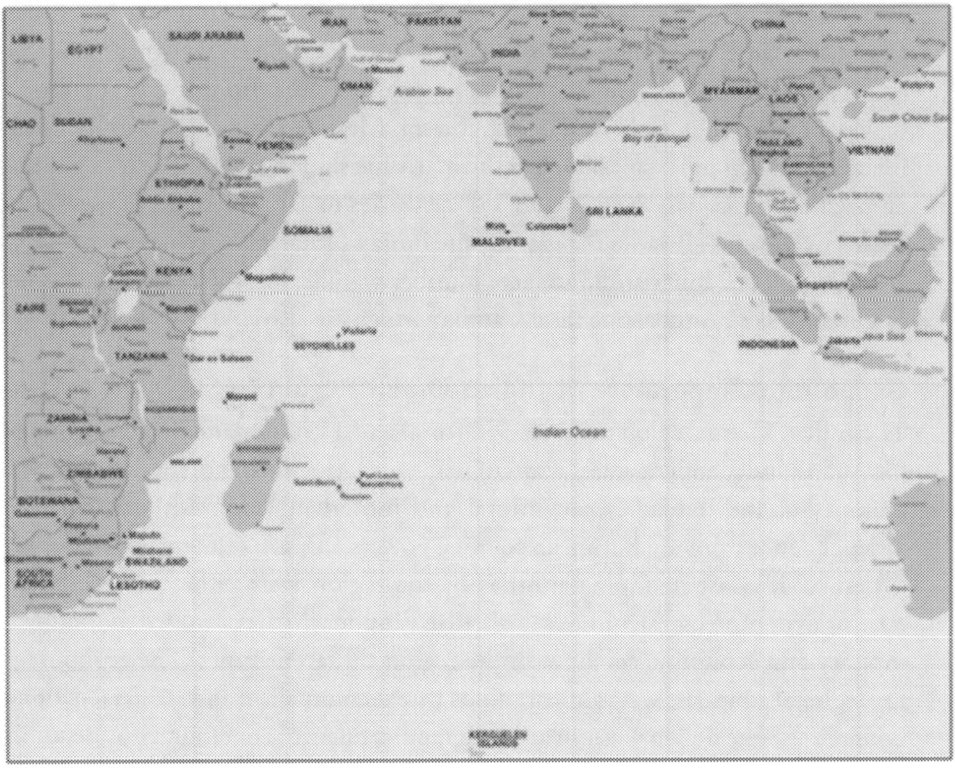

Economically, the region has a great many diversities and disparities. The African region with its 8.7 million square km is marked with uneven and underdeveloped resources and low technological development low standard of living with very high annual growth rate of population. The Asian region with its 12.5 million square km of area has an uneven distribution of population, high pressure of population on its resource base, high growth rate of population, underdevelopment nature of economy, low standard of living and low technology development. The Australian region is fairly developed like the South African area. The economy in the Indian Ocean region is predominantly agricultural in nature and the industrial base is weak.

Considering the population, the food production is less than the requirement, which put definite limitation on the countries in the region. The region is estimated to include more than 60 per cent of the world crude oil reserves[13] and is an important source of raw material and strategic minerals such as chromium, bauxite, uranium and manganese. Most of these materials are exported to the industrialized countries. The local economics lack the infrastructure necessary for the processing and full industrial exploitation of these materials. The relative dependence of these countries on the great powers for capital, technological know-how and technology transfer and manufactured goods is a very important factor influencing their external behaviour. The vast mineral resources and commercial crops added to the Indian Ocean region's strategic importance in relation to the industrially advanced countries in Europe, USA, Japan, China and Russia.

The surveys conducted in the Indian Ocean sea-bed reveals rich stocks of nodules of manganese, nickel, cobalt, copper, molybdenum, etc. Calculations show that one square mile of the sea-bed, where nodules are located could produce about 70,000 tons of minerals which would yield in value about $ 4, 00,000. One square mile of such nodules will yield among other mineral 30,000 tons of Iron ore, 3,600 tons of aluminium 2,300 tons of manganese, 400 tons of cobalt, 1,200 tons of nickel and 650 tons of copper.[14] The Indian Ocean has got extensive marine food potentiality. The estimates show that the sea-bed can provide more than 12 million tons of catch fish every year. Again one-fifth of the world's total arable land lies in this region producing crops like wheat, rice, tea, coffee and cotton. In the Indian Ocean littoral and hinterland countries huge deposits of gold and diamonds are concentrated.[15]

The Indian Ocean carries a substantial proportion of international trade, even though the industrial production in the Indian Ocean region is less in relation to the world production. [16]The natural resources of the region greatly contribute to this factor. Approximately one-fourth of the entire cargo carried in world marine trade and about two-third of oil are loaded or unloaded in the ports of the Indian Ocean region. Most of the countries in the Indian Ocean were colonies till 1945 and are not as developed as the countries in the West. The region could not play an effective role in world affairs because of it's under developed economies.

Again, unlike the developed world, the Indian Ocean region abounds with conflict situations and bilateral and multilateral negotiation as a means to settle disputes peacefully has been very rarely employed. This has provided ample opportunities for external powers to interfere in the affairs of the countries in the Indian Ocean region.

India's Indian Ocean Policy

In 1947, when India became independent the Cold War had already started and the world was divided into two antagonistic blocs, one led by the USA and the other by former USSR. India decided not to join any of the blocs but to pursue an independent foreign policy.[17] India played a major role in the Bandung Conference of Afro-Asian nations held in April 1955 which laid the foundation of the Non-aligned Movement. India was one of the founder members of the Non-aligned Movement.

In the immediate post-independence period India's interests in the Indian Ocean were largely commercial and defensive. Its economic interests in Indian Ocean were few; largely due to inadequate technological capabilities it did not investigate and exploit its oceanic resources, with the exception of fisheries. India's commercial interest stemmed from its dependence on the Indian Ocean sea lanes for sea borne trade. India's security interests and requirement centered mainly around its land frontiers particularly Pakistan in the North-West.

A study group of the Indian Council of World Affairs in 1957 stated rightly the importance of Indian Ocean to India:

> To India the security of this region is of paramount importance as oceanic routes across this ocean carry the bulk of her overseas trade. If these routes come under the control of countries not friendly to India, this would threaten very seriously her economic and industrial development, in fact, her very independence. Three sides of India's frontier are bordered by water-a serious matter. This cannot be lightly dismissed ... India although committed to a policy of non-alignment cannot possibly neglect her seaward defence. She has unquestionably got to think of having adequate naval forces to protect the miles and miles of her coastline....[18]

Even though the importance of the Indian Ocean to India's security was repeatedly[19] stressed India was constrained to give less attention to navy than land forces. This was due to a number of factors; first, the threat posed by Pakistan in the North West, second the threat posed by China in the North, third, the fact that Britain was a dominant power in the Indian Ocean which provided India some comfort because its presence was without any adverse spin off and fourth, in the overall planning of immediate dangers the threat from the Indian Ocean appeared least alarming, and hence the continued neglect of the Indian Ocean as a security threat.

The then Prime Minister of India, Jawaharlal Nehru commenting upon the entry of the US Seventh Fleet into the Indian Ocean, said on 19 December 1963; "If anything is obviously to our detriment we protest if not we do not." He also stated, "Indian Ocean is a vast area, we cannot say anybody cannot go round the area."[20] India took such a stand because at that time India favoured the US presence as a counter measure to the threat posed by China.[21] This stand of India had undergone a minor change in mid-1960's and India expressed mild protest[22] on the British decision to develop defence facilities in British Indian Ocean Territory along with the US in the Indian Ocean. But by the late sixties India strongly opposed the presence of outside great powers from outside in the Indian Ocean.[23] Towards the end of 1969 India had also decided to increase its naval capability and sought the cooperation of the countries in the Indian Ocean region to take steps for making Indian Ocean an area of peace and opposed the induction of outside forces into the Indian Ocean.[24]

Peace and Security Efforts in the Indian Ocean during the Cold War Period

In the early 1970 most of the Non-aligned countries of the Indian Ocean region were apprehensive of the great power military presence and rivalry in the Indian Ocean, because they felt that it could threaten their security and reduce their independent action. The idea of a peace zone in the Indian Ocean was mooted in the 1964 Cairo Conference of the Non-aligned countries and was given a concrete shape in the form of a resolution at the 1970 Lusaka Conference of the Non-aligned countries.

The Non-aligned countries in the Indian Ocean region were successful in getting the UN General Assembly to pass a resolution in December 1971, which called upon the members of the UN to make the Indian Ocean a zone of peace (IOZP) through the elimination of great power military presence conceived in the context of great power rivalry and competition. The 1971 UN General Assembly resolution on IOZP was mainly an approach towards peace in the region by insulating the area from the great power military presence, as majority of the littoral and hinterland countries of the region which were members of the Non-aligned Movement felt that peace could prevail in the region by the elimination of outside great power military presence in the Indian Ocean.[25]

Towards the end of the 1960, India took the decision to seek the co-operation of the countries in the region to make the Indian Ocean a zone of peace by insulating the area from the presence of the outside great powers. At the same time, India had also strengthened its naval capability. India, a non-aligned country, supported the Lusaka Summit resolution on Indian Ocean peace zone as it was in tune with India's security perception. Pakistan, an ally of the US, was in favour of the US presence in the region. Ironically, when the IOZP resolution was adopted by the UN General Assembly in December 1971, India and Pakistan were involved in an armed conflict ending up with the Indian army occupying the whole of East

Pakistan. The dismemberment of Pakistan as a result of the conflict enhanced the fear of Pakistan about India in the South Asian region of the Indian Ocean. India, on the contrary, felt that outside military presence in the region, especially the US presence posed a threat to its security as it distorted the natural power hierarchy in the region. India strongly supported the 1971 UN resolution on IOZP as it felt that if implemented it not only ensured India's security but also enhanced its power position in the region. India could effectively meet any threat from China, too, with the friendly help from former Soviet Union even if the Soviet forces withdrew from the Indian Ocean as the Soviet Union shares a border with China and the Sino-Soviet rift continues. Paradoxically, though Pakistan supported the IOZP resolution in principle, it desired the US military presence in the Indian Ocean as it felt that only the US presence would ensure its security. Though Pakistan was unhappy that the US did not prevent the dismemberment of Pakistan it felt that even the security of West Pakistan would have been endangered after the Indian forces had occupied East Pakistan but for the US' clear warning to India not to proceed further in West Pakistan.

In 1971, when the UN General Assembly meetings discussed the IOZP proposal, Pakistan had raised the issue of the threat posed by India to its security.[26] Pakistan desisted from raising the regional issues in 1972 General Assembly meeting as there were some improvements in the Indo-Pakistan relation with the signing of the Simla agreement.[27] However, the Simla spirit did not last long and Pakistan once again reverted back to focusing on the threat from within the region in the 1973 ad hoc Committee on Indian Ocean meeting and the First Committee meeting of the UN General Assembly. In the Ad hoc Committee meeting Pakistan enthusiastically raised the issue of the regional threat to peace as the Committee was mainly constituted to find ways and means to implement the IOZP resolution with due regard to the security considerations of the littoral and hinterland countries in the Indian Ocean. During the initial period, India's response towards the IOZP ranged from a strong support to the 1971 UN declaration as it envisaged the elimination of great power military presence in the Indian Ocean to a covert acquiescence to the Soviet thrust in the Indian Ocean in the absence of any progress towards the implementation of the declaration.

In 1974, the nuclear explosion conducted by India led Pakistan to introduce a parallel proposal to the Indian Ocean zone of peace in the form of South Asia as a Nuclear Weapon Free Zone (SANWFZ).[28] Pakistan maintained that the acceptance of its SANWFZ as the first step towards making Indian Ocean a zone of peace. Pakistan was successful for the first time in incorporating in the IOZP resolution of 1974 the necessity to look into the regional issues of the littoral and hinterland countries of the Indian Ocean. It continued to focus on the threat emanating from regional dominant power, India, and proposed a code of conduct to ensure an effective system of security within the Indian Ocean region. The code of conduct among other things, envisaged that military balance between dominant regional powers and weaker regional states should be maintained at a reasonable level in order to create an atmosphere of mutual confidence. India opposed the code of conduct and made it clear that any addition to the 1971 UN resolution on IOZP was unacceptable to it. In 1976, Pakistan termed the 1971 UN resolution on IOZP as impractical and undesirable and abstained from voting for the first time.[29] India while supporting the 1971 UN resolution on IOZP strongly opposed the continued US presence in the Indian Ocean. The divergent stand of India and Pakistan on IOZP reflected their contrary perception on security. India, as a dominant power in the Indian Ocean, considered the external power presence as a major threat to security of nations in the Indian Ocean region, contrary to this Pakistan, a relatively weaker country in the region, supported external power presence, especially the US presence in the region.

A minor change in India's response towards the great power military presence was discernible when the Janata government came to power in 1977. The Janata government while following a 'balanced approach' opposed equally both the US and the Soviet military presence in the region. When General Zia-ul-Haq assumed power in Pakistan in July 1977 he reverted back to Pakistan's earlier stand of voting in favour of the IOZP resolution though it continued to harp on regional threat to peace in South Asia.[30]

The 1979 Littoral and Hinterland States Meeting in its final document incorporated the major items in Pakistan's code of conduct proposal, namely, the denuclearization of the Indian Ocean littoral and hinterland states, non-use of force and peaceful settlement of disputes, and agreements on the balancing of the military strength between the major littoral powers and the weaker regional countries. While Pakistan was happy with the inclusion of these items in the final document of the Littoral and Hinterland States Meeting, India was not in favour of its inclusion. India was against extending the territorial limits of the peace zone to the national boundaries of the littoral and hinterland states.[31]

The 1977-78, US-USSR talks on arms limitation in the Indian Ocean and the response of India and Pakistan reflected once again the divergent approaches of India and Pakistan in making the Indian Ocean a zone of peace.[32] India supported the super power talks on arms limitation and termed it as a step towards the eventual elimination of great power military presence from the Indian Ocean. Pakistan, contrary, to this, was opposed to the super power talks on arms limitation as it considered that mere elimination of great power military presence or the limitation of it did not ensure the security of the smaller countries in the region against the threat emanating from dominant regional powers. Pakistan demanded the reduction of the military forces of dominant powers within the region.

The Soviet intervention in Afghanistan in December 1979 and Pakistan becoming one of the frontline states in the US' counter strategy to contain Soviet expansionism in the Indian Ocean region led to Pakistan's strong support to the US presence in the Indian Ocean. Pakistan felt that its security was threatened by the Soviet troops stationed in Afghanistan as well as the presence of dominant power India. India's silence on the Soviet action in Afghanistan intrigued Pakistan.[33] Hence Pakistan, in addition to the code of conduct demanded the Soviet troop's withdrawal from Afghanistan as a precondition to any initiative to make Indian Ocean a zone of peace. Unlike India, Pakistan was opposed to the early convening of the conference on Indian Ocean. India was concerned about the security threat posed by the militarization of the Indian Ocean and the US supply of sophisticated arms to Pakistan. Hence, India pleaded for an early convening of the conference on the Indian Ocean in order to implement the 1971 UN resolution on IOZP. By 1981, as the security environment in South Asia aggravated with the increased super power involvement, India was even agreed to consider the security concerns of the smaller countries in the region, once the reduction of great power military presence in the Indian Ocean was achieved.

Despite change of government in India and Pakistan in 1985 and 1988 respectively, both governments continued to maintain their respective stands on IOZP without any change. India continued to maintain that the sole purpose of IOZP resolution was the elimination of great power military presence in the Indian Ocean. Pakistan, on the contrary, maintained that the SANWFZ and other items included in the code of conduct were the necessary preconditions to make Indian Ocean a zone of peace. These stands of India and Pakistan were also reflected in the 1989 NAM, Commonwealth and UN General Assembly meetings.[34]

During the cold war period India's major contention was that the great power military presence was the cause of regional disharmony and tension, hence it wanted the great powers to withdraw from the Indian Ocean. Pakistan's contention, on the contrary, was that the regional disharmony was the cause of great power military presence and hence it wanted the resolution of regional issues first, before considering the elimination of great power military presence.

Thus, it is clear that India tried to enhance its power position not only by supporting the elimination of great power military presence as envisaged in the 1971 UN resolution on IOZP but also by keeping its nuclear weapon option open. Pakistan supported the US presence as it perceived threat from India. Pakistan believed that a just solution to regional issues including the Kashmir problem based on the UN resolution can be possible only with the US support. The divergent stand taken by countries in the region also helped the super powers to continue and enhance their military presence in the region. Simultaneously the cold war situation as a result of super power rivalry also augmented the regional disputes.

The security situation in the Indian Ocean region during the Cold War period was appeared to be based on three inter-related factors; first the asymmetries in the military power between intra-regional powers especially in the context of unresolved regional issues; second the outside great power interest and activities in the region; and third the interaction between intra-regional asymmetries and outside great power interests. In such a situation of mutual distrust among countries in the region any efforts towards peace would be an exercise in futility.

Peace and Security in the Indian Ocean: The Post-Cold War Scenario

Peace and security efforts in the Indian Ocean underwent a major turn in the post-Cold War period. The context in which the countries in the region initiated the IOZP has considerably been changed. The super power rivalry has come to an end with the disintegration of Soviet Union. However, a change in the international power structure, from bipolar system to unipolar/multiploar system, does not necessarily ensure peace in the Indian Ocean. [35] The threat perceived by countries in the region in the context of great power rivalry has been ended. However, the presences of the external powers continue in the Indian Ocean region. With the change in the international power structure, the threat perceptions of the countries in the region have also underwent a marked change. The post-cold war blurred boundaries between national security and international security on the one hand, and national security and human security on the other demands better cooperation among nations.

Peace and Security in the Indian Ocean: US Role in the Post-Cold War Period

The US policy immediately after the end of Cold War was to ensure that no rival super power is allowed to emerge in Western Europe, Asia or the territory of the former Soviet Union, the US is to maintain sufficient military might to deter any nation or group of nations from challenging the US supremacy and to prevent proliferation of nuclear weapons and other weapons of mass destruction and deter attack from regional forces.[36] This general policy of the US was well reflected in the Indian Ocean region also.

The geo strategic environment in the Indian Ocean underwent a radical change in the early 90 due to two factors. One was the disintegration of the former Soviet Union which resulted in the formal end of cold war. The other was the Gulf war. As a consequence, all the earlier propositions of security in the cold war period have become totally redundant. The end of cold war has removed the necessity to attempt to prevent the negative consequences of superpower rivalry. Simultaneously the Gulf war shattered the illusion of regional security.

The Gulf War has left the US with the problem of protecting its security interest in the Persian Gulf for a long term. These interests include the continued supply of oil at reasonable price, the security of the Gulf Cooperation Council (GCC) countries and the prevention of any single power from gaining control over the bulk of the Gulf oil resources and using the revenue to undermine the regional order.

In the Cold War period a variety of strategies had been used to protect these interests. This includes reliance on the British presence in the region until 1971, support for Iran under the Shah until 1979 and support for Iraq during its war with Iran. The regional power equilibrium in the Persian Gulf was collapsed when the balance of power shifted decisively in favour of Iraq and the countries in the region were unable to pose a credible deterrent to Iraqi aggression. This necessitated the outside power intervention in the region to maintain status quo.

The US strategy after its punitive action against Iraq was to evolve a security system in the north western part of the Indian Ocean with all the six members of the GCC. The US also received cooperation from Egypt and Syria in maintaining a big force to ward off any threat from any quarters in the region. But they could not get much support from all the GCC member countries, as a few countries were reluctant to have foreign troops in the region. Finally the US signed a 10 year agreement with Kuwait on 19 September 1991. The then US Defence Secretary, Dick Cheney told the US Congressional Committee in February 1992 that the US was going to expand its presence in West Asia and also its Rapid Deployment Force for swift decisive victory if the US has to fight against any third world country in the regional wars. Elaborating on his statement he further said "...in South West Asia we are striving with friends and allies to build a more stable security structure than the one that failed on 2 August 1990. But we have major interest in that part of the world and we must remain engaged to protect those interests. Therefore, we will increase our presence compared to the pre-crisis period. Hence we must be prepared to face adversaries on their term possibly involving the use of weapons of mass destruction and ballistic or cruise missiles". [37] This was the immediate strategy of the US to meet the post-Cold War situation.

This strategy of the US had practical application in the region within a short span of time. The 11 September 2001 (9/11) terrorist attack on US world trade centre and the consequent Afghanistan war to do away with terrorism from there, and ensuing Iraq war to dethrone the dictatorial regime of Saddam Hussein, have demonstrated the US capability to intervene effectively in the region to protect its foreign policy objectives through coercive means. These developments marked the active and effective involvement of an external power in the region to maintain international peace and security in accordance with its own perception.

After the terrorist attack on the US there were two important questions, on the state sponsored terrorism and on the security threats to nation states from non-state actors. The international organizations are not well equipped in terms of military power and resources to effectively meet any challenges to international peace and security posed by non-state actors. In such a situation, US, the sole superpower in the post-Cold War period, had taken over the responsibility to maintain peace and security in the region. The 9/11 attacks on the US attracted the attention of international community to wipe out terrorism from the region. The US led 'war on terror' once again legitimized not only the US presence in the region but also its active interventions. In the post-Cold War period there was realignment and regrouping in the Indian Ocean region. The Indo-US relation improved further and India had entered into close collaboration with the US on defence and security issues.[38]

Inevitability of External Power Presence

The existence of international terrorism in the region in the post-Cold War period, the shift in the international power structure from bipolar to uniploar, had also influenced the perceptions of countries in the Indian Ocean region about the external power presence. The sponsor of the IOZP, Sri Lanka now perceives the external power presence inevitable in the region. Likewise one of the strong supporters of the 1971 UN resolution on IOZP, India has no hesitation to work in tandem with the US to monitor peace and security in the region. This change in the perception of countries in the region about the outside power presence made the 1971 UN declaration on IOZP a dead proposal. The emerging security situation appended with the accelerated pace of globalization demands better cooperation between regional and extra regional countries in the Indian Ocean region. It also demands ensuring national security by enhancing self-defence capability, especially in the context of failure of global collective security mechanism to address threat to international peace and security posed by state as well as non-state actors and the existence of unresolved border disputes.

India's National Security and Indian Ocean

Indian Ocean is very important to India's military, economic, energy, environment, and human security. India has a coast line of 7516 km and an exclusive economic zone (EEZ) of 2 million sq km. The significance of Indian Ocean was predicted by Sir Alfred Mahan way back in 1890s he stated Indian Ocean as the Ocean which decides the destiny of the 21st century.[39] The importance of Indian Ocean to India has long been recognized. India occupies a central position in the Indian Ocean region, a fact that exercises an increasingly profound influence on India's security environment. Writing in the 1940s, K.M. Panikkar, like Mahan, stated the importance of the Indian Ocean to India that,

> While to other countries the Indian Ocean is only one of the important oceanic areas, to India it is a vital sea. Her lifelines are concentrated in that area, her freedom is dependent on the freedom of that water surface. No industrial development, no commercial growth, no stable political structure is possible for her unless her shores are protected.[40]

In tune with the above observations the first Prime Minister of India Jawaharlal Nehru observed "History has shown that whatever power controls the Indian Ocean has, in the first instance, India's sea borne trade at her mercy and, in the second, India's very independence itself." [41] It was in pursuance of this idea India had supported the 1971 UN declaration on IOZP during the Cold War period. In the post-Cold War period also India had emphasized the strategic significance of Indian Ocean. This was reflected in the Annual Report (2004-2005) of India's Defence Ministry, which noted that, "India is strategically located vis-a-vis both continental Asia as well as the Indian Ocean Region."[42] Again the Indian Maritime Doctrine asserts: "All major powers of this century will seek a toehold in the Indian Ocean Region. Thus, Japan, the EU, and China, and a reinvigorated Russia can be expected to show presence in these waters either independently or through politico-security arrangements." There is, moreover, "an increasing tendency of extra regional powers of military intervention in [IO] littoral countries to contain what they see as a conflict situation." [43] Accordingly India framed its naval strategy in the Indian Ocean.

Maritime Security and India's Indian Ocean Policy in the Post-Cold War Period – Elimination to Engagement with External Powers

Maritime security has become an important dimension of India's bilateral interaction with all Indian Ocean countries and regional organizations. Maritime security has become a multifaceted issue especially in the realm of non-traditional threat to security. The challenges in the field of non-traditional threat to security include maritime terrorism, smuggling transnational crime, drug trafficking and illegal immigration. In addition, the natural disasters oil spills and effect of climate change are threats and challenges that impinge on the national security of the Indian Ocean countries. The economic dimension of security challenges in the Indian Ocean region will become important in order to ensure security of vital trade routes particularly the choke points in the Indian Ocean.

In the post-Cold War period, nations are very careful in their interaction with one another as the bipolar system ended. During the Cold War period there was some kind of discipline among nation states imposed by the ideological confrontation. The international politics of the post-Cold War is not the same in the Cold War period. There is no ideological confrontation at the international level. Nations are more concerned about resolving their basic economic problem rather on pure military security. International cooperation is required for the protection and promotion of national interests, concerning peace, security and development. No nation whatsoever powerful can protect its national interest by pursuing an isolationist policy. This understanding among nations forced them to unite and work together to resolve domestic as well as external problems through international cooperation.

India's maritime policy also underwent a sea change in the post-Cold War period. The policy of exclusive engagement and elimination of outside powers has given place to overt engagement with extra regional powers. This has been well reflected in India's joint military exercises along with the US, Japan, France, and Australia. India no longer considers the external power presence as a threat to its security. Rather it considers that a joint effort is required to wipe out the major threat to India and international community posed by terrorism. It is not possible for any single nation whatsoever powerful to address the menace of international terrorism singlehandedly. India began to realize the importance of a realist approach in framing its foreign policy objectives and pursuing it through increased naval power and active collaboration with extra regional as well as intra-regional powers. This policy shift in India's stand is visible in the maritime doctrine as well as in the Navy's vision document published by the Indian Navy.

It essentially encompasses:

(i) Shaping a favourable maritime environment in the IOR for operations in peace as well as during conflict.
(ii) Preventing incursions by powers inimical to India's national interests by actively engaging countries in the IOR littoral, and rendering speedy and quality assistance in fields of interest to them.
(iii) Engaging extra-regional powers and regional navies in mutually beneficial activities to ensure the security of India's maritime interests.
(iv) Projecting the Indian Navy as a professional, credible force and the primary tool for maritime cooperation.[44]

India has also ear marked the area which falls within its immediate concern. "India's growing international stature gives it strategic relevance in the area ranging from the Persian Gulf to the Strait of Malacca...." While enumerating the basic features of India's post-Cold War Indian Ocean policy "India has exploited the fluidities of the emerging world order to forge new links through a combination of diplomatic repositioning, economic resurgence and military firmness."[45]

India's Maritime Security Interests

India maritime security interests embraces the protection of India's vast coastline of7,516 km. India's maritime zones, over which it has certain rights and obligations, include a territorial sea up to 12 nm (22 kms) from the baseline, a contiguous zone from 12 to 24 nm (22-44 kms), an Exclusive Economic Zone (EEZ) from 12 to 200 nm (22-370 kms) and a continental shelf up to 200 nm. These zones currently comprise 2.013 million sq km area of sea which is the 12th largest in the world and equivalent to two-thirds of the total land area. India's has thousand-plus island territories and offshore installations. Again nearly 70 per cent of India's energy requirements of crude oil are currently shipped from abroad, increased focus would be required on the ability to maintain the safety and security of energy shipments and the prevention of any disruption of supply through multilateral cooperation. Another important maritime security interest of India is the prevention of maritime terrorism through multilateral efforts.

India's maritime interests are as follows: [46]

1. Protect India's sovereignty and territorial integrity against threats in the maritime environment.
2. Promote safety and security of Indian citizens, shipping, fishing, trade, energy supply, assets and resources in the maritime domain.
3. Pursue peace, stability and security in India's maritime zones, maritime neighbourhood and other areas of maritime interest.
4. Preserve and project other national interests in the maritime dimension.

India's Maritime Security: Major Objectives

The major maritime security objective of India is to safeguard national maritime interests at all times.

This includes:

1. To deter conflict and coercion against India.
2. To conduct maritime military operations in a manner that enables early termination of conflict on terms favourable to India.
3. To shape a favourable and positive maritime environment, for enhancing net security in India's areas of maritime interest.
4. To protect Indian coastal and offshore assets against attacks and threats emanating from or at sea.
5. To develop requisite maritime force levels and maintain the capability for meeting India's maritime security requirements.[47]

The task of providing security to the vast coastline, unlike the land borders, is a complex phenomenon involving multiple stake-holders, such as shipping, fisheries, offshore exploration and production, tourism, and scientific community. It is not only important to protect and promotes the multifarious interests of different stake holders but also involve them in the maritime security programme. Again many external factors that condition the peace and security in the Indian Ocean region have an impact on the maritime security of India. Therefore, any policy initiative towards maritime security of India is interplay of domestic factors and external factors. As far as the external factors are concerned it has less control. The success of India's Indian Ocean policy depends on framing a dynamic policy in tune with the external factors manifested and also considering the domestic prerequisites.

It appears that India has adopted a three-pronged strategy to ensure maritime security through a more inclusive and pragmatic Indian Ocean policy. Firstly through diplomatic means, India has pursued a policy of cooperation with all major players in the Indian Ocean, including extra regional powers. This policy would help India to increase its international stature. The Indo-US strategic partnership in the Indo-Pacific region is an earnest attempt in this direction. The alliance of India, US, Japan and Australia, the democratic countries initiative towards rule-based ocean governance and free and uninterrupted SLOC and sea borne trade also attempted to deter any potential challenge to peace and security in the Indian Ocean from any corner that pays less heed to rule based Ocean governance. The process of globalization has also accelerated better and cordial interaction with outside powers as the movement of people as well as commodities would further cement relation between nations.

India has developed a friendly and cordial relation not only by bilateral exchange with nations but also strengthened the bilateral cooperation through interactions in regional organizations, such as ASEAN, EAS, SCO, BRICS, ASEM, IBSA, APTA, BIMSTEC and IOR ARC. India is vigorously pursuing the objective to become a developed nation by 2020. This requires the Indian economy to maintain an annual average growth rate of 8 percent per annum. India has framed the "Look East" policy and later the Act East policy in pursuance of this objective. Now the Act East Policy is a vital part of India's foreign policy. More than an external economic policy or a political slogan, the Act East Policy was a strategic shift in India's vision of the world and its place in the evolving global economy. It was also a manifestation of India's belief that developments in East Asia are of direct consequence to its security and development. Therefore India actively engaged in creating a bond of friendship and cooperation with East Asia that has a strong economic foundation and a cooperative paradigm of positive inter-connectedness of security interests. India becomes a member of the ARF in 1996 and considers it as an experiment in fashioning a pluralistic, cooperative security order reflective of the diversity of the Asia Pacific region. India is also a member of the East Asia Summit (EAS) which includes the ASEAN members and India, China, Japan, Republic of Korea, Australia, and New Zealand. It focuses on energy, environment, climate change, and sustainable development. The Act East Policy of India has included not only vigorous interaction with ASEAN but also improved relation with China. The ultimate objective was to evolve an Asian Economic Community on the lines of EU.

India has also pursued a policy of strengthening its economic and military power. It appears that in order to increase the national power India not only declared itself as a nuclear weapon power but also augmented its non-nuclear defence capabilities manifold. The maritime doctrine of India focuses mainly on building blue water navy.[48] India's role in ensuring the security of Indian Ocean region has been recognized by major players in the region mainly because of the major shift in its external policy through a pragmatic approach. As a result India was not hesitant to cooperate with any regional and extra regional powers. India has undertaken several innovative steps towards economic resurgence of the country. India's initiative to interact with nations at the bilateral and multilateral levels through various regional groupings appears to be based on this policy.

India's foreign policy has been adapted to the demands of the rapidly changing global, regional and domestic environments. The main drivers for reshaping India's foreign policy appears to have been the sustained dynamism of the Indian economy, emergence as a responsible Nuclear Weapon State, global expectations of India's role on the international stage and the capability to shoulder both regional and global responsibilities. India's engagement with the world community has grown to ensure a peaceful and supportive international environment that contributes to India's development goals. India advocates the need to evolve a new paradigm of cooperation, relevant to the contemporary world, in which global threats are addressed by global responses, and multilateralism becomes the preferred norm for addressing global challenges including terrorism, environmental degradation and economic meltdown.

Though India had made several strides in improving its relation with regional and extra regional countries, the India-Pakistan relation still remain one of distrust and mutual suspicion as it was during the Cold War period. This shows the great power rivalry was not the sole cause for regional disputes though great power rivalry accentuated regional rivalry. Again the India–China border dispute also remains without a solution though China is India's largest trading partner. It shows that neither the unresolved bilateral political issues, nor the divergent political systems based on democratic and totalitarianism, are hindrance to economic relations between India and China. It also shows the growing significance of economic security rather than pure military security.

It appears that in the post-Cold War period pure military security considerations has been replaced by economic security. The existence of nontraditional threat to security demands better cooperation among nations. The blurred boundary between international security and national security on the one hand and the national security and human security also demand better interaction among nations. In order to address the basic problems related to human security the countries in the Indian Ocean region has to come out of their Cold War period mind set. Thus peace and security in the Indian Ocean region depends largely on better interaction among countries in the region and extra regional countries to ensure human security. In the post-Cold War period any initiatives towards peace and security in the Indian Ocean region are dependent more on collaborations in economic security than on pure military security. The Indian Ocean Rim Association for Regional Cooperation (IOR-ARC) though a feeble attempt to establish economic community in the Indian Ocean, it is a welcome step towards stronger regional economic forum.

It appears that in the post-Cold War period the initiative towards peace and security in the Indian Ocean is to be undertaken at three stages:

1. At the initial stage greater transparency is required in the economic and security relations among Indian Ocean countries.
2. In the second stage confidence building measures is to be undertaken at the bilateral and multilateral levels with the active involvement of extra regional countries.
3. Towards the final stage organizational set up to maintain peace and security through greater interaction among sub regional forums such as SAARC, ASEAN, GCC, and BIMSTEC.

Eventually maritime security of India depends largely on the security situation prevalent in the Indian Ocean region. Though the role of India in influencing the security situation in the Indian Ocean region is limited, it can play a leading role through diplomatic manoeuvering. With the advent of accelerated pace of globalization, the emergence of nontraditional threat to the security of nations, the growing significance of human security concerns, it is imperative to address issues related to maritime security in a comprehensive manner. The blurred boundary between human security concerns and national security concerns once again necessitates such an approach. In short, maritime security of India is interplay of domestic as well as external policy preferences and responses. The national security predicament in the Indian Ocean region is very difficult to comprehend. It seems to be a clash of democratic values and totalitarian traditions and the divergent means adopted by them in addressing their respective national security concerns. Thus Indian Ocean offers both a challenge as well as an opportunity to frame India's maritime security policy.

NOTES

1 UN Document. A/AC,159/1/Rev.

2 Ibid.

3 Standard Encyclopedia of the World's Oceans and Islands (London, 1969) p.161. Also McGraw Hill, Encyclopedia of Ocean and Atmosphere Sciences (London, 1980), p.200.
4 Ibid.
5 Ibid.
6 A detailed list of Straits and Channel in and adjoining Indian Ocean. See, UN Doc.A/AC.159/1.
7 Manorajan Bezboruah, US Strategy in the Indian Ocean New York, 1977, p. 4.
8 Lok Sabha Secretariat, Indian Ocean as a Zone of Peace, New Delhi, 1979
9 Freedom to use the seas: India's Maritime Military Strategy, Integrated Headquarters Ministry of Defence (Navy) New Delhi, 2007, pp 25-28.
10 In UN terminology 'littoral' applies to those of the Indian Ocean states which have a direct access to the Ocean or the adjacent Red sea and Persian Gulf, and 'hinterland' to the states which have no such access but are separated from the ocean by not more than one littoral state. See Segei Vladimirov "Indian Ocean Zone of Peace Conference – A Step Forward" New Times (Moscow) Vol.34, 1979, p.4.
11 Pakistan becomes a member of the NAM only in 1979.
12 R.Suresh, *NAM and Indian Ocean as a Zone of Peace* in N.Krishnan & S.Gabriel (eds.) Indian Ocean Problems and Perspectives for Co-operation Pondicherry, 1992 p.145.
13 Two-third of the World oil reserves is in Persian Gulf and Red sea, North-East African and Indonesia also have oil resources. The Indian Ocean region has around three-fourth of the total oil reserves of the world. The rest of the world mainly the developed countries are greatly dependent on the Indian Ocean region for oil. Studies showed that in 1976 the US imported about 38 per cent, Japan 75 per cent, UK 71 per cent, West Germany 78.3 per cent, and Italy 82 per cent of crude oil from West Asia. See Lok Sabha Secretariat, n.8, p.3.
14 Ibid., p.3.
15 Ibid.
16 The countries in the Indian Ocean region mostly trade with the industrially developed countries of Western Europe, Japan, USA and USSR. The Intra-regional trade among them is comparatively very less.
17 Jawaharlal Nehru, the founder of India's Foreign Policy stated in September 1946: "In the sphere of Foreign Affairs, India will follow an independent policy, keeping away from power politics of groups aligned one against the other....", See The Indian Annual Register 1946, Vol.II, Calcutta, Annual Register Office 1947, pp.252-53.
18 Indian Council of World Affairs, report on Defence Security in the Indian Ocean. (New Delhi, 1957) p.iii. K.M. Panikkar in his seminal work India and the Indian Ocean: An Essay on the Influence of Sea Power in 1945 argued that "the Indian Ocean must remain truly Indian" On the same line K.B.Vidya in his book Naval Defence of India, in 1947, argued that Indian Ocean can be an Indian lake if India is the Supreme and undisputed power over the waters of the Indian Ocean.
19 The Interim government had also recognized the necessity for a sufficiently strong naval force to guard India's long coastline and its sea-borne trade.
20 Lok Sabha, Parliamentary Debates 19 December 1963, Cols. 56, 75, 67, 75.
21 At that point of time India wanted the US presence because in the Sino-Indian conflict US indirectly backed India. See. The Times (London) 10 November 1962, p.7.
22 See .Rajya Sabha, Parliamentary Debates 18 November 1965, Cols. 1815-22.
23 The External Affairs Minister of India, Dinesh Singh stated: "We are against the setting up of any foreign bases in this area". Lok Sabha, Parliamentary Debates, 19 March 1969, Cols.3-5.

24 The External Affairs Minister, Dinesh Singh stated on 19 March 1969: 'Within the limitation of our resources we shall certainly take every possible step to safeguard our interest in the Indian Ocean". Lok Sabha, Parliamentary Debates 19 March 1969, Cols. 1-10; The Deputy Minister of External Affairs Surendra Palsingh on 18 December 1969 stated: "We want the Indian Ocean area to be made an area of peace and cooperation and any introduction of military forces from any side will be against our policy. We are also in touch with all the countries concerned about this matter and there is a great deal of identity views between us and the other countries". Rajya Sabha, Parliamentary Debates 18 December 1969, Cols. 4650-4653.

25 UN Resolution A/2832(XXVI)

26 UN Doc. A/C.1/26/PV.1849

27 As per the Simla agreement both India and Pakistan agreed that they would strive to resolve their outstanding disputes bilaterally.

28 UN Doc. A/29/PV.2247

29 The abstention of Pakistan was mainly to attract the attention of international community towards the threat emanates from within the Indian Ocean region.

30 SIPRI Yearbook of World Armament and Disarmament 1978 Stockholm 1979 p. 474.

31 India had always refers to the 1971 UN Declaration on Indian Ocean as a Zone of Peace.

32 Foreign Affairs Record, Vol. 24, No.3, 1978, p.134.

33 Zalmay Khalizad, "Intervention in Afganistan Implication for the security of South West Asia", in William L.Dowly and Russel B.Trood (eds.) The Indian Ocean Perspectives on a Strategic Arena (New Delhi, 1987), pp.338-351.

34 NAM Doc. NAC 9/PC/Doc.1/Rev.3

35 According to Richard N. Haass it is Non polar system. The principal characteristic of twenty-first-century international relations is turning out to be non polarity: a world dominated not by one or two or even several states but rather by dozens of actors possessing and exercising various kinds of power. This represents a tectonic shift from the past.

36 *Hindustan Times*, Sept 21, 1991.

37 *The Times of India*, Feb 5, 1992 .

38 For instance, the Indo-US Civilian Nuclear Deal; Joint Indo-US Naval Exercises in the Indian Ocean.

39 Suresh R (2011) Peace in the Indian Ocean: A South Asian Perspective, Serials Publications, New Delhi.

40 K.M. Panikkar (1945) India and the Indian Ocean, George Allen & Unwin, London.

41 Quoted in Suresh R, n.12.

42 Annual Report 2004-2005 Ministry of Defence, Government of India, New Delhi 2005.

43 Freedom to use the seas: India's Maritime Military Strategy, Integrated Headquarters Ministry of Defense, Government of India, New Delhi, 2007. Also see The Indian Navy's Vision Document, May 2006. www.indiannavy.nic.in

44 Ibid.

45 Ibid.

46 Ensuring Secure Seas: Indian Maritime Security Strategy, Indian Navy, Naval Strategic Publication (NSP), 1.2, October 2015, pp. 9-10.

47 Ibid.

48 Suresh R, India's Coastal Security: A Perspective in Dr C Vinodan (Ed) Defence and National Security of India: Concerns and Strategies, New Century Publications, New Delhi 2017.

24

ASEAN-India-China Triangle and Geopolitics of Indo-Pacific

Sudhir Singh

ASEAN came into being in 1967 with the sole aim to safeguard its territorial integrity from the Chinese expansionist designs. Today after 54 years of its formation this baggage of history still prevails in the mindset of the ASEAN's ruling elites. ASEAN-India-China trilateral relationships are going to reshape new geopolitics in Indo-Pacific. Total volume of trade between China and the countries of the Association of Southeast Asian Nations (ASEAN) hit a record high of 587.87 billion US dollars in 2018, up 14.1 per cent year on year, as per official with the Chinese Ministry of Commerce.[1] Despite this high-profile volume of bilateral trade, they have a prevailing situation of trust deficit. India also fought war with China in 1962 and still over 14000 square km Indian territory is captive under China. Again Sino-Indian bilateral trade stands over $87 billion dollar by FY 2018–19. In 2012 leadership has changed in China and a new duo of Xi & Li have taken over and will be in the helm of affairs till their life time as new resolution was passed regarding it by Chinese puppet parliament. India has also witnessed amazing political changes. Thanks to the political acumen of the Indian common man, they have given full majority to Narendra Modi led BJP. Since 1984, the Indian political horizon was dominated by the regional parties who have less or parochial leanings of foreign policy. In May 2019, again Modi government returned to power for second term (2019–24). It is bound to accelerate the policies adopted by Modi-1 government.

In September 2014, Chinese President Li has visited India and inked many deals and pledged $20 billion dollar investment in next 5 years. But during his stay in India, Chinese army had made incursions in the western sector of Ladakh. In May 2013, Chinese Prime Minister Li had also visited India and during his stay the same kind of incident took place. In recent years, particularly after the inking of Nuclear treaty between the United States and India in 2008, these incidents have gone up. During Kargil conflict (1999) Prime Minister Nawaz Sharif and the Chief of Army Staff General Pervez Musharraf had visited Beijing to garner support against India. But the Chinese had not only declined their demand but advised them to resolve the issue with India through amicable means.[2]

After Pakistani foreign minister's Beijing visit in August 2019 in the backdrop of scrapping of Article 370, a joint statement stressed, "China recognises that the Kashmir dispute must be properly resolved "based on the UN Charter, relevant UN Security Council resolutions and bilateral agreement".[3] Before it China had blocked Masood Azhar to be designated as global terrorist by the United Nations in the backdrop of Pulwama terror attack (February 2019) but lifted it in May 2019 and Azhar was declared an international terrorist.

India and China are cooperating partner's in BRICS, Trilateral Cooperation and gamut of ASEAN platforms. They are on the same page on global warming issues.

Despite many convergences they have more arenas of divergences therefore their relations remain conflictual as opined by Kenneth Walsh. Long back Kautilaya stated that foreign policy is determined by the convergences of interests and other equalities hardly matter. If it is not then why Soviet Union and China, Vietnam and China, India and the United States, Iran and Saudi Arabia etc. have been in hostile state of relationship despite their many ideological and other convergences.

After the end of the Cold War and 9/11 terror attack the tilt of global power is inclined towards Indo-Pacific. China had been nursing its global aspiration since its present incarnation in 1949 and willing to dominate Indo-Pacific in the contemporary scenario. India, Japan, South Korea, Indonesia and Iran are also important powers and willing to keep Indo-Pacific multi-polar.

The problem of Indo-Pacific is that major countries are in cold war status for their dominance over the region before the region has established its dominance over the global system. After the Industrial Revolution, Europe had established its dominance over the global system and after that they started fighting against each other. Asian powers are replicating the same module but before their dominance over the global system. They are trying to establish their own versions of power equilibrium over Indo-Pacific. It is the root of prevailing trust deficits in Indo-Pacific. India and ASEAN along with Japan, South Korea and Australia stood together in this evolving power equilibrium of Indo-Pacific and China is in opposition with some puppet countries like Pakistan, North Korea and Cambodia.

The power game is like a different kind of cold war, where economic relations are going up without helping strategic relations. It is strategically important that president of India's Vietnam visit in September 2014 visit coincided with the Chinese president's India visit. During the Chinese president's visit $20 billion dollar was announced as investment in India but incidents of incursion were reported during the president's stay. It has vindicated the fact that China is not interested to resolve the boundary dispute for the sake of economic benefits. China keeps saying that McMahon line drawn after 1914 Shimla conference is illegal but it has resolved its border dispute with Myanmar in 1960s only on the basis of this line. This attitude of China has again rejected the notion of economic integration theory which propagates that growing economic relations will reduce the tension between hostile countries. After returning from India President Xi had given the impression that he had no prior knowledge of border incursion in the western sector of Ladakh during his India visiting September. In fact, it was his well planned move. To understand the framework, what the Chinese Communist Party (CCP) leader Xi Jinping said (Speech delivered at a party Politburo Study session convened on 28 January 2013) are important. He declared that, *"China will never pursue its development at the cost of sacrificing interests of other countries.... We will never give up our legitimate rights and will never sacrifice our national core interests. No country should presume that we will engage in trade involving our core interests or that we will swallow the 'bitter fruit' of harming our sovereignty, security or development interests."*[4]

> The Chinese are reminding India that it is not a powerful country. For Mearsheimer, rising powers tend to seek regional hegemony and China is heading in this direction.[5] The Chinese have refused to adhere to international laws to resolve South China Sea and East China Sea dispute with ASEAN and Japan respectively. In Tibet's case too, China has violated all norms of the international standards to respect human rights. To vindicate the prevailing situation in the Asia-Pacific the following statement of the Philippines President is self-explanatory.

The Philippines is one of the disputant countries against China over South China Sea. Philippines President Benigno S. Aquino III called for nations around the world to do more to support the Philippines in resisting China's assertive claims to the seas near his country, drawing a comparison to the West's failure to support Czechoslovakia against Hitler's demands for Czech land in 1938.

Like Czechoslovakia, the Philippines faces demands to surrender territory piecemeal to a much stronger foreign power and needs more robust foreign support for the rule of international law if it is to resist.

"If we say yes to something we believe is wrong now, what guarantee is there that the wrong will not be further exacerbated down the line?" he said, "At what point do you say, 'Enough is enough'? Well, the world has to say it—remember that the Sudetenland was given in an attempt to appease Hitler to prevent World War II."[6] Tokyo and Manila are even more expressive about their willingness to uphold territorial claims, no matter what it costs. On many occasions, Abe has vowed publicly that he will 'never make concessions' over the sovereignty of the Diaoyus/Sankakus and will defend 'Japanese territory at all costs.'[7]

Philippines president has been positive for China and is seeking cordial relations. In June 2019, Chinese trawler sank a Philippines boat and over 20 of its fishermen in serious crisis have been finally rescued by the Vietnamese boats.[8] After this incident, political status of the president has gone down terribly.

In recent years China has clubbed its Pakistan policy with India policy. Since 2006 every visiting Chinese leader is compulsorily visiting Islamabad.[9] India demanded that China respect India's 'core national interests' in relation to its territorial integrity, in much the same way that Delhi defers to Beijing on Tibet and Taiwan. This new equivalence between Tibet and Kashmir marks a new moment in the long-running territorial disputes between India and China.[10] Weeks before September 2014 Chinese President India visit, Foreign minister, Sushma Swaraj demanded that Beijing must respect Indian sensitiveness if it wishes that New Delhi will reciprocate. In August 2019 when Modi government scrapped Article 370 and made Ladakh a union territory, it was opposed by China. India cautioned China that it is an internal affair and it has no right to interfere. Indirectly a stern message was passed to China that India could raise the Tibet issue as disputed one and it will be extremely embarrassing for China.

Modi government has upgraded zero-sum-game policy with China. For that purpose, Japan has emerged as a golden asset for India and has emerged as new fulcrum of India's newly launched 'Act East Policy'. In his August-September Japan visit, PM Modi and Japanese PM, Shinzo Abe proved that they have immense convergences and bound to cooperate. Chinese are extremely jealous with this deepening relationship. The growing bonhomie between United States and India has created a situation akin of 'Prisoner's Dilemma' for China. During Cold War era India-United States relations were termed as 'Estranged Democracies' which has been converted as 'Engaged Democracies' in the 21st century. President George W. Bush (2000-2008) contributed immensely to cement these ties.

> President Bush and his Indian interlocutors were careful not to define their relations in terms of opposition to China. Bush's surprising warmth to India, his willingness to invest huge political capital in transforming the bilateral relationship, and his controversial decision to facilitate nuclear energy trade with India were widely interpreted as driven by a desire to make India a counterweight to a rising China. While there were no official proclamations to this effect, a key architect of Bush's India policy, Robert Blackwill, would later reveal the centrality of the China factor. 'President George W. Bush based his transformation of US-India Relations on the core strategic principle of democratic India as a key factor in balancing the rise of Chinese power', he noted. He made it clear that this was not based on the concept of 'containing' China. Nonetheless, Blackwill added, without this China factor at the fore, 'the Bush Administration would not have negotiated the Civil Nuclear Agreement and the Congress would not have approved it.'[11] During President Barrack Obama tenure (2009-2016) the Bush era's warmth had declined a bit but it improved again in the second half of his tenure. The warmth President Obama had shown during PM Modi in his September 2014 United States visit is self-explanatory. President Donald Trump administration has also sustained the tempo. It has launched trade war against China since July 2018 and also warned China to adhere with relevant international law in the dispute of South China Sea. In April 2018 Trump administration stressed that India has the "capability and potential" to play a weightier role in the Indo-Pacific region.
>
> Briefing reporters on the Trump administration's Indo-Pacific Strategy, the Deputy Assistant Secretary of State for East Asian and Pacific Affairs, Alex Wong said it is in the US' interest as well as of the entire region that India plays an increasingly weighty role in the region.

According to Mr. Wong, "India as a nation has invested in a free and open order. It is a democracy. It is a nation that can anchor free and open order in the Indo-Pacific region. And it's our policy to ensure that India does play that role and that it becomes over time a more influential player in the region,"[12] China was never comfortable with this nomenclature which has been emphasised by the United States since the last one decade.

China has been extremely jealous of this cooperation among democracies. Coincidently, a majority of the ASEAN countries, United States, Japan, Australia and India, all have adopted democracy as a way of governance. *Global Times*, the mouth piece of Chinese regime had expressed this frustration in December 2010.

"The title of 'the biggest democratic nation' looks like a glass of red wine enjoyed together by India and the West. But it doesn't generate anything substantial that is of India's national interests. With a huge population and much work left to be done in developing the economy, perhaps India won't get too drunk to act superior in front of China, because such superiority will delight India much less than it delights the West. See Who wins the Dragon-elephant contention".[13]

> Sino-Indian rivalry is millennia old. Both countries have millennia old historical linkage, but they never accepted each other as their friends. After many decades of the spread of Buddhism in China, Han Yu, an anti-Buddhist intellectual in the 9th century (who later became the harbingers of Confucianism). Put the issue starkly in his 'Memorial on Buddhism' written in 819.

"The Buddha was of a barbarian origin. His language differed from Chinese speech; his cloth of a different cut; his mouth did not pronounce the prescribed words of the Former Kings; his body was not clad in the garments prescribed by the former kings. He did not recognize the relationship between prince and the subject, nor the sentiment of father and son."[14]

This status has been further emboldened with the anticipation of shifting of global power towards Asia. ASEAN has become more powerful to tilt the balance in this game of balance of power. Historian KM Panikkar highlighted the Indian importance in ASEAN in pre-world war periods. According to him, " A free and stable government in India conscious of its responsibilities and capable of playing its part in Southeast Asia, is the essential prerequisite for the success of such a collective security system. In the absence of such a government in India he insisted Southeast Asia will remain the cockpit of colonial ambitions, incapable of defending itself, and a prey to the predatory urge of any power which is strong enough to attack it."[15] Christopher Jaffrelot has argued, convincingly, that India's post-Cold War Look East Policy could be traced back to the Asianist ideals of the Indian national movement.[16] Lord Curzon had also dreamt of India as an engine of Asian growth during British rule over India.

> Asian situation is quite anarchic and quite close to Hobbes Leviathan's point of view. According to the neorealist thinker, Kenneth Waltz, 'Because the future is uncertain, states are more concerned about relative gains and how gains will be divided. For this reason cooperation is hard to achieve in international relations. The basic nature of the international relations is therefore essentially conflict.'[17]

Despite high voltage trade relations, China and ASEAN have hostile relations on strategic affairs. India must nurse ASEAN by all counts. There are hardly any divergences between India and ASEAN. ASEAN countries are very much interested that India must accelerate its presence in their part. India has rightly done while extending its imprint in South China Sea and developing all-weather relations with Vietnam. ASEAN countries are bound to sustain their Look West Policy towards India. Due to expanding security concerns, ASEAN countries have accelerated the pace of accumulation of weapons. This market is over $40 billion and India must put aside shyness and export weapons to these countries. Modi government has started this work with new will power and slated to sustain this tempo. Needless to say, that it will not only contain China within its own backyard but embolden India's strategic importance on the larger canvass of Indo-Pacific. It will be extremely helpful to India and ASEAN to reshape the geopolitics of Indo-Pacific on the basis of peace, development and international order.

NOTES

1 Xinhua, March 19, 2019.

2 Singh, Sudhir, *India in Emerging Asia-Pacific*, Pentagon Press, New Delhi, 2014, p. 17.

3 Naveed Siddiqui, China to 'Uphold justice for Pakistan on Kashmir Issue, *Dawn*, Karachi, August 9, 2019.

4 D.S. Rajan; *The Meaning of Latest Chinese Transgression in Ladakh, Ahead of Chinese President's Visit to India,* C3S Paper No. 2040 dated 17 September 2014.

5 Mearsheimer, John J. China's Unpeaceful Rise, *Current History*, 2006, 105 (690), p. 161.

6 Keith Bradsher, Philippine Leader Sounds Alarm on China, *New York Times*, New York, February 5, 2014.

7 Teddy Ng, 'Shinzo Abe Slams Beijing "Provocations" on Island Tour', *South China Morning Post*, Hong Kong, 18 July 2013.

8 Indrani Bagchi, ASEAN Links its Indo-Pacific Strategy to India's Outreach, Times of India, New Delhi, June 24, 2019.

9 Xinjiang has been boiling since last few years and emerged as bleeding grounds of China. It is an open secret that all Non-State Actors of Pakistan have extended its support to this movement. Despite this serious factor since 2006 every Chinese leader (President, PM) while visiting India visiting Pakistan also. In September 2014, Chinese President could not visit Islamabad due to ongoing unrest in Islamabad.

10 Pranab Dhal Samanta, India equates Jammu & Kashmir with Tibet, *The Indian Express*, November 15, 2010, available at http://www.indianexpress.com/news/india-equates-jammu-&-kashmir-with-tibet/711151/ accessed on January 11, 2011.

11 Robert Blackwill, The Future of US-India Relations, Address to the Confederation of Indian Industry, New Delhi, May 5, 2009, available athttp://www.stratpost.com/the-future-of-us-indiarelations, accessed on January 9, 2011.

12 India can play a weightier role in Indo-Pacific region: U.S., PTI, New Delhi, April 3, 2018.

13 Global Times, December 16, 2010, available at http://opinion. globaltimes.cn/editorial/2010-

12/602061.html accessed on January 10, 2011.

14 Sen, Amartya, *The Argumentative Indian,* Penguin, London, 2005, p. 170.

15 K.M. Panikkar, *The Future of South East Asia; An Indian View*, Macmillan, New York, 1943, pp. 11-12.

16 Chirstopher Jaffrelot, " India's Look East Policy; An Asianist Strategy in Perspective, *India Review,* Vol. 2, No. 2, 2003, pp. 35-68.

17 Kenneth N. Waltz, Reflections on Theory of International Politics in Robert O. Keohane ed. *Neorealist and Its Critics*, New York, Columbia University Press, 1986, p.102.

25

Five Decades of ASEAN Saga: Perambulating Its Significance from the Prism of Indian Foreign Policy

Tridib Chakraborti

In the domain of Southeast Asia, the concept of regionalism as a means of associating cohesive relations, in order to promote their common politico-economic interests, had not gained momentum in this region immediately after the end of the Second World War, due to a number of inter-state hostilities stemming not only from the ironic nature of the constituents, but also the different and mutually discordant external military and security factors. However, after years of conflict and turmoil, the natural craving for peace provided the immediate impetus for regional cooperation in this region, which ultimately formalized with the formation of the Association of Southeast Asian Nations (ASEAN) on 8 August 1967 in Bangkok with the five original member countries namely Indonesia, Malaysia, Singapore, Thailand and the Philippines. Following this initiative, Brunei Darussalam joined ASEAN on 8 January 1984, Vietnam on 28 July 1995, Laos and Myanmar on 23 July 1997 and Cambodia on 30 April 1999. The formation and expansion of this membership and promotion of the principle of non-intervention is the core centrality of this organization for its main collective regional response. This configuration of ASEAN was the product of the lack of peace and stability from which the whole Southeast Asian region was suffering since sometime past, together with the ASEAN states' apparent dislike for the Big Power interference, leading to the convergence of the non-communist states' political outlook, which made the establishment of ASEAN possible. From this point of view, ASEAN can be regarded as the demonstration of a type of nationalistic urge on the part of its members to build up their collective self-reliance, independent of Big Power's individual regional equations and cooperative initiative for the development of this region.

The establishment of ASEAN in 1967 was hinged on the urge to promote economic cooperation and the welfare of the people in the Southeast Asian region. The members of this regional organization came under one umbrella with three core objectives in mind: to promote the economic, social and cultural development of the region through cooperative programmes; to safeguard the political and economic stability of the region against big power rivalry; and to serve as a forum for the resolution of intra-regional differences. Thus, this regional organization was no doubt a product of the Cold War and envisaged the written goal of containment of communism. Before its establishment, several attempts were made by some countries of Southeast Asia to establish a regional organization. Regional grouping like Association of Southeast Asia (ASA) in 1961, followed by MAPHILINDO in 1963, ended almost at the time of their birth. However, these regional initiatives created a space for congenial environment to strengthen relations between countries in the region and to promote cooperation in areas such as economics, science and culture and which ultimately paved the way for the establishment of ASEAN with the signing of the Bangkok Declaration on 8 August 1967. This Bangkok Declaration presented the aims and purposes of ASEAN that shall be to promote active collaboration and mutual assistance on matters of common interest in the economic, social, cultural, agricultural and industrial, scientific and transport spheres and to raise the living standards of their peoples.[1] In its elongated chequered history of development of more than 50 years, ASEAN can be regarded as a successful organization, where its purpose has shifted from fighting communism to principally fostering economic cooperation. Its member states have not fought one another and have grown stronger through integration. It has set its sights on achieving a "people-centred" community and narrowing the development gaps between its member states. It has also given importance to developing closer ties with countries outside the region, to promoting ASEAN's centrality in shaping the regional architecture and to contributing to the global community of nations, which resulted in development from the Pacific Rim to the Indian Ocean Rim and across the entire Indo-Pacific region and the continued nurturing of the group's importance.[2]

During these more than 50 years of its existence and performance, based on certain central principles through trial and error method, ASEAN has emerged as one of the most successful experiments in regional cooperation in the developing world and currently in the emerging global architecture. Through its multiple policies of trial and triumph, ASEAN has come to play a very constructive and prominent role in developing a sense of regional identity in Southeast Asia. ASEAN has also faced some major problems like Vietnam's invasion of Cambodia, the Asian financial crisis, transmigration and influx of refugees, drug trafficking and transnational crimes, East Timor crisis, Myanmar's military repression, transnational problems such as the forest fires in Indonesia, low-intensity conflicts, terrorism and ISIS issue, South China Sea dispute, etc. These intra and inter-state problems severely posed threats not only to the survival of the region and the states, but also to the prospect for regional order as a whole. Furthermore, in the mid-1990s, issues like Thailand's devaluation of the Baht, Myanmar's military repression, Cambodia's coup d'etat and the sacking of Malaysian Deputy Prime Minister, Anwar Ibrahim, etc., have all generated critical comments on government policy from different political leaders in the neighbouring countries, and placed a big question mark about ASEAN's principles of non-interference and non-confrontation. Moreover, the Southeast Asian region also witnessed plethora of domestic problems that have obvious transnational dimensions, adversely affecting neighbouring countries as well as the entire region. Therefore, all these above mentioned issues sporadically disturbed the normal functioning of ASEAN, and raised a big question mark about ASEAN's principles of no-interference and non-confrontation, based on the Treaty of Amity and Cooperation (TAC), signed among members of ASEAN in February 1976. These intra and inter-state problems have sparked occasional political and structural debates on ASEAN's operation and functioning in the mid-1990s, with special reference of its core 'principle of non-intervention'. However, after a prolonged debate, finally all its members regard the retention of the principle of non-intervention, based on consensus, as the essential bonding glue of its functioning. What is at issue is the need for some adjustments to take account of the changed circumstances. Overall, the need to rethink non-interference should be seen not as an abstract moral concern associated with human rights protection, but as a matter of a "practical" necessity without which ASEAN cannot stay relevant and address real world changes and challenges.

What appeared to be the most important to the ASEAN members is that many of their internal problems, which have regional and transnational dimensions, occasionally cause serious tensions and divided opinions among the countries of Southeast Asia. However, in most of the cases, realizing the depth of the problem, the ASEAN members clearly understand that these are no longer an individual undertaking of the affected countries, and mostly demand a coordinated and concerted response by the members. This resulted in that the ASEAN members have always tried to work together to address the problems and mobilize its own regional resources to prevent the crises. The ASEAN members' overall outlook has been entirely based on dialogue, consultation, cooperation, engagement and mutual interaction. It prefers engagement to become more 'flexible', and interaction 'enhanced'. Both engagement and interaction are therefore maintained. It is also trying to balance between what is desirable and what is possible, between the ideal and the practical, between desired ends and available means and between international involvement and national sovereignty. It tries to tackle many of its problems by regional consensus, without breaking away from the principle of non-intervention. The majority members of ASEAN felt that these principles are inherent in the very nature of the organization and have contributed to ASEAN's success in the past and will continue to do so in the future. It is a fact that during its more than five decades of existence, the overall ASEAN economics have come a long way—from 1967 to 2016—the aggregate gross domestic product of the five original members (Indonesia, Malaysia, Singapore, Thailand and the Philippines) grew by a factor of 14.5, in real terms, to $2.2 trillion. That is roughly 3% of the global economy. Similarly, these five countries' combined GDP per capita soared 39-fold to $4,760 in 2016, from just $122 in 1967. Having had several miracle years of economic growth as well as having successfully faced the global economic downturn, the merchandise trade of ASEAN's economy remained strong at USD2.2 trillion in 2016, of which 23.1% was intra-ASEAN. Intra-region trade is also expected to stage a rebound in 2018 mirroring the projected broad-based improvements in global trade. In 2016 the region attracted USD 98.0 billion foreign direct investment (FDI) inflows, of which 25.2% was intra-ASEAN, reflecting continued investors' confidence in the region.[3] Moreover, in 2003 the ASEAN members adopted ASEAN Economic Community (AEC) aspirations, which highlighted economic cooperation measures including lower trade and investment barriers; harmonized rules and regulations; and ways to place the region in the global value chain of production. The aim is to create a 'single market and production base' and generate more welfare gains than those facilitated through tariff liberalization under the ASEAN Free Trade Area (AFTA) of the 1990s. Yet ASEAN is far from delivering a single market to its stakeholders. This is because the non-tariff barriers continue to prevail. The region continues to suffer from infrastructure deficiency. These factors dilute the full benefit of tariff liberalization. Moreover, this region continues to experience difficulties from the development gaps among its members. Thus, it can be said that despite achieving a significant percentage of its stipulated targets, ASEAN has not yet achieved its single market objective. However, this AEC outcome should not be viewed as a negative strategic project; rather it can be interpreted as a tool for its members to plug into global supply chains, and thereby to bargain its strength in international economic and financial matters. Despite criticism for lack of achievement of many of their targeted areas, it has largely emerged as a core regional and eminently successful regional organization in contemporary global politics.

However, during its long history of more than past five decades, ASEAN's success was multifarious. **First,** ASEAN's major achievement is the maintenance of regional peace and stability for the past 50 years. It took a common position on the crisis in Cambodia in 1978 which raised solidarity and strengthened regional security and finally amicably resolved the Cambodian conflict via peaceful negotiation. **Secondly,** together with other countries, ASEAN established the ASEAN Regional Forum (ARF) as a forum of consultation of ASEAN Member Countries and other global security players, including the European Union. Moreover, **ASEAN** is in the driver's seat in the **ASEAN** Plus Three mechanism, cooperation with China, Japan, and Republic of Korea (ROK) and currently the East Asian Summit (EAS), initiated by this regional organization functioning quite effectively. **Thirdly**, it has helped to balance the interests of Great Powers in Southeast Asia by engaging them in various dialogues and programme, such as ASEAN's Zone of Peace and Nuclear Weapons Free Zone. **Fourthly**, in response to the financial crisis of 1997, ASEAN countries earnestly focused on economic and financial recovery, while resolving to move towards economic integration for a single market. This is achieved only by accelerating the implementation of ASEAN Free Trade Area (AFTA), the ASEAN Investment Area (AIA), and the ASEAN Industrial Cooperation (AICO) scheme. **Fifthly,** ASEAN countries over the years have worked together in addressing trans-boundary problems and regional crisis, such as the trans-boundary Haze crisis, successfully prevented and eradicated the Severe Acute Respiratory Syndrome (SARS) disease and played a significant role in the tsunami-affected countries, like Indonesia, Malaysia and Thailand in December 2004 and agreed to strengthen the scheme of regional disaster management by setting up regional structures, mechanisms and strategies on disaster management. **Finally,** Narrowing the Development Gap (NDG) the ASEAN is currently aiming to reduce the development gap between the more developed member countries with the less-developed member countries, through its Initiative of ASEAN Integration (IAI) programme. In this initiative, the prime challenges are how to reduce the development gap including income disparity and inadequate infrastructure.[4] Therefore, on the whole, ASEAN remains a political and economic force because it is the only regional organization in this present global order, which gives the countries of Southeast Asia a collective voice and solid clout in dealing with extra-regional powers. Summarily then, the hallmark of the ASEAN Way, consensus guarantees that all member states, big or small, are equal in ASEAN's decision-making. Consensus was credited for bringing and keeping ASEAN members united on the path of regional cooperation despite their vast diversity. Consensus was the bonding glue that inculcated mutual trust and comfort. Consensus therefore has been indispensable to both ends of ASEAN's existence—unity in diversity. As against such background, the purpose of this article is to analyze the importance and utility of ASEAN from the mirror of Indian foreign policy.

India's Perception of ASEAN in the Cold War Period

India and ASEAN remained "awkward strangers" during the Cold War period and their relationship lacked substance. India was not among those countries that enthusiastically welcomed the formation of ASEAN in 1967. While India did not align with those countries that openly condemned this Association, it simultaneously frugally acknowledged it as an exposition of regional will. Its attitude was rather blurry which mainly originated from the fact that this regional grouping was of an exclusive sort with a pronounced pro-Western orientation.[5] New Delhi's lack of depth in political relations and weak economic linkages (due to closed and regulated economy) with ASEAN were caused due to their differences in perception and behaviour in security and other related issues of great power activities and policies in the Southeast Asian region. Besides this, India felt piqued at being left out of this regional grouping body, on account of the presence of two SEATO members-the Philippines and Thailand in the ASEAN orbit and also certain reservations existed among Indian policy makers towards ASEAN since it detracted from the non-aligned image of the organization as well as because New Delhi felt that Pakistan could influence ASEAN in a way contrary to Indian interests through its two SEATO allies within that organization.[6] Furthermore, at the time of the formation of ASEAN, its original members apprehended that this Association might be dominated by India, evoking the Western countries reservation about the Association. A country like Indonesia profoundly apprehended that her leadership may be challenged with the presence of India. Singapore, on the other hand, being dominantly Chinese in ethnicity, was deeply scared that India's anti-Chinese sentiment might dismay the advancement of the Organization and

Thailand and the Philippines were opposed to India's non-alignment and, as such they did not want to include India.[7] Moreover, India's pervasive linkage with the former Soviet Union, the India-Soviet Treaty of 1971, support of Brezhnev's plan for collective security in Asia, flaccid support to the Soviet action in Afghanistan and the Vietnamese invasion of Kampuchea by New Delhi irked many Southeast Asian countries. Besides this, India's recognition of the Heng Samrin government in Cambodia was a further setback to the ASEAN members. In fact, New Delhi, at this time, did not risk surrendering its close ties with Hanoi and Moscow because it valued its intimate relations with these countries as much more strategically important than its standing among the ASEAN members.[8]

Shifting Mindset of India towards ASEAN in the Post-Cold War Phase

In the early 1990s, global and regional politics underwent qualitative changes. The collapse of the former Soviet Union leading to the resolution of the decade long Cambodian crisis and the 1991 economic liberalization policy inaugurated by Narasimha Rao government in India, led to significant alterations in India–ASEAN relations. India under Narasimha Rao's government embarked on a substantive and wide-ranging programme of economic reforms, restructuring and liberalization and thereby bringing the Indian economy in line with those of the ASEAN countries. India's decision to give a special policy thrust to its relations with the ASEAN and "desired improved relations with individual countries in the ASEAN region and with ASEAN as a collective entity" virtually obliterated its hitherto indifferent outlook towards this regional organization. India, during this time under the Prime Minister, P.V. Narasimha Rao, announced its 'Look East' policy which was very well calculated and well thought out.

To ASEAN, India's size, population, educated middle class, industrial base, military strength, technical capability, ancient cultural ties and presence of overseas Indians were factors in its favour. Also, ASEAN's perception of New Delhi as an emerging regional power and China as a source of security threat, the volatile situation in the South China Sea due to conflicting claims over the Spratly Islands, the grisly atmosphere in the Taiwan Straits and the Korean peninsula and the no-win ties among US, Japan and China, had convinced ASEAN of the need for a paradigm shift in India–ASEAN linkages. Thus, mutual needs affected their convergence. New Delhi's 'Look East' policy therefore coincided with ASEAN's 'Look West' line and this new-found regionalization drive ultimately led to an overall normalization of relations between India and ASEAN. This convergence of bilateral interests resulted in ASEAN governments responding to Indian prelude in 1992, and between 1992 and 1996, New Delhi first became a 'sectoral dialogue' partner of the grouping and thereafter a 'full dialogue' partner. India also joined the security entity of the ASEAN, the ASEAN Regional Forum (ARF) in 1996, thereby helping to raise the profile of the security forum. But New Delhi's priority of its 'Look East' policy in its initial years concentrated more towards the developed economies within the ASEAN members and failed to coordinate a policy of promoting better partnership with the less economically developed countries of the region. However, the decision for a separate ASEAN–India Summit clearly demonstrated an opportunity for India to prove its economic influence and dynamics in the region.[9]

India's 'Look East' policy reached its distinction when the First ASEAN–India Summit took place in Phnom Penh on 5 November 2002. This preferment of India as a new actor in the orbit of ASEAN's economic, political and strategic process was a product of history of more than one decade. In this Summit, Prime Minister Atal Behari Vajpayee represented India and had the distinction of being the first leader not only of India, but also from the entire South Asia to address the ASEAN Summit. Hun Sen, the Prime Minister of Cambodia inaugurated this Summit and launched 'The Phnom Penh Agenda: Promoting Shared Prosperity and Peace Across ASEAN'. In this Summit, the Indian Prime Minister proposed to create an ASEAN–India Free Trade Area (FTA) by the year 2012, which covering about 1.5 billion consumers with a combined GNP at 1.7 trillion dollars, would gradually eliminate the trade barriers between the member countries of ASEAN and India. Prime Minister Vajpayee also agreed to offer greater tariff concessions to less-developed members of ASEAN, namely Laos, Cambodia, Vietnam and Myanmar. Thus, this India–ASEAN Summit was no doubt a watershed event in the history of bilateral relations between India and Southeast Asia since the fall of former Soviet Union, and having reached greater heights, it was urgent to implement India's long drawn 'Look East' policy not only in theory, but also in practice.[10] This dimension of India's 'Look East' policy, since 2014 under the leadership of Prime Minister Narendra Modi has re-accelerated its track, and is known as 'Act East' policy, where the countries of ASEAN and those further East, along with the countries of the Gulf and West Asia, have been integrated under the broad ambit of this newly prescribed foreign policy. This 'Act East' policy clearly emphasizes Connectivity, Commerce and Culture as the focus areas of action for a greater ASEAN-India integration. It takes into account the blueprints of the three pillars of ASEAN community building process, the ASEAN vision document, ASEAN 2025-Forging Ahead Together, the ASEAN Master Plan for Connectivity 2025, the ASEAN ICT Master Plan 2020 and the Initiative for ASEAN Integration Work Plan III. Besides this, in 2012, India became a Strategic Partner of ASEAN and emerged an important investment partner, where ASEAN and its 6 Dialogue Partners including India, Japan, China, South Korea, Australia and New Zealand are currently initiating the Regional Comprehensive Economic Partnership (RCEP). While relations with many of ASEAN's founding members remain strong, relations with Myanmar are important as it could contribute effectively towards the political security and economic development of India's North Eastern Region. Thus, India's ASEAN policy over the decades has exhibited some major achievements in the domain of its overall foreign policy.

Major Accomplishments of India's ASEAN Policy: Time for Space Appraisal

India's engagement with the ASEAN members through its 'Look East' and 'Act East' diplomacy has provided a large impetus to its political, economic and strategic relations with ASEAN and clearly demonstrates an impressive performance in its development of relations with most of the countries of Southeast Asia. In the last three decades (since 1991), India's ASEAN policy has demonstrated certain major accomplishments and they are as follows:

The **first** major achievement of India's 'Look East' policy involves security cooperation, and expansion of its area of influence in the Southeast Asian region, with a view to becoming a major player in the emerging security architecture of Asia. This security cooperation involves joint operations to protect sea-lanes and pooling resources in the war against terrorism and other non-traditional security threats. In recent years, the Indian Navy has been clasping an effective role in combating piracy in the Malacca Straits, and has offered to cooperate with the littoral states in the implementation of the 'Eyes in the Sky' programme for patrolling the piracy-infested Straits of Malacca., including the safety of the sea-lanes-of-communication (SLOC), which have been indispensable for the development of economic richness of the region. Moreover, India's recent growing naval activities in the Indian Ocean region, based on Indian Maritime Doctrine of 2004, 2007 and revised in 2015 and its 'Look East' security thrust involving the ASEAN and the 'rim land' states—like Japan and South Korea and beyond—has been no doubt a successful exercise in its naval diplomacy. India's naval movements which float in different parts of Indo-Pacific region, carrying Indian designed missile destroyers, holding annual joint exercises with the smaller littoral navies, exercising off shore during extended "goodwill" tours with the host country's naval vessels and, thereby establishing its existence in proximal as well as distant seas, constantly reminds one of India's strategic importance in the region. It is a fact that the military contacts and joint exercises that India initiated with ASEAN countries on a low-key basis in the early 1990s are now expanding into full-fledged defence cooperation. New Delhi has also quietly begun to put in place arrangements for regular access to ports in Southeast Asia. India's defence contacts have widened to include Japan, South Korea and China, which hitherto was never engaged by India in such a multi-directional diplomatic endeavour. In the sphere of defence, over the last few years, India has steadily expanded its ties with the East, Southeast Asian and beyond.

Furthermore, the expansion of the Indian Navy, establishment of Indian Far Eastern Naval Command (FENC), mainly in Andaman-Nicobar Islands, and its warming relations with the ASEAN members indicates that New Delhi desires to balance China and act as a balancer, in the Indian Ocean/Pacific regions, with the collaboration of the United States (US) in Southeast Asian region and beyond. The bilateral naval exercises were a manifestation of a more pragmatic and vision-based 'Look-East' policy. Since 2000, joint naval exercises and patrols as well as regular port calls by their respective navies have become a regular feature and where the Indian Navy has sent warships, tankers and submarines to Japan, South Korea, Thailand, Malaysia, Indonesia, Singapore, Cambodia and Vietnam for bilateral exercises. There were several objectives of these joint naval exercises with the Southeast Asian countries. An example can be cited in this juncture that with reference to Vietnam, since 1998 onwards, Indian naval ships had visited various Vietnamese ports regularly and thereby tested the future viability and strategic cooperation in the naval domain with Vietnam. The process of joint naval exercises with Vietnam first started, when the Naval Ship 'INS-Rajput' undertook a goodwill visit to Ho Chi Minh City from 28 September to 1 October 2000.[11] Since then, up to September 2016, various Indian ships, have visited multiple ports ofVietnam, as a goodwill visit and thereby clearly displayed its strength, existence, mobility and its consideration ofVietnam's importance to their anti-China stand, exacerbated by Hanoi's anti-China past and its geo-strategic location, in terms of its proximity to the Sea Lines of Communication (SLOCs), on account of the growing Chinese naval manoeuver in the eastern Indian Ocean region. Besides this, the expedition of INS Sudarshini set sail from Kochi on September 15, 2012 was a historic event in recent times. In the course of this naval voyage, Sudarshini visited 13 ports in 9 countries in Southeast Asia, besides the 3 ports in India. The major ports it visited were Padang, Bali, Manado (Indonesia), Port Muara (Brunei), Cebu, Manila (Philippines), Da Nang (Vietnam), Sihanoukville (Cambodia), Bangkok

(Thailand), Singapore, Port Klang, (Malaysia) Phuket (Thailand), and Sittwe (Myanmar), over a period of six months to commemorate 20 years of India–ASEAN partnership. The objective of the expedition is to enhance people-to-people and naval links between India and the ASEAN and remains one of the major flagship events being undertaken by ASEAN and India together to mark this important stage of bilateral relations.[12]

It has been pragmatically realized by the Indian policy-makers that its 'Look East' and 'Act East' policy domain should not be confined only to trade, but also extended to the new military-security power projection in the Southeast Asian region, particularly through naval deployments and maritime diplomacy. Moreover, maritime security is an important aspect of the bilateral cooperation between India and the countries of the Indo-Pacific region. The deepening dependence on Gulf oil and gas raises important security issues. The oil and gas from the Persian Gulf area passes through several vulnerable maritime choke points such as the Hormuz Strait, the Gulf of Aden, the Suez Canal and the Strait of Malacca. Problems of gun running, drug trafficking, piracy and terrorism constitute major threats to maritime security in this region.[13] This is a field in which large numbers of countries in the region are positioned to offer a meaningful and mutually beneficial cooperation with India, on account of its growing naval mobility in recent times. So as a gesture of goodwill, through regional confidence-building and cooperation mechanisms like the ASEAN Regional Forum (ARF), the Regional Cooperation Agreement on Combating Piracy and Armed Robbery against Ships in Asia (ReCAAP), the MILAN exercises, the Malabar Exercises, etc., through which India tries to keep its presence in the region. Moreover, the agreement in October 2011, between India and Vietnam to expand and promote joint oil exploration and gas in Blocks 127 and 128 in the South China Sea, by the ONGC Videsh Ltd, was not auspiciously looked upon by China, since it construed the challenge to the Chinese sovereignty claim on the disputed water. As a gesture of firm commitment of New Delhi's joint exploration exercise with Vietnam, on 24 May 2013, four Indian Navy ships, INS Rana, Shakti, Shivalik and Kurmak toured across the South China Sea on their way to Shanghai, where they arrived for a goodwill visit for a couple of weeks. Of these official tour, INS Rana and Shakti, have been temporarily halted in Subic Bay of the Philippines, and Shivalik and Kurmak at Haifong in Vietnam, which was not favourably accepted by China.[14]

Besides this, Indian Naval Ship (INS) *Airavat's* participation in the ADMM Plus Exercises on Maritime Security and Counter Terrorism held in Brunei from 1-5 May 2016; the first ever joint exercise between Indian Navy and Royal

Malaysian Navy and Indian Naval Ships Sahyadri, Shakti and Kirch visit to Malaysia from 15-19 July 2016; the participation of Indian Naval Ship INS *Sumitra* in the International Fleet Review to celebrate 75th Year of New Zealand Navy at Auckland from 16-22 November 2016; the signing of revised Defence Cooperation Agreement (DCA) signed between India and Singapore in November 2015 and visits by Indian ships—INS *Airavat* in May 2016 and INS Satpura in September 2016 to Singapore; the participation of Vietnamese Ship in the International Fleet Review at Vishakhapatnam, India, in February 2016 and Indian Naval Ships INS Satpura and INS Kirch a port call to Cam Ranh from 30 May-3 June 2016 and Indian Coast GuardShip ICGS SAMRAT a port call to Danang port from 23-27 October 2016,[15] INS Satpura and INS Kadmatt at Hai Phong City Port of Vietnam from 23-27 September 2017, INS Sumedha at Ho Chi Minh City on 12 January 2018, INS Sahyadri, Shakti and Kamorta at Tien Sa Port, Da Nang, Vietnam from 21-25 May 2018, are some of the landmark events in the text of security cooperation between India and ASEAN in recent times under the banner of 'Act East' policy.

Furthermore, Vietnam along with some other ASEAN members' participation in the MILAN naval exercises in 2010 and 2018, a multi-nation naval exercise in the Indian Ocean, the PASSEX Naval exercises, which includes signal drills, surface manoeuvres and communications between India and Vietnam, the first-ever joint naval exercise in May 2018 between India and Vietnam are important examples of India's entry in the radar of ASEAN strategic and security policy. Besides this, in the wake of the Tsunami disaster in December 2004, Indian ships were immediately sent to Sri Lanka, Maldives, Thailand and Indonesia and which was widely acclaimed by all the countries of Southeast Asia. Besides this, many of the Southeast Asian countries' economic survival largely depends on the safety and security of the Indian Ocean trade routes and felt that this route should not be controlled by any hegemonic power. So, India's growing naval strength and its maritime security diplomacy gave many ASEAN members, a security relief and brought them closer to each other.

The **second** achievement of India's ASEAN policy remains the growing economic cooperation. Over the last two decades, India and ASEAN as regional trade partners, offer a huge and attractive interconnected, geographically contiguous market of more than 1.5 billion people. Growth in India's exports to ASEAN countries in recent past has been much higher in comparison with other important destinations, though in case of imports, those from other regions have achieved faster growth. Thus, economic cooperation and trade scenario has acquired a prominent place between India and Southeast Asia, owing to their emerging complementary economies. Presently, Indian companies have invested in Singapore, Thailand, Malaysia and Indonesia in pharmaceuticals, textiles, paper and pulp manufacturing and palm oil refining. Besides this, New Delhi also developed better economic ties with Thailand, Indonesia and the Philippines. Unfortunately it lacked attention towards Brunei, another developed country within Southeast Asia, the per capita Gross Domestic Product (GDP) of which remains second only to Singapore, due to unknown reasons. In spite of this growing economic engagement, India's bilateral relations with the countries of ASEAN, have not yet evolved into a meaningful partnership in which both sides have a vital stake.

Trade ties over the years have clearly exhibited a sharp increase in India's exports to this area. ASEAN accounted for 3.6% of India's exports to the world in 1980, which by 1992 increased nearly 6%. In terms of value, India's export to ASEAN countries had more than quadrupled in 1992 and in the later years, India's trade in terms of both exports and imports increased very rapidly. In the last five years, India's exports to ASEAN and imports from ASEAN have increased very sharply. India's trade with the ASEAN members, during the year 2017-18 was US $79, 911.83 million, which remained 20 times more than the year 1992-93. However, the Balance of Trade, except for the year 1993-94, has tilted in favour of the Southeast Asian countries. Besides this, ASEAN remains the fifth most important market in the world in terms of Indian exports and fourth in terms of imports. Among the Southeast Asian countries, Malaysia and Singapore have been India's most prominent trading partners and India's trade with Laos has been the least in value terms (as per 2015-16 trade statistics). However, the trade turnover declined quite sharply in 1997 and 1998, as a result of the 'East Asian Financial Crisis', mostly due to a steep fall in New Delhi's exports. Since 1999, the situation recovered and in 2015-16, India remained ASEAN's seventh-largest trading partner with ASEAN accounting for 12% of India's global export market. During this period, exports and imports grew at an average rate of 23.7% and 18.6% respectively.[16]

The growing economic ties between India and ASEAN are reflected in the continued buoyancy in trade figures. With the process of economic liberalization, ASEAN countries are increasingly undertaking Foreign Direct Investment (FDI) in India in crucial infrastructure sectors, such as telecommunications, heavy industry, fuels, hotel and tourism services, chemicals, fertilizers, textiles, paper and pulp and food processing. Malaysia, Thailand and Singapore have become the major FDI sources. From a negligible amount in 1991, cumulative approved

FDI from ASEAN has so far reached more than US$ 5 billion. Unfortunately, compared to other dialogue partners of ASEAN, the volume of trade and investment flows between India and ASEAN remained very low. However, this situation has been changed in recent years. As of 2014, India's outward investment to Singapore, Indonesia, Malaysia, Philippines, Thailand, and Vietnam stood at a record $128 billion, which is even higher than Indian investment in China, some $119.56 billion. At the same time, approximately 12.5% of India's total inflows of foreign investment come from ASEAN. Besides this, New Delhi has also set up joint working groups with Malaysia, Indonesia, etc., for working towards Comprehensive Economic Cooperation Agreement (CECA). The Comprehensive Framework Agreement was actually signed by the leaders of India and ASEAN, at the Bali Summit in 2003, and laid a strong base for the eventual establishment of an ASEAN-India Regional Trade and Investment Area (RITA), which includes FTA in goods, services and investment. In 2009 and 2015, the ASEAN-India Trade in Goods Agreement and ASEAN-India Trade-in-Services and Investments were signed. With the signing of these Agreements, the ASEAN-India FTA is complete. Following these agreements, the ASEAN-India trade rebounded in 2017-18 to reach USD 79 billion. FDI inflows into India from ASEAN from April 2000 to December 2017 were US$ 65.92 billion, which represents 17.88% of the cumulative inflows received by India. Likewise, cumulative FDI outflows from India to ASEAN countries from April 2007 to March 2015, was about US$ 38.67 billion.[17] Therefore, though New Delhi has been a campaigner of multilateralism and acted as a responsible member of the WTO, regionalism as a reaction to the multilateral process has gained its ground of its foreign policy agenda in the present juncture, and this FTA remains a major step of India's ASEAN policy in reducing its dependence on trade with the US, EU and China and turning towards Southeast Asia, in order to strengthen its regional dynamics.

The **Third achievement** of India's ASEAN policy has been its engagement with Southeast, East Asia and beyond, through East Asia Summit (EAS). The First EAS meeting, held in December 2005 in Kuala Lumpur, consisted of 16 countries (ASEAN, China, Japan, Korea, India, Australia and New Zealand) and remained a historic event in the emerging global politics. The road to this first Summit has been followed by recent events, especially the ASEAN plus formula and the EAS initiative can be termed as the first step for establishing an East Asian Community on the lines of the European Economic Community, with the aim of promoting peace, stability and economic prosperity in East Asia and its surrounding areas. The then Prime Minister, Manmohan Singh, after attending the inaugural

EAS (2005) meeting, described this platform as a "potential to play a major role in global affairs. Its composition, its evolving agenda and format give it the potential to play a major role in global affairs. India's presence in this group from its very outset is an opportunity we value."[18] Thus, India's presence and participation both in the ASEAN+1 and EAS are no doubt a good beginning for its ultimate integration with that region. In fact, rapid integration with East Asia as part of India's 'Look East' Phase II and current 'Act East' policy has made the region India's largest trade partner, ahead of the EU and the US. India is evolving a complete FTA with ASEAN, and is presently studying Free Trade Area's (FTAs) with Japan, China and South Korea and trying to integrate as a part of the growing larger web of FTAs in the region. In other words, in the context of emerging regionalism in Asia, India could emerge as a hub between East on the one hand, and South, West and Central Asian countries on the other, where Southeast Asia could act as a bridge. The importance of EAS for the policy makers of India was reflected again through the former Indian Prime Minister, Manmohan Singh's speech delivered at the 8th EAS, held in Brunei on 10 October 2013, where he said: "Asia has been a late starter in terms of building regional architectures of cooperation. We have embarked on this collective journey in large part because of the outstanding vision and leadership of ASEAN, first in pursuing ASEAN integration and then expanding it to the wider region. We will be successful if we adhere to the principles of unity, cooperation and integration that have guided ASEAN and if ASEAN centrality continues to shape the East Asia Summit processes. I reaffirm India's commitment to contribute to this process."[19] Therefore, India deems the EAS as a firm move in the direction of realizing its long cherished dream of building the Asian community and its participation in the EAS is a real opportunity to broaden and deepen its engagement within the emerging Asian architecture.

The **Fourth achievement** of India's ASEAN policy has been its active participation in the Initiative for ASEAN Integration (IAI) programme, which is a regional framework for integration, aimed at narrowing the development gap within ASEAN and enhancing regional integration. It was felt by the ASEAN members that the accelerated process of market liberalization for regional integration ran a risk of provoking distributional problems by producing negative effects on the economy of less developed members through intensified competition. This issue had serious implications for ASEAN, which experienced the development gap when it achieved the ASEAN-10 by accepting the Indochina States (Vietnam, Cambodia and Laos) and Myanmar in the late 1990s. During that time, there was a serious gap in development between the old members and the newly joined CLMV (Cambodia, Laos, Myanmar and Vietnam) countries. To overcome this gap, at the Fourth Informal Summit in November 2000, at Singapore, the Singapore Prime Minister, Goh Chok Tong proposed the IAI. Besides narrowing development divide between ASEAN's old and new members, the IAI aimed to promote equitable economic development, and help alleviate poverty of the new members. India being a responsible 'Dialogue Partner' of ASEAN had actively played a very constructive role in this programme. India has successfully completed the "Railway Training Programmes for 48 trainers from CLMV countries in India." Additionally, India is presently implementing a project namely "India-Singapore Joint Training Programme for CLMV in English language Training". New Delhi is also involved in an Entrepreneurial Development project in each of the CLMV countries, with the objective of providing technical and advisory services to CLMV for the establishment of Entrepreneurial Development Institute in each of these countries, as part of efforts to train entrepreneurs and prepare small enterprises that face the challenge of globalization. So far, New Delhi has already established Entrepreneurship Development Centres in Cambodia, Laos and Vietnam, and in Myanmar it will be set up soon. This active focus of New Delhi on the IAI has been looked upon by ASEAN countries as a sign of India's commitment to ASEAN and its processes. Therefore, India's ASEAN policy in the 21st Century has truly become multi-dimensional and is clearly multi-pronged in character.[20]

The **Fifth achievement** of India's ASEAN policy remains the sub-regional forum initiatives in order to develop better connection with this region. To advance its "Look East" ASEAN policy, India used multilateralism as a principal tool in its geo-strategic perception. In terms of geopolitics, the contiguous sea spaces of the Bay of Bengal " South China Sea could be regarded as hubs of geo-economic and geo-strategic advantages and opportunities for New Delhi. It was felt by the Indian foreign policy makers that poor trade ties with ASEAN countries during the Cold War years had largely reduced its idea of an extended neighbourhood, and kept dormant the transport links with this region. However, this outlook was radically altered when New Delhi perceived that the immediate neighbourhood policy would be of vital national interest in the context of the emerging global economic order. This pragmatic viewpoint resulted in that in the later part of its 'Look East' Phase I and current "Act East' policy, India actively supported the creation of bilateral and sub-regional groupings, to complement its larger goal of enhancing ASEAN-India ties. The creation of the Bangladesh–China–India–Myanmar (BCIM) Forum for Regional Cooperation, established in 1999 and formerly known as the 'Kunming Initiative', a sub-regional initiative by India, as against the backdrop of its 'Look-East' Policy was essentially to promote the long-term demand of India's North Eastern Region (NER) for the opening of trade, connectivity and people-to-people contacts with the neighbouring countries which constitute nearly 98% of the region's borders. Besides this, the formation of BIMSTEC in 1997 and the Mekong-Ganga Cooperation (MGC) in 2000 has been instrumental in promoting cultural tourism as well as in defining regions in the new global economy and seeks to broaden and intensify joint efforts at economic cooperation between India and ASEAN in the Mekong region. Furthermore, these linkages between India and the countries of Indochina over land might accord New Delhi a chance to expedite economic development with the NER and its integration into the Eurasian land bridge system. Thus, the formation of BIMSTEC and MGC permits New Delhi to break out of the stringent confines of the subcontinent that it had long dented and be credited with the creation of geographical connectivity for the promotion of sustainable economic partnership between India and the Indochina States in the present century. The launching of India-ASEAN Car Rally in 2005—starting from Guwahati and ending in Indonesia—aimed to promote India-ASEAN relations, with reference to better scope for enhanced trade, road transport and connectivity, investment, tourism and people-to-people links, evidently demonstrated a forward stride in this innovative initiative.

The **Sixth achievement** of India's ASEAN policy remains the connectivity policy (mainly in improving road, railway, sea and air linkages) initiated by both sides. Connectivity with ASEAN—geographical, institutional or people-to-people—is a strategic priority for India. In December 2012, New Delhi hosted the India-ASEAN Commemorative Summit to mark 20 years of its association with the grouping and 10-years of its summit level partnership. In this meeting, connectivity policy was firmly emphasized in order to promote ASEAN centrality in the regional architecture, facilitate the building of an ASEAN Community and pragmatically presenting it as a foundation for constructing enhanced connectivity outside the region and encouraging trade and investment. Currently, India has already been involved in multiple connectivity projects with ASEAN members and they are: India-Myanmar-Thailand Trilateral highway project, building bridges and upgrading 120 km road between Kalewa and Yargyi, land connectivity between Northeast India and Myanmar, the building of Mekong-India Economic Corridor, a Delhi-Hanoi road and railway link and also the transportation networks including the East-West Corridor project and the Trans-Asian highway, etc. These important initiatives are viewed as the advancement of transport and infrastructure links which would alleviate the cross-border movement of goods and services between India and ASEAN in the Mekong Basin, for further operation of the ASEAN-India FTA. The opening of 2nd Car rally by Manmohan Singh on 21 December 2012 from New Delhi, in the presence of Heads of State and Governments of the ASEAN members has been another momentous event in recent times. While describing the India-ASEAN ties at an "exciting stage", Manmohan Singh in the inauguration programme of this car rally said: "Our future will be driven by the bonds of connectivity we build in the coming years. These physical bonds will be strengthened by digital links, which will help our younger generations to network better. Together, this web of linkages will help unleash the vast economic potential of our region, accelerate development and deepen our strategic partnership".[21] Another milestone event, which took place in the same year between India and ASEAN, was the establishment of an ASEAN-India Centre in New Delhi, followed by the ASEAN-India Strategic Partnership Agreement, representing an elevated echelon of a strategic understanding between them.[22] Therefore, this Car Rally endeavour clearly revealed the indispensability of India-ASEAN connectivity for further integration, which the Prime Minister, Narendra Modi, through his 'Act East' policy has underscored with greater vigour than the past years. Moreover, strengthening connectivity, including land and sea connectivity, jointly by India and ASEAN is taking place along with strengthening the Maritime Connectivity.

The **Seventh achievement** of India's ASEAN policy is that there is a domestic political and public consensus on India's 'Look East' and 'Act East' policy. No party has ever questioned the desirability of closer engagement with Southeast Asia and beyond. This is no doubt a prime achievement of India's ASEAN policy.

The **Eighth achievement** of India's ASEAN policy, especially in the first phase of Prime Minister Narendra Modi remained that most of the countries of Southeast Asia currently acknowledge India's presence in the region to act as balancer, in the context of growing expansion of Chinese wings, both economically and strategically. In recent times, the gradual emergence of the 'Indo-Pacific' as a new vocabulary in international relations seeks to define a regional strategic framework encompassing both the Pacific and Indian Oceans. In the broadest sense, this concept covers the military, economic, and strategic interests of regional stakeholders and their complicated and interdependent relationships. These interests include the United States' ambitious 'pivot' towards Asia, China's advance westwards through initiatives such as the 'Maritime Silk Road', and India's vivacity to 'Act East' rather than simply 'Look East'.[23] In this theatre of competing national interests, India and ASEAN have an integral role in creating a favourable regional building process, which was mentioned by Prime Minister Narendra Modi, during his keynote address at Shangri La Dialogue on 1 June 2018:

> "Inclusiveness, openness and ASEAN centrality and unity, lie at the heart of the new Indo-Pacific. India does not see the Indo-Pacific Region as a strategy or as a club of limited members. Nor as a grouping that seeks to dominate. And by no means do we consider it as directed against any country.... India's vision for the Indo-Pacific Region is, therefore, a positive one and where Southeast Asia is at its centre and, ASEAN has been and will be central to its future."[24]

With Prime Minister Narendra Modi's push for economic reforms and proactive international diplomacy since 2014, India stands as the only partner equal to China and the United States. In fact, China's increasing strategic influence across the Indian Ocean demands a regional counterbalance. So, increasing defence and naval cooperation among the United States, Japan, Australia, ASEAN members and India clearly demonstrates the relevance of this new initiative. While explaining the growing importance of ASEAN, both strategically and economically for India, in the same speech, Prime Minister Narendra Modi said:

> I see ASEAN as an example and inspiration. ASEAN represents the greatest level of diversity of culture, religion, language, governance and prosperity of any grouping in the world. It was born when Southeast Asia was a frontline of global competition, a theatre of a brutal war and a region of uncertain nations. Yet, today, ASEAN has united ten countries behind a common purpose. ASEAN unity is essential for a stable future for this region. I am convinced that ASEAN can integrate the broader region. In many ways, ASEAN is already leading the process. In doing so, it has laid the foundation of the Indo-Pacific Region. The East Asia Summit and the Regional Comprehensive Economic Partnership – two important initiatives of ASEAN – embrace this geography.[25]

Therefore, in order to forge a 'natural alliance' to make this initiative a reality, India's growing understanding with the ASEAN members, which according to Narendra Modi "free from contests and claims," firmly anchored in an upward spiral of improving relations with the Southeast Asian region and beyond. Moreover, on 26 January 2018, hosting the ten ASEAN leaders on India's Republic Day celebration and ASEAN-India Commemorative Summit on 25 January 2018, amply demonstrates the testimony of India's strategic, economic and political commitment to ASEAN and its Act East policy.

The last but not the least achievement has been that in the last few years, New Delhi participated in a number of ARF meetings, ASEAN Defence Ministers

Meet plus (ADMM+), ASEAN Maritime Forum and other strategic activities related to confidence-building measures (CBMs), maritime search and rescue, peacekeeping, non-proliferation, preventive diplomacy and disaster management and found them productive and useful for facilitating the introduction of appropriate CBMs among ASEAN members. Over these years, the key strategic parameters shared between India and ASEAN are —Combating piracy; Intelligence sharing and counter terrorism; Maintenance of coastal security and protection of the legitimate sovereign use of International waters; Enforcement of International law; Disaster relief operations; Climate change; Conservation of environment, including marine; Comprehensive economic development; Re-establishing hearty cultural relations; Cooperation in education, science and technology and other multifarious areas, promoting people-to-people contact, etc. This participation of India through its 'Look East' and 'Act East' policies has ensured New Delhi a unique place to play a noteworthy role in the Indo-Pacific balance of power equation.

The Future Conduit

In this emerging global order, today ASEAN is widely recognized in the international community as an example of enlightened regionalism. It has proved its critics wrong. After five decades of its brilliant performance, it is a now a vibrant reality that this regional organization is acknowledged and recognized not only in its own region but also in the world as one of the most successful regional cooperative schemes. After it's more than five decades of existence, despite obvious challenges and global economic downturns, scarred by maritime, connectivity and developmental issues, the ASEAN has moved briskly from strength to strength and successfully overcome its inherent constraints. The achievements of ASEAN as a regional framework and institution are wide-ranging. From the stated objectives of socioeconomic and cultural cooperation, as embodied in the Bangkok Declaration of 1967, ASEAN has in fact grown effectively through the more sensitive approach of political and geo-political cooperation in the last fifty years. Currently, it is the only regional organization in Asia that provides a political forum where Asian countries and the world powers can discuss and consider problems about security, political issues and military concerns. The success story of this organization lies on account of its members' strong commitment of cooperative mindset and where it has not allowed any theoretical and political differences to interfere in its efforts to cooperate for the common good. Therefore, on the whole as a regional organization, ASEAN represents a success story in defending the principles of territorial integrity and non-interference in each other's internal affairs and remains a political and economic force because it is the only regional organization in this current global order, which gives the countries of Southeast Asia a collective voice and solid clout in dealing with extra-regional powers.

As against such backdrop, the above analysis clearly discloses that India's ASEAN policy since 1991 has been an account of admirable fortune. Barring the Cold War period, it is evident that in the initial post-Cold War years, India's ASEAN policy has been temporarily soft-pedalled towards the countries of Southeast Asia. In the ASEAN mindset, India has evolved as an emerging power and its keenness to develop relations has been viewed as beneficial to the ASEAN countries as a whole. The ASEAN members felt that India possesses strategic capabilities and can be a strong stabilizing regional balancing force. Economically, India, with its burgeoning middle class, can be a significant market for ASEAN manufactures and consequently, an important source of benefit for the region, following which, this region can gain from India's development in its service sector. India understands that the ASEAN grouping consists of countries which have achieved noteworthy growth in the past few decades. Therefore, it is essential for New Delhi to establish beneficial linkages with these countries to gain from their past experience and current standing and synergies with these countries' economy would naturally strengthen New Delhi's emerging profile more on solid pedestal. Today, India-ASEAN relations are marked by a novel resilience and energy as they move towards greater economic integration not only at India-ASEAN level but also at the pan-regional level. While referring to the successful conclusion of the India-ASEAN FTA in Services and Investment, the Indian Prime Minister, Manmohan Singh characterized India-ASEAN relations at an 'exciting stage' with the possibility of their bilateral trade going up to US$200 billion in a decade. Moreover, India is also part of ASEAN's fresh initiative for negotiation towards a pan-Indo-Pacific economic integration involving sixteen founding members of the EAS, known as Regional Comprehensive Economic Partnership. Currently, there is growing acceptance on the part of ASEAN that India has a much larger task and greater role to play in Southeast Asia in the current juncture of this century. In fact, New Delhi's role is becoming more critical in shaping the regional strategic discourse that has been drifting towards uncertainty, multi-layered rivalry and multi-polarity. Naturally, many ASEAN members expected India to play a more pro-active role in the regional security discourses, especially with reference to the South China Sea issue, on account of China's growing assertion in the region.

Summarily then, ASEAN-India partnership holds plentiful prospects for a successful future and reap mutual benefits. Huge potential remains untapped in the ASEAN-India partnership. Geographical proximity, emerging transport connectivity, and especially geostrategic considerations will be important factors in bringing ASEAN and India closer in the future. As things stand, it is evident that both sides are keen to establish a strong relationship with a long-term emphasis on greater cooperation and integration, apart from the escalation of economic and strategic ties. India with its present "Act East" policy must propel a meaningful investment environment to integrate more deeply with the countries of Southeast Asia. As for ASEAN members, they must be seen as capable of "Looking West" to engage India more in their efforts to maintain strategic equilibrium in the region. However, there are definite challenges to be addressed before achieving a consolidated ASEAN policy, for which, New Delhi must change its Cold War mindset. It should play a more pragmatic, practical and pro-active role through its 'Look East' and 'Act East' ASEAN policies, so as to establish herself as a stable and strong powerhouse in the Asian region. Thus, to make India's 'Look East' cum 'Act East' ASEAN doctrine an effectual one, New Delhi should follow a more realistic, sensible and vision-oriented policy, to minimize the space, which it had lost during the Cold War period, because a better and deeper relationship between ASEAN and India might ultimately lead to the benefit of the greater East Asia and Indo-Pacific regions, culminating in providing the space for a stable and peaceful Asia. Therefore, it is heartening to reckon that although belated, after 50 years of ASEAN's existence, India has pragmatically realized the gravity and importance of this regional organization in the context of current geoeconomic, geostrategic and geopolitical global order.

NOTES

1 See http://www.mfa.go.th/asean/en/organize/62206-The-Birth-of-ASEAN.html (accessed on 29 September 2018)

2 See http://www.mfa.go.th/asean/en/organize/62208-Evolution-of-ASEAN.html (accessed on 29 September 2018)

3 Ambassador Anil Trigunayat, "ASEAN @ 50", Asian Century Institute, 6 April 2017, seehttp://asiancenturyinstitute.com/international/1353-asean-50 (accessed on 16 October 2018)

4 For details see www.aseansec.org/21254.htm (accessed on 30 September 2018)

5 Kripa Sridharan, "India and ASEAN: The Long Road to Dialogue", *The Round Table*, No. 340, October 1996, p.467.

6 Mohammed Ayoob, *India and Southeast Asia: Indian Perception and Politics,* Routledge, London, 1990, pp.11-12
7 Asis Kumar Majumdar, *South-East Asia in Indian Foreign Policy: A Study of India's Relations with South-east Asian countries from 1962-82,* Naya Prokosh, Calcutta, 1982, p.175.
8 Tridib Chakraborti, "Disparate Priorities: Explaining the Penumbra of India's Look East Policy", in K. Raja Reddy (ed.), *India and ASEAN: Foreign Policy Dimensions for the 21st Century,* New Century Publications, New Delhi, 2005, pp.52-53.
9 *Ibid.*, pp.53-54
10 *Ibid.*, pp.54-55
11 *Annual Report: 2000-2001*, Ministry of External Affairs, Government of India, New Delhi, 2001, p.25
12 See http://www.aseanindia.com/press-release-ins-sudarshini/ (accessed on 13 October, 2016)
13 W. Anderson, W, "A growing congruence of interests with Korea", in S.Ganguly, (ed.) *India's Foreign Policy: Retrospect and Prospect,* Oxford University Press, New Delhi, 2010, pp.175-205
14 Indrani Bagchi, "Four Navy ships in South China Sea to mark Indian presence", *The Times of India,* 24 May 2012
15 For details see *Annual Report: 2016-2017,* Ministry of External Affairs, Government of India, New Delhi, 2017, p.28-43
16 For details see Tridib Chakraborti, "India's Rendezvous with ASEAN in the New Global Order: Achievements and Pitfalls", *POLITICO,* Vol. 2, No.2, 2014, pp.145–48
17 For details see httpwww.mea.gov.inPortalForeignRelationASEAN_India_August_2017.pdf, p.3 (accessed on 2 October 2018)
18 See http://www.rediff.com/money/2005/dec/14asean2.htm (accessed on 20 June 2018)
19 For detail speech see http://mea.gov.in/Speeches-Statements.htm?dtl/22305/Prime+Ministers+Statement+at+8th+East+Asia+Summit+in+Brunei+Darussalam+October+10+2013 (accessed on 20 June 2018)
20 Tridib Chakraborti, n.16, pp.150-151
21 See http://www.tehelka.com/india-asean-relations-at-exciting-stage-manmohan-singh/ (accessed on 21 June 2018)
22 For details see http://mea.gov.in/bilateral-documents.htm?dtl/20982/Vision+ Statement ASEANIndia+Commemorative+Summit (accessed on 21 June 2018)
23 Soyen Park and Ramandeep Singh, "India's inevitable role in an emerging Indo-Pacific", East Asia Forum, 3 December 2016, seehttp://www.eastasiaforum.org/2016/12/03/indias-inevitable-role-in-an-emerging-indo-pacific/ (accessed on 2 October 2018))
24 For Details see "Prime Minister's Keynote Address at Shangri La Dialogue", 1 June, 2018, https://mea.gov.in/Speeches-Statements.htm?dtl/29943/Prime_Ministers_ Keynote_ Address_ at_Shangri_La_Dialogue_June_01_2018(accessed on 4 May 2019)
25 *Ibid.*

26

Influence of Cholas as a Maritime Power on Southeast Asia

S. Utham Kumar Jamadhagni and C.S. Anuradha

Maritime Mastery

In the 38th edition of *Man Ki Baat* of November 26, 2017, PM Narendra Modi remarked that the "ancient India sea power reached its zenith during the Chola Dynasty".[1] While mercantile relations with China and Arab world had already been established, it was the subjugation of Southeast Asian region that illustrated the might of the Chola Naval power.

One of the southern kingdoms the Cholas, undertook naval expeditions to Southeast Asia. They had attempted this after bringing neighbouring islands like Sri Lanka, Maldives and Lakshadweep under their control during the 10th and 11th centuries. The Southeast Asian sojourn was ostensibly to protect their commercial interests ably supported by maritime power. Other reasons like *digvijaya* or lap of victory as well as plunder to fund the large donations that characterised the Chola governance are also put forward.

However, the fact that such a naval enterprise was undertaken points to several aspects. The vast distances covered indicate the use of large ships that would carry logistics including soldiers to fight battles in foreign lands, weapons and equipment that would have been needed for such campaigns and food to feed the entire expeditionary force. The expertise in ship-building technology, the construction of huge ships and the ability to navigate the seas sans sophisticated equipment laid the foundation for building a mighty navy one of a modern blue water kind. In fact it is even thought that the Chola navy was considered the largest defence force in Asia at that time.[2] A maritime power indicates not only military strength of the naval arm of the state but comprehensively the ability to safeguard its maritime commercial interest; ensure freedom of navigation and maintain a sphere of influence that would serve its national interests as well as protect it from threats. The Southeast Asian episode amply illustrated the status of the Cholas as a strong and often unopposed maritime power.

Strategic Environment

The early relations between the Cholas and the kingdoms of the Southeast Asian region were cordial. The most powerful was the Hindu Sri Vijaya kingdom. There were other kingdoms like the Khmer, Tamralinga and such other smaller ones too. This can be understood from the Khmer ruler Mara Vijayatunga varman sponsoring the building of a Buddhist Chulamani *vihara* in the port of Nagapattinam in 1005 AD. Many more gifts followed later. This also underscores the point that the maritime commercial interests warranted maintenance of cordial ties during this period. However later, this very interest could have sprung up rivalries that were addressed resorting to the use of force.

The deterioration in relations resulted in the Cholas being at constant rivalry with the Sri Vijaya kingdom of Southeast Asia for more than a century in the early part of the first millennia. It ended with the defeat of the Sri Vijaya Empire which had twin consequences. Not only did this firmly entrenched Chola's influence in the region but later also paved way for Moslem supremacy in Indian Ocean waters. One of the reasons for the conflicts is thought to be the restriction of unhindered access to Chinese trading ports by the Sri Vijayas through the manning of the straits. KRA Narasiah a veteran maritime historian further observed that the naval invasion was to ensure security for the vast Chola mercantile fleet that was threatened by pirates.[3]

Herman Kulke cites the Chinese sources that describe the Sri Vijaya ability to launch attacks on ships that refused to dock in their ports enroute the Chinese destinations[4]. The other factor cited is the simultaneous rise of Egyptian Fatimid Empire, the Cholas in India and Sri Vijayas in the Southeastern region that meant competing maritime powers in the Indian Ocean.

The Chinese Song Empire was one of the principal trading destinations in the East. It regulated maritime trade by setting up a Bureau of Licensed Trade through which foreign goods were bought and then sold locally by only the state. This is also touted as an element in the competition game. Sri Vijayas adopted a "kind of ritual diplomacy"[5] where they built Buddhist temples in India in Chola territory, and even in the Malayan peninsula for the welfare of the Chinese emperor. This can clearly be seen as an attempt to maintain cordial relations with the two big powers of the age in order to preserve its dominant status in maritime trade in the area that lay between the two. The despatch of several envoy missions to both the Song court as well as the Chola kingdom by the Sri Vijayas could only be seen as a reflection of this effort.

The Khmer King Mara Vijaytunga Varman built a Buddhist Vihara in the port city of Nagapattinam during the time of Rajaraja Chola. The Chulamani inscription explains the arrangements made for land grants that would support the upkeep of the temple. Suryavarman I the later Khmer king even presented his war chariot as gift to the Chola king Rajaraja for his support. During the reign of Kulathunga Chola, a gemstone presented by the Kamboja king was fixed in the front row of the stone wall of the Chidambaram temple front.[6] It is even said that the maritime power of Sri Vijayas had a permanent agent called *kanmi* in the port city of Nagapattinam to oversee relations. Three inscriptions discovered in Nagapattinam mention the donation by the *kanmi* of: (i) lamp stands for a Siva temple; (ii) ornaments with the makara - king's emblem fixed in the centre of the pieces; and (iii) donation of two gold pieces of *Chinakanagam* (Chinese gold) for worship and feeding.[7]

Merchant Guilds

Yet another explanation added to the naval expedition in the maritime trade approach is the presence of merchant guilds called *ainnuruvar, nanadesi, manigramam, anjuvannam, padinenvishayam* and *valenjiyar*.[8] With flourishing trade contacts the trading merchants set up guilds that protected their interests. It is said that they even possessed private armies that would defend their commercial ships from pirates and other vagaries of overseas travel. Evidence of their presence in Southeast Asian kingdoms is also available. Thus any threat to their mercantile practise could have been instrumental in seeking the protection of Rajendra the Chola king who would have obliged with such a naval venture.[9] A 1088 AD Tamil inscription in Sumatra mentions the famous merchant guild Nanadesa Tisaiyayirattu Ainnutruvar.[10] The Takuapa inscription of an artificial lake dug by a member of the merchant guild Manikramam further substantiates the power of the guilds in foreign lands.[11]

Kadaram Conquest

The commercial relations with the Southeast Asian kingdoms and further with

Chinese Song Empire were well developed long before the advent of Cholas. It is said that there was intense competition between many of the Southeast Asian kingdoms. The then Khmer King Suryavarman I in order to challenge the Tamralinga kingdom sought the help of the Cholas. The belligerent side roped in the powerful Sri Vijayas and this put the Cholas in direct confrontation with the Sri Vijaya. A small naval expedition was sent in 1017 AD. However, the warnings were ignored.[12]

The next naval expedition of the Cholas in 1025 AD left a lasting impact on the Southeast Asian region. There were a series of campaigns which saw many cities conquered. One noteworthy war is the Battle of Kedah in 1025 AD. A Siamese painting depicts the naval battle launched by the Cholas under Rajendra I. He was also attributed the title "Kadaram Kondan" or "securer of Kadaram", the Tamil name for Kedah a part of modern day Malaya. The presence of flamethrowers, the first of its kind on naval ships[13] is a testament to the naval prowess. The ability to engage armies in foreign lands also means the use of the Navy in the Chola period to secure beachheads, prevent piracy, protect sea-trade routes, and project power and as a diplomatic symbol. Though precise accounts of naval battles of the Chola kings in Southeast Asia are not readily available, indirect references in *prasastis* and inscriptions as well as other texts help us to build a composite picture.

The Tanjavur inscription talks of "*having dispatched many ships in the midst of the rolling sea and having caught Sangrama- Vijayattunga Varman, the King of Kadaram, together with the elephants in his glorious army*". Kedah or Kadaram was the most important entrepot that served as a replenishment and repair point for ships and stopover for sailors waiting for favourable winds before continuing their voyages and as a storage depot. Thus the exploits of many Chola kings saw the Bay of Bengal "converted into a Chola lake".[14] The meikirti also mentions the places that were captured in the conquest. The Alur Tamil inscription mentions of a life-time endowment made to a military General Kadaram Konda Chola Brahmarayar. A cross reference of the areas invaded by Rajendra Chola can be made using the Chinese source Chau Ju-Kua. Interestingly almost all are located in the island of Sumatra and on either coast of Malaya. These include Pannai on Sumatra's eastern coast; Maliayur in mid-Sumatra; Mayirudingam in Malaya; Talai takkolam; Madamalingam in Southern Malay Peninsula Ilamuridesam in Northern Sumatra near Acheh port Ilangasokam close to Kra Isthmusand Mevilambagam and Valaippanduru in Northern Malaya adjoining Kra.

Several historians like Hultzsch, Venkiah, Coedes and Nilakanta Sastri have amply identified these places. B. Arunachalam has even attempted to reconstruct the "passage plan" of the naval expedition by using epigraphic evidences and nautical information. He is of the opinion that though the port of embarkation would have been mainly Nagapattinam with maybe the flagship with the Commander of the armada, other ships might have joined the fleet in Sri Lanka. The port of calls could have been Nicobar islands and Burma ports. The author concludes that the armada could have sailed south of Sumatra and attacked the different ports of the Sri Vijayas.[15] The sheer distance of five thousand nautical miles traversed to reach the Southeast Asian region exemplifies that the Cholas were adept at maintaining supply lines as well as possessing a navy that could conduct campaigns far away from homeland shores. The attempts at tracing the navigational route have borne some fruit.

The well-established Hindu kingdom of Sri Vijaya in Southeast Asia clearly indicates the maritime underpinning of long-lasting cultural and historical influences. The Cholas in particular have expanded their influence right upto the Malay Peninsula. The extensive trade contact established both with the Chinese empire and the Caliphate realm show the strength of maritime commerce of the Cholas. In fact many authors are of the opinion that it is the need to protect SLOCs that warranted naval campaigns against the eastern kingdoms. The busy trading routes through the Straits of Malacca between the Malaya Peninsula and Sumatra island and the Sunda Straits between Sumatra and Java islands came under the control of the Sri Vijayas during the early part of 10th century. The Sri Vijaya Empire is said to have imposed "exacting exorbitant tolls on merchant ships"[16] destined for China. This could have triggered the Chola naval expeditions as an attempt to check the growing influence of the Sri Vijaya realm in the Malay peninsula region. It could also have been to reestablish the freedom of navigation in these waters especially of the Chola traders in their relations with the Song dynasty of China.

The Kadaram campaign saw "expeditious attacks"[17] on significant ports and other important places and gave the opponents little time to strategise. The defeat of Sangrama Vijayatonga varman meant the weakening of the Sailendra kings of Sri Vijayas and ultimately their decline. However unlike the European maritime powers, the Cholas did not annex these areas. This clearly indicates lack of expansionist ambitions, while simultaneously establishing influence over the Indian Ocean region.

Naval Organisation

As a sea power, the Cholas built a variety of ships ranging from the modest *kattumaram* to the massive *Marakkalam* that could carry hundreds of soldiers and equipment. The *Thoni* meant for coastal waters plied in the Chola waters off South India. *Padavi* was roughly a quarter of the size of a *Marakkalam*. Each naval division had a commander with the highest rank earmarked for the King or his Fleet Admiral. They were named Jaladhipathy or Admiral of the Navy; Pirivu Adhipathy or Fleet Commander; Ganathipathy manning a fleet-squadron; Mandaladhipathy equivalent to today's Vice Admiral; Kalapathy or Ship Commander. Kaapu, Seevai and Eitimnaar were officers in charge of weapons, masts and marines.

Another significant aspect that aided the Chola Naval supremacy was the exceptional navigational skills acquired. They were experts in reading the climatic conditions of the Bay of Bengal and employed the astronomical knowledge of direction and location of stars and constellations as vital tools in sea faring. The records of many Chola expeditions gleaned from Chinese and Malayan sources meant the frequency and ease with which the great nautical distances were forged.

Interestingly they also made use of rudimentary navigational aids like the

- *Rappalagai* to site stars;
- Tappu palagai to measure speed;
- Flat Bronze plates to fathom water depth;
- Pigeons to identify land; and
- Human hand to measure altitude of stars.

The Cholas also possessed sufficient skills in ship building as the ships had to be ocean-going ships, large in size and high in carrying capacity. A variety of ships were built for diverse set of purposes. The coastal waters were manned by *Thoni*, the vessel which was 70 feet long, 20 feet broad, and 12 feet deep flying a single mast and long sail as described by C.D Maclean and plying the Coromandel Coast.[18] Larger ships made from Timber and other hard woods carried soldiers and war equipment as far away as the Southeast Asian shores. The large ships had wood that seemed as if it were sewn together with wooden nails. The trees that provided wood for ship building were chosen for their lightness in weight, flexibility, crack resistance, self-lubrication, impervious to insects and imputrescible. These were Iluppai (Mahua), Punnai (Oil nut Tree), Siru Tekku Teak, Aini, Karimarudu (Indian Laurel).

The Cholas also invaded Sri Lanka and Maldives. Rajendra Chola defeated King Mahinda V and consolidated the Chola suzerainty over the island. Karikala Chola was the earliest Chola ruler to have invaded Sri Lanka. Later Parantaka I undertook a naval expedition on Ceylon. The Ukkal temple inscription refers to "twelve thousand ancient islands of the sea" a reference to Maldives subjugated by Rajaraja Chola in the 29th year of his reign. In a Chennapatna inscription of Rajendra's 13th year as king, there is mention of a grand armada "across the middle of the sea lashing with waves" that set sail to subjugate the Far East territories.

Ship building must also have been an advanced industry even if ships were not specifically built for navies but commercial maritime ships were modified to carry weapons and equipment. The ports of Nagapattinam, Kodikarai and smaller ports nearby must have contributed to the provision of beach heads and other facilities for ships to be constructed. The port of Nagapattinam was a vibrant trading post and it is probable that the armada fleet that sailed to Southeast Asia must have embarked upon the journey from here. The route of the naval campaign has also been attempted to be discerned.

Cultural Influence

The maritime contact of the Cholas with the Southeast Asian region was mostly peaceful. Several temples, statues, inscriptions, copper plates have been found both in India and modern Indonesia, Malaysia, Thailand and Cambodia. Many of them confirm direct Cholan influence in architectural style, depiction of important figures and the use of Tamil as a language for inscribing. In the northern coast of Sumatra near Medan, an imposing Ganesha statue in the pure Chola style, has been found. The 1086 AD Kedah inscription talks of Kulothunga Cholan I and commercial contacts the Chola empire had with Malaya.[19] Of further proof is the appearance of the figure of Karaikal Ammaiyar the only woman saint in the Nayanmar pantheon of ardent Saivite saints whose glory was spread far and wide during the Chola reign. Across the present day Isan region of northeast Thailand; the temple of Banteay Srei in the Siem Reap province of Cambodia and Malaysia the emaciated, skeletal and often demonic depiction of the female devotee of Shiva especially near the *Adavallan* form of one of the Hindu Trinity is a clear indication of the direct Chola influence on the culture of the region.[20]

The effect of the Chola invasion was twin-pronged. First by ensuring the safety of sea lanes and establishing the freedom of navigation around the Malaya Peninsula, the Chola naval campaign confirmed the primacy of the maritime route to the region in the Indian Ocean later named the "Spice route" over the danger-infested land route of the Silk Road that connected the various ancient Asian kingdoms to the rest of the world. The ease with which the Cholas completed the round trip of transporting a huge army, arms and other equipment to the

Suvarnadwipa and beyond was proof of its relative safety and the energy and cost it saved the traders involved in commerce. In fact it is said that the Chinese Emperor during this time "urged Arab envoys shift their trade from the Central Asian Silk Road to the Silk Road of the Sea".[21] Secondly, with the fall of the Sri Vijayas the onset of Arab influence increased. With the Cholas not establishing an empire here the vacuum was filled by the Arabs. Several Arab navigational texts derived directly from Chola navigational distances and calculations. This later led to growing Islamic influence in the region.

Present Parallel

This examination of the expansion of the Chola sphere of influence into the Southeast Asian region must not merely be viewed from a historical perspective. Rather, several similarities to existing strategic conditions could be identified. Just like in the past, India is still looked upon as a benign power. There are no serious divergences with any of the ASEAN countries of today. The close trade contacts with the region continue. As an energy importer and one that looks at diversification of its supply sources, India is bound to continue its focus on the region.

The position of a "balancer" vis-à-vis the feared ambitions of ever-present China harks back to the Chola era when Indian rulers were sought to act as neutralisers of adverse change in power dynamics in the region. Today, countries like Vietnam look to India as a counter to the Chinese stance over the maritime issue of the South China Sea. Cultural influences that were deepened during the Chola era have endured and could serve as a soft power potential for India. Thus this article presents the case for "heavy lifting" in the case of India in her relations with the ASEAN countries that could enhance scope for "deeper integration rather than rousing summitry.[22]

NOTES

1 Mann Ki Baat: PM Narendra Modi salutes Indian Navy, remembers women warriors of Chola Dynasty, *Financial Express*, November 26, 217 https://www.financialexpress.com/india-news/mann-ki-baat-pm-narendra-modi-salutes-indian-navy-remembers-women-warriors-of-chola-dynasty/948069/

2 When Chola ships of war anchored on the east coast, *The Times of India*, March 12, 2018 https://timesofindia.indiatimes.com/city/chennai/when-chola-ships-of-war-anchored-on-the-east-coast/articleshowprint/63260602.cms

3 T E Narasimhan, The king who looked east 1,000 years ago, *Business Standard*, November 22, 2014 https://www.business-standard.com/article/beyond-business/the-king-who-looked-east-1-000-years-ago-114112101224_1.html

4 Hermann Kulke, The naval expeditions of the Cholas in the context of Asian history, in

Hermann Kulke, K. Kesavapany and Vijay Sakhuja eds., *Nagapattinam to Suvarnadwipa: Reflections on the Chola Naval expeditions to Southeast Asia*, Institute of Southeast Asian Studies, Singapore 2009, p.4.

5 Ibid., p. 7.

6 https://glorioustamils.com/category/karaikkal-ammaiyar-in-southeast-asia/

7 Meenakshi Sundararajan's Rajendra Chola's Naval expedition and the Chola trade with Southeast and East Asia, in *Nagapattinam to Suvarnadvipa*, pp.172–73.

8 For a detailed discussion on the various aspects of merchant guilds refer Noboru Karashima's South Indian merchant guilds in the Indian Ocean and Southeast Asia in Nagapattinam to Suvarnadvipa, pp.135–157

9 Anirudh Kaniseti, The Geopolitics of Rajendra Chola: The Apogee and decline of a South Indian Golden Age, *Indian National Interest*, December 9, 2017, https://nationalinterest.in/why-the-cholas-collapsed-69fef10b163d

10 The Contribution of the Cholas in the Expansion of Indian Culture outside India, http://www.yourarticlelibrary.com/culture/the-contribution-of-the-cholas-in-the-expansion-of-indian-culture-outside-india/4043

11 S. Rajavelu, Maritime Contacts on the Coromandal coast, http://www.sabrizain.org/malaya/library/coromandal.pdf

12 There's a Dragon in the sea, *The Economic Times*, April 26, 2016 https://economictimes.indiatimes.com/blogs/et-commentary/theres-a-dragon-in-the-sea/

13 Prakash Katoch, "*An Indian Marine Corps* ?", Centre for Land Warfare Studies, September 2, 2012 http://www.claws.in/896/an-indian-marine-corps-prakash-katoch.html

14 Prithwis Chandra Chakravarti, Naval Warfare in ancient India, *The Indian Historical Quarterly*, Vol. 4, No. 4, 1930.12, p.663.

15 For a detailed attempt to reconstruct a navigational route refer B.Arunachalam, Chola Navigational Package, Maritime Historical Society, Mumbai, 2004, pp.25–42.

16 Excerpt from the book by Sanjeev Sanyal, *The Ocean of Churn: How the Indian Ocean Shaped Human History*, Penguin Random House, 2017 as cited in https://swarajyamag.com/books/rajendra-cholas-painting-for-mazgon-docks-a-tribute-to-the-naval-might-of-cholas

17. Praful Shankar, The wars that were won : Rajendra Chola's naval conquest of South-East Asia, *Swarajya*, October 29, 2017 https://swarajyamag.com/ideas/the-wars-that-were-won-rajendra-cholas-naval-conquest-of-south-east-asia

18 Nagapattinam to Suvarnadwipa, cited by Subbarayalu A note on the Navy of the Chola State, p. 94.

19 http://uncoverancienthistory.blogspot.com/2017/05/kadaram-kedah-uncover-lost-ancient.html

20 Subbulakshmi, Ammai in Banteay Srei and the Tamil Maritime links in South East Asia, Varalaru.com, http://www.varalaaru.com/design/article.aspx?ArticleID=1428

21 K N Chaudhuri, *Trade and Civilization in the Indian Ocean: An Economic History from the Rise of Islam to 1750*, Cambridge,1985, p.56

22 ASEAN rising—on India-Southeast Asia cooperation, Editorial, *The Hindu*, January 27, 2018 https://www.thehindu.com/opinion/editorial/asean-rising/article22530919.ece

Index